PERSONAL INJURY AND CLINICAL NEGLIGENCE LITIGATION

PERSONAL INJURY AND CLINICAL NEGLIGENCE LITIGATION

David Dow LLB, Solicitor

Jeff Lill BA, Solicitor

2002

Published by
Jordan Publishing Limited
21 St Thomas Street
Bristol BS1 6JS

© The College of Law 2002

David Dow and Jeff Lill have asserted their moral
rights in accordance with ss 77–89 of the
Copyright Designs and Patents Act 1988.

All rights reserved. No part of this publication may be
reproduced, stored in a retrieval system, or transmitted in
any way or by any means, including photocopying or recording,
without the written permission of the copyright holder,
application for which should be addressed to the publisher.

British Library Cataloguing-in-Publication Data
A catalogue record for this book is available from the British Library.

ISSN 1353–3622
ISBN 0 85308 748 2

Printed in Great Britain by Hobbs The Printers Ltd of Southampton

PREFACE

The purpose of this book is to provide an introduction to the large and complex area of personal injury and clinical negligence litigation. It does not set out to cover the subject fully.

This text has been written as an integrated element of The College of Law's Legal Practice Course elective 'Personal Injury and Clinical Negligence Litigation' and its aim is to provide a framework upon which the course is built. Students are expected to carry out their own research into some aspects of the course and will receive further tuition in others and, therefore, this book is not intended to be used as a stand-alone text on the subject.

We are grateful to all of our colleagues who have contributed to the book and A. Foster who assisted with earlier editions.

We have updated this text approximately 2 years after the introduction of the Civil Procedure Rules 1998. However, it is clear that it is still a time of change for personal injury solicitors. Not only are amendments still being made to the Civil Procedure Rules, practitioners are having to deal with the withdrawal of public funding for many personal injury cases and expansion in the number of conditional fee agreements.

Under the Civil Procedure Rules, the term 'claimant' is used to identify the person bringing the claim. Prior to this, the word 'plaintiff' was used, and thus, where quotes have been referred to in this text, the term 'plaintiff' is seen, but this is just the phrase used to identify the victim of the accident.

As noted above, the Civil Procedure Rules are still being amended and it is important that readers make reference to the relevant provisions which are in place at the time of publication.

In the interests of brevity, we have used the masculine pronoun throughout to include the feminine.

This text is based upon the 1995/96 edition by Paul White and Harvey Silverman.

The law is generally stated as at 15 June 2001.

JEFF LILL and DAVID DOW
The College of Law
York

CONTENTS

PREFACE v

TABLE OF CASES xiii

TABLE OF STATUTES xix

TABLE OF STATUTORY INSTRUMENTS, CODES AND CONVENTIONS xxiii

TABLE OF ABBREVIATIONS xxvii

Chapter 1	AN INTRODUCTION TO THE WORK OF A PERSONAL INJURY AND CLINICAL NEGLIGENCE SOLICITOR	1
	1.1 Introduction	1
	1.2 Personal injury claims	2
	1.3 Clinical negligence claims	3
	1.4 A less adversarial culture to personal injury and clinical negligence litigation	4
	1.5 Conclusion	5
	1.6 Overviews of personal injury and clinical negligence actions	6
Chapter 2	PERSONAL INJURY AND CLINICAL NEGLIGENCE JARGON	9
	2.1 Introduction	9
	2.2 Common injuries and medical terms used	9
	2.3 Diagrammatic representation of the human skeleton	16
	2.4 Conclusion	16
	2.5 Further reading	17
Chapter 3	LIABILITY: PERSONAL INJURY AND CLINICAL NEGLIGENCE	19
	3.1 Introduction	19
	3.2 Liability at common law – negligence	19
	3.3 Breach of statutory duty	27
	3.4 Occupiers' liability to lawful visitors	37
	3.5 Vicarious liability	38
	3.6 Enforcement of health and safety at work	39
	3.7 Claims for psychiatric illness or 'nervous shock'	41
	3.8 Liability in clinical negligence cases	45
	3.9 *Res ipsa loquitur*	50
	3.10 Other common issues	51
	3.11 Conclusion	54
	3.12 Further reading	55
Chapter 4	THE FIRST INTERVIEW	57
	4.1 Introduction	57
	4.2 First interview	57
	4.3 Funding	58
	4.4 Urgent matters	73
	4.5 Advising the client	75
	4.6 The client's proof of evidence	76

	4.7	Welfare benefits	82
	4.8	Road Traffic (NHS Charges) Act 1999	86
	4.9	Rehabilitaion, early intervention and medical treatment	87
	4.10	Conclusion	88
	4.11	Further reading	88
	4.12	Overview of matters to be considered at the first interview	89

Chapter 5   FACT GATHERING AND ANALYSIS   91

5.1	Introduction	91
5.2	Identifying the defendant	91
5.3	Letter of claim	94
5.4	Notice in road traffic cases	95
5.5	The Motor Insurers Bureau	96
5.6	Acquiring evidence	101
5.7	Early access to documents and other items	104
5.8	Obtaining medical records in clinical negligence claims	105
5.9	Conclusion	109
5.10	Further reading	109
5.11	Overview of initial liability investigations	110

Chapter 6   LIMITATION OF ACTIONS   111

6.1	Introduction	111
6.2	The limitation period	111
6.3	Date of knowledge	111
6.4	Claims in fatal accidents	115
6.5	Persons under disability	116
6.6	The court's discretion to override the limitation period	116
6.7	Special periods of limitation	119
6.8	Avoiding limitation problems	119
6.9	Conclusion	120
6.10	Further reading	120

Chapter 7   COMPLAINTS PROCEDURES AND DISCIPLINARY PROCEDURES OF HEALTHCARE PROVIDERS   121

7.1	Introduction	121
7.2	The NHS complaints procedure	121
7.3	Local resolution	122
7.4	Convener of the independent review panel	123
7.5	The independent review panel	124
7.6	Complaints involving clinical matters	125
7.7	Role of the independent clinical assessors	125
7.8	The independent review panel report	126
7.9	Time-limit	126
7.10	Formal ending of complaints procedure	127
7.11	Changes implemented as a result of the report	127
7.12	The Health Service Commissioner (Ombudsman)	127
7.13	Access to Health Records Act 1990	128
7.14	Effect of coroner's inquest	128
7.15	Disciplinary proceedings against doctors	128
7.16	Disciplinary proceedings against the nursing profession	132
7.17	Conclusion	133
7.18	Further reading	133
7.19	NHS complaints procedure	134

Chapter 8	**INSTRUCTING EXPERTS**		137
	8.1	Introduction	137
	8.2	Who is an expert?	137
	8.3	How to find an expert	137
	8.4	Key qualities to look for in an expert	139
	8.5	Joint selection of experts	139
	8.6	Particular matters relating to instructing experts in personal injury actions	140
	8.7	Particular matters relating to instructing experts in clinical negligence actions	142
	8.8	Use of experts' reports	145
	8.9	Conference with experts and counsel where expert instructed by one party	146
	8.10	Meeting of experts	147
	8.11	Experts' costs	147
	8.12	Types of experts	147
	8.13	Conclusion	148
	8.14	Key points	149
	8.15	Further reading	149
Chapter 9	**PRE-COMMENCEMENT AND COMMENCEMENT STEPS**		151
	9.1	Introduction	151
	9.2	Pre-action protocol to be used in personal injury claims	152
	9.3	Pre-action protocol to be used in clinical disputes (clinical negligence)	155
	9.4	Pre-action disclosure	159
	9.5	Issuing proceedings	160
	9.6	Conclusion	164
	9.7	Further reading	164
Chapter 10	**CASE TRACKING AND CASE MANAGEMENT**		165
	10.1	Introduction	165
	10.2	Case management	165
	10.3	Allocation to track	166
	10.4	The case management conference and pre-trial review	168
	10.5	Group litigation	168
	10.6	Interim payments	169
	10.7	Disclosure and inspection of documents	170
	10.8	Witness evidence	171
	10.9	Use of plans, photographs and models as evidence at trial	172
	10.10	Expert evidence	172
	10.11	Offers to settle and payments into court	172
	10.12	Conclusion	175
	10.13	Further reading	176
Chapter 11	**NEGOTIATIONS, ADR AND TRIAL**		177
	11.1	Introduction	177
	11.2	Professional conduct	177
	11.3	Negotiating with insurance companies and defence solicitors	177
	11.4	Conducting the negotiation	179
	11.5	Negotiating in clinical negligence claims	180
	11.6	Alternative Dispute Resolution (ADR)	180
	11.7	Funding any settlement	184
	11.8	Court orders	185

	11.9	Preparation for trial	186
	11.10	The trial	189
	11.11	Conclusion	190
	11.12	Further reading	191

Chapter 12	CLAWBACK OF BENEFITS – SOCIAL SECURITY (RECOVERY OF BENEFITS) ACT 1997	193
	12.1 Introduction	193
	12.2 The legislation	193
	12.3 Definitions	194
	12.4 Compensation subject to recoupment	194
	12.5 'Like-for-like' recoupment	195
	12.6 The role of the compensator	195
	12.7 The meaning of 'recoverable benefits'	197
	12.8 Exempt payments	198
	12.9 Contributory negligence	198
	12.10 Multiple defendants ('compensators')	199
	12.11 Clinical negligence	199
	12.12 Structured settlements	199
	12.13 Part 36 payments	199
	12.14 Interim payments	199
	12.15 Appeals system	200
	12.16 The Compensation Recovery Unit and the Road Traffic (NHS Charges) Act 1999	200
	12.17 Conclusion	200
	12.18 Further reading	201

Chapter 13	QUANTIFICATION OF DAMAGES	203
	13.1 Introduction	203
	13.2 Special damages	204
	13.3 General damages	213
	13.4 Interest	223
	13.5 The award of damages at trial	225
	13.6 Further reading	225

Chapter 14	POST-DEATH INVESTIGATIONS	227
	14.1 Introduction	227
	14.2 The coroner's court	227
	14.3 Prosecution for manslaughter or prosecutions under the Health and Safety at Work etc Act 1974	239
	14.4 Criminal prosecution for causing death by dangerous driving	241
	14.5 Conclusion	242
	14.6 Key points	243
	14.7 Further reading and information	244

Chapter 15	FATAL ACCIDENT CLAIMS – PROCEDURE AND QUANTIFICATION	245
	15.1 Introduction	245
	15.2 Limitation period	245
	15.3 Cause of action	246
	15.4 The appointment of personal representatives	246
	15.5 Damages under the Law Reform (Miscellaneous Provisions) Act 1934	247
	15.6 Damages under the Fatal Accidents Act 1976	248

	15.7 Interest	258
	15.8 Pension loss	258
	15.9 Establishing the case	258
	15.10 Conduct	259
	15.11 Simplified example of a schedule of loss in a fatal accident case – traditional method	260
	15.12 Conclusion	261
	15.13 Further reading	261
Chapter 16	CLAIMS INVOLVING UNUSUAL ELEMENTS	263
	16.1 Criminal Injuries Compensation Authority	263
	16.2 Claims on behalf of child claimants	268
	16.3 Claims on behalf of mental patients	270
	16.4 Provisional damages	270
	16.5 Structured settlements	273
	16.6 Choice of jurisdiction	277
	16.7 Conclusion	278
	16.8 Key points	279
	16.9 Further reading	279

APPENDICES 281

Appendix 1	CONDITIONAL FEE DOCUMENTS	283
	Conditional Fee Protection Plan	285
	Conditional Fee Protection Plan Proposal Form	295
	The Law Society's Conditional Fee Agreement	299
Appendix 2	MEDICAL INFORMATION	307
	Common abbreviations used in medical records	309
Appendix 3	PRE-ACTION PROTOCOL FOR THE RESOLUTION OF CLINICAL DISPUTES AND THE PRE-ACTION PROTOCOL FOR PERSONAL INJURY CLAIMS	319
Appendix 4	QUESTIONNAIRE – ACCIDENT AT PLACE OF WORK	353

INDEX 359

TABLE OF CASES

References in the right-hand column are to paragraph numbers.

A (Disclosure of Medical Records to the GMC), Re [1998] 2 FLR 641, FD	7.15.5
Adefunke Fashade v North Middlesex Hospital (2001) PMILL, January	16.4.2
Alcock v Chief Constable for South Yorkshire [1992] AC 310, HL	3.7.3
Alderson and Another v Skillorgan Sales Ltd and Another [2001] All ER (D) 104 (June), CA	8.7.2
Allen v British Rail Engineering Ltd [2001] EWCA Civ 242, (2001) LTL, 23 February, CA	6.3.1
Amber v Stacey [2001] 2 All ER 88, CA	10.11.2
Ash v Buxted Poultry (1989) *The Times*, November 29, QBD	11.9.8
Auty v National Coal Board [1985] 1 All ER 930, CA	13.3.3, 15.6.2
Avon County Council v Hooper [1997] 1 WLR 1605, CA	13.2.4
B, Re (unreported)	16.5.7
Ballantine v Newalls Insulation Co Ltd (2000) *The Times*, June 22, CA	13.5
Barings plc and Another v Coopers and Lybrand and Others (2001) unreported, 9 February, ChD	8.1
Barnett v Chelsea and Kensington Hospital Management Committee [1969] 1 QB 428, QBD	3.8.3
Beahan v Stoneham (2001) LTL, 16 May	13.4
Beatham v Carlisle Hospitals NHS Trust (1999) *The Times*, May 20	16.2.6
Beattie (A Patient) v Secretary of State for Social Security [2001] EWCA Civ 498, [2001] 1 WLR 1404, CA	4.7.3, 16.5.6
Best v Samuel Fox & Co Ltd [1952] 2 All ER 394, HL	13.2.4
Billings (A.C.) & Son Ltd v Riden [1968] AC 240, HL	3.2.5
Birkett v Hayes [1982] 2 All ER 70, CA	13.4
Blamey (1988) unreported, 16 December	13.3.4
Bland v Stockport Borough Council (1998) unreported, January	2.2.14
Bolam v Friern Hospital Management Committee [1957] 1 WLR 582, QBD	3.8.2, 3.10.1
Bolitho v City and Hackney Health Authority [1997] 3 WLR 1151, HL	3.8.2, 3.8.3
Bonnington Castings Ltd v Wardlaw [1956] AC 613, HL	3.3.1
Bradburn v Great Western Railway Co (1874) LR 10 Exch 1	13.3.2
Brayson v Wilmot-Breedon [1976] CLY 682, Crown Ct	13.2.2
Breaveglen Ltd (t/a ANZAC Construction Co) v Sleeman Ltd (1997) *The Times*, May 10, QBD	5.2.2
Brooks v Home Office [1999] 2 FLR 33, QBD	3.8.3
Brown v Lewisham & North Southwark HA [1999] Lloyd's Rep Med 110, CA	3.8.3
Buckley v Farrow and Buckley [1997] PIQR Q78, CA	13.2.4
Burgess v Florence Nightingale Hospital for Gentlewomen [1955] 1 QB 349, QBD	15.6.1
Burke v Tower Hamlets Area Health Authority (1989) *The Times*, August 10, QBD	16.5.2
C, Re [1997] Sol Jo, 4 April	3.10.3
C (Adult: Refusal of Medical Treatment), Re [1994] 1 All ER 819	3.10.2
Cachia and Others v Francis Ola Faluyi (2001) *The Times*, July 11, CA	15.6.1
Calderbank v Calderbank [1976] Fam 93, CA	12.13
Callery v Gray; Russell v Pal Pak Corrugated Ltd [2001] All ER 213 (D), CA	4.3.4
Campion v Bradley (1999) 8 CL 203	12.13
Cape Distribution Ltd v O'Loughlin (2001) JPIL, Issue 2/01, p 191, CA	15.6.2
Carlton v Fulchers (A Firm) [1997] PNLR 337, CA	6.8
Carlson v Townsend [2001] EWCA Civ 511, [2001] All ER (D) 99 (April), CA	8.5, 9.2.2, 9.2.7
Cassidy v The Ministry of Health [1951] 2 KB 343, CA	3.8.1, 3.8.3
Caswell v Powell Duffryn Associated Collieries Ltd [1940] AC 152, CA	3.2.4
Chan Wai Tong v Li Ping Sum [1985] AC 446, PC	13.3.2
Chelsea Girl Ltd v Alpha Omega Electrical (1995) PMILL, February	3.2.5
Close v Steel Co of Wales [1962] AC 367, HL	3.3.3
Coad v Cornwall and Isles of Scilly Health Authority [1997] 1 WLR 189, CA	6.6
Coates v Curry (1998) *The Times*, August 22	13.5
Coker v Barkland Cleaning Ltd (1999) unreported, 6 December, CA	8.1

Colledge v Bass Mitchells & Butlers [1988] 1 All ER 536, CA	13.2.2
Compania Naviera SA v Prudential Assurance Co (Ikerian Reefer) [1993] 2 Lloyd's Rep 68	8.8
Cookson v Knowles [1979] AC 556, HL	15.6.2
Corbin v Penfold Metalizing (2000) *The Times*, May 2, CA	6.3.2
Cosgrove and Another v Pattison and Another (2001) *The Times*, February 13, ChD	8.7.2
Coward v Comex Houlder Driving Ltd (1988) unreported, 18 July, CA	15.6.2
Cox v Hockenhill (1999) *Law Society Gazette*, 30 June	15.6.1
Coyne v Cawley [1995] CLY 1624, Cty Ct	13.2.1
Croft v Shavin & Co (1995) unreported, 16 November, QBD	6.4.2
Cunningham v Camberwell Health Authority [1989] 2 Med LR 49, CA	13.3.3
Cunningham v Harrison [1973] 3 All ER 463, CA	13.2.2, 13.2.4
Daly v General Steam Navigation Co; The Dragon [1980] 3 All ER 696, CA	13.2.4
Dalziel and Dalziel v Donald (2001) JPIL Issue 2/01, p 190	15.6.2
Daniels v Walker [2000] 1 WLR 1382, CA	8.7.2, 8.8
Davie v New Merton Board Mills [1959] AC 604, HL	3.2.3
Davies v Powell Duffryn Associated Collieries [1942] AC 601, HL	15.6.2
Davis v Inman [1999] PIQR Q26	13.3.1
Dews v National Coal Board [1988] AC 1, HL	13.2.2
Dhaliwal v Personal Representatives of Hunt (deceased) [1995] PIQR Q56, CA	15.6.2
Dimond v Lovell [2000] 2 WLR 1121, HL	13.2.1
Dobbie v Medway Health Authority [1994] 1 WLR 1234, CA	6.3.1
Doleman v Deakin (1990) *The Times*, 30 January, CA	15.6.4
Donnelly v Joyce [1973] 3 All ER 475, CA	13.2.4
Donovan v Gwentoys [1990] 1 WLR 472, HL	6.6
Duller v South East Lincs Engineers (1985) CLY 585	13.2.2
Dureau v Evans [1996] PIQR Q18, CA	13.3.1
Eagle Star Insurance v Department for Social Development, Northern Ireland (2001) NICE, 12 February	12.17
Edmunds v Simmonds [2001] 1 WLR 1003, QBD	16.6.1
Evans v Motor Insurers Bureau (1997) *The Times*, November 10, QBD	5.5.5
Everett v Everett and Norfolk County Council (1991) unreported	16.5.7
F, Re [1990] 2 AC 1, HL	3.10.2
Farthing v North East Essex Health Authority [1998] Lloyd's Rep Med 37, CA	6.6
Fitzgerald v Ford [1996] PIQR Q72, CA	13.2.4
Forbes v Wandsworth Health Authority [1997] QB 402, CA	6.3.1
Ford v GKR Construction [2000] 1 All ER 802, CA	10.11.5
Foster v National Power plc [1997] LTL, 7 May	3.2.2
Foster v Tyne and Wear County Council [1986] 1 All ER 567, CA	13.3.2
Franklin v Gramophone Co Ltd [1948] 1 KB 542, CA	3.3.3
Fretwell v Willi Betz (2001) unreported	15.6.1
Froom v Butcher [1976] 1 QB 286, CA	3.2.5
Frost v Chief Constable of South Yorkshire [1997] 1 All ER 540, CA	3.7.3, 3.7.5
Frost v Chief Constable of South Yorkshire; White v Chief Constable of South Yorkshire; Duncan v British Coal Corp [1998] 3 WLR 1509, HL	3.7.4, 3.7.5
General Cleaning Contractors Ltd v Christmas [1953] AC 180, HL	3.2.1
Gillick v West Norfolk and Wisbech Area Health Authority and Department of Health and Social Security [1986] AC 112, HL	3.10.3
Goldborough v Thompson and Crowther [1996] PIQR Q86	13.3.2
Graham v Dodds [1983] 2 All ER 953, HL	15.6.2
Greatorex v Greatorex [2000] 4 All ER 769, QBD	3.7.3
Griffiths and Others v British Coal Corporation and Another (1998) unreported, 23 January, QBD and [2001] 1 WLR 1493, CA	12.7, 15.6.4

Case	Reference
Halford v Brookes [1991] 3 All ER 559, CA	6.3.1, 6.6
Hammond v West Lancashire Health Authority [1998] Lloyd's Rep Med 146, CA	6.6
Handelskwekwerij GJ Bier BV v Mines de Potasse d'Alsace SA [1978] QB 708, ECJ	16.6.1
Hannon v Pearce (2001) LTL, 25 June	13.3.3
Harris v Empress Motors; Cole v Crown Poultry Packers [1984] 1 WLR 212, CA	15.6.2
Hartley v Birmingham City District Council [1992] 2 All ER 213, CA	6.6
Hartley v Sandholme Iron Co Ltd [1975] QB 600, QBD	13.2.2
Harwick v Hindson and Another (1999) NLJ, 28 May	13.2.4
Hawkes v Southwark LBC (1998) unreported, 20 February, CA	3.2.2, 3.3.2
Heil v Rankin and Another [2000] 2 WLR 1173, CA	13.3.1
Henderson v Temple Pier Co Ltd [1998] 1 WLR 1540, CA	6.3.3
Hewson v Downs [1970] 1 QB 73, Sheffield Assizes	13.2.2
Hicks v Wright; Wafer v Wright [1992] 2 All ER 65, HL	15.5.1
Hilton International v Martin-Smith (2001) LTL, 12 February	12.17
Hodgson v Trapp [1988] 3 WLR 1281, HL	13.2.3
Holleran v Bagnell [1879] 4 LR Ir 940	15.4
Hotson v East Berkshire Health Authority [1987] AC 750, HL	3.8.3
Houghton v Meares [1995] 1 CL 115	13.3.7
Housecroft v Burnett [1986] 1 All ER 332, CA	13.1, 13.2.4
Hubble v Peterborough Hospital NHS Trust (2001) unreported, 16 March	5.8.4
Hucks v Cole (1968) 118 NLJ 469, CA	3.8.2
Hudson v Ridge Manufacturing Co [1957] 2 QB 348, Manchester Assizes	3.2.1
Hughes v Addis (2000) LTL, 23 March, CA	13.2.1
Hulse and Others v Chambers (2001) *The Times*, July 13, QBD	16.6.1
Hunt v Severs [1994] 2 All ER 385, HL	13.2.4
Hunter v British Coal [1999] QB 89, CA	3.7.4
Hunter v Hanley 1955 SLT 213, Ct of Sess	3.8.2
Hussain v New Taplow Paper Mills Ltd [1988] AC 514, HL	13.2.2
IRC v Hambrook [1956] 3 All ER 338, CA	13.2.4
James v East Dorset Health Authority (1999) *The Times*, December 7, CA	6.3.1
James v Hepworth & Grandage Ltd [1968] 1 QB 94, CA	3.2.2
Jameson and Another v Central Electricity Generating Board and Another [2000] AC 455, HL	15.3
Jefford v Gee [1970] 2 QB 130, CA	13.5
Jones (A Minor) v Wilkins (Wynn and Another) (2001) *The Times*, February 6, CA	3.2.5
Kelly v Dawes (1990) *The Times*, September 27, QBD	16.5.7
Kirkham v Boughey [1958] 2 QB 338, QBD	13.2.4
Lancaster v Birmingham City Council (1998) unreported, 23 July	2.2.13
Latimer v AEC Ltd [1953] AC 643, HL	3.2.2
Lawrence v Chief Constable of Staffordshire (2000) *The Times*, July 25, CA	13.4
Lim Poh Choo v Camden and Islington Area Health Authority [1979] 2 All ER 910, HL	13.2.3
Lister and Others v Hesley Hall Ltd [2001] 2 All ER 769, HL	3.5.3
Liverpool Roman Catholic Archdiocesan Trust v Goldberg (2001) NLJ, 20 July, ChD	8.4
Longden v British Coal Corporation [1997] 3 WLR 1336, HL	13.2.2, 13.3.6
Loveday v Renton [1990] 1 Med LR 117, QBD	8.6.1
Lybert v Warrington HA (1996) 7 Med LR 71, CA	3.10.1
M v S (2001) CLI, May	15.6.2
McCamley v Cammell Laird Shipbuilders Ltd [1990] 1 All ER 854, CA	13.2.2
McDermid v Nash Dredging & Reclamation Co Ltd [1987] 2 All ER 878, HL	3.2.3
McGhee v National Coal Board [1973] 1 WLR 1, HL	3.8.3
Martin and Brown v Gray (unreported), QBD	15.6.4
May v Pettman Smith (a firm) and Jacqueline Perry (2001) Lawtel, 4 July	8.1

Mattocks v Mann [1993] RTR 13, CA	13.2.1, 13.3.7
Maynard v West Midlands Regional Health Authority [1984] 1 WLR 634, HL	3.8.2
Mehmet v Perry [1977] 2 All ER 529, DC	15.6.2
Moeliker v A Reyrolle & Co Ltd [1977] 1 WLR 132	13.3.2
Molloy v Shell UK Ltd (2001) LTL, 6 July	13.4
Morgan v Lucas Aerospace Ltd (1997) JPIL 4/97, CA	3.2.1
Morris v Breaveglen [1993] ICR 766, CA	3.2.3
Morris v Johnson Matthey & Co Ltd (1967) 112 SJ 32, CA	13.3.4
Mutch v Allen [2001] EWCA Civ 76, (2001) Lawtel, 24 January, CA	8.6.1
Nash v Eli Lilly [1993] 1 WLR 782, CA	6.3.1
National Justice Compania Naviera SA v Prudential Assurance Co; The Ikarian Reefer [1993] 2 Lloyd's Rep 68, QBD	8.6.1
Navaei v Navaei (1995) *Halsbury's Laws*, June, 1784	15.6.4
Naylor v Preston Area Health Authority [1987] 1 WLR 958, CA	5.8.1
Neal v Bingle [1998] 2 All ER 58, CA	13.2.1
Newbury v Bath DHA (1999) 47 BMLR 138	3.10.1
Newman v Marshall and Dunlop Tyres Ltd (2001) LTL, 19 June	13.2.2
Oliver v Ashman [1962] 2 QB 210, CA	13.3.3
Owen v Martin [1992] PIQR Q151, CA	15.6.2
Oxley v Penwarden (2000) MLC 0250, CA	8.7.2
Page v Sheerness Steel Co Ltd; Wells v Wells; Thomas v Brighton Health Authority [1998] 3 WLR 329, QBD	13.2.5, 13.3.5, 13.7.5, 15.6.3
Page v Smith [1996] AC 155	3.7.5
Paris v Stepney Borough Council [1951] AC 367, HL	3.2.2
Parry v Cleaver [1970] AC 1, HL	13.2.2
Penney v British Steel (1997) unreported, 1 July, CA	6.3.1
Penney and Others v East Kent Health Authority [2000] Lloyd's Rep Med 41, CA	3.8.3
Phillips v Taunton and Somerset NHS Trust (1996) *The Times*, August 15, CA	6.8
Phipps v Brooks Dry Cleaning Services Ltd [1996] PIQR Q100, CA	13.3.3
Pickett (Administrator of the Estate of Ralph Henry Pickett, decd) v British Rail Engineering Ltd [1980] AC 136, HL	13.3.3
Polock v North East Essex Mental Health NHS Trust (1998) unreported, March	2.2.13
Practice Direction (QBD) (Provisional Damages) [1985] 1 WLR 961, QBD	16.4.7
Practice Direction (QBD) (Provisional Damages: Amended Procedure) [1995] 1 WLR 507, QBD	16.4.7
Prendergast v Sam and Dee Ltd (1989) *The Times*, March 14, CA	3.10.7
Prokop v Department of Health and Social Security and Cleaners Ltd (1983) unreported, 5 July, CA	13.4
R (A Minor) (Wardship: Consent to Treatment), Re [1992] Fam 11, CA	3.10.2
R v Adomako [1995] 1 AC 171, HL	14.3
R v Birmingham and Solihull Coroner ex parte Benton [1997] 8 Med LR 362	14.2.6
R v British Steel plc [1995] ICR 586, CA	14.3
R v Caldwell; Commissioner of Police of the Metropolis v Caldwell [1982] AC 341, HL	14.3
R v Criminal Injuries Compensation Board ex parte K [1998] 2 FLR 1071, QBD	15.6.2
R v Director of Public Prosecutions ex parte Manning and Another [2000] 3 WLR 463, QBD	14.2.6
R v Gateway Foodmarkets Ltd [1997] 3 All ER 78, CA	3.6.3
R v HM Coroner for Avon ex parte Bentley [2001] EWHC Admin 170, (2001) LTL, 23 March, QBD	14.2.5, 14.2.6
R v HM Coroner for Avon ex parte Smith (1998) 162 JP 403	14.2.3
R v HM Coroner for Coventry ex parte Chief Constable of Staffordshire Police (2000) LTL, 28 September, QBD	14.2.6
R v HM Coroner for Derby and South Derbyshire ex parte Hart (2000) 164 JP 429, QBD	14.2.6
R v HM Coroner for Greater Manchester North District ex parte Worch and Brunner [1988] QB 513, CA	14.2.2

Case	Reference
R v HM Coroner for Inner London North District ex parte Cohen (1994) 158 JP 644, DC	14.2.6
R v HM Coroner for Inner London South District ex parte Douglas-Williams (1998) 162 JP 751, CA	14.2.6
R v HM Coroner for Inner West London ex parte Cleo Scott [2001] EWHC Admin 105, (2001) LTL, 13 February, QBD	14.2.6
R v HM Coroner for North Humberside and Scunthorpe ex parte Jamieson [1995] QB 1, CA	14.2.6
R v HM Coroner for Swansea and Gower ex parte Tristram (2000) 164 JP 191, QBD	14.2.6
R v Howe & Son (Engineers) Ltd [1999] 2 All ER 249, CA	3.6.3
R v Inner London North Coroner ex parte Touche [2001] 3 WLR 148, CA	14.2.3
R v Lincolnshire Coroner ex parte Hay (1999) 163 JP 666, QBD	14.2.5, 14.2.6
R v HM Coroner for Kent (Maidstone District) ex parte Johnstone (1994) 158 JP 1115, QBD	14.2.6
R v Newcastle upon Tyne Coroner ex parte A (1998) 162 JP 387, QBD	14.2.6
R v P & O European Ferries (Dover) Ltd (1991) 93 Cr App R 72	14.3
R v Poplar Coroner ex parte Thomas [1993] 2 WLR 547, CA	14.2.3
R v Portsmouth City Coroner ex parte Keane (1989) 153 JP 658, DC	14.2.6
R v Rollco Screw & Rivet Co Ltd [1999] 2 Cr App R (S) 436, CA	3.6.3
R v Surrey Coroner ex parte Wright [1997] 2 WLR 16, CA	14.2.1, 14.2.6
Ramsden v Lee [1992] 2 All ER 204, CA	6.6
Ratcliffe v Plymouth and Torbay Health Authority [1998] PIQR P170, CA	3.9
Reed v Sunderland Health Authority (1998) *The Times*, October 16, CA	13.3.1
Regan v Chetwynd (2001) JPIL 2/01	8.1
Regan v Williamson [1976] 1 WLR 305, QBD	15.6.2
Rialas v Mitchell (1984) *The Times*, July 17, CA	13.2.4
Roberts v Johnstone [1989] QB 878, [1988] 3 WLR 1247, CA	13.2.4, 13.2.5, 13.4
Roberts v Winslow (1999) *The Times*, January 12	6.3.1
Rose v Plenty [1976] 1 All ER 97, CA	3.5.3
Rush v JNR (SMD) Ltd (1999) unreported, 11 October, CA	6.3.3
S (a Minor) v Birmingham Health Authority (1999) CTL, 23 November, QBD	8.7.2
Schneider v Eisovitch [1960] 2 QB 430, QBD	13.2.4
Secretary of State for Social Security v Oldham MBC and Others (2001) unreported, 15 May	12.17
Shakoor v Situ (t/a Eternal Health Co) [2000] 4 All ER 181, QBD	3.10.8
Sharman v Sheppard [1989] CLY 1190, Cty Ct	15.7
Sharpe v Southend Health Authority [1997] 8 Med LR 299, CA	3.8.2, 8.6.1
Shepherd v Post Office (1995) *The Times*, June 15, CA	15.6.1
Sidaway v Governors of the Bethlam Royal Hospital [1985] AC 871, HL	3.8.2, 3.10.1
Silverton v Goodall and MIB (1997) PIQR P451, CA	5.5.1
Simpson v Norwest Holst Southern Ltd [1980] 2 All ER 471, CA	6.3.3
Smith v Crossley Bros (1951) 95 Sol Jo 655, CA	3.2.1, 3.2.3
Smith v Leech Brain & Co Ltd [1962] 2 QB 405, QBD	3.2.3, 13.3.1
Smith v Manchester Corporation (1974) 17 KIR 1, CA	13.3.1, 13.3.2
Smoker (Alexander) v London Fire and Civil Defence Authority; Wood v British Coal Corpn [1991] 2 All ER 449, HL	13.3.2
Sniezek v Bundy (Letchworth) Ltd (2000) LTL, 7 July, CA	6.3.2
Spargo v North Essex District Health Authority [1997] 8 Med LR 125, CA	6.3.2
Sparrow v St Andrews Homes Ltd (1998) unreported, 21 May, QBD	2.2.14
Speed v Thomas Swift & Co [1943] KB 557, CA	3.2.1
Spittle v Bunney [1988] 1 WLR 847, CA	13.4
Stanley v Saddique [1992] 1 QB 1, CA	15.6.2
Stapley v Gypsum Mines Ltd [1953] AC 663, HL	3.3.1
Stark v Post Office [2000] ICR 1013, CA	3.3.2
Steeds v Peverel Management Services Ltd (2001) *The Times*, May 16, CA	6.6
Stinton v Stinton and the Motor Insurers' Bureau [1993] PIQR P135, CA	3.2.5
Stobart v Nottingham Health Authority [1992] 3 Med LR 284, QBD	14.2.5
Sumner v William Henderson & Sons Ltd [1964] 1 QB 450, QBD	3.2.3
T (Adult: Refusal of Treatment), Re [1992] All ER 649, CA	3.10.4

Taylor v Serviceteam Ltd and London Borough of Waltham Forest [1998] PIQR P201, Cty Ct	5.2.2
Thai Trading Co (A Firm) v Taylor [1998] 2 WLR 893, CA	4.3.4
Thomas v Kwik Save Stores Ltd (2000) *The Times*, June 27	15.6.1
Thomas v Plaistow (1997) LSG 94/17, 30 April, CA	6.5
Thorn v Powergen plc [1997] PIQR Q71, CA	13.3.2
Thrul v Ray (2000) PIQR Q44, QBD	13.2.4
Usher v Crowder [1994] CLY 1494, Cty Ct	13.2.1
Vadera v Shaw (1998) BMLR 162, CA	3.8.3
Vernon v Bosley (No 1) [1997] 1 All ER 577, CA	3.7.3
Wadley v Surrey County Council (2000) *The Times*, April 7, HL	13.4
Wain v F Sherwood and Sons Transport Limited (1998) *The Times*, July 16, CA	13.5
Walker v Northumberland County Council [1995] 1 All ER 737, QBD	2.2.13
Wells v Wells, *see* Page v Sheerness Steel plc, Thomas v Brighton Health Authority [1997] 1 All ER 673, QBD	
West (H) & Son v Shephard [1964] AC 326, HL	13.3.1
Wheat v Lacon (E) & Co Ltd [1966] AC 522, HL	3.4.1
Wheatley v Cunningham [1992] PIQR Q100, QBD	15.6.2
White v Chief Constable of South Yorkshire, *see* Frost v Chief Constable of South Yorkshire; White v Chief Constable of South Yorkshire; Duncan v British Coal Corp [1998] 3 WLR 1509, HL	
Whittaker v Westinghouse Brake and Signal Holdings (1996) CLR, 9 August, CA	
Wickham v Dwyer (1995) *Current Law Weekly*, 1 January	5.8.5
Widdowson v Newgate Meat Corporation and Others [1998] PIQR P138	3.2.3
Williams v BOC Gases Ltd [2000] PIQR 253, CA	13.2.2
Williamson v East London and City HA [1998] 1 Lloyd's Rep Med 6, ChD	3.10.1
Willson v Ministry of Defence [1991] 1 All ER 638	16.4.2
Wilsher v Essex Area Health Authority [1988] AC 1074, HL	3.8.1, 3.8.2
Wilson v Pringle [1986] 3 WLR 1, CA	3.10.2
Wilson v Tyneside Window Cleaning Co [1958] 2 QB 110, CA	3.2.1
Wilson, Holdham & Adams v West Cumbria Healthcare NHS Trust (1995) PMILR, 3 August, Cty Ct	5.2.2, 5.2.3
Wilsons & Clyde Coal Co v English [1938] AC 57, HL	3.2.1, 3.4.4
Worrall v Powergen plc (1999) *The Times*, February 10	13.3.3
Young v Charles Church (Southern) Ltd (1998) 39 BMLR 146, CA	3.7.4

TABLE OF STATUTES

References are to paragraph and Appendix numbers.

Access to Health Records Act 1990	5.8.4, 5.11, 7.13, 9.3.4
Access to Justice Act 1999	
ss 1–11	4.3.2
ss 19–26	4.3.2
s 27	4.3.4
s 29	4.3.4
s 71	14.2.3
Sch 2	4.3.2
Administration of Justice Act 1982	15.5.2, 15.6.1
s 5	13.2.2
Adoption Act 1976	15.6.1
Carriage by Air Act 1961	6.7, 15.1, 15.2
Civil Evidence Act 1995	5.6.2, 15.9
Civil Jurisdiction and Judgments Act 1982	16.6.1
Civil Liability (Contribution) Act 1978	6.7
Consumer Credit Act 1974	13.2.1
Consumer Protection Act 1987	3.10.6
Coroners Act 1988	14.2
s 8(1)	14.2.2, 14.2.3, 14.6
s 17A	14.2.3
s 21(3)	14.2.2
Corporate Homicide Bill (2000)	14.3.1
County Courts Act 1984	
s 51	16.4.2
s 52	5.8.4, 9.4
(2)	5.7.1
s 69	13.4
Courts and Legal Services Act 1990	
s 58(1)	4.3.4
Criminal Injuries Compensation Act 1995	
ss 1–6	16.1
s 8	16.5.3
s 12	16.1
Damages Act 1996	
s 1	13.3.3
s 3	16.4.8
s 6	16.5.3
Data Protection Act 1998	5.8.4, 9.3.4
s 1(1)	5.8.4
s 7	5.8.4
s 8(2)	5.8.4
s 12A	5.8.4
s 14	5.8.4
s 68	5.8.4
s 69	5.8.4
s 70(2)	5.8.4
Deregulation and Contracting Out Act 1994	3.3.2
Employers' Liability (Compulsory Insurance) Act 1969	3.6.2
Employers' Liability (Defective Equipment) Act 1969	3.2.1
Factories Act 1961	3.3, 5.6.7
Family Law Reform Act 1969	
s 8(1)	3.10.3
Fatal Accidents Act 1976	6.4.2, 9.5.2, 12.8, 15.1, 15.2, 15.3, 15.4, 15.5, 15.6, 15.6.1, 15.6.2, 15.6.3, 15.6.5, 15.6.6, 15.6.7, 16.4.8
s 1	15.3
(4), (5)	15.6.1
s 1A(4)	15.6.4
s 2	15.6.1
(2)	15.4
s 3(3)	15.6.2
(4)	15.6.1
(5)	15.6.5
s 4	15.6.6
Foreign Limitations Act 1984	16.7
Health Act 1999	7.1
Health and Safety at Work etc Act 1974	3.1, 3.3, 3.6.3, 14.1, 14.2.6, 14.3, 14.6
ss 2–7	3.3.1
s 2(1)	3.6.3, 14.3, 14.6
s 3(1)	3.6.3, 14.3, 14.6
s 15	3.3
s 16	3.2.2, 3.3
s 19	14.2.6
s 37(1)	14.3, 14.6
s 47	3.3.1
(1)	3.3.1
Health and Social Services Adjudication Act 1983	
s 17	13.2.4
Health Services Act 1980	5.2.3
Highways Act 1980	
s 41	4.6.2
Human Rights Act 1998	5.8.4, 15.6.1

Law Reform (Contributory Negligence) Act 1945	3.2.5
s 4	3.2.5
Law Reform (Contributory Negligence) Act 1948	3.2.4
Law Reform (Miscellaneous Provisions) Act 1934	6.4.1, 6.4.2, 15.1, 15.2, 15.3, 15.4, 15.5, 15.5.6, 15.5.7, 15.6.5, 15.6.6
s 1(2)	15.3, 15.5.6
(a)(ii)	15.5.2
(c)	15.5.3
s 11(4)	6.4.1
Law Reform (Personal Injuries) Act 1948	
s 2(4)	13.2.3
Legal Aid Act 1988	4.3.2, 11.6.6
s 4(2)(b)	14.2.4
Limitation Act 1980	5.2.1, 6.1, 6.3.2, 6.4.2, 6.6, 10.5, 15.2
s 2	6.2
s 11	6.2, 6.3.1, 6.4.2, 6.6
(4)	6.2, 6.4.1
(5)	6.4.1
(7)	6.4.1
s 12	6.2, 6.3.1, 6.4.2, 6.6
(2)	6.4.2
s 14	6.3.1, 6.3.2, 6.3.3
(1)(b)	6.3.2
(2)	6.3.1
(3)	6.3.2, 6.3.3
s 28	6.4.2, 6.5, 16.3
(2)	6.5
s 33	6.3.2, 6.4.1, 6.4.2, 6.5, 6.6, 6.8, 6.9, 15.2
(3)	6.5, 6.6
(a)	6.6
(d)	16.3
s 38	6.1
Maritime Conventions Act 1911	6.7
Medical Act 1858	7.15.1
Medical Act 1983	7.15.1
ss 36–45	7.15.1
Sch 4	7.15.1
Medical (Professional Performance) Act 1995	7.15.1
Mental Health Act 1983	6.5, 16.3
s 28	6.5
(2)	6.5
Merchant Shipping Act 1995	6.7
National Health Service Act 1977	
s 1	3.8.1
s 3	3.8.1
Sch 5, para 15	5.2.3
National Health Service and Community Care Act 1990	5.2.3
National Health Service (Residual Liabilities) Act 1996	16.5.3
Nurses, Midwives and Health Visitors Act 1979	7.16.1
Occupiers' Liability Act 1957	3.1, 3.4.1, 3.4.4
s 1(1)–(3)	3.4.1
s 2(1)	3.4.5
(2)	3.4.2
(3)	3.4.3
(4)	3.4.3
(b)	3.4.4
(5)	3.4.2
Offices, Shops and Railway Premises Act 1963	3.3
Opticians Act 1989	3.3.2
Pneumoconiosis etc (Workers' Compensation) Act 1979	13.5
Powers of Criminal Courts Act 1973	
s 35	12.8
Private International Law (Miscellaneous Provisions) Act 1995	16.7
s 12(1)(b)	16.6.1
Road Traffic Act 1988	5.5.1
ss 1, 2	14.4
s 2A	14.4
s 151	5.2.1, 5.4, 5.4.1, 10.6
(2)	5.4.1
s 152	5.2.1, 5.4, 5.4.2, 5.5.1
(2)	5.4.2
s 154	5.3.1, 5.5.4
ss 157, 158	4.8
Road Traffic (NHS Charges) Act 1999	4.8, 12.16
Sale of Goods Act 1979	3.10.6
Social Security Act 1998	
Sch 7, paras 148–152	12.2
Social Security Administration Act 1992	4.7.3
s 103	12.7
ss 104, 105	12.7
Social Security (Recovery of Benefits) Act 1997	4.7.3, 4.8, 12.2, 12.3.1, 12.4, 12.12, 12.17, 15.5.6, 15.6.7
s 1	12.3.1, 12.3.3

Social Security (Recovery of Benefits) Act 1997 *cont*		s 33(2)	5.7.1
		s 34	11.9.8
s 3	12.4	s 35A	13.4
s 4	12.6.1		
s 6	9.5.1		
s 8	10.11.8, 12.13	Unfair Contract Terms Act 1977	
Sch 1, Pt 1	12.8	s 2	3.4.5
Sch 2	12.3.3, 12.5, 12.7, 12.13		
Supreme Court Act 1981	16.4.2		
s 32A	16.4.2	Workmen's Compensation Acts	4.7.1
s 33	9.4		

TABLE OF STATUTORY INSTRUMENTS, CODES AND CONVENTIONS

References in the right-hand column are to paragraph and Appendix numbers.

Abrasive Wheels Regulations 1970, SI 1970/535	3.3
Access to Justice (Membership Organisations) Regulations 2000, SI 2000/693	4.3.4
reg 4(2)	4.3.4
Civil Procedure Rules 1998, SI 1998/3132	1.1, 1.4, 1.5, 4.3.4, 5.5.4, 5.8.2, 8.1, 8.5, 8.6.2, 8.8, 8.10, 8.13, 9.2.1, 10.2, 10.3.2, 10.5, 10.8.2, 10.12, 10.13, 11.3, 11.8.2, 11.12, 12.17, 16.2.4, 16.4.2
Part 1 Overriding Objective	9.2.8, 11.6, 11.6.2
Part 2 Application and Interpretation of the Rules	
r 2.3	10.3.1
Part 8 Alternative Procedure for Claims	4.3.4, 16.2.3, 16.8
Part 16 Statements of Case	16.4.4
PD 16 – Statements of Case	9.5.2, 16.4.4
Part 19 Addition and Substitution of Parties	10.5
PD 19B – Group Litigation	10.5
Part 20 Counterclaims and Other Additional Claims	9.5.8
Part 21 Children and Patients	16.2.4, 16.8
PD 21 – Children and Patients	16.2.4
Part 23 General Rules about Applications for Court Orders	10.11.5, 16.4.6, 16.5.2, 16.8
Part 25 Interim Remedies	5.11
r 25.5	9.4.3
Part 31 Disclosure and Inspection of Documents	5.11
r 31.16	9.4
Part 32 Evidence	
r 32.1	8.8
Part 35 Experts and Assessors	8.1, 8.8, 8.14, 9.2.7
r 35.16	5.7.1
r 35.10(4)	8.8
PD 35 – Experts and Assessors	8.8, 8.13
Part 36 Offers to Settle and Payments into Court	9.2.8, 10.11 et seq, 11.6.6, 11.9.1, 12.13, 16.4.9
r 36.7	16.4.9
r 36.20	10.11.5
PD 36 – Offers to Settle and Payments into Court	10.11.8, 11.9.1, 12.13
Part 40 Judgments, Orders, Sale of Land etc	
PD 40C – Structured Settlements	16.5.2
Part 41 Provisional Damages	16.4.3
PD 41 – Provisional Damages	16.4.3
Part 44 General Rules About Costs	4.3.4
PD Costs	
para 20.1	4.3.5
Pre-action protocol for Personal Injury Claims	5.3.1, 8.5, 8.15, 8.16, 9.2.2, 9.2.3, 9.2.7, 9.2.8, 9.7, App 3
para 3.21	9.2.8
Pre-action protocol for Resolution of Clinical Disputes	8.5, 8.16, 9.3.1, 9.3.2, 9.3.3, 9.3.4, 9.7, App 3
Civil Procedure (Amendment No 3) Rules 2000, SI 2000/1317	4.3.4
Conditional Fee Agreements Order 2000, SI 2000/823	4.3.4
Conditional Fee Agreements Regulations 2000, SI 2000/692	4.3.4
regs 2–4	4.3.4
reg 3(2)(b)	4.3.5

Control of Substances Hazardous to Health Regulations 1988, SI 1988/1657	3.3
Control of Substances Hazardous to Health Regulations 1994, SI 1994/3246	3.3.2
Coroners Rules 1984, SI 1984/552	14.2, 14.2.6
r 6	14.2.2
r 7(4)	14.2.2
r 20(2)	14.2.6
r 22	14.2.6
r 26(3)	14.2.6
r 43	14.2.6
r 57(1)	14.2.2
Sch 2, Form 22	14.2.6
Data Protection (Subject Access) (Fees and Miscellaneous Provisions) Regulations 2000, SI 2000/191	5.8.4
Health and Safety (Display Screen Equipment) Regulations 1992, SI 1992/2792	3.3.2, 3.12
reg 2	3.3.2
reg 5	3.3.2
reg 6	3.3.2
reg 7	3.3.2
Income Support (General) Regulations 1987, SI 1987/1967	
reg 41(2)	4.7.3
Lifting Operations and Lifting Regulations 1998, SI 1998/2307	3.3.2, 3.12
Management of Health and Safety at Work Regulations 1999, SI 1999/3242	3.2.2, 3.3.1, 3.3.2, 3.12
regs 3–7	3.3.2
reg 10	3.3.2
reg 12	3.2.5
reg 13	3.3.2
reg 14	3.3.2
reg 16	3.3.2
reg 19	3.3.2
regs 21, 22	3.3.1
Manual Handling Operations Regulations 1992, SI 1992/2793	3.3.2, 3.12
reg 2(1)	3.3.2
reg 4(1)	3.3.2
(a)	3.3.2
(b)	3.3.2
(iii)	3.3.2
(5)	3.3.2
Motor Cycles (Protective Helmets) Regulations 1980, SI 1980/1279	3.2.5
Motor Vehicles (Wearing of Seat Belts) Regulations 1993, SI 1993/176	3.2.5
Motor Vehicles (Wearing of Seat Belts by Children in Front Seats) Regulations 1993, SI 1993/31	3.2.5
National Health Service (Injury Benefits) Regulations 1974, SI 1974/1547	12.8
Noise at Work Regulations 1989, SI 1989/1790	2.2.5

Package Travel, Package Holidays and Package Tours Regulations 1992, SI 1992/3288	16.6.3
Personal Protective Equipment at Work Regulations 1992, SI 1992/2966	3.2.1, 3.3.2, 3.12
reg 4	3.3.2
regs 6, 7	3.3.2
reg 9	3.3.2
Provision and Use of Work Equipment Regulations 1998, SI 1998/2306	3.2.1, 3.3.2, 3.12
reg 2	3.3.2
reg 4	3.3.2
reg 5	3.3.2
reg 6	3.2.1
(1)	3.3.2
(2)	3.3.2
reg 8	3.3.2
reg 9	3.3.2
reg 11	3.3.2
reg 13	3.3.2
regs 15–17	3.3.2
regs 20–25	3.3.2
Reporting of Injuries, Diseases and Dangerous Occurrences Regulations 1995, SI 1995/3163	5.6.6
Sch 2	5.6.6
Social Security (Recovery of Benefits) Regulations 1997, SI 1997/2205	12.2
reg 8	10.11.8
Transfer of Undertakings (Protection of Employment) Regulations 1981, SI 1981/1794	5.2.2
Workplace (Health, Safety and Welfare) Regulations 1992, SI 1992/3004	3.2.1, 3.3.2, 3.12
reg 3	3.3.2
regs 5–9	3.3.2
regs 11–13	3.3.2
regs 20, 21	3.3.2

Codes and Conventions

Approved Codes of Practice	
Control of Carcinogenic Substances	3.3
Brussels Convention on Jurisdiction and the Enforcement of Judgments in Civil and Commercial Matters 1968	16.6.1
Art 5(3)	16.6.1
Community Legal Service Funding Code	4.3.2, 11.6.6
Part 1	4.3.2
Part 2	4.3.2
Draft Code of Guidance for Experts	8.14
European Convention for the Protection of Human Rights and Fundamental Freedoms 1950	15.6.1
European Framework Directive (89/391/EC)	3.3.2

Law Society Code for Advocacy	14.2.9
Law Society Guide to the Professional Conduct of Solicitors	4.3.4
Principle 21.18	14.2.9
Law Society Conditional Fee Agreement	4.3.4, App 1
Conditions 4, 5	4.3.4
Condition 6	4.3.10
Condition 7	4.3.4
Law Society protocol for obtaining hospital medical records	5.8.2
Solicitors Practice Rules 1990	4.3.4
Warsaw Convention	6.7
Written Professional Standards	4.3.9

TABLE OF ABBREVIATIONS

See Appendix 2 for commonly used medical abbreviations.

ABWOR	assistance by way of representation
ACOPS	Approved Codes of Practice
ADR	alternative dispute resolution
ALP	Accident Line Protect
APIL	Association of Personal Injury Lawyers
AVMA	Association of Victims of Medical Accidents
CFA	conditional fee agreement
CICA	Criminal Injuries Compensation Authority
CJJA 1982	Civil Jurisdication and Judgments Act 1982
CNST	Clinical Negligence Scheme for Trusts
CPR 1998	Civil Procedure Rules 1998
CPS	Crown Prosecution Service
CRU	Compensation Recovery Unit
CTG	cardiotachograph
DSE	display screen equipment
DSS	Department of Social Security
ECG	electrocardiogram
FAA 1976	Fatal Accidents Act 1976
FOIL	Federation of Insurance Lawyers
GLO	group litigation order
GMC	General Medical Council
HAVS	hand/arm vibration syndrome
HSE	Health & Safety Executive
ICTA 1988	Income and Corporation Taxes Act 1988
IRP	independent review panel
LA 1980	Limitation Act 1980
LAA	legal advice and assistance
LR(MP)A 1934	Law Reform (Miscellaneous Provisions) Act 1934
MIB	Motor Insurers Bureau
MPA	multi-party action
NHSLA	NHS Litigation Authority
OLA 1957	Occupiers' Liability Act 1957
PAR	police accident report
PD	Practice Direction
PPE	personal protective equipment
PTSD	post-traumatic stress disorder
RIDDOR 1995	Reporting of Injuries Diseases and Dangerous Occurrences Regulations 1995
RSI	repetitive strain injury
SSP	statutory sick pay
UKCC	United Kingdom Central Council for Nursing, Midwifery and Health Visiting
VWF	vibration white finger

Chapter 1

AN INTRODUCTION TO THE WORK OF A PERSONAL INJURY AND CLINICAL NEGLIGENCE SOLICITOR

1.1 INTRODUCTION

The aim of this text is to provide an introduction to personal injury and clinical negligence litigation. It is, however, assumed that the basic civil litigation procedure has been studied before and reference to the LPC Resource Book *Civil Litigation* (Jordans) and the Civil Procedure Rules 1998 (CPR 1998) may be necessary for those unfamiliar with the essential elements of High Court and county court procedure.

The terms 'personal injury litigation' and 'clinical negligence litigation' are widely used to describe claims for compensation for injuries which a client has suffered. In this text, personal injury litigation is the term used to refer to the following types of claims.

(1) Road traffic accident claims. These are usually the most straightforward type of claim and include any case where, in addition to property damage, an injury has been suffered by the client.
(2) Employers' liability claims. This term is used for accidents that have occurred where the claimant was injured in the course of his employment and his employer is the defendant. Common examples of this type of personal injury claim are slipping accidents on the factory floor, repetitive strain injury suffered by machine operatives and clients who suffer from deafness due to their employers providing inadequate ear protection.
(3) Public liability claims. These claims arise out of public use of products or premises, for example, a person who cuts his foot on a cracked tile whilst using the public swimming baths.

Clinical negligence claims refer not only to the negligence of doctors but to all the related medical professions, such as nurses, physiotherapists and dentists. Whilst the basic litigation procedure for both types of claim is the same, the skills required to pursue the claim differ. Where the procedure for a clinical negligence claim differs from that of a personal injury claim, specific reference is made in the text.

This text will not deal with every type of claim that is encountered in practice. It should, however, serve as a basic introduction to a fascinating area of law which is developing quickly.

The CPR 1998 require personal injury and clinical negligence solicitors to adopt an 'approach' to litigation which requires the parties and the court to have regard to the speed and cost involved in pursuing the case. One of the major changes to support this ideal, introduced by the Civil Procedure reforms in 1999, is the concept of pre-action protocols in personal injury and clinical negligence cases. Full details of the protocols are set out in Chapter 9. However, it must be noted that these protocols set out the steps which should be taken by the parties **prior** to the issue of proceedings.

Chapter 1 contents
Introduction
Personal injury claims
Clinical negligence claims
A less adversarial culture to personal injury and clinical negligence litigation
Conclusion
Overviews of personal injury and clinical negligence actions

1.2 PERSONAL INJURY CLAIMS

1.2.1 The claimant's perspective

The aim of the claimant's personal injury solicitor is to prove that the defendant was responsible for the client's injuries and to maximise the amount of compensation that the client receives. The solicitor should also attempt to obtain the compensation payment as quickly as possible. Therefore, there are two essential elements to a personal injury claim: liability and quantum. This may sound obvious, but it is important that these two elements are paramount in the solicitor's mind throughout the case.

Personal injury claims can take time to progress. At the initial interview, it should be explained to the client how it is anticipated the case will proceed and a realistic time-scale should be given (although this can be difficult) as to when the matter might be settled or reach trial. The client should be informed of the basic requirements of the relevant pre-action protocol and the time-limits imposed on each side. It is important that the client is kept informed as the matter proceeds. Regular letters should be sent updating the client on the current position. If a proactive approach is taken, this will avoid difficulties in the future.

Liability

It is for the claimant to prove his case and the onus, therefore, will be on the client to persuade the court that the defendant is in breach of a statutory or common law duty owed to the client. The majority of personal injury actions include negligence as a cause of action and a reminder of the basic elements of negligence is included in Chapter 3, together with an examination of other potential causes of action. Sometimes it will be possible for the claimant's solicitor to advise the client with a degree of certainty whether a case will be made out against the defendant.

For example, if a client informs his solicitor that he was stationary in his vehicle when he was hit from behind by the defendant's vehicle, or that the client was a passenger in a car that was involved in an accident, then it is likely that the client will establish liability. However, liability can never be taken for granted.

Quantum

Many claimants have reported being dissatisfied with the compensation they received. This may have been as a result of the operation of the law in the personal injury and clinical negligence field, or of imprudent investment of the damages by the claimant. However, it is clear that the claimant's solicitor should have as his aim the maximisation of damages for his client and he must do all that is possible to achieve that aim. Most solicitors working in this area acknowledge that a weariness on the part of the victims themselves can set in, caused, for example, by anxiety at having to attend trial, which can result in the client accepting inappropriately low offers rather than progressing with the litigation process. This should be acknowledged as a factor to be dealt with by the solicitor and the client's concerns should be anticipated.

Medical evidence is required by the court to prove the injuries suffered by the client. Instructing a doctor may appear to be a simple task but the choice of the appropriate doctor is significant. The court, if the matter proceeds to trial, or the defendant's insurers, if the case is settled, will assess the value of the client's injuries on the basis of the medical evidence supplied to them. The instruction of experts is dealt with in

Chapter 8. Those unfamiliar with this type of work will be surprised at the number and different types of experts in existence. They range from orthopaedic consultants, (who can, for example, provide an opinion on a fractured bone) to consulting engineers (who can, for example, provide a report on the safety of ladders).

The claimant's solicitor should ensure that he moves the case on with speed. A diary system is essential to ensure that deadlines are complied with. Many firms use electronic case management systems to assist in this process.

1.2.2 The defendant perspective

The defendant's personal injury solicitor will usually be instructed only when proceedings have been issued against the defendant. At all times prior to this, the claimant's solicitor will normally correspond with the defendant's insurance company, and many cases will be settled without the need to instruct a defence solicitor. However, if the insurance company believes that its insured can escape liability, it will defend the action. Similarly, if it believes that liability will be established, it will attempt to dispose of the claim for as little money as possible. The insurance company's aims are clearly opposed to the aims of the claimant's solicitor.

The defendant's solicitor will be sent a file of papers by the insurance company when proceedings have been issued, and his first task will normally be to prepare a report dealing with liability and quantum. The defendant's solicitor's aim in dealing with the case will be similar to that of the insurance company.

It is important that the defendant's solicitor contacts the insured, who is the named defendant in the court proceedings. Many insurance companies require the insured to sign a letter of authority allowing them to act on the insured's behalf and to dispose of the case in any way that the defendant's solicitor sees fit. This is often a formality, as the terms of the insurance policy will allow the insurance company and its solicitor to have control of the case. The insurance company will, on occasion, take into account the views of its insured as to how the action should proceed, as it will be concerned to ensure that the insured remains a client (this is more appropriate where the insured is a large and significant client of the insurance company).

1.3 CLINICAL NEGLIGENCE CLAIMS

1.3.1 The claimant's perspective

The essential aims in a clinical negligence claim are the same as in a personal injury claim – namely, to establish liability and maximise damages. However, these are frequently not the only aims and considerations. The client's trust in a respected profession has been lost and many clients will frequently not be certain what has happened to them. It must be explained to the client that he has to prove his claim if he is to establish liability. One of the first distinctions which has to be made between personal injury and clinical negligence cases is that the issue of liability is normally far more complicated in the latter, and there is a greater chance that the claimant's claim will fail at trial. However, the law relating to the quantum of damages is the same in both personal injury and clinical negligence cases.

The costs involved in a clinical negligence case are usually higher than those incurred in a personal injury case. The clinical negligence pre-action protocol will have to be complied with and the initial investigations prior to commencing the action will involve the solicitor taking instructions, obtaining the client's medical notes and then instructing an expert to assess the notes and evidence available. This can cost a significant amount. It is only then that any preliminary view on liability can be obtained. Unlike a personal injury case, the victim's clinical negligence solicitor will never be able to give a view on liability at the first interview. It will only be when the notes and an expert's view are obtained that any advice on liability can be given to the client.

A common concern expressed by clients is how they will continue to be treated by the doctor/health care professional if there is a continuing 'doctor/patient' relationship and an explanation of the alternatives available to clients may be required. Clients will need advice not only in respect of pursuing claims for damages but also on how to complain about the conduct of the health care professional or hospital, or the appropriateness of mediation in respect of their claim. The options available to the client in such circumstances should be familiar to a solicitor working in this area of the law. The solicitor will need to establish whether the client wishes to pursue a damages claim or if the client's aim is solely to report the alleged misconduct to the regulatory body.

1.3.2 The defendant perspective

The defendant clinical negligence solicitor will have the same basic aims as those of the defendant personal injury solicitor. If liability can be refuted then the case will be vigorously defended and, if liability is established, the case will be settled at the lowest possible cost. However, there are also special factors that the defendant clinical negligence solicitor must consider. The principal factor is that the defendant is a professional person and, whilst damages will not be paid by him personally, his reputation will be brought into question by any admission or finding of negligence on his part. This is one of the reasons why more clinical negligence claims proceed to trial than personal injury claims and, as will be seen, establishing liability in a clinical negligence case is not easy. Whilst the patient may complain that the treatment was unsuccessful, it does not follow that the doctor was negligent, and the arguments available to the defendant's solicitor to refute negligence are wider and more complicated than in a personal injury case.

1.4 A LESS ADVERSARIAL CULTURE TO PERSONAL INJURY AND CLINICAL NEGLIGENCE LITIGATION

As noted above, the aims of the claimant and defendant solicitors are opposed. However, following the implementation of the CPR 1998, solicitors are adopting a more 'open' and 'realistic' view to personal injury and clinical negligence litigation. Many solicitors report that there appears to have been a greater willingness by defendants to settle at an early stage in the litigation process and it is clear from the judicial decisions following the introduction of the CPR 1998 that the concept of the 'overriding objective' is key to all areas of litigation.

1.5 CONCLUSION

Personal injury and clinical negligence litigation is a diverse and expanding area. At its least complex, it may involve a claim for compensation for minor injuries suffered as a result of a road traffic accident, or, at the other extreme, it may involve representing clients in complex claims against drug manufacturers, such as the Benzodiazepine drug litigation.

The increased significance of personal injury and clinical negligence work has resulted in the setting up of a number of specialist groups.

(1) It is possible for solicitors who fulfil certain criteria and who hold current practising certificates (or Fellows of the Institute of Legal Executives who fulfil certain criteria) to apply to join the personal injury and/or clinical negligence panel set up by The Law Society (the criteria for membership of the clinical negligence panel does not have a minimum post-qualification period, but most members would have at least 3 years' experience to fulfil the other points of the criteria). Various requirements relating to expertise must be satisfied by applicants.

(2) Membership of the Association of Personal Injury Lawyers (APIL) is open to students and qualified solicitors. It is an organisation which campaigns on behalf of victims of personal injuries and can provide a useful source of information.

(3) Membership of the Association of Victims of Medical Accidents (AVMA). A useful service is provided by this charitable organisation which gives assistance not only to members of the public who believe they have been a victim of a medical accident but also to solicitors through its lawyers' service. This provides access to unique information relating to barristers, members of the medical profession who are prepared to provide expert medical reports and other matters relating to evidence that may be used in the case. AVMA operates a system whereby each request from a solicitor looking for an expert in a particular field is assessed by a qualified case worker and this service is used by many firms of solicitors who represent victims of clinical negligence.

(4) Membership of the Federation of Insurance Lawyers (FOIL). This group represents defendant solicitors who act on behalf of insurance companies.

This text aims to provide an introduction to personal injury and clinical negligence litigation, but reference should also be made to practitioners' works and original sources. Where appropriate, reference must be made to the actual CPR 1998 and pre-action protocols.

1.6 OVERVIEWS OF PERSONAL INJURY AND CLINICAL NEGLIGENCE ACTIONS

1.6.1 Overview of the main steps in clinical negligence action

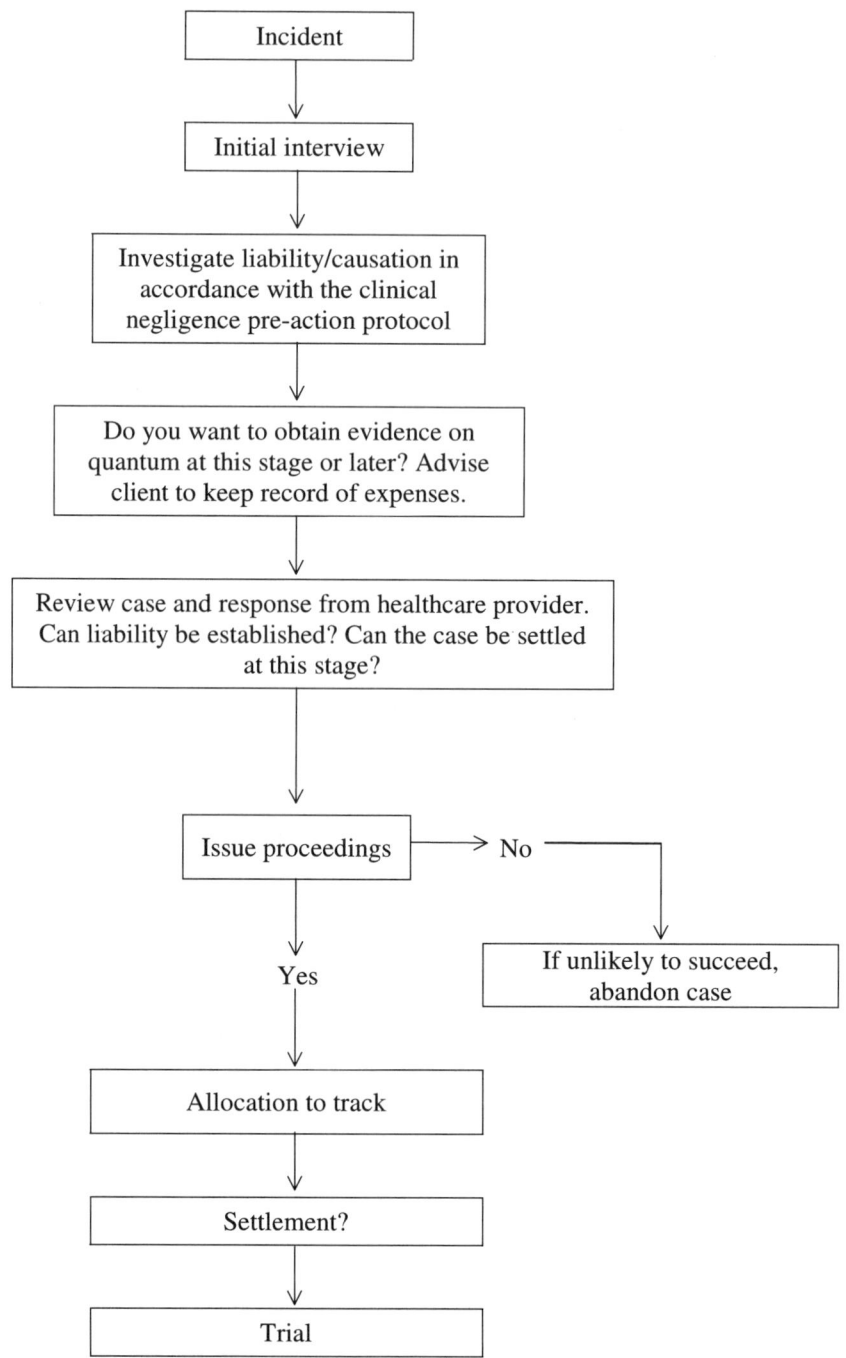

Defendants are normally insured or part of the NHS, so normally there are no problems with enforcement.

Introduction to the Work of a Personal Injury/Clinical Negligence Solicitor 7

1.6.2 Overview of the main steps in personal injury, for example road traffic or employer's liability case

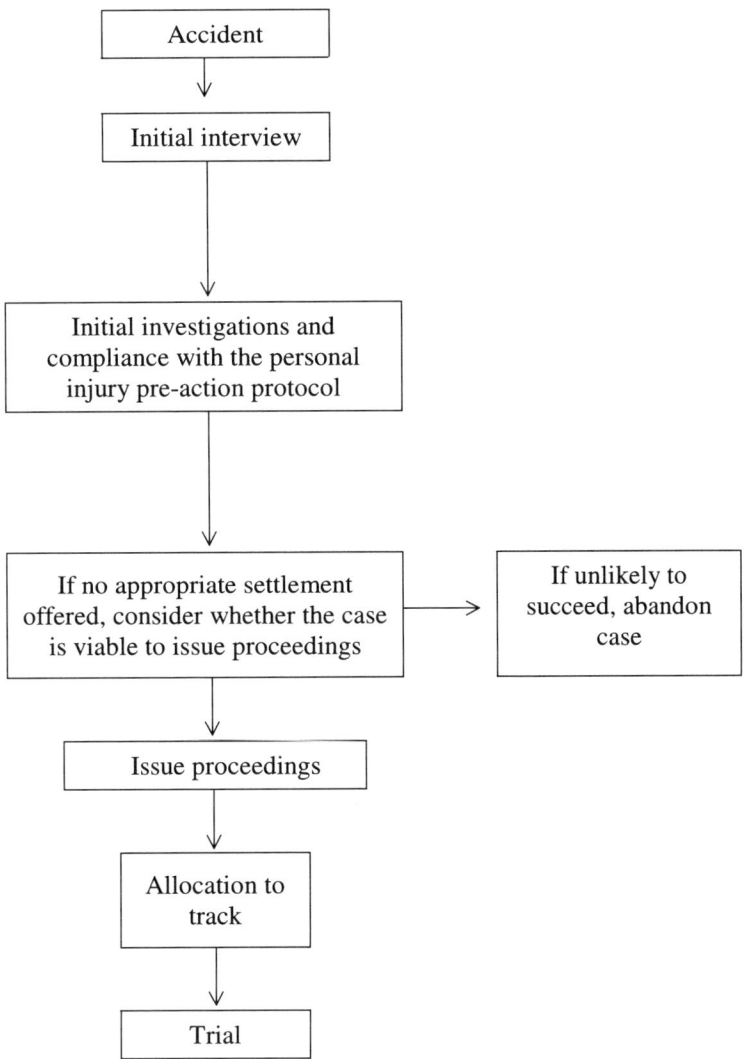

Most defendants insured, so normally there are no problems with enforcement.

Chapter 2

PERSONAL INJURY AND CLINICAL NEGLIGENCE JARGON

2.1 INTRODUCTION

A trainee solicitor who enters the personal injury/clinical negligence department of a legal firm has to cope not only with the pressures of being able to understand fully and advise accurately on, the law, but also with a barrage of unfamiliar medical terms. There can be no doubt that proficient solicitors who practise in the personal injury field have extensive medical knowledge and a detailed understanding of the terms used. This knowledge enables solicitors to understand fully clients' complaints, experts' reports and medical notes and also enables them to explain matters thoroughly to clients. For example, upon receipt of a medical report obtained following a simple road traffic accident, the solicitor must read the report carefully and then send it to the client. If the client subsequently contacts his solicitor stating that he does not understand the terms used in the medical report, it is not acceptable for the solicitor to say, 'neither do I'!

The medical profession favours abbreviations and to the trainee this can be particularly difficult. If a trainee is faced on his first day with his colleagues referring to claims dealing with repetitive strain injury (RSI), vibration white finger (VWF), post-traumatic stress disorder (PTSD), etc, and if he is unfamiliar with the terminology, he will obviously be at a disadvantage. The purpose of this chapter is to assist in the understanding of the terms and abbreviations commonly found in personal injury/clinical negligence work. However, a medical dictionary is an essential requirement for the personal injury solicitor and more detailed medical texts may also be of use. See **2.3** (human skeleton) and Appendix 2 for a list of common abbreviations.

Chapter 2 contents
Introduction
Common injuries and medical terms used
Diagrammatic representation of the human skeleton
Conclusion
Further reading

2.2 COMMON INJURIES AND MEDICAL TERMS USED

2.2.1 Orthopaedic injuries

Orthopaedic (bone) injuries are the most common injuries encountered in a personal injury claim and are normally incurred as a result of falling or being involved in a road traffic accident.

The most common terms found in orthopaedic medical reports are as follows.

(1) *Arthrodesis* – means a joint that has been fused, either because of pre-existing joint disease or because of injury as a result of trauma to the joint.
(2) *Arthroplasty* – means that the joint has been reconstructed, often by the use of a joint implant to replace one or more parts of the components of a joint.
(3) *Contusion* – means an injury to the skin and the deeper tissues in the surrounding area which is accompanied by bleeding from damaged blood vessels. The skin, however, is not broken. The simplest form of contusion is a

bruise, developing through to a contusion accompanied by a large haematoma, which is a collection of blood under the surface of the skin.
(4) *Dislocation* – means an injury which results in the bones of a joint being out of alignment or connection with one another. There is usually associated ligament and soft tissue damage.
(5) *Subluxation* – a joint which has subluxed has undergone a partial dislocation, and subluxation is a term which is sometimes used to describe a sprain.
(6) *Sprain* – means an injury in the region of a joint with associated ligament and soft tissue damage.
(7) *Fracture* – means a break in the continuity of a bone.

As a consequence of an orthopaedic injury, the client's injury may have been immobilised by a plaster of Paris cast. Certain of the terms relating to casts are self-evident (eg, below knee cast) but examples of the less obvious terms are:

(1) *scaphoid cast* – a cast which covers the arm from just below the elbow to the start of the fingers; or
(2) *shoulder spica cast* – a body jacket which encloses the trunk and shoulder and elbow.

A client who has an orthopaedic injury may also undergo traction – a system of weights and pulleys is used to pull muscle groups, so as to reduce/immobilise fractures and put the bones back into alignment.

In general, the most common fractures occur to:

(1) *the clavicle (collar bone)* – these fractures are especially common in children and young adults and are almost always due to falls or direct trauma to the point of the shoulder. Treatment involves the wearing of a sling until the pain has subsided. Surgical intervention is very rarely required and is usually only indicated if there is a risk to nearby nerves or blood vessels. If surgical intervention is required, the client undergoes an open reduction and fixation of the fracture, where the skin over the site of the fracture is opened and the fracture is immobilised with metal pins, which are usually removed at a later date;
(2) *the surgical neck of the humerus (the long bone stretching from the shoulder to the elbow)* – these fractures are usually treated with a sling but, if badly displaced, are surgically treated and fixed with metal pins;
(3) *the shaft of the humerus* – these fractures can occur at any point along the humerus and are usually treated by immobilising the fracture in a plaster of Paris cast for 6 to 8 weeks;
(4) *fractures to the radius (the bone running from the elbow to the base of the thumb)* – there are many different types of radial fracture but the most common is the Colles fracture which involves fracture of the lower end of the radius with posterior displacement of the distal fragment. This involves the fractured piece of bone being displaced into the joint space of the wrist which causes pain and loss of function. It is typically seen in clients who have fallen forward onto outstretched hands;
(5) *the femur (the thigh bone)* – these fractures can occur at any point along the length of the femur. The most common sites are the neck or the shaft of the femur. Treatment tends to be surgical, with surgery ranging from open fixation with metal pins to total hip replacement. Clients with fractures of the shaft of the femur will be placed in a Thomas splint, which immobilises the fracture;

(6) *the tibia and fibula* – these two bones make up the part of the leg from beneath the knee to the ankle. Fracture of these two bones can result from direct or indirect trauma. The tibia has a very large area of skin and subcutaneous tissue overlying it which makes it one of the most common sites for compound fractures. The fibula has a relatively poor blood supply so there is a high risk of non-union of fractures;

(7) *the pelvis* – a number of bones which are formed together to form a ring-like structure at the base of the spine. It contains the vertebrae of the sacral spine and the hip joints and fractures can occur at any point. Because of the relative stability of the pelvis, small, undisplaced fractures can be relatively minor. Fractures to the pelvis are of two main types: first, isolated fractures of one of the bones which make up the pelvis and, secondly, double fractures of the bones which make up the pelvic rim. Treatment can be conservative, with the client being confined to bed for a period of time, or surgical, depending upon the severity and the position of the fracture.

Occasionally, following trauma, a client will have a limb amputated. This will have a tremendous impact on his life. It will involve a great deal of treatment and rehabilitation mainly in the form of physiotherapy in order to maintain the existing function and to maximise the potential for rehabilitation. Often, a client will have a prosthesis fitted – an artificial structure which can range from part of a limb to a complete limb.

2.2.2 Work-related upper limb disorders

Work-related upper limb disorders can occur following the constant repetition of tasks such as typing. It leads to a chronic condition which can be permanent for the sufferer. It can result in numbness, swelling and tingling.

Repetitive work can also result in tenosynovitis which is the inflammation of a tendon.

Reference should be made to the relevant Regulations that govern health and safety at work in relation to work-related upper limb disorders, see Chapter 3.

2.2.3 Terms used to describe injuries to the skin

The following terms are used to describe injuries to the skin:

- *abrasion* – occurs when the surface of the skin or a mucous membrane is rubbed off due to a mechanical injury;
- *hypertrophic* – the overgranulation of scar tissue which can lead to disfigurement;
- *laceration* – a wound to the skin which has jagged, irregular edges.

2.2.4 Terms used to describe head injuries

The following terms are used in relation to head injuries:

- *aphasia* – the loss of power of speech;
- *anosmia* – the loss of the sense of smell;
- *cerebral oedema* – a swelling of the brain;
- *closed head injury* – a head injury in which there is no open skull fracture;
- *concussion* – instantaneous loss of consciousness due to a blow on the head;

- *diffuse axonal injury* – a brain injury which involves shearing of the brain tissue itself;
- *dysarthria* – a difficulty in the coordination of the speech muscles which leads to an inability to pronounce words clearly;
- *dysphagia* – a difficulty in swallowing;
- *dysphasia* – a difficulty in understanding language and in self-expression;
- *extradural haematoma* – a blood clot which lies immediately above the brain and its protective membranes and below the surface of the skull;
- *Glasgow Coma Scale* – a system of assessing neurological function;
- *hydrocephalus* – a condition which arises due to an increase in the amount of cerebro-spinal fluid within the cranial cavity;
- *hemiplegia* – paralysis of one side of the body;
- *intracerebral* – within the substance of the brain itself;
- *monoplegia* – a paralysis of one limb;
- *open head injury* – a head injury with an associated depressed skull fracture;
- *subdural haematoma* – a blood clot lying in between the brain and its protective membranes.

2.2.5 Industrial deafness

Industrial deafness claims are brought by those who have suffered hearing loss due to exposure at work to a high level of noise for a long period of time. For example, employees working in the steel industry, shipbuilding or other manufacturing industry may suffer from industrial deafness. Expert medical evidence is required to prove the loss of hearing, and evidence relating to the employees' working conditions is also required. Employers should, for example, have a system of assessing the risk from noise, provide ear-protectors and have clearly marked zones where ear protection must be worn. An employer should be aware of the 'daily personal noise exposure' of its employees, which involves calculating the noise exposure to the client (the abbreviation 'Leq (8hr)' is used). Employers should take precautions where there is any possibility of their employees suffering a hearing loss, but especially if the daily personal noise exposure is of 85dB (a) or above.

In such cases, it is important to obtain a detailed employment history and details of the client's working conditions, such as the degree of noise the client believed he encountered, for example whether he had to shout at workmates to make himself heard, details of ear protection supplied, the types of machinery operated and any warnings given, etc. It must be remembered that the client's claim will succeed only if he can prove that his hearing loss was caused by his employment with the relevant defendant and that it was foreseeable that such a hearing loss might be sustained. It is vital to ensure that it was the client's employment which caused the deafness and not any natural degeneration or intervening illness.

Reference should be made to the Noise at Work Regulations 1989, SI 1989/1790, for further details relating to industrial deafness.

2.2.6 Post-traumatic stress disorder

Post-traumatic stress disorder (PTSD) has become more prominent in recent years. This expression refers to a psychological illness where the claimant suffers from a variety of symptoms which include:

- constantly reliving the initial incident which provoked the stress;

- panic attacks;
- palpitations;
- chest pain;
- nausea;
- constipation;
- insomnia;
- lack of concentration;
- loss of libido;
- agoraphobia;
- headaches;
- indigestion;
- diarrhoea;
- eating disorders;
- restlessness;
- extreme fatigue.

It is important that medical evidence to support the injury is obtained so that the defendants cannot make the allegation that the claimant has simply been 'shaken up'. This type of injury must be considered by the claimant's solicitor, even if the client concentrates only on the physical injuries when he is asked at the first interview what injuries he has suffered as a result of the accident.

2.2.7 Vibration white finger

Vibration white finger (VWF), often referred to as hand/arm vibration syndrome, is suffered predominantly by employees who have frequently used pneumatic drilling machines and often results in a tingling sensation in the finger, together with a discoloration (whitening). This type of injury has been recognised for some time and became a prescribed disease in April 1985. Although each individual case is determined on the facts, the courts have considered that employees should be screened prior to use of such tools, that they should have periodic medical examinations and that a system of job-rotation should be operated. This type of injury was highlighted in 1998 by the unsuccessful appeal by British Coal against a finding of liability against it, following claims brought by miners who had suffered from VWF.

2.2.8 Asbestosis/pneumoconiosis

Asbestosis is a form of pneumoconiosis which is a general term applied to any chronic form of inflammation of the lungs affecting people who are liable to inhale irritating substances or particles at work.

Asbestosis occurs specifically following the inhalation of mainly blue or brown asbestos dust. It leads to the development of widespread scarring of the lung tissue leading to severe breathing difficulties. The main hazard, however, is the potential for the development of a type of cancer called mesothelioma, which affects the lungs, the pleura or, more rarely, the ovaries.

2.2.9 Occupational asthma

Occupational asthma may develop following exposure to a precipitating factor in the work-place, for example flour.

Asthma is a disorder of breathing and is characterised by a narrowing of the airways within the lungs. The main symptom is breathlessness and an associated cough. It is an extremely distressing condition and, if left untreated, can be fatal.

Occupational asthma is usually treatable by the identification of the allergen which is provoking the attacks. Common allergens are flour and grain in bakeries or isocyanates found in industries involving paint-spraying.

2.2.10 Occupational dermatitis

Dermatitis is an inflammation of the skin, which is usually caused by direct contact with some irritating substance.

Occupational dermatitis is the most common of all the occupational diseases.

2.2.11 Hand injuries

In interpreting medical reports regarding hand injuries, a basic understanding of the anatomical position of the hand is required.

The functional parts of the hand are the wrist and the fingers. If the wrist is flexed, the hand is brought forward; if the hand is positioned as if to push someone away, it is said to be extended. The wrist is described as being 'pronated' if the palm of the hand is pointing towards the floor, and is described as being 'supinated' if the hand is positioned to receive something.

If the hand is made into a fist, the fingers are described as flexed; if the hand is opened out as if to receive something the fingers are described as extended.

The fingers are described as the distal half of the hand, and are made up of three joints. Working from the palm of the hand out towards the end of the fingers, the three joints are the metacarpo-phalangeal joint (the knuckles), the proximal interphalangeal joint, and the distal interphalangeal joint which is the joint nearest to the finger nails. The thumb has the same number of joints but appears shorter because it attaches to the hand lower down. Seventy per cent of the function of the hand is provided by the thumb.

If a scar to the hand is described as transverse, it runs across the hand; if it is described as longitudinal, it is running along the length of the hand.

2.2.12 Obstetrics

A normal labour and delivery takes place in three stages. The first stage refers to the period of time it takes the cervix to dilate fully to 10 cms and is the longest stage of labour. The full dilation of the cervix is also associated with the rupture of the amnion, which is the tough fibrous membrane lining the cavity of the womb during pregnancy, containing 0.5 to 1 litre of amniotic fluid which supports the foetus. The rupture of the amnion is often referred to as the breaking of the waters. The second stage of labour is the actual birth of the baby. The third stage is the delivery of the placenta.

An obvious sign of foetal distress is the presence of meconium, which is a brown semi-fluid material which collects in the bowels of the baby before birth and is usually discharged either at birth or shortly afterwards. If a baby becomes distressed, it ejects the meconium into the amniotic fluid.

Cerebral palsy is a group of conditions which are characterised by varying degrees of paralysis occurring in infancy or early childhood. In some 50% of cases, this takes the form of spastic paralysis. It is thought that the factors involved in the development of cerebral palsy are trauma to the child during birth or lack of oxygen.

If a baby is deprived of oxygen, it is said to have become hypoxic. Hypoxia refers to a state where there is an inadequate supply of oxygen to maintain normal tissue function. If a baby is deemed to be in danger, it will be intubated and ventilated. This involves the insertion of an endotracheal tube into the baby's trachea to facilitate the maintenance of the baby's airway.

Once a baby is born, it is assessed using the Apgar score. This is a method of assessing a baby's condition by giving a score of either 0, 1 or 2 to each of five signs: colour, heart rate, muscle tone, respiratory effort and response to stimulation. A total score of 10 is the best Apgar score. If a baby is described as apnoeic, it means that it is not breathing; bradycardia refers to the fact that the baby's heart is beating too slowly.

Perinatal mortality refers to the death of a foetus after the 28th week of pregnancy and to the death of the newborn child during the first week of life.

2.2.13 Occupational stress

Following the case of *Walker v Northumberland County Council* [1995] 1 All ER 737, in which a social services officer received compensation for stress induced by his employment (he suffered a nervous breakdown), it is currently believed that occupational stress claims may increase in frequency, as is evidenced by the unreported case of *Polock v North East Essex Mental Health NHS Trust* (1998) unreported, March. This case involved a nurse who took his own life after complaining of stress at work. This case did not proceed to trial as a settlement was agreed in what is believed to have been the first out-of-court settlement to a family for a suicide related to stress.

In the case of *Lancaster v Birmingham City Council* (1998) unreported, 23 July, a clerical worker successfully sued her employers for stress as she was deployed to a job in the housing department of the City Council without any training. Similarly, in January 2000 a council worker for Hereford and Worcester County Council received £203,000 for work-related stress, in an out-of-court settlement.

2.2.14 Tobacco-related diseases

In recent years, there has been increasing concern over smoking-related diseases. A number of cases involving 'passive smoking', have been reported, normally involving the claimant having been exposed to cigarette smoke over a period of years in the work environment, normally resulting in such diseases as bronchial asthma (see the unreported case of *Sparrow v St Andrews Homes Ltd* (1998) unreported, 21 May). Also, in the case of *Bland v Stockport Borough Council* (1998) unreported, January, the claimant accepted £15,000 from her employers for personal injuries arising out of exposure to cigarette smoke.

2.3 DIAGRAMMATIC REPRESENTATION OF THE HUMAN SKELETON

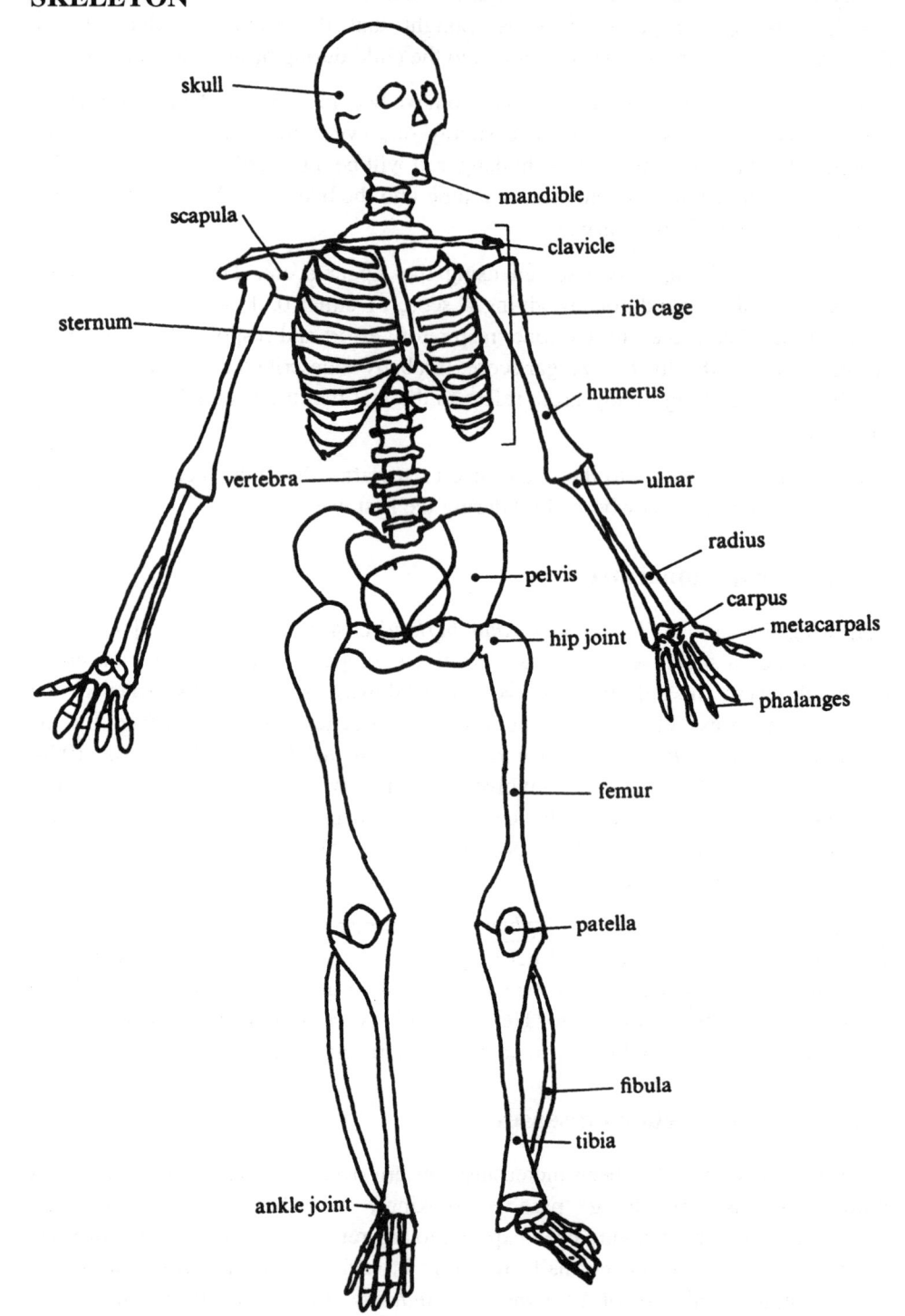

2.4 CONCLUSION

A basic understanding of the medical terms involved in personal injury and clinical negligence cases can assist the trainee in understanding medical reports and also provide an insight into the client's problems which can often be useful in the negotiation of any settlement.

2.5 FURTHER READING

Kemp and Kemp *The Quantum of Damages* (Sweet & Maxwell).

Chapter 3

LIABILITY: PERSONAL INJURY AND CLINICAL NEGLIGENCE

3.1 INTRODUCTION

Many personal injury claims arise as the result of an accident at work. The employer may be personally liable to an injured employee on the basis of:

(1) common law negligence; and/or
(2) breach of statutory duty, for example under the Health and Safety at Work etc Act 1974, the Occupiers' Liability Act 1957, or European Directives covering safety by way of regulations under the Health and Safety at Work etc Act 1974. Many of the regulations also have Approved Codes of Practice (ACOPs) of which the solicitor must be aware.

The heads of liability are not mutually exclusive. For example, in certain circumstances the employer may be liable to the injured employee under both heads, whilst in other circumstances the employer may be liable only in common law negligence but not otherwise. The employer may be vicariously liable to the injured employee where the injury was caused by a tort (eg negligence) of another employee who was acting in the course of his employment. However, many accidents (eg in the construction industry) involve workers who are independent contractors working either for themselves or for an employer other than the person with control of the site itself.

Chapter 3 contents
Introduction
Liability at common law – negligence
Breach of statutory duty
Occupiers' liability to lawful visitors
Vicarious liability
Enforcement of health and safety at work
Claims for psychiatric illness or 'nervous shock'
Liability in clinical negligence cases
Res ipsa loquitur
Other common issues
Conclusion
Further reading

3.2 LIABILITY AT COMMON LAW – NEGLIGENCE

As with any other claim in negligence, the burden is upon the claimant to prove that:

(1) the defendant owes him a duty of care;
(2) the defendant is in breach of that duty;
(3) the breach has caused consequential losses which are reasonably foreseeable.

It is well established that an employer owes his employee a duty of care. For losses arising out of an accident, reference should be made to Chapter 13. The remainder of this chapter will concentrate on the nature of the duty of care, and breach of that duty.

3.2.1 The nature of the duty of care

An employer is under a duty to take reasonable care of his employees' health and safety. This means providing health checks (especially if employees are engaged in hazardous work), equipment to protect employees from injury and medical equipment in order to mitigate the effects of any injury. This duty to take 'reasonable care' was explained by Lord Wright in *Wilsons and Clyde Coal Co v English*

[1938] AC 57 as requiring an employer to exercise due care and skill in three particular areas, ie to provide:

(1) competent staff;
(2) adequate plant; and
(3) a safe system of work.

Many of the common law duties are confirmed or strengthened by statute and regulations, but common law rules are an important indication of how courts are likely to interpret new regulations (eg the Provision and Use of Work Equipment Regulations 1998, SI 1998/2306 (see below)).

Competent staff

The duty is on the employer to take reasonable care to provide competent fellow workers. If an employee is injured as a result of the incompetence of a workmate, the employer may be personally liable. Whether the employer has failed to take reasonable care may depend upon the knowledge that he has (or ought to have) of the workmate's incompetence or inexperience etc (*Hudson v Ridge Manufacturing Co* [1957] 2 QB 348; *Smith v Crossley Bros* (1951) 95 Sol Jo 655).

Adequate plant

'Plant' simply means anything used in the course of work and not merely heavy machinery. It will include everything from large and complicated machinery (eg a paper mill) to the most basic equipment (eg an office chair). The duty rests on the employer to take reasonable steps to provide adequate equipment and materials to do the job and then to maintain that equipment. The employer will also be vicariously liable if employees fail to maintain or repair such plant or equipment. For example, if an office swivel chair gives way under an employee, the employer may be liable for failing to maintain the chair, or for having inadequate provision for maintenance or renewal.

Accidents may occur because either no plant or equipment is provided, or inadequate equipment is provided. For example, if an employee suffers injuries falling from a makeshift means of gaining access to high shelves, the employer will be liable if no ladder has been provided for this purpose. If an employee stood on an office swivel chair to gain access to the shelves and fell off the chair, it could be argued that the manufacturer would not be liable under the Employers' Liability (Defective Equipment) Act 1969 as the use was not a use that the manufacturer intended for the product.

Where plant is provided there is a duty to maintain it in good order. This duty is now supplemented by the Provision and Use of Work Equipment Regulations 1998, SI 1998/2306 (see below). When considering whether plant has been adequately maintained the court will look to current practice, which will be different according to the type of equipment involved.

Depending on the type of equipment, all or any of the following matters may be relevant and evidence should be looked for, both when using the pre-action protocol and at the disclosure stage of litigation:

(1) inspection and servicing records;
(2) reports of defect, breakdown or poor running;
(3) replacing worn out parts or equipment;

(4) steps taken to repair or replace equipment shown to be defective;
(5) cleaning schedules or rotas.

The frequency and method of inspection or testing will be a question of fact depending on the equipment. Items which are subject to stress, such as ropes, should be inspected and, if necessary, replaced more regularly (see reg 6 of the Provision and Use of Work Equipment Regulations 1998) than items which are subject simply to ordinary wear and tear, such as floor coverings that might cause a person to trip.

For example, in a food processing plant, machinery and floors may become contaminated with grease if not cleaned regularly. The employer will be negligent if he fails to clean the plant; this may necessitate closing the production line down whilst cleaning takes place.

The requirement to provide adequate plant also extends to a duty to make reasonable provision of safety and protective equipment. This duty at common law is now supplemented by the Personal Protective Equipment at Work Regulations 1992, SI 1992/2966 (see below).

Safe system of working

The duty to provide a safe system of working is very wide and will be a question of fact to be considered in each case. It covers such things as:

(1) the physical layout of the plant;
(2) the sequence in which work is to be carried out;
(3) the method by which work is carried out;
(4) the provision of instructions;
(5) the provision of proper warnings, notices and instructions (*Speed v Thomas Swift & Co* [1943] KB 557).

The employer must take into account the fact that an employee may become careless after a time, especially if the work is of a repetitive nature (*General Cleaning Contractors Ltd v Christmas* [1953] AC 180).

Example

In *Morgan v Lucas Aerospace Ltd* (1997) JPIL 4/97 the claimant was employed in the defendants' factory to clean waste swarf (oil contaminated with metal waste) from trays underneath machinery. He had been given no formal training. Swarf caught in the machine cut through his heavy-duty glove, causing a cut to the hand. The claimant alleged this injury was caused by the defendants' failure to provide and maintain a safe system of work. In the first instance, it was held that the defendants were not absolved from the duty to provide a safe glove merely because it was difficult or expensive to obtain. If no better glove could be obtained at a reasonable price, the whole system was unsafe. The defendants appealed. On appeal, it was held that it was not necessary for the claimant to prove what alternative system of work could be adopted and which would have been safer. The claimant proved that the defendants allowed an unsafe practice to be adopted which they ought to have known to be unsafe and which they could have altered. If gloves provided were the best available, the obligation of the defendants was to devise a system which would remove or reduce the risk of injury.

Safe premises

It is accepted that the duty of care extends to the provision of premises. The duty applies not only to premises occupied by the employer, but also to premises occupied by a third party where the employee is working temporarily (*General Cleaning Contractors v Christmas* [1953] AC 180; *Wilson v Tyneside Window Cleaning Co* [1958] 2 QB 110). The duty is now supplemented by the Workplace (Health, Safety and Welfare) Regulations 1992, SI 1992/3004 (see below).

Slipping and tripping cases are frequent causes of negligence claims at work, as is shown by the amount of advice and preventative information available to employers by the Health & Safety Executive (HSE). The employer must act reasonably to ensure that floors and means of access are reasonably safe.

3.2.2 The requirement of 'reasonableness'

It should be remembered that the duty on the employer is not absolute, but merely to take reasonable care. Generally, a high standard will be required but it will vary according to the circumstances. Factors to be taken into account include the following.

(1) *Existing disabilities of the employee.* If the employer knows, or should know, of an employee's existing disability, extra precautions should be taken (*Paris v Stepney Borough Council* [1951] AC 367; cf *James v Hepworth & Grandage Ltd* [1968] 1 QB 94).

(2) *Knowledge of the risk which the employer has or ought to have.* Due to the level and quality of safety information in the form of books, leaflets and videos from the HSE, employers may have difficulty in alleging that they were not aware of the risk, or if they were aware of it that they did not know what to do about it. The Management of Health and Safety at Work Regulations 1999, SI 1999/3242, now require employers to carry out a risk assessment to identify potential risks and suggest precautionary measures to diminish the risk. Although employers should be aware of current improvements in matters of health and safety they are not obliged to implement them. However, once a new safety measure has proved itself practicable and reasonably available, an employer would be negligent if he failed to adopt it. For example, if there is a risk that the operator of a pneumatic drill will become deaf as a result of prolonged use of the drill, this is a matter the employer should be aware of but need not do anything to remedy. Once it is established that providing adequate ear-defenders would prevent the deafness occurring, however, the employer would be negligent if he failed to adopt the precaution. The grey area is whether and to what extent the employer should take his own initiatives to try to solve the problem or look elsewhere for information to do so.

(3) *Cost and effort of adopting precautions to overcome the risk and the seriousness of the injury risked.* If there is a high risk of serious injury, then greater (and, probably, more expensive) precautions should be taken. Conversely, if the risk of injury is small, expensive precautions may not be justified (*Latimer v AEC Ltd* [1953] AC 643). The burden is on the defendant to show that it has taken appropriate steps to reduce the risk of injury to the lowest level reasonably practicable (see *Hawkes v Southwark LBC* (1998) unreported, 20 February, CA).

(4) *Current trade practice.* Compliance with current trade practice may indicate that the employer has acted reasonably (although this is not conclusive). It is

more important that practice reflects what is accepted as correct by informed opinion. Whilst the following were all accepted trade practices, they were still found to be negligent: failing to fence hatchways between decks of a ship at sea; failing to provide a harness for a window cleaner when standing on a window-sill; and loosely roping kegs of beer whilst lowering them, thus exposing employees to the risk that the kegs might slip out and injure them.

Section 16 of the Health and Safety at Work etc Act 1974 authorises Approved Codes of Practice (ACOPs) which will be evidence of what is good practice in a particular trade. A failure to observe an ACOP will not give rise to criminal liability but will be admissible in evidence in criminal proceedings. ACOPs will also be admissible in civil proceedings as evidence of good practice in the trade and, as such, are a reflection of current informed thinking in the health and safety industry. Similarly, Guidance Notes issued by the HSE, although not binding, will be indicative of whether good working practices were being followed.

Judicial comment has been made that defendants ought to have foreseen risks, where information was available in documents published by the HSE. It would, therefore, follow that it was questionable whether such documents had to be acted upon instantly and whether a claimant's conduct was negligent if he failed to do so (see *Foster v National Power plc* [1997] LTL 7 May 1997).

3.2.3 Personal nature of duty

The employer will escape liability only if he shows that both he and the person to whom he delegated the duty exercised reasonable care in the discharge of that duty (*Davie v New Merton Board Mills Ltd* [1959] AC 604). Therefore, the duty is not discharged, for example, merely by delegating it to an apparently competent manager if that manager in fact fails to act competently (*Sumner v William Henderson & Sons Ltd* [1964] 1 QB 450; *McDermid v Nash Dredging & Reclamation Co Ltd* [1987] 2 All ER 878).

An employer can remain liable for the safety of an employee, even whilst the employee is under the control of someone else. For example, where a worker on a building site is injured whilst working on a different building site under the control and instruction of different contractors because he had been sent to work for the contractors by his own employer, his employer can be found liable for failing to ensure that he was properly trained and for failing to maintain a safe system of work even though the employer had no control over management of that site (*Morris v Breaveglen* [1993] ICR 766, CA).

Remoteness of damage

The defendant will be liable to the claimant only if it can be proved that it was foreseeable that the claimant would suffer damage of the kind that the claimant did in fact suffer. The claimant will generally recover for:

(1) damage which was reasonably foreseeable; or
(2) damage which can be shown to flow as a direct consequence of the breach.

Once damage is established as foreseeable (no matter how small), the claimant can recover for the full extent of the injury even if this was unforeseeable (*Smith v Leech Brain & Co Ltd* [1962] 2 QB 405).

Res ipsa loquitur

It will be relatively rare that the maxim *res ipsa loquitur* (the thing speaks for itself) will be relevant. It is no more than a presumption that in the ordinary course of events the accident would not have happened. The fact of its happening is enough to raise a prima facie case in negligence if it was not possible for the claimant to show what precisely had happened, but it was more likely than not that the effective cause was some act or omission by the defendant amounting to negligence. It is therefore up to the defendant to raise evidence to explain why the accident occurred other than by his negligence (see *Widdowson v Newgate Meat Corporation and Others* [1998] PIQR P138, CA). The maxim will not apply if the employer was not in control of the operation or equipment that gave rise to the accident. For example, the claimant may seek to raise *res ipsa loquitur* if he falls from a ladder because one of the rungs gives way beneath him. However, if the ladder was his own rather than one supplied by an employer, this maxim could not be used by the claimant.

3.2.4 Defences

While *volenti non fit injuria* may be a defence in theory, in practice it is rarely successful; it is rare that an employee will consent freely to run the risk of injury with full knowledge of that risk. Contributory negligence may reduce the employee's damages under the Law Reform (Contributory Negligence) Act 1948, but in judging whether the employee has failed to take reasonable steps for his own safety, due allowance will be given for fatigue, repetition of job, etc. To a certain extent, an employee may be expected to be careless, and the employer's duty is to protect the employee from himself (*Caswell v Powell Duffryn Associated Collieries Ltd* [1940] AC 152).

3.2.5 Claimant's contributory negligence

The contributory negligence of the claimant may sometimes reduce the damages to be awarded against the defendant. It is up to the judge to decide the proportion of responsibility of the claimant and to reduce the amount of damages accordingly.

The Law Reform (Contributory Negligence) Act 1945 provides that:

> '[If] any person suffers damage as a result partly of his own fault and partly of the fault of any other person ... damages recoverable in respect thereof shall be reduced by such extent as the court thinks just and equitable having regard to the claimant's share in responsibility for the damage.'

'Fault' is defined by s 4 as 'negligence, breach of statutory duty, or other act or omission which gives rise to a liability in tort or, apart from this Act, gives rise to the defence of contributory negligence'.

The question for the court when considering contributory negligence is whether the claimant acted reasonably in taking the risk (*A.C. Billings & Son Ltd v Riden* [1968] AC 240).

In assessing the claimant's conduct, allowance will be made for his working conditions. Mere inadvertence by the employee will generally not be sufficient for contributory negligence, for example where the employee is engrossed in his work or is in a hurry to get on with his job. The relative age and experience of the claimant will also be a relevant consideration for the court when deciding questions of contributory negligence. Disobedience or reckless disregard for the employer's orders are far more likely to give rise to a finding of contributory negligence.

The following have all given rise to findings of contributory negligence:

(1) disregarding orders to test equipment prior to use;
(2) a machine operator placing his hand under the guard without isolating the machine;
(3) disobeying orders by going to a part of the factory where an employee ought not to be; and
(4) riding on a produce conveyor when this is known to be prohibited and dangerous.

Similarly, reckless disregard for one's own safety will give rise to a claim for contributory negligence. For example:

(1) turning up for work intoxicated;
(2) disregarding warning notices;
(3) cleaning or adjusting machinery which is still running;
(4) allowing loose clothing to become entangled in a machine;
(5) failure to use safety equipment provided;
(6) failing to use a push stick with a power saw; or
(7) failing to use steel toe-capped boots on a building site.

When considering contributory negligence, it should be remembered that many statutory duties apply to duties of employees and not employers. For example, the Management of Health and Safety at Work Regulations 1992, SI 1992/2051, reg 12 places a duty on employees to use equipment in accordance with training and instructions.

The following are illustrations of common areas that give rise to questions of contributory negligence.

(1) Seat belts

The law requires seat belts to be used if they are fitted to the vehicle. It is illegal to carry an unrestrained child in the front seat of any vehicle. The law relates to the front seats of all vehicles and the rear seats of cars and small mini-buses. See the Motor Vehicles (Wearing of Seat Belts) Regulations 1993, SI 1993/176, and the Motor Vehicles (Wearing of Seat Belts by Children in Front Seats) Regulations 1993, SI 1993/31.

Summary of the law relating to seat belts

	Front seat	*Rear seat*	*Whose responsibility*
Driver	Seat belt must be worn if fitted	Not applicable	Driver
Child under 3 years of age	Appropriate child restraint must be used	Appropriate child restraint must be used if available	Driver
Child aged 3–11 and under 1.5m (approximately 5 ft in height)	Appropriate child restraint must be worn if available. If not, an adult seat belt must be worn if available	Appropriate child restraint must be worn if available. If not, an adult seat belt must be worn if available	Driver
Child aged 12 or 13 or younger child 1.5m or more in height	Adult seat belt must be worn if available	Adult seat belt must be worn if available	Driver
Adult passengers 14+	Seat belt must be worn if available	Seat belt must be worn if available	Passenger

Exemptions from wearing seat belts include:

(1) persons with a current medical certificate;
(2) disabled persons wearing a disabled persons belt;
(3) persons carrying out a reversing manoeuvre;
(4) taxi drivers; and
(5) children under one year old in a carry cot, provided that the cot is restrained by straps.

See also *Jones (A Minor) v Wilkins (Wynn and Another)* (2001) *The Times*, February 6. The claimant (aged 3) was seated on her mother's lap in the front passenger seat of a car. The lap part of the seat belt was across the claimant. In assessing liability for contributory negligence at 25% by the claimant, the judge considered himself bound by *Froom v Butcher* [1976] 1 QB 286. In this case, where no seat belt was worn, the judge decided that the reduction in damages for contributory negligence should not exceed 25%.

(2) Crash helmets

Regulations require that every person driving or riding a motorbike on a road must wear protective headgear. See the Motor Cycles (Protective Helmets) Regulations 1980, SI 1980/1279 (as amended).

Exceptions include:

(1) mowing machines;
(2) vehicles propelled by a person on foot; and
(3) members of the Sikh religion who wear a turban.

The general rule is that there will be a 25% reduction in damages if there would have been no injury had a seat belt or helmet been worn, and a 15% reduction if the injury would have been less severe.

(3) Intoxication

The claimant's damages will generally be reduced if he knowingly gets into a car with a driver who is under the influence of drink or drugs. See *Stinton v Stinton and the Motor Insurers' Bureau* [1993] PIQR 135, in which damages were reduced by 33% for contributory negligence.

(4) Automatism

If, for example, the claimant suffers a heart attack or hypoglycaemia, there must be total loss of voluntary control. Evidence of impairment only, no matter how severe, will not be enough to escape liability. See *Chelsea Girl Ltd v Alpha Omega Electrical* (1995) PMILL, February.

3.3 BREACH OF STATUTORY DUTY

The relationship between an employer and employee is usually closely regulated by statute. The basic principles are set out below.

Legislation generally falls into one of the following categories:

(1) the Health and Safety at Work etc Act 1974;
(2) regulations (made under the Health and Safety at Work etc Act 1974, s 15), for example the Control of Substances Hazardous to Health Regulations 1988, SI 1988/1657;
(3) Approved Codes of Practice (ACOPs) (made under the Health and Safety at Work etc Act 1974, s 16), for example Control of Carcinogenic Substances;
(4) statutes existing prior to the Health and Safety at Work etc Act 1974, for example the Factories Act 1961, the Offices, Shops and Railway Premises Act 1963;
(5) regulations existing prior to the Health and Safety at Work etc Act 1974, for example the Abrasive Wheels Regulations 1970, SI 1970/535.

Much of the legislation prior to the Health and Safety at Work etc Act 1974 has been repealed and replaced by regulations produced under that Act to comply with European Directives on health and safety. The old legislation (eg the Factories Act 1961) applied only to employees working specifically in factories. In contrast, the Health and Safety at Work etc Act 1974, and the regulations implemented under it to comply with EU Directives, apply to employees regardless of their actual place of work.

3.3.1 Civil liability for breach of statutory duty

To be successful in a civil claim based on a breach of statutory duty, the injured employee must show that:

(1) the breach is actionable in a civil court;
(2) the duty is owed to the claimant by the defendant;
(3) the claimant's loss is within the mischief of the Act;
(4) the defendant is in breach of the duty;
(5) the breach caused the loss.

Is the breach of duty actionable in a civil court?

A breach of statutory duty is primarily a crime, but it can also give rise to civil liability except where the statute expressly provides otherwise. There is express exclusion of civil liability for breaches of general duties under the Health and Safety at Work etc Act 1974 (s 47(1)). However, most of the health and safety regulations under EU Directives, described below as 'the six pack', do not expressly exclude civil liability (the exception to this is the Management of Health and Safety at Work Regulations 1999, SI 1999/3242, which expressly exclude civil liability (reg 22)). These Regulations also place duties on employees to take care of themselves whilst at work, and therefore allegations of contributory negligence by employers against employees are likely to increase.

Statute

The statute should first be checked to see if it states specifically whether the breach is actionable. For example, the Health and Safety at Work etc Act 1974, s 47 provides that a breach of the general duties owed by employers and employees under ss 2 to 7 is not actionable in a civil court (it should be noted that these general duties closely reflect the duties required to be performed at common law (see **3.2**) and any breach is probably actionable in common law negligence in any event). Section 47, however, also provides that a breach of duty imposed by health and safety regulations is actionable except insofar as the regulations provide otherwise. Furthermore, there is no 'contracting out' of this provision unless the regulations allow.

Case-law

In the absence of a specific provision, case-law should be checked to ascertain if there is a precedent stating that the particular breach is actionable.

In general terms, a 'safety provision' (such as a requirement to fence dangerous machinery) is normally found to be actionable; a 'health and welfare' provision may not be.

Has the defendant breached his statutory duty?

The standard required of the employer to fulfil his statutory duty is a question of construction of the statute. The common formulae are:

(1) 'absolute' (or strict) duty: where a state of affairs is required to exist and that state does not exist, then the employer is in breach (even if he has not been negligent);
(2) 'so far as reasonably practicable': where in judging whether there has been a breach the court will balance the risk against sacrifice (eg in terms of time, trouble or money) to avoid the risk;
(3) 'as far as practicable': is a duty stricter than 'reasonably practicable', although more lenient than 'physically possible'. For example, current knowledge of the risk of injury will be relevant in judging whether a safety precaution was 'practicable'. The onus is on the person on whom the duty is imposed to show that compliance was not 'practicable'.

Causation

The test for causation is the same for both negligence and breach of statutory duty. The onus of proof is on the claimant to prove that there is a causal connection between the breach and the loss on the balance of probabilities.

Whether the claimant can establish causation is a question of fact to be decided by the judge in each case. The claimant is not required to show that the breach is the sole cause of the loss; it is sufficient if the breach materially contributed to the loss (*Bonnington Castings Ltd v Wardlaw* [1956] AC 613). To determine who caused the accident the courts apply common sense to the facts of the case. If a number of people can be shown to have been at fault that does not necessarily mean that they all caused the accident; it is a question of looking at the facts and deciding which factors are too remote and which are not (*Stapley v Gypsum Mines Ltd* [1953] AC 663).

3.3.2 Health and safety legislation

The Management of Health and Safety at Work Regulations 1999 (SI 1999/3242) (the 'Framework Directive')

The revised Management Regulations came into force on 29 December 1999 and replaced the Management of Health and Safety at Work Regulations 1992. The Regulations introduce changes to clarify the UK's implementation of the European Framework Directive (89/391/EEC).

The Regulations implement European Health and Safety Directives relating to the employer's obligations in respect of health and safety for workers and in relation to minimum health and safety requirements for the workplace as to fire safety.

The main provisions regarding employer's duties are as follows.

(1) RISK ASSESSMENT (REG 3)

All employers are required to make a suitable and sufficient risk assessment of the risks to health and safety of their employees and persons who are not in their employment but who are affected by the conduct of their undertaking. Having made an assessment of the health and safety risks, it is incumbent upon the employer to try to diminish the risks that have been identified.

Due to the large number of accidents involving young and inexperienced workers there are specific requirements in regard to assessment of risk for children and young persons. According to the Regulations, a 'child' means a person who is not over compulsory school age, and 'young person' means any person who has not attained the age of 18. Regulation 3 makes the further requirement that an employer shall not employ a young person unless he has, in relation to the risks to the health and safety of young persons, made or reviewed a risk assessment.

In making or reviewing the assessment, an employer who employs or is to employ a young person shall take particular account of:

(a) the inexperience, lack of awareness of risks and immaturity of young persons;
(b) the fitting-out and layout of the workplace and the workstation;
(c) the nature, degree and duration of exposure to physical, biological and chemical agents;
(d) the form, range, and use of work equipment and the way in which it is handled;
(e) the organisation of processes and activities;

(f) the extent of the health and safety training provided or to be provided to young persons (see reg 19).

The duty on employers to carry out a risk assessment is likely to be one of the areas highlighted by personal injury lawyers to substantiate whether or not the employer has acted reasonably to provide a safe system of work and to establish the question of foreseeability of harm in negligence actions. The HSE booklet *Five Steps to Risk Assessment* is available free to employers and will help to show how pro-active the employer is in regard to the Regulations. If the employer has five or more employees, there is a duty to record the risk assessment (reg 5), and to note any significant findings of the assessment and whether any group of employees is identified as being especially at risk. The assessment should be carried out by consulting employees as to how they carry out their functions, together with taking advice from a relevant health and safety expert and ergonomists. The assessment should be updated and reviewed regularly.

(2) PRINCIPLES OF PREVENTION (REG 4)

According to reg 4, the principles of prevention of risk to be applied are to:

(a) avoid risks;
(b) evaluate the risks which cannot be avoided;
(c) combat the risks at source;
(d) adapt the work to the individual, especially as regards the design of workplaces, choice of work equipment and choice of working and production methods with a view to alleviating monotonous work and work at a pre-determined work rate to reduce their effects on health;
(e) adapt to technical progress;
(f) replace the dangerous by the non-dangerous or less dangerous;
(g) develop a coherent overall prevention policy which covers technology, organisation of work, working conditions, social relationships and the influence of factors relating to the working environment;
(h) give collective protective measures priority over individual protective measures; and
(i) give appropriate instruction to employees.

(3) REVIEW OF HEALTH AND SAFETY ARRANGEMENTS (REG 5)

Employers must make appropriate arrangements for monitoring and review of preventative and protective measures.

(4) HEALTH SURVEILLANCE (REG 6)

Employers are required to have an appropriate policy on risk surveillance, having regard to the findings of risks identified by the risk assessment. For example, if the risk assessment of employees showed that their were risks to health from airborne dust, that identified risk should be kept under review by regular health checks for rises in respiratory problems in employees.

(5) HEALTH AND SAFETY ASSISTANCE (REG 7)

Employers must appoint competent persons to assist the employer in carrying out compliance with statutory safety provisions. The Regulations require that a safety audit be carried out by accredited auditors who are suitably qualified. The audit will identify potential hazards in the workplace.

(6) INFORMATION FOR EMPLOYEES (REG 10)

Employers must give information which is comprehensible to employees on health and safety risks and protective measures that should be adopted.

(7) EMPLOYEE CAPABILITIES AND HEALTH AND SAFETY TRAINING (REG 13)

Employers must provide adequate health and safety training, when first recruited and subsequently on being exposed to new risks. Such training should be repeated periodically.

(8) RISK ASSESSMENT FOR NEW OR EXPECTANT MOTHERS (REG 16)

For the purpose of reg 16, 'new or expectant mother' means an employee who is pregnant; who has given birth within the previous 6 months or who is breastfeeding. Where the workforce includes women of child-bearing age and the work is of a kind which could involve risk to the health and safety of a new or expectant mother, or of the baby, the risk assessment required by reg 3 must include an assessment of that risk. If at all possible, the employee's working conditions or hours of work should be altered so as to avoid the risk. If it is not reasonable or it is not possible to avoid the risk by these means the employer may suspend the employee from work for so long as is necessary to avoid the risk.

Where a new or expectant mother works at night and obtains a certificate from a registered medical practitioner or registered midwife showing it is necessary for her health and safety that she should not work for any period identified in the certificate, the employer shall suspend her from work for so long as is necessary for her health and safety.

(9) PROTECTION OF YOUNG EMPLOYEES (REG 19)

A 'young person' means any person who has not attained the age of 18. In relation to young persons, reg 19 states that employers are under a duty to ensure that young persons are protected from risks which are, as a consequence of the young persons' lack of experience, or absence of awareness of existing or potential risks or the fact that young persons have not yet fully matured. Subject to this, employers are not allowed to employ young persons for work which is beyond their physical or psychological capacity, or involves harmful exposure to agents which are toxic, carcinogenic, cause heritable genetic damage or harm to an unborn child or which in any other way may chronically affect human health. Employers are not to allow young persons to work where they may be involved in harmful exposure to radiation; nor involve the risk of accidents which it may reasonably be assumed cannot be recognised or avoided by young persons owing to their insufficient attention to safety or lack of experience or training.

(10) CIVIL AND CRIMINAL LIABILITY (REGS 21 AND 22)

In relation to civil and criminal liability under the Regulations, reg 21 clearly states that nothing in the statutory provisions shall operate so as to afford an employer a defence in any criminal proceedings for a contravention of the provisions by reason of any act or default of an employee of his or a person appointed by him to assist with health and safety measures. According to reg 22, the breach of a duty under the Regulations does not confer a right of action in any civil proceedings. Although a breach of the Regulations is not actionable in a civil court, it is likely that they will be of use as evidence of approved or good working practice. A failure to heed such standards can be used as evidence of negligence. Although this is the general position, the two notable exceptions are in relation to new and expectant mothers and young employees. In those circumstances, the Regulations will impose civil liability.

(11) DUTIES OF EMPLOYEES (REG 14)

Although the main thrust of the Regulations is to confirm the obligations on employers in relation to health and safety, there are also obligations on employees who have a duty to:

(i) use machinery, equipment, dangerous substances or other equipment in accordance with the training and instructions which have been given to them by their employer; and
(ii) inform the employer of anything which the employee considers to represent a danger to health and safety or any shortcomings in the employer's arrangements for health and safety.

Health and Safety (Display Screen Equipment) Regulations 1992

The Health and Safety (Display Screen Equipment) Regulations 1992, SI 1992/2792, are applicable to new display screen equipment (DSE) as from 1 January 1993, and to existing DSE from 1 January 1996. However, the requirement of ongoing risk assessment applies to both old and new DSE as from 1 January 1993.

The main provisions are:

(1) employers must make a risk assessment of work stations used by display screen workers and to reduce risks identified (reg 2);
(2) employers must ensure that display screen workers take adequate breaks, and must provide appropriate eye care, for example an appropriate eyesight test (reg 5). In the UK, an appropriate eye test is as defined in the Opticians Act 1989;
(3) employers must provide users with adequate health and safety training in the use of any work station upon which he may be required to work (reg 6);
(4) employers must also provide adequate health and safety information to DSE operators, which should cover such things as information, and reminders on how to reduce risks such as early reporting of problems and provision of adjustable furniture (reg 7).

The main health problems associated with DSE operation are:

(1) general fatigue caused by poor work station design;
(2) upper limb disorders, such as peritendinitis or carpal tunnel syndrome. Repetitive strain injury (RSI) is the most common problem experienced by keyboard users;
(3) eyesight problems, such as temporary fatigue, sore eyes and headaches.

Employers should have, and be able to show that they have, an adequate policy designed to reduce risks associated with DSE work. The policy should identify hazards, such as visual fatigue, and action to be taken to reduce risk, such as provision of eyesight tests, screen filters and training in workstation adjustment.

Provision and Use of Work Equipment Regulations 1998

The Provision and Use of Work Equipment Regulations 1998, SI 1998/2306, came into force on 5 December 1998. The Regulations replace the Provision of Work Equipment Regulations 1992, which are re-enacted and augmented in the 1998 version. The Regulations apply to all types of machine, appliance, apparatus, tool or installation for use at work (reg 2) in all types of work-places. The Regulations are intended to ensure the provision of safe work equipment and its safe use. The main provisions are as follows.

(1) The employer shall ensure the suitability of work equipment for the purpose for which it is provided. The equipment must be suitable by design and construction, suitable for the place in which it will be used and for the intended purpose (reg 4).

(2) The employer must ensure that the equipment is maintained in an efficient state (reg 5), and that if machinery has a maintenance log, that the log is kept up to date (reg 6(2)).

(3) If the work equipment must be assembled and installed correctly in order for it to be safe to use, the employer must ensure that:

 (a) it is inspected after installation and prior to being put into service; or
 (b) after assembly at its new location (reg 6(1)).

If the work equipment is exposed to conditions making it likely that it will deteriorate over time, then the equipment must be inspected at suitable intervals and each time the equipment has been the subject of exceptional stresses. The result of the inspection must be recorded and kept until the next inspection is recorded. For example, safety ropes and harnesses used by employees working at heights, should be periodically checked for wear, and also re-checked whenever they have had a load applied to them (because an employee has fallen) to ensure the continued integrity of the equipment (reg 6(1)). The wording of reg 6(1) has been considered by the Court of Appeal in *Stark v Post Office* [2000] ICR 1013. The claim concerned an accident at work where a postman was thrown from a bicycle provided by his employer when part of the front brake broke in two. It was accepted that the defect to the bicycle would not have been detected by a rigorous inspection. Nevertheless, the court found that the form of words used in the regulation gave rise to a finding of strict liability in relation to the provision of work equipment.

(4) The employer must ensure that employees have adequate health and safety information and, if appropriate, instruction in the use of equipment. This should include information on conditions when the equipment may be used and foreseeable abnormal situations, and the action to be taken if such a situation occurs (reg 8).

(5) The employer must ensure that anyone using the equipment has had adequate training, including any risks which use may entail and precautions to be adopted (reg 9). In particular, the ACOP attached to these Regulations states that induction training is particularly important when young people first enter the work-place.

(6) Employers must ensure the protection of persons from dangerous parts of machinery in the following order of precedence (reg 11):

 (a) by fixed guards if possible; but if not
 (b) by other guards or other protection devices if practicable; but if not
 (c) by use of jigs, holders, push sticks or similar protective devices; but if not
 (d) by information, instruction, training and supervision.

(7) Employers must ensure that where equipment or the substances produced are at a very high or low temperature there must be protection to prevent injury to any person (reg 13).

(8) Employers must ensure that, where appropriate, equipment is provided with one or more easily accessible stop controls, and, where appropriate, emergency stop controls, and that they be clearly visible and identifiable (regs 15, 16 and 17 respectively).

(9) Employers must ensure that, where appropriate, the equipment is provided with suitable means to isolate it from all sources of energy. This must be clearly identifiable and readily accessible. Appropriate measures must be taken to ensure that re-connection of the energy source to the equipment does not expose any person using the equipment to any risk.

(10) The equipment must be suitably stabilised and suitably lit (regs 20 and 21 respectively).

(11) When maintenance is being carried out, equipment must be shut down if reasonably practicable (reg 22).

(12) The equipment must be suitably marked with appropriate health and safety information and warning devices as appropriate (regs 23 and 24).

(13) Due to the rising number of accidents arising out of the use and misuse of forklift trucks, there are comprehensive regulations relating to the use of mobile work equipment. The Regulations require employers to ensure that employees are not carried on mobile equipment unless it is both suitable, and incorporates reasonably practicable safety features (reg 25). The Regulations also seek to reduce the risk of equipment rolling over or overturning by placing on the employer an obligation to increase the stability of the equipment by making structural alterations if necessary (regs 26–28).

Personal Protective Equipment at Work Regulations 1992

The Personal Protective Equipment at Work Regulations 1992, SI 1992/2966, came into force on 1 January 1993. The Regulations make provision for the supply of protective and safety equipment: for example, eye-protectors, respirators, gloves, clothing for adverse weather conditions, safety footwear, safety hats, high-visibility jackets, etc.

The main provisions are as follows.

(1) Employers must ensure that suitable personal protective equipment (PPE) is provided to employees at risk to their health and safety while at work. PPE is not suitable unless (reg 4):

  (a) it is appropriate to the risk involved;
  (b) it takes account of ergonomic requirements and the health of persons who may wear it;
  (c) it is capable of fitting correctly; and
  (d) it is effective to prevent or control the risk involved without increasing overall risk.

(2) Before choosing PPE the employer should make an assessment to ensure that it is suitable (reg 6).

(3) Employers must ensure that PPE is maintained in efficient working order and good repair (reg 7).

(4) Employers must ensure that where PPE is provided, employees obtain such information, instruction and training as is adequate to ensure that they know what risks the PPE will avoid or limit, the purpose of the PPE and any action they must take to ensure efficient working of the PPE (reg 9).

Manual Handling Operations Regulations 1992

The Manual Handling Operations Regulations 1992, SI 1992/2793, came into force on 1 January 1993. A large number of back problems are work-related. Such problems can be caused by the transporting or supporting of loads, such as lifting too heavy a weight or lifting a weight incorrectly. Despite moves toward mechanisation in industry. there are still many jobs, such as packaging and warehouse work, requiring the day-to-day lifting of heavy objects. Regulation 2(1) provides a definition of handling as any transporting of a load (including the lifting, carrying and moving thereof) by hand or bodily force. Many claims are brought by health service staff who may have to lift and carry heavy patients as part of their everyday duties. Over one-quarter of accidents reported to the HSE involve manual handling. Most such accidents involve arm and back injuries involving fractures, strains and sprains. Many injuries are caused by poor posture and excessive repetition. A full recovery is not always made and such injuries can lead to permanent disability.

The Regulations require as follows.

(1) So far as reasonably practicable, employers must avoid the need for employees to undertake any manual handling involving risk of injury (reg 4(1)(a)).
(2) If avoidance is not practicable, employers must make an assessment of manual handling risks, and try to reduce risk of injury. The assessment should address the task, the load, the working environment and the individual's capability (reg 4(1)(b)).
(3) If it is not reasonably practicable to avoid manual handling operations which involve risk of injury, employers must take steps to reduce manual handling to the lowest level reasonably practicable (reg 4(1)(b)(ii)).
(4) Employees must be provided with information on the weight of each load, and the heaviest side of any load (reg 4(1)(b)(iii)).

Employees have a duty to make full use of any system of work provided by the employer to reduce manual, handling risks (reg 5). As to the meaning of 'so far as reasonably practicable' in reg 4(1), see *Hawkes v Southwark LBC* (1998) unreported, 20 February, CA. In this case, it was found that the defendant had not carried out any risk assessment as required under the Regulations. The judge made it clear that the burden of proving what was 'reasonably practicable' lay on the defendant, and that failure to carry out an assessment did not by itself prove liability, rather it was the failure to take appropriate steps to reduce risk of injury to the lowest level reasonably practicable that was at issue. See also the Lifting Operations and Lifting Equipment Regulations 1998, SI 1998/2307 which deal with health and safety requirements with respect to lifting equipment.

Workplace (Health, Safety and Welfare) Regulations 1992

The Workplace (Health, Safety and Welfare) Regulations 1992, SI 1992/3004, replace much of the old legislation covering such things as lighting, cleaning, the condition and slipperiness of floors, and traffic routes. The Regulations came into effect on 1 January 1993. However, transitional provisions mean that the Regulations apply immediately to existing work-places but only to work-places first used after 31 December 1992 as from 1 January 1996. The Regulations are supported by an Approved Code of Practice which came into effect on the same dates. The Regulations apply to all work-places except ships, construction sites and mining operations (reg 3).

The main provisions are as follows.

(1) Work-place equipment, devices and systems must be maintained in efficient working order and good repair (reg 5).
(2) There must be adequate ventilation (reg 6).
(3) The indoor temperature during working hours must be reasonable, and thermometers must be provided to enable employees to determine the temperature (reg 7).
(4) Work-places must have suitable lighting, which, if reasonably practicable, should be natural light (reg 8).
(5) Work-places, including furniture, fittings, floors, walls and ceilings, must be kept sufficiently clean, and waste materials must not be allowed to accumulate (reg 9).
(6) Every work-station must be arranged so that it is suitable for any person likely to work there (reg 11).
(7) Every floor or traffic route surface must be suitable for the purpose for which it is used. In particular, it must have no hole or slope, or be uneven or slippery so as to expose any person to a risk to his health or safety. So far as practicable, every floor or traffic route must be kept free of obstructions or articles which may cause a person to slip, trip or fall (reg 12).
(8) So far as reasonably practicable, effective measures must be taken to avoid injury to persons caused by falling or being struck by a falling object (reg 13).
(9) Suitable and sufficient sanitary conveniences must be provided at readily accessible places. They must be adequately lit, ventilated and kept in a clean and tidy condition (reg 20).
(10) Suitable and sufficient washing facilities must be provided, including showers if required by the nature of the work for health reasons (reg 21).
(11) An adequate supply of wholesome drinking water must be provided at the work-place, which should be readily accessible and conspicuously marked where necessary.

Control of Substances Hazardous to Health Regulations 1994

The Control of Substances Hazardous to Health Regulations 1994, SI 1994/3246, came into force on 16 January 1995. Although these Regulations are not part of the original 'six pack', they are of primary importance and are included for that reason.

Substances hazardous to health include chemicals, airborne dusts, micro-organisms, biological agents and respiratory sensitisers.

Employers' duties are:

(1) to carry out a formal risk assessment of risks to employees;
(2) to prevent or control exposure to risks;
(3) to ensure proper use of personal protective equipment;
(4) to monitor exposure of employees;
(5) to provide health surveillance of employees where necessary (ie where a particular task is known to make employees susceptible to a particular injury or disease);
(6) to provide information and training to employees regarding hazardous substances.

3.3.3 Statutory duty and common law negligence

The claimant employee's case will frequently make a claim in both common law negligence and breach of statutory duty. Although the two are distinct causes of action, they are inevitably linked. It is usually difficult, but not impossible, to show that, if the employer has complied with regulations, he has nevertheless been negligent (*Franklin v Gramophone Co Ltd* [1948] 1 KB 542) (*Close v Steel Co of Wales* [1962] AC 367). However, the employer may be liable for breach of statutory duty even though he has not been negligent. The onus of proof may also be different in the two causes: in negligence the onus is upon the claimant to show a breach, but for breach of statutory duty the onus is often on the defendant to show that he acted 'as far as (reasonably) practicable'.

3.4 OCCUPIERS' LIABILITY TO LAWFUL VISITORS

3.4.1 Introduction

The Occupiers' Liability Act 1957 (OLA 1957) replaces common law rules concerning the duty owed by an occupier to a lawful visitor.

Under s 1(1), 'occupier' is given the same meaning as at common law (s 1(2)), the test for which was said by Lord Denning in *Wheat v E. Lacon & Co Ltd* [1966] AC 522 to be, 'who is in sufficient control?'.

A 'visitor' is a person who would be treated as an invitee or licensee at common law (s 1(2)) and who therefore is a lawful visitor (as opposed to a trespasser). The duty of care extends not only to the visitor's person but also to his property (s 1(3)).

3.4.2 The nature of the duty of care

The common duty of care is a duty to take such care as in all the circumstances of the case is reasonable to see that the visitor will be reasonably safe in using the premises for the purposes for which he is invited or permitted by the occupier to be there (s 2(2)).

The common duty of care does not impose on an occupier any obligation to a visitor in respect of risks willingly accepted as his by the visitor (s 2(5)).

3.4.3 Discharging the duty of care

The duty is to take '... such care as ... in all the circumstances ... is reasonable' taking into account the degree of care, and of want of care, which would ordinarily be looked for in such a visitor (s 2(3)). A warning may discharge the duty of care if it is enough to enable the visitor to be reasonably safe (s 2(4)).

3.4.4 Employing an independent contractor

Where injury is caused to a visitor by a danger due to the faulty execution of any work of construction, maintenance or repair by an independent contractor employed by the occupier, the occupier will not be treated by this reason alone as answerable for the danger if in all the circumstances (s 2(4)(b)):

(1) he had acted reasonably in entrusting the work to an independent contractor; and

(2) he had taken such steps (if any) as he reasonably ought in order to satisfy himself that:

    (a) the contractor was competent; and
    (b) that the work had been properly done.

The duty of care under the Act is therefore delegable to an independent contractor. This should be contrasted with the personal nature of the common duty of care owed to an employee, which is non-delegable (see *Wilsons & Clyde Coal v English* [1938] AC 57).

3.4.5 Exclusion or modification of duty of care

By s 2(1) of OLA 1957, an occupier may extend, restrict, modify or exclude his duty to any visitor. However, this must be read subject to s 2 of the Unfair Contract Terms Act 1977 under which, in the case of business liability:

(1) a person cannot by reference to any contract term or to a notice given to persons generally or to particular persons exclude or restrict his liability for death or personal injury resulting from negligence;
(2) in the case of other loss or damage, a person cannot so exclude or restrict his liability for negligence except insofar as the term or notice satisfies the requirement of reasonableness.

3.5 VICARIOUS LIABILITY

3.5.1 Definition

An employer will be vicariously liable for his employee's torts if committed in the course of his employment. Therefore, it falls to be established:

(1) whether the tort was committed by an employee; and
(2) whether that employee was acting in the course of (ie within the scope of) his employment.

3.5.2 'Course of employment'

The employee must have committed the tort 'in the course of his employment' – which is less clear than may first appear. There are many cases on the point, but the nearest to a formulation of a rule is that the employer will be liable for acts of employees if they perform an authorised act in an unauthorised way, but will not be liable for acts not sufficiently connected with authorised acts.

3.5.3 Disobedience of orders by employees

Having established that an employer will be liable for acts of his employees if they are acting within the course of their employment, it is necessary to examine the situation where the employee disobeys the orders of his employer in relation to the way he carries out his work. In *Rose v Plenty* [1976] 1 All ER 97 a milkman had been told by his employers not to allow children to help him on his rounds. Subsequently he allowed a child to assist him and the child was injured whilst riding on the milk float due to the milkman's negligent driving. On appeal to the Court of

Appeal, the employer was found to be vicariously liable. The court held that the employee was doing his job but was using a method that his employers had prohibited. Nonetheless, he was still found to be working within the scope of his employment as it was performed for the benefit of the defendant's business.

Contrast the above with the facts of *Lister and Others v Hesley Hall Ltd* [2001] 2 All ER 769. The facts of the case were that the warden of the school abused boys while they were resident at the school. The House of Lords held the defendant vicariously liable for the acts of their employee. The Lords said that the court should not concentrate on the nature of the actual act complained of (abuse) but that they should concentrate on the closeness of the connection between the nature of the employment and the tort complained of. The Lords found that the defendant employed the warden to care for the claimants. The abuse took place whilst he was carrying out the duties required by his employment. On that basis the proximity between the employment and the tort complained of was very close and therefore the defendant ought to be liable.

3.6 ENFORCEMENT OF HEALTH AND SAFETY AT WORK

The function of enforcement is carried out by:

(1) the HSE, which deals broadly with industrial working environments and is also responsible for policy development;
(2) various specialist agencies appointed on behalf of the HSE (eg UK Atomic Energy Authority);
(3) local authorities, which deal broadly with non-industrial working environments.

3.6.1 Health and safety inspectors

Health and safety inspectors have wide powers to enter premises and carry out investigations. As a result of an investigation revealing a contravention, an inspector may:

(1) issue an improvement notice requiring any contravention to be remedied;
(2) serve a prohibition notice requiring the contravention to be remedied and fixing a time after which the activity is prohibited unless remedied;
(3) commence a criminal prosecution (which may give rise to a relevant conviction that can be used against the employer by the employee in subsequent civil proceedings).

3.6.2 The employer's duty to report, maintain and implement safety provisions

The following are the principal requirements of an employer.

(1) An employer who employs more than five persons must have written details of his policy in regard to the organisation, control, monitoring and review of health and safety measures.
(2) An employer is under a duty to report certain accidents, diseases and dangerous occurrences to the HSE on Form F2508. Employers are also able to report accidents to the HSE by posting information direct to their internet site at www.riddor.gov.uk. This enables the HSE to consider an investigation of the

incident. All occurrences which are required to be reported must be recorded and details of the injuries must be kept in an accident book. The records must be kept for at least 3 years.

(3) The employer may (and in certain circumstances must) have a safety representative to represent the health and safety interests of the employees. Such a representative has wide powers to investigate potential hazards and dangerous occurrences and to follow up complaints made by employees.

(4) In addition to the safety representative, the employer may (and in certain circumstances must) have a safety committee, the function of which includes:

- (a) the studying of accidents and notifiable diseases in order to recommend corrective measures to management;
- (b) making recommendations on safety training;
- (c) examining reports of the HSE and safety representatives;
- (d) making recommendations on developing/changing safety rules.

(5) Where an employee is injured at work and claims benefit, in certain circumstances the employer is obliged to complete Form B176 to be sent to the Department of Social Security.

(6) Subject to certain exceptions, an employer is required by the Employers' Liability (Compulsory Insurance) Act 1969 to take out insurance against liability to his own employees.

3.6.3 Employer's liability – enforcement through criminal proceedings

The Court of Appeal established in *R v Gateway Foodmarkets Ltd* [1997] 3 All ER 78 that s 2(1) of the Health and Safety at Work etc Act 1974 imposed a duty of strict liability. This is qualified only by the defence that the employer has done everything reasonably practicable to ensure that no person's health and safety is put at risk. The defendants appealed against their conviction that they failed to do everything reasonable to ensure the safety of their employees. The court dismissed the company's appeal and held that both s 2(1) and s 3(1) of the Act were to be interpreted so as to impose liability in the event of a failure to ensure safety unless all reasonable precautions had been taken, not only by the company itself but by its servants and agents on its behalf.

Following concern at the low level of fines being imposed for offences under the Health and Safety at Work etc Act 1974, the Court of Appeal has given guidance on the factors to be taken into account by courts when considering the appropriate penalty for this type of offence. In *R v Howe & Son (Engineers) Ltd* [1999] 2 All ER 249, the Court of Appeal stated that the aim of the Act was to ensure safety for employees and the public and therefore fines needed to be large enough to convey that message. In general, they should not be so large as to put the employer out of business. In determining seriousness, the court should consider:

- (a) how far short of the appropriate standard the defendant had been;
- (b) that the standard of care was the same for small organisations as for large;
- (c) the degree of risk and extent of danger involved; and
- (d) the defendant's resources and the effect of a fine on its business.

Aggravating factors could include:

- (a) failure to heed warnings;

(b) deliberate breach of regulations in pursuit of profit or saving money; and
(c) loss of life.

Mitigating factors could include:

(a) early admission of responsibility;
(b) plea of guilty;
(c) taking action to remedy any breach brought to the company's notice; and
(d) a good safety record.

The court further held that it was incumbent upon a defendant seeking to make representations about its financial position to provide copies of accounts to the court and the prosecution in good time.

The above guidelines where considered by the Court of Appeal in *R v Rollco Screw & Rivet Co Ltd* [1999] 2 Cr App R (S) 436. The defendant company and two of its directors protested that the length of time given for payment of fines was inappropriate and that no distinction should be made between personal and corporate defendants (as there was a risk of double penalty if directors and shareholders where the same people). On appeal, the court agreed that a personal defendant's period of punishment had to remain within acceptable boundaries, this was not true of a corporate defendant as the same sense of anxiety was unlikely and a fine could be ordered to be payable over a longer period. The level of fines must make it clear that directors had a personal responsibility; there was a risk of double penalty in smaller companies where directors were also shareholders and would be the principal losers.

3.7 CLAIMS FOR PSYCHIATRIC ILLNESS OR 'NERVOUS SHOCK'

Claims for psychiatric injury or illness have risen markedly in recent years on the basis that if the defendant would be liable for foreseeable physical injury then he ought also to be liable for foreseeable psychological injury.

3.7.1 What is nervous shock?

There must be evidence that the claimant has suffered a recognised psychiatric illness which is more than temporary grief or fright. In recent years 'nervous shock' and 'post-traumatic stress disorder' (PTSD) have become commonly used to mean psychological illness brought about by a negligent act. The Law Commission's consultation paper on liability for psychiatric illness (1995) favoured the term 'psychiatric illness'.

There are two main systems of classification of psychiatric illnesses currently used in the UK:

(1) the Diagnostic and Statistical Manual of Mental Disorders of the American Psychiatric Association, fourth edition (DSM IV); and
(2) The World Health Organisation International Classification of Mental and Behavioural Disorders, tenth edition (ICD-10)

One recognised psychiatric illness which forms part of the claim by claimants is PTSD. Major factors in the onset of PTSD tend to be a life-threatening experience, or exposure to grotesque death. The symptoms of PTSD are listed in Chapter 2.

3.7.2 Primary and secondary victims

(i) Primary victims

To be regarded as a primary victim the claimant must be able to show a risk of foreseeable physical harm. The key importance of this classification between primary and secondary victims is that if he can show that he is a primary victim then the claimant is likely to be treated more favourably by the courts. Primary victims will normally be involved in the events as participants, but it will be relatively rare for a primary victim directly involved in the events not to suffer any physical injury as well.

(ii) Secondary victims

Secondary victims are normally witnesses of injury caused to others.

The distinction between primary and secondary victims may not always be appropriate in relation to victims who are also employees and victims who are also rescuers and/or employees (as to which see below).

3.7.3 Foreseeability of primary and secondary victims

(i) Primary victims

A primary victim must show that some personal injury was reasonably foreseeable as a result of the defendant's negligence so as to bring him within the scope of the defendant's duty of care. No distinction should be brought between a physical or a psychiatric injury.

(ii) Secondary victims

A secondary victim must show that a person of reasonable fortitude would have foreseeably suffered some psychiatric injury. Foreseeability of psychiatric injury is of critical importance to secondary victims as they will normally be outside the scope of persons who might suffer foreseeable physical injury.

If a claimant is a secondary victim, he will need to show sufficiently close ties of love and affection with a primary victim. Following the House of Lords' decision in *Alcock v Chief Constable for South Yorkshire* [1992] AC 310, there is a rebuttable presumption of sufficiently close ties between, for example, relationships as between parents, children and spouses. For example, in *Vernon v Bosley (No 1)* [1997] 1 All ER 577, CA, although damages for normal grief and bereavement suffered as a result of another's negligence were not recoverable, the claimant in a position of a secondary victim could recover damages for PTSD or pathological grief disorder provided the two pre-conditions for recovery of damages for psychiatric illness were satisfied: namely, that the claimant was in a close and loving relationship with the primary victim and was connected with the accident in time and space, ie the bystander and direct viewer.

If the claimant did not perceive the events in question with his own unaided senses, generally there will be no recovery for psychiatric illness. In *Frost v Chief Constable of South Yorkshire* [1997] 1 All ER 540, it was held that the claimant must witness the event with his own unaided senses, either by sight or hearing.

In *Greatorex v Greatorex* [2000] 4 All ER 769, the court considered whether or not a primary victim owed any duty of care to a third party where the third party suffers psychiatric injury. Although the case is based on a very singular set of facts, it is useful reading to anyone new to this area of law as Cazelet J considered many of the prior cases on nervous shock in the course of his judgment. The relevant facts are that the claimant was a fireman and father of the defendant who was the crash victim in a road traffic accident. It was accepted that the accident was the defendant's fault. The claimant did not witness the accident but went to the scene in the course of his employment as a fire officer. The claimant was diagnosed as suffering from post-traumatic stress disorder as a result of what he had seen. In essence the question was 'does a victim of self-inflicted injuries owe a duty of care to third party not to cause him psychiatric injury?'. Having considered the facts the court decided that a victim does not owe a duty to a third party in circumstances where self-inflicted injuries cause psychiatric injury as to conclude otherwise would 'create a significant limitation upon an individual's freedom of action'. The judge went on to conclude that such an action would only be maintainable at all by a close relative, which would lead to undesirable litigation within the family. Such policy considerations were adjudged to outweigh arguments in favour of there being such a duty of care.

3.7.4 Employee victims

Following the House of Lords' decision in *White v Chief Constable of South Yorkshire* [1998] 3 WLR 1509, it is clear that unless employees can show a risk of physical injury (and therefore fall into the category of primary victims), they will be treated as secondary victims. In *Young v Charles Church (Southern) Ltd* (1998) BMLR 146, it was established that an employee who suffered psychiatric illness after seeing a workmate electrocuted close to him could recover damages against his employer as a primary victim because of the risk to himself of physical injury. The court decided that the ambit of the regulations was not limited to physical electrocution. The statute gave protection to employees from kinds of injury which could be foreseen as likely to occur when the electrical cable or equipment was allowed to become a source of danger to them. This included mental illness caused to the claimant by the shock of seeing his workmate electrocuted in circumstances where he was fortunate to escape electrocution himself.

Contrast the above case with *Hunter v British Coal* [1999] QB 89, CA. The claimant was a driver in a coalmine. His vehicle struck a hydrant causing it to leak. With the help of a workmate, he tried to stop the flow but failed. He left the scene in search of help. When the claimant was 30 metres away, the hydrant burst, and he was told that someone was injured. On his way back to the scene, he was told that the workmate who had been helping him had died. The claimant thought he was responsible and suffered nervous shock and depression. He brought proceedings for damages against his employers. It was held that a claimant who believes he has been the cause of another's death in an accident caused by the defendant's negligence could recover damages as a primary victim if he was directly involved as a participant in the incident. However, a claimant who was not at the scene could not recover damages as a primary victim merely because he felt responsible for the incident. In this case, the claimant was not involved in the incident in which the workmate died as he was 30 metres away, and only suffered psychiatric injury on being told of the death some 15 minutes later. Therefore, there was not sufficient proximity in time and space with the incident. Also, the illness triggered by the death was not a foreseeable consequence of the defendant's breach of duty of care as it was an abnormal reaction to being told of the workmate's death triggered by an irrational feeling that he was responsible.

3.7.5 Professional rescuers

In relation to physical injury, there is a duty of care owed to a foreseeable rescuer not to cause the rescuer foreseeable harm. In relation to psychological injury, in the case of *Frost v Chief Constable of South Yorkshire Police*, the Court of Appeal considered *Page v Smith* [1996] AC 155 and bypassed the categorisation of primary or secondary victims and held that claimants could recover on the basis of their work as rescuers. Also, it was claimed that because the claimants were employees of the defendant, the defendant owed them a duty of care to protect them from the risk of physical as well as psychiatric injury. *Frost v Chief Constable of South Yorkshire* has been appealed to the House of Lords (reported as *White v Chief Constable of South Yorkshire Police and Others* [1999] 2 AC 455). The Lords rejected the police officers' claims for psychiatric injury.

The Lords disagreed with the finding in the Court of Appeal that the claimants, as rescuers, were to be treated as a special category. In his judgment, Lord Hoffman said that the claimants asserted that they were in a special position from friends or relatives who may have developed psychiatric injuries. They claimed that, because it was admitted that the disaster had been caused by the negligence of persons for whom the defendants were vicariously liable, thus the claimants were owed a special duty as employees. The Lords debated whether it was appropriate to recognise a duty to guard employees against psychiatric injury. It was felt that it would not be fair to give police officers the right to a claim merely because the disaster had been caused by the negligence of other policemen and that, if it was given effect, the law would not be seen to be treating like cases with like.

The claimants also argued that their position was analogous to that of rescuers. The Lords rejected this argument, also stating that there was no authority for placing rescuers in a special position. The Lords decided this, based on two factors:

(1) the problem of applying a definition to define the class of rescuers that could claim; and
(2) if the law did allow the claims to succeed, the result would be unacceptable to the ordinary person who would think it wrong that policemen should have the right to compensation for psychiatric injury out of public funds when bereaved relatives did not. Fairness demanded that the appeal be allowed and the claims were therefore dismissed.

3.7.6 Bystanders as victims

A 'mere bystander' is someone who is not a primary victim or a secondary victim, but is merely a witness.

3.8 LIABILITY IN CLINICAL NEGLIGENCE CASES

The law of negligence as it relates to clinical negligence must be explained to the client in terms which are easily understood.

If the client is to be successful against a doctor, he must show that the essential elements of negligence are proved, ie:

(1) that the doctor owed him a duty of care;
(2) that the doctor breached that duty;

(3) that he suffered loss as a result of that breach of duty.

The solicitor must make it clear to the client that it is for the client to prove these three elements. The client may find this difficult to accept. If he is still in pain, he may take the view that the doctor must have been negligent. However, this is not necessarily the case and the client must be made aware of this.

Each of the three elements above are examined in detail below.

3.8.1 The duty of care

The doctor

It is clear that a doctor owes a duty of care to his patients in the normal course of events.

The health authority

Does the health authority/trust owe a duty of care and can it be sued for negligence itself without proving negligence on the part of the doctor? The leading case in this area is *Wilsher v Essex Area Health Authority* [1988] AC 1074, in which it was held that a health authority has a duty to provide services of doctors of sufficient skill, and there is no reason why a health authority cannot be liable for a failure to provide such services (see also ss 1 and 3 of the National Health Service Act 1977 and *Cassidy v The Ministry of Health* [1951] 2 KB 343).

3.8.2 Breach of the duty of care

In the case of a clinical negligence action, the normal 'reasonable man' test is modified. In order to show a breach of duty, the claimant must show that the doctor has followed a course of action which is not supported by any reasonable body of medical opinion – this has become known as the *Bolam* test after the case of *Bolam v Friern Hospital Management Committee* [1957] 1 WLR 582, in which it was held that:

> 'The test as to whether there has been negligence or not is not the test of the man on top of the Clapham omnibus because he has a special skill. The test is the standard of the ordinary skilled man exercising and professing to have that special skill. A man need not possess the highest expert skill; it is well established law that it is sufficient if he exercises the ordinary skill of an ordinary competent man exercising that particular art... . A doctor is not guilty of negligence if he has acted in accordance with a practice accepted as proper by a reasonable body of medical men skilled in that particular art ... a doctor is not negligent, if he is acting in accordance with such a practice, merely because there is a body of opinion which takes the contrary view.'

Thus, if the defendants can show that the doctor acted in accordance with a reasonable body of opinion, they will have a defence to the action. Practitioners refer to the 10% rule. It is said that if 10% of the doctors in the country would have taken the same course of action then it will not be a negligent act. In *Hunter v Hanley* [1955] SLT 213, it was stated that in the realms of diagnosis and treatment there is ample scope for genuine difference of opinion and one man clearly is not negligent merely because his conclusion differs from that of other professional men: '... the true test for establishing negligence in diagnosis or treatment on the part of a doctor is whether he has been proved to be guilty of such failure as no doctor of ordinary skill would be guilty of if acting with ordinary care'.

This approach must be considered with some caution as each case will turn on its own facts.

There are a number of reported cases which suggest limits on the *Bolam* test. In *Hucks v Cole* (1968) 118 NLJ 469, Lord Denning MR said:

> 'A doctor is not to be held negligent simply because something has gone wrong. He is not liable for mischance or misadventure or for an error of judgment. He is not liable for taking one choice out of two or favouring one school rather than another. He is only liable when he falls below the standard of a reasonably competent practitioner in his field. On such occasions, the fact that other practitioners would have done the same thing as the defendant is a very weighty matter to be put in the scales on his behalf; but it is not conclusive. The court must be ever vigilant to see whether the reasons for putting a patient at risk are valid in the light of any well known advance to out of date ideas.'

Sachs LJ added that when the evidence showed that a lacuna in professional practice existed by which risks of grave danger were knowingly taken then, however small the risks, the court must examine that lacuna, particularly if the risks could be easily and inexpensively avoided.

One of the most significant cases on the law relating to the duty owed by doctors is *Wilsher v Essex Area Health Authority* [1988] AC 1074. The facts of this case were that a junior hospital doctor was working in an intensive care neo-natal unit when he made the mistake of inserting a catheter into a vein instead of an artery. The junior doctor asked the senior registrar to check to see that what he had done was correct, but the senior registrar also failed to notice the mistake. As a result the child was given excess oxygen which the claimant alleged caused near blindness. In this case, the junior doctor had discharged the standard of care by consulting his more experienced colleagues. The court suggested that there are two potential tests of liability. Mustill LJ said in his judgment that the standard for the higher test is not just that of the averagely competent and well-informed junior houseman (or whatever the position of the doctor), but of such a person who fills a post in a unit offering a highly specialised service.

Many commentators suggest that the higher test is generally used as the courts take the view that the public should be protected, that the duty of care should relate to the post and that the public should be able to rely on the doctor filling the post.

The burden of proof is on the claimant to show that on the normal balance of probabilities there was a breach of duty. In a number of cases the courts have continued to reaffirm the view that the allegations of a breach of duty against a doctor is a serious matter and the evidence should be clear. The courts have given a clear message that, merely because an operation goes wrong or things turn out badly, that does not necessarily mean that there has been a breach of duty, providing the doctor has taken a course of action that a responsible body of doctors would have taken. (See *Maynard v West Midlands Regional Health Authority* [1984] 1 WLR 634.)

A good example of the position on liability in such cases was expounded by Cresswell J in *Sharpe v Southend Health Authority* [1997] 8 Med LR 299. It was contended that the defendant authority was negligent in that it had adopted a 'wait and see policy' in relation to the claimant's tumour until it was too late. It was alleged that they had failed to notice its increase in size, and had failed to operate before it became malignant. The defendants argued that they had complied with standard medical practice and that x-rays showed no significant increase in the size of the tumour. In his summing-up the judge found:

(1) the standard of care is that of a reasonably competent radiologist/ radiotherapist *at the time*;
(2) the defendants were not negligent if they adopted a practice accepted as reasonable by a responsible body of practitioners skilled in the relevant field;
(3) the recommended procedure was continued observation;
(4) the condition had been correctly identified and the advice highly competent;
(5) the radiological changes were of negligible significance.

In those circumstances a continued policy of observation was probably a reasonable one. In the circumstances, there had been no negligence.

The *Bolam* test is concerned only with matters of clinical judgment. Clinical negligence claims can relate to errors that are clearly in breach of a doctor's duty, for example a case where a swab is left in the patient during an operation. Such an omission will constitute a breach of duty.

The standard of care of a specialist, such as an ophthalmologist, is the standard of a reasonably competent specialist (see *Sidaway v Governors of the Bethlem Royal Hospital and Maudsley Hospital* [1985] AC 871).

3.8.3 Causation (proof of loss as a result of breach of duty)

The claimant in a clinical negligence action will be maintaining that, as a result of the injuries he received because of the negligent treatment by the doctor or hospital, he failed to recover from his pre-existing condition, or the chances of him recovering from that condition diminished to a substantial degree. Alternatively, the claimant may argue that his original injury or condition has become worse as a result of the treatment which he received, or, where the claimant has died, the claimant's relatives may argue that the claimant's death was caused by negligent treatment.

The issue of causation was considered by the House of Lords in *Bolitho v City and Hackney Health Authority* [1997] 3 WLR 1151. In that case, the child claimant (aged 2) underwent surgery to correct a heart defect. Subsequently the claimant got croup and was admitted to hospital. The claimant suffered breathing difficulties and the nurse called for the Senior Registrar. The Senior Registrar was unable to attend and the Senior House Officer was paged instead. The Senior House Officer did not attend either because the batteries of his pager were not working. The child subsequently suffered cardiac arrest, and, although he was subsequently resuscitated, he suffered brain damage. At first instance, it was accepted by the court that it was negligent not to attend the child, but the issue at stake was whether the failure was causative of any damage. It was agreed that if the child had been intubated (passing a tube into the child to create an airway) the child would not have suffered the cardiac arrest and consequently would not have become brain damaged. At this point, there was dispute as between the experts in the case as to what would have been the appropriate action to take in those circumstances. The court considered the *Bolam* test for assessing whether the doctor had been negligent (as to which see above). At first instance the judge decided in *Bolitho* that the defendant should succeed on the issue of causation as, on the evidence before the court, it would not have been negligent for the doctor not to have intubated the child.

The case was appealed to the Court of Appeal, where the decision at first instance was approved by majority. The claimant then appealed to the House of Lords and the Lords dealt with the case by making a two-stage approach.

(1) The court first considered what the doctor would have done if she had attended the child. This was a fact-finding exercise and the *Bolam* test was not relevant at this stage. From the doctor's evidence, it was accepted by the court that she would not have intubated the child.

(2) Secondly, would that omission to intubate have been negligent? At this point the *Bolam* test is relevant. The court should consider whether a responsible body of medical opinion would support the decision to not intubate. The Lords once again found for the defendant.

It is important to remember that the appropriate test should be related to the state of knowledge in the medical profession at the time of the alleged incident. Many clinical negligence claims come to light only many years after the alleged negligence and, when an expert is instructed, it is important to remind the expert that the relevant state of medical knowledge is what prevailed at the time when the incident occurred.

Examples

(1) In *Brooks v Home Office* [1999] 2 FLR 33, the standard of obstetric care that a prisoner in prison is entitled to receive is the same as she would have received if not in prison.

(2) In *Vadera v Shaw* (1998) BMLR 162, the claimant had been prescribed a contraceptive pill in 1996 by the defendant who was her GP. Six weeks later, she suffered a stroke and sought to claim that the pill had caused the stroke, as there had been suggestions within the medical profession that this might be the case. On appeal, the claim was quickly dismissed due to lack of evidence. On the issue of causation, the judge approached the problem based on his findings of fact. He found that there was no history of hypertension or a history of headaches, therefore the issue of causation could not be proved. It was also noted that an infection or some other condition could have caused the stroke.

(3) In *Brown v Lewisham & North Southwark HA* [1999] Lloyd's Rep Med 110, the plaintiff alleged negligence in the use of an anti-coagulant drug (Heparin) and also in failing to diagnose deep vein thrombosis. The plaintiff was admitted to Guy's Hospital for quadruple bypass surgery (having been referred to Guy's from Royal Victoria Hospital, Blackpool). Heparin was administered to the plaintiff during the operation. The plaintiff was discharged form Guy's unaccompanied and travelled by train back to the Royal Victoria Hospital. The plaintiff experienced difficulties over the coming days and Heparin was administered to assist him. The plaintiff had an adverse reaction to the drug (which was not widely known about at that time), gangrene set in and the leg had to be amputated, as a consequence of the adverse reaction to Heparin.

On the question of causation, the plaintiff asserted that had he not been discharged he would have remained in hospital and would have received treatment earlier. Also, he would not have had to endure the effects of journey from Guy's Hospital back to Royal Victoria Hospital. The court found that it was unlikely that the journey was an effective cause of the loss of the leg. The complex circumstances made it impossible to infer that the plaintiff's loss was a result of the journey. In the final analysis, the court found that there was no causal link between the negligence and the amputation, as by the time the haematologist gave his negligent advice the gangrene was evident and was an unfortunate consequence of the plaintiff's reasonably unrecognised reaction to the Heparin. The plaintiff's claim therefore failed.

(4) Cervical smear tests were taken from a number of claimants. Each of the tests was reported by the primary cytoscreeners as being negative but each of the claimants went on to develop invasive cancer. The judge found that the slides exhibited abnormalities which no reasonably competent cytoscreener would have treated as innocuous, such that a negative test would not have been given. With early detection, pre-cancerous or cancerous conditions could have been dealt with by minor surgery, but as a result of the negative smear test there was no timely follow up or therapeutic intervention (*Penney and Others v East Kent Health Authority* [2000] Lloyd's Rep Med 41).

In each of these examples, there is an issue of causation, ie the connection between the defendant's alleged breach of duty and the claimant's eventual injury or condition.

In order to succeed in his case, a claimant must prove that the breach of duty caused his injury. If a failure to treat a patient has made no difference because he would have died in any event, his death will not have been caused by negligence.

In *Barnett v Chelsea and Kensington Hospital Management Committee* [1969] 1 QB 428, three night-watchmen attended a casualty department complaining of vomiting. As they had drunk some tea 3 hours previously, the doctor told them to go home and go to bed and, if necessary, to call their own doctors. They went away but one of them died later that night and the cause of death was subsequently found to be arsenic poisoning. It was held that since the defendants provided a casualty department, they owed the deceased a duty of care to exercise such skill as ought reasonably to be expected of a nurse and casualty officer. In this instance, because the casualty officer had not exercised such skill, he was found negligent and in breach of duty. However, the court also found that the deceased would have died of the poisoning, even if he had been treated with all the necessary care. Therefore, the claimant had failed to establish on the balance of probabilities that the defendants' negligence caused the deceased's death.

The conventional doctrine, therefore, is that no action will be successful unless the negligence causes the damage or injury.

The doctrine goes one step further in clinical negligence cases in that a claimant cannot claim for the loss of a prospect of recovery if the chance of recovery is less than probable. In *Hotson v East Berkshire Health Authority* [1987] AC 750, a 13-year-old boy was playing at school in his lunch break and, for fun, climbed a tree to which a rope was attached. He lost his grip on the rope and fell 12 feet to the ground. He was subsequently taken to hospital where the staff failed to diagnose a fracture. The boy was sent home to rest. When he returned to the hospital, the correct diagnosis was made. As a result of the initial failure to give a correct diagnosis, the boy was left with a disability of the hip and a risk of future osteoarthritis. At first instance, the trial judge, Simon Brown J, found that if the health authority had correctly diagnosed and treated the claimant when he first attended hospital, there was a high probability (which he assessed at a 75% risk) that the claimant's injury would have followed the same course as it had followed. In other words, the doctor's delay in making the correct diagnosis had denied the claimant a 25% chance that, if given immediate treatment, the avascular necrosis would not have developed and if it had not developed the claimant would have made a complete recovery. Accordingly, Simon Brown J awarded 25% of the appropriate damages. The defendants successfully appealed. The claimant received no damages in respect of his lost chances of recovery because they were less than 50% (see also *Bolitho v City and Hackney Health Authority* [1993] PIQR 334 on the issue of causation).

It can thus be said that the test applied is that 'but for' the negligence the patient would not, on the balance of probabilities, have suffered the harm in any event. Experts need to be reminded of the importance of the causation test.

The issue of causation is far more difficult for the claimant's clinical negligence solicitor than in normal personal injury work. In personal injury cases, the claimant is normally fit and the injury which results is due to the accident. In contrast, in clinical negligence cases, the injury complained of can be as a result of many different variables (see *McGhee v National Coal Board* [1973] 1 WLR 1).

In practice, care must be taken that if the defendants admit liability prior to trial, the claimant's solicitor should seek confirmation that the defendants also admit causation. This must be specifically considered by the claimant's solicitor.

Can the maxim *res ipsa loquitur* be used in a clinical negligence case? The reason why this question has been raised is that, in certain circumstances, it can be very difficult to identify the specific negligent act, although it appears from the facts that negligence must have occurred. An example would be where a patient goes into hospital with a problem relating to two of his fingers on one hand but when he is discharged that hand has become completely useless (see *Cassidy v Ministry of Health* [1951] 2 KB 343). It appears from that case that although the maxim *res ipsa loquitur* may be used only in exceptional circumstances, the court, on limited occasions, will hold that the maxim is appropriate in a clinical negligence case.

3.9 RES IPSA LOQUITUR

The proper approach to *res ipsa loquitur* in clinical negligence litigation was reviewed by the Court of Appeal in *Ratcliffe v Plymouth and Torbay Health Authority* [1998] PIQR P170. Dismissing the appeal, the judge made the following points in relation to *res ipsa loquitur* to clinical negligence cases.

(i) The maxim applies where the claimant relies on the happening of the thing itself to raise the inference of negligence, which is supported by ordinary human experience, and with no need for expert evidence.
(ii) The maxim can be applied in that form to simple situations in the clinical negligence field (a surgeon cutting off a right foot instead of the left; a swab left in the operation site; a patient who wakes up in the course of a surgical operation despite a general anaesthetic).
(iii) In practice, in contested clinical negligence cases the evidence of a claimant which establishes the *res* is likely to be buttressed by expert evidence to the

effect that the matter complained of does not ordinarily occur in the absence of negligence.

(iv) The position may then be reached at the close of the claimant's case that the judge would be entitled to infer negligence on the defendant's part unless the defendant can then adduce some evidence which discharges the inference.

(v) This evidence may be to the effect that there is a plausible explanation of what may have happened which does not rely on negligence on the defendant's part.

(vi) Alternatively, the defendant's evidence may satisfy the judge on the balance of probabilities that he did exercise proper care. If the untoward outcome is extremely rare, or is impossible to explain in the light of the current state of medical knowledge, the judge will be bound to exercise great care in evaluating the evidence before making such a finding.

(vii) It follows from this that, although in very simple situations the *res* may speak for itself at the end of the lay evidence adduced on behalf of the claimant, in practice the inference is then buttressed by expert evidence adduced on his behalf.

3.10 OTHER COMMON ISSUES

3.10.1 Consent

Many of the actions of a doctor or nurse could constitute trespass on the patient if they were performed without consent. For example, a trespass may occur if, without his consent, the patient underwent an operation, was given an injection of drugs or had his body manipulated.

The patient's consent must be freely given and informed. The consent need not be in writing.

The consent will be only for the actual operation to which the patient has consented. As such, normal NHS consent forms are termed widely so as to allow the doctor to deal with any 'procedure that is necessary ... in the patient's best interests'.

If the patient asks questions about the proposed treatment then the doctor must, so far as is possible, answer any questions fully as to the risk involved in treatment and the likelihood and nature of any side-effects, however minor or unlikely.

What obligation is placed upon the doctor to tell the patient about the risks of the proposed operation? The leading case is *Sidaway v Board of Governors of the Bethlem Royal Hospital and Maudsley Hospital* [1985] AC 871, where the claimant complained of persistent pain in the right shoulder and left arm. The claimant was admitted to hospital and an operation was carried out on her back to attempt to free her from pain and discomfort. During the operation the spinal cord was damaged which left the claimant severely disabled. The claimant sued the hospital and the surgeon's estate. It was not claimed that the operation had been negligently performed. The claim was instead based on the failure to warn the claimant of the risk of damage to a nerve root and the spinal cord. The evidence produced at the trial showed a combined risk of damage of between 1 and 2%, and that the risk of damage to the spinal cord alone was less than 1%. The medical witnesses stated that they would warn a patient that there was a small risk of untoward consequences and of an increase of pain instead of relief. It was held to be accepted practice not to mention to patients the possibility of death or paralysis resulting from the operation. The trial judge dismissed the claim and the Court of Appeal by a majority endorsed this decision. The House of Lords, by a majority of one, endorsed the medical test. Lord Diplock said that the *Bolam* test should be applied to disclosure as well as to treatment and diagnosis. Lord Scarman expressed the view that the *Bolam* principle may be taken that a doctor is not negligent if he acts in accordance with a practice accepted at that time as proper by a reasonable body of medical opinion, even though other doctors adopted a different practice.

In cases where consent to medical treatment has been obtained, it is of primary importance to ensure that the ambit of the consent is fully explained and that the subsequent surgery does not go further than was agreed to. In *Williamson v East London and City HA* [1998] 1 Lloyd's Rep Med 6, the plaintiff agreed to an operation to replace a leaking silicone breast implant. The consulting surgeon noted that the situation was worse than had originally been thought, but no further consent form was signed. A mastectomy was performed without the patient's consent and the patient sued the health authority. The court found that the clinician did not properly or sufficiently inform the plaintiff of her intention to increase the operation, the plaintiff had not consented to the operation and accordingly damages were awarded for the pain and suffering caused by negligent failure to acquire consent.

In a further refinement of the law regarding consent in *Newbury v Bath DHA* (1999) 47 BMLR 138, the court found that where surgery is contemplated the nature of the operation and its risks should be explained. If the plaintiff was led to believe that the operation was trivial and risk free, and such was not the case, then that advice would be wrong and negligent within the terms of *Sidaway v Board of Governors of Bethlem Royal Hospital* [1985] 2 WLR 480. The judge went on to give examples of circumstances where the patient was entitled to be told when surgery was not in the mainstream of treatment:

- if it involved a method which was entirely new or relatively untried;
- if the method had fallen out of use because it has been shown to be defective and was not accepted by a responsible body of medical opinion.

In relation to the warning of such risks, see *Lybert v Warrington HA* (1996) 7 Med LR 71 for guidance as to the form such warnings should take. In this case, the plaintiff claimed damages for failure to advise on the risk of the possibility of failure of a sterilisation operation. The court held that it was the duty of those running the sterilisation unit to ensure that there was a proper and effective system for warning patients at some stage. Ideally, the warning should be both oral and in writing and could have been given on admission or before she agreed to sterilisation or before discharge. There was evidence that no warning at all had in fact been given.

3.10.2 Emergency treatment

In some instances, for example in emergencies, consent may not be possible. However, where treatment is necessary to save the life or preserve the health of the patient in such circumstances, a failure to obtain consent will not render the doctor liable for an assault. In *Wilson v Pringle* [1986] 3 WLR 1, CA, the court held that a casualty surgeon who performed an emergency operation on an adult who had been brought into hospital unconscious was not liable for battery and his actions were acceptable. See also *Re C (Adult: Refusal of Medical Treatment)* [1994] 1 All ER 819, where the patient applied for an injunction preventing the hospital carrying out an operation.

In *Re F (Mental Patient: Sterilisation)* [1990] 2 AC 1, it was held that, where the patient cannot give consent, the doctor should do no more than is reasonably required in medical terms, but that it is possible for the doctor to carry out the necessary treatment. If required to examine the doctor's decision, the court is likely to hold that the doctor has acted appropriately if a 'reasonable body of the medical profession would have done likewise'. (See also *Re R (A Minor) (Wardship: Consent to Treatment)* [1992] Fam 11.)

3.10.3 Consent by children

The Family Law Reform Act 1969, s 8(1) provides a presumption that a child may give valid consent for medical treatment at the age of 16. This area of the law was examined closely in *Gillick v West Norfolk and Wisbech Area Health Authority and Department of Health and Social Security* [1986] AC 112, in which it was held that the important point is the degree of understanding by the child of what is going to happen (see also *Re C* [1997] Sol Jo, 4 April).

3.10.4 Refusal of consent

The basic proposition is that an adult should have a choice as to whether he wishes to undergo medical treatment. However, the case of *Re T (Adult: Refusal of Treatment)* [1992] 4 All ER 649 concerned a pregnant mother who was injured in a road traffic accident. At the hospital the mother went into labour. The mother expressed her views that she did not want a blood transfusion prior to the birth. The mother had to undergo a Caesarian section and, as a consequence, had to be admitted to the intensive care unit and was ventilated. The doctor treating her wished to give the mother a blood transfusion but was aware of the patient's views prior to the birth. The Court of Appeal held that, whilst an adult had the right to decide on her own treatment, even if it led to death, if the patient did not have capacity at the time of the decision and that patient was under pressure from others, a doctor was justified in exercising his clinical judgement in the patient's best interests.

The consent form is evidence of only the consent and does not imply that true consent has been given. Just because the doctor has had the form signed, it does not mean that consent has in fact been given.

3.10.5 Contractual relationship

Liability for most clinical negligence claims is under the law of tort. However, in the case of private treatment there will be a contractual relationship between the parties and both causes of action will normally be pleaded. It is important in respect of private treatment that the doctor who has been alleged to have been negligent is identified as a defendant, as no vicarious liability applies in this situation. The contract is between the patient and the doctor, not the patient and the private hospital.

3.10.6 Sale of Goods Act 1979

If a patient suffers injury as a result of purchasing goods, such as a wheelchair, he may bring an action under the Sale of Goods Act 1979 or, in the absence of a contractual relationship, recourse may be made to the Consumer Protection Act 1987.

3.10.7 Shared liability between health care professionals

It is possible for the court to hold more than one type of health care professional jointly responsible for personal injuries that result from negligence. This is well illustrated in the case of *Prendergast v Sam and Dee Ltd* (1989) *The Times*, March 14, in which a pharmacist misread a prescription and gave the claimant a drug which resulted in irreversible brain damage. The pharmacist was held to be 75% responsible and the doctor who wrote the prescription was held to be 25% at fault because his handwriting was so illegible.

3.10.8 Liability of alternative healthcare practitioners

Increasing use of 'alternative' therapy for ailments has led to increased awareness of problems that can arise from use of alternative forms of healthcare. In *Shakoor v Situ (t/a Eternal Health Co)* [2000] 4 All ER 181, the court considered the appropriate standard of care by which an alternative practitioner should be judged. The court decided that, given that the alternative practitioner would often be practising alongside orthodox medicine, it would not be appropriate to simply judge him based on the standard of an ordinary practitioner 'skilled in that particular art'. Rather, it was appropriate to take account of whether the alternative practitioner had taken account of the implications of prescribing complimentary medicine, namely that any person who suffered an adverse reaction would be likely to report to a mainstream hospital and the incident was likely to be reported in orthodox medical journals. The alternative practitioner should satisfy himself that there had not been adverse reports raised in relevant journals likely to be read by an orthodox practitioner practising at the level at which the alternative practitioner held himself out to be.

3.11 CONCLUSION

As stated at the beginning of this chapter, the possible heads of liability of an employer are not mutually exclusive. When acting for a claimant, it is important for the solicitor to consider all heads of claim in order to maximise the client's chances of success. It is necessary to succeed under only one head for the claimant to be successful overall. In practice, it is far harder to establish liability in a clinical negligence claim than in a personal injury claim. It is important that the claimant's solicitor regularly reviews the evidence available and remembers the essential elements which need to be proved at all times.

3.12 FURTHER READING

The above is merely an overview of the law as it relates to liability in personal injury and clinical negligence claims. For a more detailed consideration of the subject, reference should be made to the following sources of information.

Redgrave, Hendy and Ford, *Redgrave's Health and Safety* (Butterworths).
Munkman, *Employer's Liability* (Butterworths).
Tolley's Health and Safety at Work Handbook (Tolley).
Management of Health and Safety at Work Regulations 1999, SI 1999/3242 (Stationery Office).

Health and Safety (Display Screen Equipment) Regulations 1992, SI 1992/2792 (Stationery Office).
Provision and Use of Work Equipment Regulations 1998, SI 1998/2306 (Stationery Office).
Personal Protective Equipment at Work Regulations 1992, SI 1992/2966 (Stationery Office).
Manual Handling Operations Regulations 1992, SI 1992/2795 (Stationery Office).
Workplace (Health, Safety and Welfare) Regulations 1992, SI 1992/3004 (Stationery Office).
Lifting Operations and Lifting Equipment Regulations 1998, SI 1998/2307 (Stationery Office).
www.hse.gov.uk
www.safety-now.co.uk

Chapter 4

THE FIRST INTERVIEW

4.1 INTRODUCTION

The claimant's solicitor should never lose sight of the following points when making initial enquiries.

(1) He should make full enquiries as soon as possible, as this will give a tactical advantage.
(2) He should not focus on settlement being the likely outcome of the case. The assumption should be that the matter will proceed to trial and the case should be prepared accordingly.
(3) He should not give the client a firm indication of the level of damages the client is likely to receive. Clients' over-expectations as to the level of damages they can expect are often lawyer-led.

4.2 FIRST INTERVIEW

The first interview is the cornerstone of the solicitor/client relationship and it is therefore worthwhile making the effort to get it right. Reference should be made to the LPC Resource Book *Skills for Lawyers* (Jordans) which deals with how to conduct an interview. The claimant's solicitor should ensure that he meets the client at reception, especially if the solicitor's office is not on the ground floor and there is no lift. It is quite likely that the client may have difficulty managing stairs, in which case the solicitor should make arrangements to see the client in a ground floor interview room or in a colleague's ground floor office. In personal injury work the first interview may be the longest, or possibly the only time there is personal contact between solicitor and client. The interview will normally last at least an hour. The client should tell his own story, and the solicitor will often complete a long and detailed accident questionnaire, prior to drafting a proof of evidence. Detailed preparation at this stage will save a great deal of time later. The client may be confused or upset as a result of the accident and it is the solicitor's job to explain the litigation process to the client as fully as possible. It is important that the solicitor instills confidence in the client, who may be uncertain whether he should bring a claim at all, especially if the likely defendant is his current employer. Having heard the client's story, it is important that the advice given to the client is explained in a way that the client can understand. The solicitor should explain what will happen next and the likely interval prior to contacting the client again. Having conducted the interview, it will be necessary to consider all of the post-interview steps (see Chapter 5).

4.2.1 Use of questionnaires

Client questionnaires are used frequently in personal injury work. The questionnaires are designed to elicit certain basic information about the client. For example, it will

Chapter 4 contents
Introduction
First interview
Funding
Urgent matters
Advising the client
The client's proof of evidence
Welfare benefits
The Road Traffic (NHS Charges) Act 1999
Rehabilitation, early intervention and medical treatment
Conclusion
Further reading
Overview of matters to be considered at the first interview

be necessary to find out the employment details of the client to ensure that the client's claim for loss of wages is properly assessed. The client's job title, payroll or employee number, together with past wage slips, should all be ascertained.

The questionnaire is invaluable in saving time later when it comes to drafting documentation, or for using the questions as a prompt to ensure that an important detail is not missed. Some solicitors prefer to send questionnaires out to the client prior to interview, both to save time and to focus the client's mind on the facts, while others prefer to go through the questions with the client in person so that they can explain the importance of the more central questions and answer any queries that may arise. Either method is acceptable, but the value of the questionnaire to the novice is that it greatly reduces the chance of some basic piece of information being missed which may have long-term adverse implications for the client. However, it must always be remembered that a questionnaire, for example designed for road traffic accidents is of little use in a factory accident, and therefore care should be taken when drafting or following questionnaires. They should be used as an aid to, rather than a substitute for, the solicitor's skills. A basic questionnaire is reproduced at Appendix 4.

4.3 FUNDING

Most clients will be concerned to find out first what the claim is likely to cost and will only be happy to talk at length once they have been provided with some solid advice on this point.

4.3.1 Funding the first interview

Free initial interviews
Many firms offer a free initial half-hour interview in order to persuade clients into their offices. Many people are wary of solicitors' charges, and are put off making claims accordingly. Some solicitors therefore offer free initial advice in which they will form a view as to the viability of a personal injury or clinical negligence claim, and advise clients about the various case-funding methods available.

Accident Line – personal injury cases
The Law Society operates a scheme called 'Accident Line' under which members of the public can obtain a free first interview from members of the scheme. Only members of personal injury panels are eligible to become members of Accident Line. The benefit to the firm, if eligible to join the scheme, is that it is assured a steady stream of prospective clients for initial interview. The benefit to the public is that the service is free and carries the assurance that only those who are competent to give advice in this area are able to join the scheme.

Legal Help – under the Legal Services Commission
The Legal Services Commission replaced the Legal Aid Board as from 1 April 2000. Under the 'Legal Help' scheme, the equivalent of up to 2 hours' advice may be given to the client. This can cover the first interview and initial correspondence.

4.3.2 Legal Services Commission and Community Legal Service

On 1 April 2000, the Government implemented ss 1–11 and 19–26 of the Access to Justice Act 1999. These are the key provisions which reform the public funding of civil cases. The Legal Services Commission (LSC) was established and replaced the Legal Aid Board. It is responsible for the Community Legal Service (CLS), which handles funding in civil matters from that date. (The criminal counterpart – the Criminal Defence Service – will begin operation in October 2000.)

The 'Funding Code'

Schedule 2 to the Access to Justice Act 1999 generally excludes personal injury (other than clinical negligence claims) from CLS funding. The CLS decides funding issues in accordance with the Funding Code published in October 1999. The Code has 2 parts: Part 1 defines the 'Levels of Service' which the CLS provides; Part 2 deals with the procedures for obtaining funding.

The most important Levels of Service are 'Legal Help' and 'Legal Representation'. These replace the legal advice and assistance (LAA) scheme and assistance by way of representation (ABWOR) and Civil Legal Aid respectively. Legal Representation has two sub-levels: 'Investigative Help' and 'Full Representation'.

Unlike clinical negligence cases, personal injury cases are normally outside the scope of CLS funding because they are suitable for conditional fee agreements. However, the Code does permit public funding – 'Support Funding' – to be given in personal injury cases; chiefly, where there are the following requirements.

(i) High investigative costs involved (Investigative Support) in order to get the case to a point where it is possible to assess whether or not it could be funded under a conditional fee agreement (ie disbursements over £1,000 or profit costs over £3,000).
(ii) High overall costs involved (Litigation Support) (ie disbursements over £5,000 or profit costs over £15,000).
(iii) Wider public interest issues.

The LSC *may* pay the costs or disbursements incurred in excess of the above thresholds.

The Lord Chancellor's Department has produced draft guidelines on availability of 'Exceptional Funding' in individual cases, and is designed for use in specific cases, for example, representation at inquests.

Transitional provisions

Cases commenced pre-1 April 2000 will continue to be dealt with under the Legal Aid Act 1988. From 1 April 2000, all clinical negligence work and, where covered, personal injury work will fall within the General Civil Contract (ie the contract which firms have with the LSC to run publicly funded cases).

The financial eligibility limits for Legal Representation and Support Funding for disposable income and for disposable capital are received annually. There are no separate thresholds for personal injury claims.

4.3.3 LSC funding in clinical negligence cases

Applications for Legal Representation for proceedings in clinical negligence cases are subject to the General Funding Code (see the criteria in section 9 of the Funding Code).

The scope of clinical negligence as defined in the Funding Code is:

(a) a claim for damages in respect of an alleged breach of duty of care or trespass to the person committed in the course of the provision of clinical or medical services (including dental or nursing services); or
(b) a claim for damages in respect of alleged professional negligence in the conduct of such a claim.

Only firms with a clinical negligence contract are eligible for CLS funding. Firms with a clinical negligence franchise are required to have a supervisor who is a member of either the Law Society's Clinical Negligence Panel or a member of Action for Victims of Medical Accidents (AVMA).

Claims not exceeding £10,000

If the likely value of the claim is not more than £10,000, Investigative Help may be refused if use of the NHS complaints procedure would be in the best interests of the client rather than pursuing litigation in the first instance. Although the LSC accept that the NHS complaints procedure was never designed to replace recourse to the court system, they nevertheless wish it to be recognised that in small value claims (between £5,000 and £10,000) it is much more cost-effective of public funds for the claimant to seek redress in the form of explanation and apology rather than compensation through the civil court system. In claims where the likely level of damages will not exceed £5,000, the Funding Code recommends that Investigative Help should be refused on the ground that the potential cost greatly outweighs the benefit to be achieved. However, there is a caveat that the damages cut off will not apply to claims which have a significant wider public interest or are of overwhelming importance to the client (for example, claims involving the death of an infant).

If the claim is valued at less than £10,000, the solicitor will need to provide specific reasons as to why the complaints procedure is not the appropriate avenue of redress for the client. The Funding Code contains a number of examples of circumstances, which it says would not be appropriate to refuse funding, which are reproduced below:

(a) the NHS complaints scheme is not available to the client or clients being told a complaint may not be pursued;
(b) the claim has overwhelming importance to the client, for example because it relates to infant death;
(c) there are problems with NHS complaints scheme in the clients region, for example there are unusually long delays in responding to complaints;
(d) proceedings must be issued as a matter of urgency, for example because of limitation; or
(e) it is clear the relationship between the client and NHS has broken down to such an extent that prospect of complaints procedure resolving the complaint are very remote.

Investigative Help for clinical negligence claims

Investigative Help will only be granted where the prospects of success on a claim are not clear and substantial work needs to be undertaken before the prospects of success can be determined accurately. Certificates limited to Investigative Help will be subject to a limitation that the certificate covers only the obtaining of medical notes and records, obtaining one medical report per specialism, complying with all steps under the clinical disputes pre-action protocol, considering relevant evidence with counsel or an external solicitor with higher court advocacy rights and experts if necessary and thereafter obtaining counsel's opinion, up to and including settling proceedings if counsel so advises.

The cost of the above is nevertheless limited to £3,500 (including costs and disbursmeents but not VAT).

According to para 5.6.1 of the Capital General Funding Code, the potential to obtain a conditional fee agreement will not be a ground for refusal of Investigative Help in clinical negligence claims.

Criteria for granting of Full Representation

The Funding Code makes it clear that an application for Full Representation will be refused either if:

(a) prospects of success are unclear, or
(b) prospects of success are borderline (ie not better than 50%), or
(c) prospects of success are poor (clearly less than 50%).

The cost benefit criterion gives the minimum cost benefit ratios for damages to costs in clinical negligence claims.

(a) 1:1 – for cases with 80% or more prospects of success – ie the likely damages must at least break even with and should exceed the likely cost in cases with very good prospects of success;
(b) 1.5:1 – for 60–80% prospects of success – ie the prospects of success are good, likely damages must exceed likely cost by at least 1.5; and
(c) 2:1 – for cases with 50–60% prospects of success – ie the prospects of success are moderate, likely damages must be at least twice the likely costs.

These are the minimum cost benefit ratios in the General Funding Code.

If the prospect of success and the cost benefit criteria set out above are satisfied, then the solicitor should make an application for Full Representation after the investigative stage. The certificate will then be issued limited to all steps up to and including exchange of statements and reports and Part 35 questioning of experts and thereafter obtaining counsel's opinion or the opinion of an external solicitor with higher court advocacy rights.

In the event that the claimant wishes to proceed to full trial, the cost benefit criteria above are reapplied to the case and if the criteria are satisfied, then application can be made once again to amend the scope of the Full Representation certificate to cover the cost of trial.

4.3.4 Conditional fee agreements

A conditional fee agreement (CFA) is an agreement under s 58 of the Courts and Legal Services Act 1990, whereby a client agrees that he will have to pay his own solicitor's costs only in certain circumstances (normally if he wins).

Availability of Conditional Fee Agreements

From 1 April 2000, CFAs are regulated by the Conditional Fee Agreements Order 2000, SI 2000/823 and the Conditional Fee Agreements Regulations 2000, SI 2000/692. The Order specifies that CFAs can be applied to all non-family and non-criminal cases and whether or not proceedings are actually commenced. Only agreements that comply with conditions set out in the Regulations are enforceable (Courts and Legal Services Act 1990, s 58(1)). In particular, all agreements are required to be in writing. Both claimants and defendants may take out agreements, but most agreements are taken out by claimants.

This gives rise to three possibilities.

(1) If the case is won, the client agrees that the solicitor can claim his normal hourly rate in costs and in addition a 'success fee' which is calculated as a percentage uplift on his usual hourly rate and is agreed at the beginning of the retainer.
(2) If the case is won, the client agrees that the solicitor can claim costs only (no uplift) (known as '*Thai Trading* agreements', as to which, see below).
(3) If the case is lost, the solicitor is not entitled to charge any costs at all.

Agreements with a success fee

If the action is successful, the solicitor will normally expect to receive an enhanced fee to reflect his 'success'. The enhancement on the fee is a percentage increase of the solicitor's normal fee and not a percentage of damages. The percentage increase on the solicitor's fee is agreed in writing between the client and the solicitor prior to the litigation and should reflect the difficulty in winning the case. There is nothing to prevent a CFA, even where the prospects of success are very high (say, above 80%) as might be the case in relation to a straightforward road traffic rear end shunt. By the same token, the lawyer is less likely to accept the instruction on a CFA basis, even with a greatly enhanced percentage increase on costs, if there is a very good chance that the case will be lost. The normal fee payable may be uplifted under a CFA to reflect success to a maximum of 100%. In practice, a mark-up of between 25% and 50% is common.

Under the Access to Justice Act 1999, s 27, the success fee is recoverable from the loser to the litigation. The mechanism for recovery of the success fee is dealt with in the CPR 1998 and is covered later in this chapter.

Agreements without a success fee

In the case of *Thai Trading (A Firm) v Taylor* [1998] 2 WLR 893, the defendant's solicitor agreed to act for his client in proceedings on the basis that he would recover only his ordinary profit costs if his client succeeded in the action and nothing if he lost. It was held on appeal that, although the judge felt bound by previous authority to hold that such an arrangement was void, modern conditions meant that it was no longer improper for a solicitor to agree to act on the basis that he was paid his ordinary costs if he won but that he would receive nothing if he lost.

Disbursements and opponent's costs

Although the CFA covers the costs in relation to the client's own solicitor, the client will still have to fund his own disbursements and a successful opponent's costs and disbursements. The loser's liability to pay the other side's costs and disbursements and his own disbursements can be insured against by what is often referred to as 'After The Event Insurance'. As the name suggests, After The Event Insurance is taken out only once the need for the legal action has become apparent but before the proceedings have been commenced. Here, the insurance is not against the risk of litigation but merely against the risk of having to pay the other side's costs and disbursements should the litigation fail, and can cover the cost of the parties' own disbursements as well. This type of insurance can be obtained alongside a CFA or on its own as insurance against liability for the other side's costs. Under the Access to Justice Act 1999, s 29, the premium for insuring against liability to pay the other side's costs and disbursements is recoverable from the loser.

Requirements of the Conditional Fee Regulations 2000

REGULATION 2

All agreements must specify:

(a) the particular proceedings or part of proceedings to which it relates;
(b) the circumstances in which the legal representative's fees and expenses or part thereof will be payable;
(c) what payment, if any, is due:

    (i) if those circumstances only partly occur (ie partial success);
    (ii) irrespective of whether the circumstances occur (ie irrespective of success); and
    (iii) on termination of the agreement for any reason.

The agreement must also specify amounts which are payable in all the circumstances, the method it used to calculate them and, in particular, whether amounts are limited by reference to damages which may be recovered on behalf of a client. This means that the agreement must state whether there is a 'cap' on the success fee. In other words, does the solicitor agree that should the case be successful the maximum that the solicitor can add by way of success fee can never be more than an agreed percentage of the claimant's damages. In this way, the claimant can be assured that in the event of success he will always receive *at least* the amount safeguarded by the cap.

Requirements for conditional fee agreements which provide for success fees

REGULATION 3

Under reg 3, certain matters must be specified if the CFA provides for a success fee.

The agreement must:

(a) briefly specify the reason for setting the percentage increase at the level stated in the agreement; and
(b) specify how much of that percentage increase, if any, relates to the cost to the legal representative of the postponement of his fees and expenses.

If the agreement relates to court proceedings, the agreement must make provision where the success fee becomes payable as a result of the proceedings as follows.

(a) That the legal adviser or the client may, if required by the court to do so, disclose to the court, or any other person, the reasons for setting the success fee at the level stated.

(b) That if any amount of the success fee is disallowed on the ground that the level at which the increase was set was unreasonable in the light of facts which were or should have been known to the legal adviser at the time, then that amount will cease to be payable under the agreement, unless the court is satisfied it should continue to be so payable.

This means that the level of the success fee (regardless of what is in the agreement) which is payable by the client, will be limited to that which is allowed by the court on assessment.

Information for clients before the conditional fee agreement is made

REGULATION 4

Under reg 4, before any conditional fee agreement is entered into, the legal representative must bring certain matters to the client's attention, and, if the client requires, provide such further explanation, advice or information 'as the client may reasonably require'.

Matters that must be brought to the client's attention are:

(a) circumstances in which the client may be liable to pay the costs of the legal representative in accordance with the agreement;
(b) circumstances in which the client may seek assessment of fees and expenses of his legal representative and procedure for doing so;
(c) whether the legal representative comes to the conclusion that the client's risk of incurring liability for costs in respect of the proceedings to which the agreement relates is insured against under an existing contract of insurance;
(d) whether other methods of financing costs are available and, if so, how they apply to that client and the proceedings in question;
(e) whether the legal representative considers any particular method, or methods of financing any or all or part of those costs is appropriate, and if he considers that a contract of insurance is appropriate, or recommends a particular contract, his reasons for doing so and whether he has any interest in so doing.

The above information under reg 4 must be given to the client orally (whether or not it is also given in writing) but the information in relation to other methods of financing the costs, and the availability of insurance must be given both orally and in writing.

Regulation 2 applies to all conditional fee agreements, whether or not there is an additional uplift if the case is successful (ie the success fee).

This Regulation therefore includes *Thai Trading*-type agreements (as to which see above).

Information for the parties about conditional fees

Where a party seeks to recover the cost of the success fee or insurance premium, the CPR 1998 (as amended) stipulates that he must provide the following information to the opposition and to the court:

- where a funding agreement with success fee has been taken out, that the CFA exists and its date;
- where insurance cover has been taken out, its existence and date and the name of the insurer but no further details;
- where the cover is provided by way of self-insurance (most notably by a trades union), the name of the trades union and the terms of the undertaking given.

In all cases, the information must indicate the claim/counterclaim to which the funding relates. Notice of the above matters should be given by completing Form N251. Information pre-issue should be given as soon as the party is able to do so.

The notice should be filed and served with the Claim Form or within 7 days of entering into the agreement, if later. The information must be provided when the party issues or responds to a Claim Form, files an allocation questionnaire, a listing questionnaire, and a claim for costs.

Where the funding arrangement changes part way through the proceedings such that the information provided to the opposition is no longer accurate, the party must file a notice of change and serve it on all other parties within 7 days.

The form of the CFA

The CFA must be in writing and signed by the client and by the legal representative.

THE LAW SOCIETY MODEL CONDITIONAL FEE AGREEMENT

The Law Society's Conditional Fees Committee has prepared a revised model agreement for use in personal injury cases to take into account the 2000 Regulations, which are reproduced at Appendix 1.

Use of the Law Society model agreement is not mandatory, but it is based on fulfilling the requirements of the Conditional Fee Regulations and any agreement that does not comply with the Regulations will be invalid and therefore unenforceable. If the client has decided to sign up to a CFA together with insurance to cover the other side's costs if he loses, then a requirement of that insurance may be that the Law Society model is adopted.

The following matters should be specifically considered when advising a client about conditional fee agreements.

What the agreement covers

(1) The agreement must state the particular proceedings to which it relates (ie whether it covers a counterclaim, appeal or proceedings to enforce a judgment or order).
(2) The agreement must state the date on which the injury was suffered. The solicitor should consider this carefully, as in a case alleging industrial disease it may be necessary to allege a series of dates indicating a period of time of exposure.
(3) The opponent's appeal is covered in the standard agreement. This is because the client cannot be said to have 'won' within the definition in the agreement until any appeal by the opponent has been either won by the defendant or become time-barred.

What the agreement does not cover

(1) The standard agreement excludes defending a counterclaim brought by the defendant.

(2) Appeals are not covered by the standard agreement. If a client wishes to appeal, they should negotiate a fresh agreement, or alternatively they must have bargained for this eventuality and altered the agreement accordingly prior to signing the agreement at commencement of the retainer.

PAYMENTS

Payment of disbursements

The client agrees that he will pay the disbursements in any event. Disbursements can be recovered out of interim payments if necessary.

Costs and interim hearings

If basic costs of a successful interim hearing are payable in any event, the success fee on those costs will be payable if the case is finally successful.

The meaning of 'basic charges'

Includes charges for letters and telephone calls, and requires the setting out of hourly rates for different levels of fee earner.

The meaning of 'success fee'

To calculate the success fee, the agreement states that this is a percentage uplift of the solicitor's basic charges. Basic charges should be the solicitor's usual hourly charging rate to privately paying personal injury clients. The solicitor's justification for the level of success fee should be set out in the schedule to the agreement. The percentage that relates to the postponement of basic charges and disbursements should be specified.

What happens if the client is successful? (Condition 4)

If the client's case is successful at trial, the loser will be liable to pay his basic costs, disbursements and success fee (in so far as it is reasonable).

If the client's case never gets as far as a trial because the opponent makes an offer, which includes an offer to pay basic charges and the success fee, the client agrees that he will not instruct his solicitor to accept the offer if it includes payment of the success fee at a lower rate from that set out in the agreement. This is to try to avoid problems if the opponent makes a lower offer based on a lower success fee than was originally contemplated and agreed to by the client and his solicitor.

What happens if the client loses? (Condition 5)

If the client's case is lost, he does not pay his own solicitor anything. The client's solicitor agrees to claim under any insurance policy to settle any order to pay the opponent's costs and disbursements and the client's own disbursements.

What happens if the agreement is ended early by the client? (Condition 7)

If the client wishes to end the agreement he may do so without giving any reason. If the client ends the agreement early the solicitor has two options.

(1) He may take his basic charges and disbursements straight away.
(2) He may wait and see if the client wins, in which case the solicitor may still claim his basic charges, disbursements and success fee. However, the risk with taking this option is that, should the client lose the case, the solicitor will receive no payment at all. The reason why the client is ending the agreement early will almost certainly be an important factor in determining which option to choose. Is the client planning to instruct someone else? If so, who, and how expert is that firm? Does the client intend to continue as litigant in person? If so, what are his chances of success? Does the client wish to discontinue the proceedings altogether, in which case there is no possibility of the solicitor obtaining his success fee?

What happens if the agreement is ended early by the solicitor?

The solicitor must bear in mind the Solicitors' Practice Rules and must not terminate the retainer except for good reason and on reasonable notice.

The solicitor may generally only terminate the agreement if the client is in breach of one or more of his obligations under the agreement. The agreement can also be ended by the solicitor if the solicitor advises that the case will be lost and the client disagrees. In this event the client will only have to pay his solicitor's disbursements unless he has insurance to cover this.

Under the same condition, if the client rejects the solicitor's advice to accept an offer of settlement he must pay basic costs and disbursements immediately because the solicitor has 'won' the case within the meaning of the agreement. However, because the client has not yet received any damages the success fee does not yet fall to be paid, and will only be payable on a successful resolution of the case.

The solicitor may end the agreement early if the client fails to pay the insurance premium when asked to do so.

Costs and conditional fees

The provisions of the CPR 1998 relating to recovery of costs in conditional fees cases have been re-drafted to take account of the mechanics for recovery of the success fee and insurance premiums.

The Civil Procedure (Amendment No 3) Rules 2000, SI 2000/1317 cover the mechanism for obtaining payment of the success fee and insurance premium from the losing party by way of costs. These amendments came into force on 3 July 2000.

According to the costs rules at CPR 1998, Part 44 (as amended):

(a) recovery of the success fee will not include recovery of any proportion of the success fee which relates to the cost to the solicitor of funding the case (ie the costs to the firm of having payment of costs delayed);
(b) recovery of the success fee will not include recovery of any part of the success fee for any period during which that party was in breach of a rule, Practice Direction or court order concerning provision of information on funding arrangements;
(c) if the solicitor is required by the court or PD 48 to CPR 1998 – Costs to disclose the reasons for setting a particular level of success fee and fails to do so, he may not recover the success fee;

(d) recovery of the success fee will not be possible if a party fails to provide the information regarding success fees and after the event insurance required by the Rules or a Practice Direction in any assessment proceedings;

(e) where agreement is reached prior to issue of proceedings the procedure for resolving disputes as to costs will be by application to the court by way of a Part 8 Claim Form. The Claim Form must also be accompanied by a copy of the relevant CFA.

Challenging the level of success fee or after the event insurance by the losing party

At the conclusion of the case, the court will either:

(i) make a summary assessment of all costs including any additional liability to pay a success fee/ insurance premium; or

(ii) make an order for detailed assessment of the additional liability but make a summary assessment of the other costs; or

(iii) make an order for detailed assessment of all costs.

The impact on CFAs of Callery v Gray [2001] All ER (D) 213

In *Callery v Gray; Russell v Pal Pak Corrugated Ltd* [2001] All ER 213 (D), CA, the court considered the issue of recoverability of after the event insurance premiums and success fees in a case which was the subject of a negotiated settlement and only came to court for the consideration of assessment of costs. The defendant argued that he was not liable to pay the amount of the insurance premium paid by the claimant for after the event insurance. The insurance was taken out shortly after the accident and before any negotiations had taken place and before the protocol had been complied with. The defendant also argued that the success fee, which was set at 40%, was too high.

Recoverability for cost of insurance

With regard to the recoverability of the after the event insurance premium, the judge considered the wording of s 29 of the Access to Justice Act 1999. Under s 29:

> 'where in any proceedings a costs order is made in favour of any party who has taken out an insurance policy against the risk of incurring a liability in those proceedings, the costs payable to him may, subject in the case of court proceedings to rules of court, include costs in respect of the premium of the policy.'

In this case, proceedings were never issued and the question arose whether the insurance premium was recoverable in circumstances where the only 'proceedings' were Part 8 proceedings which related to costs only. Where a claim had been settled on terms that the parties agreed which party was to pay the costs, and this was made or confirmed in writing, but they then failed to agree the amount of the costs. The court ruled that the after the event insurance premium could be recovered.

Time for taking out insurance

On a subsidiary point, the defendant argued that it was not right to allow any or part of the insurance premium to be recovered because it was taken out at a very early stage. On appeal, the court ruled that it would normally be reasonable for a CFA to be entered into with after the event insurance, on the first occasion that the client instructed his solicitor. If the cost of the uplift and premium were reasonable, each would be recoverable from the defendant if the claim succeeded or was settled on terms that the defendant paid the claimant's costs.

Level of success fee

In relation to the level of recoverable success fee, the court ruled that if the CFA were entered into in a modest and straightforward claim for injuries resulting from a road traffic accident, then 20% would be the maximum uplift that could be agreed. If there were specific features or doubts about the soundness of the case, the uplift could be higher. However, if this conclusion were based on limited information, it would be better to review the situation once sufficient information was available for a 'fully informed' assessment to be made.

When it considered whether the level of cost of after the event insurance premiums was reasonable, the court found that it did not have sufficient evidence to form a conclusion. The court directed that this matter be looked into by a senior costs judge and would provide a separate judgment on this point. At the time of writing, this separate judgment is not available.

Legal representative's right to challenge an order that part of the percentage increase be disallowed

Where the level of success fee is subsequently disallowed on summary assessment or detailed assessment, that amount ceases to be payable (CPR 1998, PD Costs, para 20.1).

However under reg 3(2)(b) of the CFA Regs 2000, the legal representative may apply for an order that the disallowed amount should continue to be payable by the client.

Client's right to challenge the level of his own solicitors costs and success fee

A client who has agreed to enter into a CFA with his solicitor and has agreed to a certain level of success fee, nevertheless has the right to have the basic costs assessed and to have the level of success fee assessed in the usual manner. If the client applies for the success fee to be reduced the client must specify why the amount claimed is too high and what he thinks it ought to be. When assessing the application, the court will have regard to the circumstances as they appeared to the solicitor at the time when the CFA was signed. It is therefore particularly important to have a full file note available setting out the relative merits and risks on liability on the facts of the case as they appeared at that date. The court will take into account:

- the risk that the case would be lost;
- the inability to call for payments on account;
- whether there is a CFA between solicitor and counsel;
- the solicitor's liability for disbursements.

  Example
  Fred (the claimant) enters into a conditional fee agreement with his solicitor. Damages are awarded at £5,000 against Joe. Fred's solicitors' costs amount to £2,500 plus disbursements of £500. Costs and disbursements of £2,750 are recovered from Joe after assessment of costs.

Calculation

	£
Damages	5,000
Fred's solicitors' costs	2,500
Fred's solicitors' disbursements	500
Success fee agreed at 20%	500
Costs and disbursements recovered from Joe	2,750
Success fee recovered from Joe but assessed by the court at 15%	375

Out of net damages of £5,000 Fred will pay his own solicitors:

	£
Shortfall of costs and disbursements	
*shortfall recovered from Joe (£3,000 – £2750)	250
**shortfall on success fee (£500 – £375)	125
Total to be paid by Fred out of net damages	375

* However, this may be covered by After The Event Insurance

** Fred can challenge this amount when the court assesses the reasonableness of the costs and level of success fee (see CFA Regs 2000, reg 3(2)(b)).

Access to Justice (Membership Organisations) Regulations 2000, SI 2000/693 (in force 1 April 2000)

Under these Regulations, trades unions who indemnify their members in relation to costs liabilities are able to recover the amount that they have paid as 'quasi-insurance' in relation to their member. However, this sum must not exceed the cost of an equivalent insurance policy (reg 4(2)).

After The Event insurance

After The Event Insurance covers the client's own disbursements and the client's liability to pay costs and disbursements of the opponent in the event that the client loses the case.

According to reg 4 of the CFA Regulations 2000, if a solicitor advises a client regarding an insurance product, he must give reasons for giving that advice, and declare any interest he may have, either in the product/insurer itself or in any agreement with a particular insurance provider. The solicitor must ensure that he complies with the recommendations in *The Law Society's Guide to Professional Conduct* concerning costs information and client care. The solicitor must be able to give information on the types of insurance products that are available so that the client can make an informed choice as to which one is best for his individual circumstances. The solicitor should make it clear to the client that he is not an insurance broker who will find the best 'deal' at any given time, but will give advice on the nature of the products available and his reasoning behind any recommendation he gives.

An example of After The Event insurance is Litigation Protection Limited's Conditional Fee Protection Plan which is reproduced at Appendix 1. This insurance offers different levels of cover for different premiums.

Cover is available as follows.

(1) Basic cover for the opponent's legal costs and the client's own solicitor's disbursements (including counsel's fees). The cover provides an indemnity on four levels between £10,000 and £100,000 for different premiums (in a non-clinical negligence claim the premium varies between £250 and £2,000).
(2) Cover in respect of client's expert witness fees.
(3) Deficiency of damages, designed to cover any shortfall between the damages awarded to the client if the client wins and the client's actual costs.

There are many other providers of After The Event Insurance providing different packages with differing levels of cover. The inclusion of details from this provider is for illustration only. The solicitor should consider each case and advise the client as to the availability of insurance products generally but not the suitability of products, in accordance with reg 4 (as to which, see above).

The premium for cover in conditional fee clinical negligence claims is rated individually. It will therefore be necessary to do a certain amount of advance work on the case such as attendance at the inquest and obtaining of expert evidence prior to making the application for insurance so that the insurer can make an adequate risk assessment to decide whether to offer insurance for that case, and if so at what premium.

4.3.5 After the event insurance and clinical negligence claims

A conditional fee insurance scheme called 'Medical Accident Protect' has also been launched for firms belonging to The Law Society's Clinical Negligence Panel. The scheme is underwritten by the same insurers as developed the ALP Scheme. However, unlike ALP, Medical Accident Protect is not available at a flat premium, but will assess risk on each case individually with premiums being assessed at between £4,000 and £7,500. The great increase in the level of premiums reflects the increase in the size of the risk being taken on by the insurer. The amount of cover provided is up to £100,000 of the other side's costs and the client's own disbursements should he lose the case.

As conditional fees have become more common, the number of insurance providers has increased and the relevant premiums are more competitive. These matters are beyond the scope of this book and each practitioner will need to satisfy himself that he is obtaining the best available cover in the marketplace at any given time.

4.3.6 Client care

The Law Society's guide to conditional fee agreements recommends that the solicitor should read through the agreement with the client, emphasise the binding nature of the agreement and check that the client understands the agreement fully. To this end, it is good practice for the solicitor to send The Law Society's leaflet *Conditional Fees Explained* to the client prior to the meeting. The leaflet includes a checklist of 'questions to ask your solicitor' and it is therefore essential for the solicitor to be prepared to answer these questions, and to be able to explain those answers to the client.

4.3.7 Conditional fees and counsel

Counsel's fees incurred on behalf of a client do not form part of the disbursements covered by Accident Line Protect. The Law Society model agreement at condition 6 specifies two ways of dealing with counsel's fees.

(1) The solicitor enters into a separate conditional fee agreement with the barrister.

    (a) if the client wins the case, the barrister's basic fee will be recovered as a disbursement from the opponent. The solicitor will pay the barrister's 'uplift' agreed in the barrister's conditional fee agreement, but will have regard to this expense when agreeing his own fee 'uplift' with the client;

    (b) if the client loses the case, he will owe the barrister nothing.

(2) There is no conditional fee agreement between the barrister and the solicitor, in which case:

    (a) if the client wins the case and has been paying the barrister's fees on account (ie up front), there will be no extra success fee to pay, and the barrister's fees can be recovered from the opponent as before;

    (b) if the client wins the case and has not been paying the barrister's fees on account, the solicitor will recover that disbursement from the opponent. Because of this greater outlay by the solicitor (and greater financial loss to the firm in the event that the client loses) the solicitor will charge an extra success fee in the event that the client wins;

    (c) if the client loses the case and has not been paying the barrister's fees on account, the solicitor is liable to pay them, and will not be able to pass this loss on to the client.

4.3.8 Trade unions

If the client has had an accident at work and belongs to a trade union, he may be entitled to receive free access to legal advice as part of his membership. This is something that the client may not be aware of initially and the solicitor should therefore cover this point at the initial interview. If the client is entitled to advice through his union, the union may have its own legal department or nominated solicitors whom it always uses. If this is the case, the solicitor first consulted by the client is unlikely to be instructed, but should nevertheless advise the client to seek advice from his union on this point. The advantage to the client, if he is able to procure the support of union funding, is that, provided he has paid his membership fees to the union, he will have the full financial support of the union behind him. His solicitor will still have to convince the union as to the merits of the case, and will also be obliged to report on the case prior to proceeding with it. However, the claimant will not have to worry that part of his damages may be taken away to pay his legal expenses, as would be the case if he was funded either through public funding or a CFA.

4.3.9 Legal expenses insurance

The client may have legal expenses insurance (known as 'before the event' insurance) as a part of either his home or motor insurance policy, or as an extra for which he has paid an additional premium. This is something that the client may either be unaware of or have forgotten, and it is therefore important that this is considered at the first interview. As with union-funded work, the insurer may have nominated firms of solicitors who must be instructed to undertake the insured's claim. If the insured is free to instruct the solicitor of his choice, it is usual for the insurer to require the solicitor to report to it regularly on the progress of the case. In terms of confidentiality, it is essential for the solicitor to explain to the client at the outset that a term of the insurance is that the insurer has the right to receive reports on the viability of the case and whether or not it is worthwhile to continue with it. The progress of the case can be slowed down considerably by the obligation on the solicitor to report back to the insurer to seek approval (and therefore funding) to continue with the claim to the next stage.

4.3.10 Private fee-paying clients

Some clients will have no alternative but to fund their cases privately, or may choose to do so in any case. In this event the solicitor is obliged, under the Written Professional Standards, to explain to the client fully his liability for costs and disbursements. The solicitor should give the best information on costs that he can, including likely disbursements and the hourly rate that the solicitor proposes to charge (as to which see the LPC Resource Book *Pervasive and Core Topics* (Jordans), Part II, Professional Conduct).

4.4 URGENT MATTERS

If an urgent matter comes to light during the first interview, the solicitor should bear in mind the question of funding prior to making lengthy or expensive investigations on the client's behalf, and should consider making an application for emergency public funding if appropriate.

4.4.1 Limitation

At the first interview in a personal injury or clinical negligence claim, it may become apparent that:

(1) the 3-year primary limitation period is about to expire (this is explained fully in Chapter 6). If so, the solicitor should consider issuing protective proceedings immediately;
(2) the 3-year primary limitation period has recently expired. If so, consideration should be given to issuing proceedings as soon as possible, including in the claim form or particulars of claim, a request for a direction that the limitation period should be disapplied. Thereafter, the solicitor should inform the defendant without delay that proceedings have been issued to minimise any claim by the defendant of prejudice due to the passage of time;
(3) there is a question as to the client's 'date of knowledge' of the injury complained of. The client should be questioned closely regarding the earliest date on which he realised he might have a cause of action, and how he came to that conclusion. Proceedings can then be issued as in point (2) above and thereafter it can be argued that the limitation period has not yet expired because the client's date of knowledge of the injury is within the last 3 years. If this is not successful, an application should be made for the court to exercise its discretion and disapply the limitation period (see Chapter 6).

4.4.2 Key dates

Having established when the primary limitation period is due to expire, it is important that the time-limit is recorded separately from the file in a diary system. The file itself may be similarly marked with the date on which limitation expires. This double recording of the primary limitation period is good practice as negligence claims against solicitors in personal injury cases account for roughly 11% of claims on the Solicitors' Indemnity Fund. Failure to identify the correct limitation period is one of the most common pitfalls – which can be avoided.

4.4.3 Photographs

In most personal injury cases, persons seeking advice following an accident will do so relatively soon after the accident occurs. If this is the case, a task, which is often overlooked, will be to secure photographic evidence.

The client

The client may attend the interview with an array of bruises and abrasions (soft tissue injuries). These will heal or fade relatively quickly and an important piece of the claimant's evidence will be lost. The claimant's solicitor should therefore ensure that good colour photographs are taken of the client's injuries for subsequent disclosure. Such photographs will form very tangible evidence of the severity of the injuries sustained, when the case comes to be considered some months or years in the future. In cases where the client may suffer embarrassment at being photographed, or indeed in any case where a degree of sensitivity is needed, specialist medical photographers are available, for example at larger teaching hospitals.

The location of the accident

In road traffic cases, it is usually necessary to produce photographs and plans of the locus of the accident for two reasons. First, the layout of the road may change between the date of accident and the date of trial and/or the road may appear different depending on whether it is photographed in summer or in winter, especially if there are lots of trees or vegetation which could obscure a driver's view. Secondly, it may be necessary to try to show the locus from the perspective of the car drivers at the time. An aerial view or plan of a road junction will do nothing, for example, to prove to a court how badly the approach of a vehicle was obscured by trees and bushes or roadside property. The solicitor should not lose sight of the fact that he must be able to prove to the court what could or could not be seen from a particular vantage point. It is open to the court to visit the site of the accident, but this may not be practicable and, in any event, would take an inordinate amount of time. The solicitor should always visit the site if possible, in order to get a feel for the case. Police accident reports (see Chapter 5) often contain good quality photographs which can be purchased on payment of an extra fee per print, and may prove helpful in showing not only the severity and location of the damage to each vehicle, but also the final position on the road that the vehicles were in immediately following the accident. This evidence may assume significance at a later date or may contradict the oral evidence of the witnesses. It is, however, important to read the police accident report closely, as it will confirm whether or not the vehicles were moved from their original resting position prior to the taking of the photographs.

In road traffic cases, the photographer should mark on a plan the precise location from which each photograph was taken and the direction in which the camera was pointing.

Site visits in non-road traffic cases are no less important. For example, in a case where the client has tripped on broken pavement, it is not uncommon that, as soon as the local authority receives intimation of a possible claim, it will send a team of operatives to remedy the offending pavement to rebut any subsequent suggestion on the part of the claimant that it failed to take all reasonable care in the circumstances. It is therefore vitally important to secure good quality photographs of the pavement etc as soon as possible, usually on the same day that the client is interviewed. Photographs must contain some indication of scale, and it is therefore necessary to place an item, such as a ruler, within the photograph.

It is not good practice to entrust the taking of photographs to the client, who may underestimate the importance of the task and forget about it until it is too late. Photographs taken by the client may be out of focus or underexposed which will not help the client's case.

4.5 ADVISING THE CLIENT

4.5.1 Personal injury claims

It is important for the solicitor not to lose sight of the fact that the client has come into his office seeking some meaningful advice, which he hopes will lead him to a decision as to whether he has an actionable case against some other party. The client therefore needs to have the best information available, in a form that he can understand, so that he can make an informed decision as to what to do next. It is best to set out the strengths and weaknesses of the case, based on what has been said by the client. The importance of the limitation period should be explained to the client if this is likely to be an issue. The solicitor should explain to the client that it is down to him to prove his case by evidence and that anything short of this is not enough. He should be informed of the basis of his case, and the level of proof needed by the court to prove that case. The client should be left in no doubt that it is *his* case, to be proved by *his* evidence, and that he bears the risk that his case may fail. As such, he should think seriously prior to instructing his solicitor to issue proceedings. The solicitor should give an indication as to whether he believes that the case is likely to succeed, but he should make it clear that the assessment is based on the limited information available at this early stage. In any event, if the solicitor is considering taking the client's case but will be paid under a conditional fee agreement, it will be necessary for the solicitor to conduct an assessment of risk at an early stage in order to decide whether or not to accept the client's instructions on that basis.

It may be that the solicitor advising the client will be required to produce to his superiors a report, from which his superiors will make a risk assessment in relation to whether or not the client should be accepted on a conditional fee basis. The risk assessment report may also consider such things as whether it is proposed that the client covers his own disbursements or whether the firm is prepared to fund them on the client's behalf. The client is likely to press for an indication of the likely level of damages that may be recovered. Giving a firm indication based on inadequate information should be resisted. Instead, the solicitor should explain to the client why an assessment would be premature at this stage.

One reason for not giving a provisional indication of the likely level of damages is that the client may be found to have been contributorily negligent. This principle should be explained to the client, first to try to elicit whether the client has any reason to believe that it will be relevant to his claim, and, secondly, to act as a warning to the client that it is likely that the opposition will try to allege that he was contributorily negligent.

The client should also be advised that he must prove every head (or type) of loss against his opponent. Although it is the case that the client is able to claim all he has lost as a direct result of the accident, he must also be in a position to prove every head of that loss to the court if he wishes to recover damages in respect of it. It should therefore be explained to the client that damages are made up of general damages (for pain, suffering and loss of amenity) and special damages (everything the client has had physically to pay for and other quantifiable losses as a direct result of the accident). For a detailed analysis of the subject of damages, see Chapter 13.

It will assist greatly when it comes to proving his losses if the client has kept a detailed record or account of his out-of-pocket expenses. To this end, the client should be advised at the first interview to keep all receipts for expenses incurred as a direct result of the accident, and that it is his responsibility to do so. Common examples are prescriptions, the cost of items lost or damaged beyond repair in the accident, and taxi fares to the out-patient department or physiotherapy. Similarly, with respect to general damages for pain and suffering, although the client's distress may be keen at the first interview, by the time of trial his recollection may have dimmed to the extent that he has forgotten many of the minor losses of function he suffered in the early stages of recovery from his injuries. The client should therefore be advised to keep a diary if he does not already do so, to record, for example, the fact that he is unable to sleep due to pain, or is unable to dress himself unaided or to do housework, and to record how long these disabilities last. Any number of tasks, either recreational or work-related, should be recorded so that they are not forgotten later when it comes to preparing the client's witness statement.

4.5.2 Clinical negligence claims

It is particularly important in clinical negligence cases that the client is made aware of the difficulties in pursuing the claim, and especially that he must establish not only a breach of duty, but also that the breach was causative of the damage that resulted (rather than the underlying illness or injury being the root cause of the loss). If the client is paying for the litigation privately, the high costs involved must be clearly explained to him. The solicitor should also explain the difficulty in giving a preliminary view on liability without first obtaining all the client's medical notes and at least one expert's views.

4.6 THE CLIENT'S PROOF OF EVIDENCE

The client's proof of evidence should not be confused with the client's witness statement. Although they are both statements taken from the client they serve different functions. The proof is the 'rough copy', which may include irrelevant material and suspicions or 'versions' rather than facts provable by the client in court. The witness statement contains only those matters which the witness can prove, and is disclosed to the opposition at the relevant stage in the proceedings. Practice

Directions setting out the form of witness statements have not been finalised at time of writing. The function of the proof is to obtain the fullest possible detail from the client, and only later to sift out what is strictly admissible as evidence. The proof can be taken at the end of the first interview when the client is still present, or from notes made at the time in conjunction with the questionnaire.

4.6.1 Contents of the proof

The proof should commence with the client's full name, address, date of birth and National Insurance number. It should state his occupation and whether he is married. If he was admitted to hospital, it should state his hospital number. The proof is intended for use by the client's solicitor and barrister, and, subsequently, in the preparation of the client's witness statement, and, as such, it should be the fullest possible statement from the client relating to the incident, the events immediately following the incident and its long-term effects. The client should begin his narrative at the earliest point in time that he feels to be relevant. Following the client's personal details, the proof should next detail the date, time and location of the incident. It should then follow through chronologically and meticulously:

(1) the events leading up to the incident;
(2) the circumstances of the accident itself;
(3) what happened immediately after the incident;
(4) why the client feels that the incident was caused by the negligence of some other person;
(5) what medical treatment was given and injuries incurred; and
(6) how the client feels that the incident has affected his day-to-day life.

The solicitor should bear in mind that the proof will form the basis of the witness statement, and that, usually, the witness statement will be ordered to stand as the witness's evidence-in-chief at the trial. It is important, therefore, that the proof is detailed in its description of how the incident actually happened, and the effect the incident has had on the client's day-to-day life. All aspects of the client's life should therefore be considered in the proof. The following areas should always be covered, including an estimate in weeks or months of how long the incapacity affected his life, or confirmation that the incapacity is still continuing.

(1) Everyday tasks which he is unable to do for himself; for example, dressing, bathing, housework, shopping, driving. This will be important if a claim is made for loss incurred in employing someone else to carry out these tasks.
(2) Recreational activities such as sports, hobbies, gardening, DIY in maintaining the home and the family car. The client's inability to participate in sports will have an effect on his loss of amenity claim for general damages. The client should also be asked whether he is a member of any sports team or club, and any prizes or trophies he has won as further evidence of his level of commitment. The inability to carry out maintenance jobs around the home will similarly affect his claim for loss of amenity. If the client gives evidence that DIY is a hobby, details should be obtained of any projects he has undertaken. This will also affect his special damages claim for the labour element of the cost of having to employ someone else to fulfil those tasks in the future.
(3) Whether and to what extent the injury has affected his sex life. This area of loss of amenity should always be broached with the client, as the stress of an accident can often bring about a degree of sexual dysfunction, even if the injury itself would not immediately suggest that such was the case.

(4) Specifically whether the incident will affect the client's ability to continue with his employment, and the extent to which he is affected. It may be obvious that the client will never work again, or will be unable to work in his pre-incident position but will have to retrain, or that he intends to return to his pre-incident employment but is unsure whether he will cope. Details should also be obtained as to the client's position if he were to be made redundant, and the degree of difficulty he would have in obtaining similar employment elsewhere because of his injuries.

It is important that all of the above issues are considered, and, if it is relevant, that they are covered in the proof in some detail, as there is little point in the client and/or his solicitor knowing the extent to which the incident has ruined the client's life, if this is not articulated sufficiently to the court. If a matter is not covered in the client's witness statement, the chances are the court will never hear of it and, if the court is not made aware of all relevant matters, the claimant's solicitor has not achieved one of his main aims, that of maximising the client's damages.

Before finishing the proof in personal injury cases, the client should always be asked whether he has had any pre-existing incident injury which may affect the current case.

The proof should always end with the client's signature and the date on which it was prepared so that, if the client dies prior to the conclusion of the case, the proof will still be of use evidentially.

4.6.2 Proofs in relation to different types of incident

The following types of incident will require the proof to cover certain areas in particular detail.

Incidents at work

The nature of the work process that gave rise to the incident must be thoroughly understood from the outset if the case is to be dealt with properly. The client should be asked to explain:

- his job title;
- what that involves in the work process;
- the level of training or instruction received;
- the level of seniority he held;
- the level of supervision over him;
- whether he can recall any written or oral confirmation of his work duties;
- a description of his usual duties;
- what he was doing on the day in question that gave rise to the incident;
- whether anything out of the ordinary occurred that day;
- details of other similar incidents known to the claimant;
- any representations made by the trade union about the machine or system of work;
- any comments made at health and safety meetings.

Example
John is an instrument artificer employed to work at a chemical plant. Part of his duties is to check the temperature of certain chemicals stored in large tanks above ground on the site. On the day of the accident, John climbed to the top of

a storage tank and removed the outer cover. Without warning, John was blown backwards by excess pressure in the tank causing him to fall from the tank approximately 4 metres to the ground. Because the chemical was corrosive on contact with the skin, John suffered burns to his face and hands as well as a damaged spine and broken left leg. John tells you that he has done the same task many times before without incident, but he believes that whoever last checked that particular tank failed adequately to secure the inner seal so that when he next opened the outer seal the sudden change in pressure was like releasing a cork from a bottle. John tells you that he is usually accompanied by a fellow employee when doing these checks as the company's safety policy requires this. On the day of the incident, his colleague had telephoned in sick, but the duty manager had not called in anyone else to take his place. John also tells you that the company used to have a nurse on site to deal with minor injuries, but when the last nurse ceased to be employed she was not replaced, John believes that this was because of the expense involved. John also believes that his burns would not be so severe if he had received first aid more quickly.

In the above example, if, when describing any part of his duties, John becomes unclear, he should be asked to explain it again, perhaps drawing a sketch to assist his narrative. It is important that there is no misunderstanding at this stage as the solicitor will probably use this information as the basis for his statement of case. In addition, if the solicitor is unsure from the client's explanation precisely how the incident happened, it is also likely that a judge will be similarly confused. It is therefore vitally important that any ambiguity is resolved at this point. If ambiguity remains, facilities should be sought for a site inspection. Where the place of work is privately owned property, and may be a dangerous environment for the visitor, the solicitor must always seek permission from the employer for a site inspection. The inspection can be carried out with the claimant's expert engineer if the accident involves a piece of machinery.

In the above example, it is necessary to include in the proof John's suspicions as to:

- the cause of the incident;
- disregard of safety policy; and
- his belief that the burns were worsened by delay in treatment.

All these matters will have to be checked, however, as the chemical engineer who inspects the plant may conclude that the incident had a completely different cause, possibly involving contributory negligence by John himself. It may be apparent to the engineer that the tank is fitted with a large pressure gauge that John should have checked prior to opening the tank. Similarly, the company safety policy may specify that rubber gloves and full face mask must be worn when working with corrosive chemicals, and that the burn time for that particular chemical is less than 30 seconds, in which case having medical personnel on site would have made no difference to John's injuries.

The function of the proof is to form the basis of the witness statement. As such, the client's assertions must be checked thoroughly in order to decide whether they are provable and can be included in the statement.

Road traffic incidents

When taking the proof in the case of a road incident, it is important first to have in mind the stretch of road in question. A large-scale map of the area in question is invaluable at this stage as it will cut short any unproductive argument as to how or where, for example, the road bends. If the client has difficulty explaining how the incident happened, it can be useful to get him to draw a sketch of the relative position of the vehicles involved, or to use toy cars to illustrate what happened. Care should be taken to ensure that the client is entirely clear about the following matters:

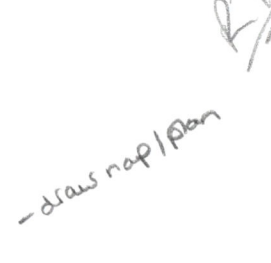

- the direction in which he was travelling;
- whether there was anyone else in the car with him;
- the speed of travel;
- familiarity with the car;
- familiarity with the road;
- whether there were any witnesses;
- the make and registration numbers of all vehicles involved;
- who he believes to be responsible for the incident and why;
- what happened immediately after the incident;
- exactly what he said to anyone after the incident;
- exactly what anyone said to him, and whether anyone else heard what was said;
- whether the police were called and, if not, why not;
- if the police were called, which police force and the name of the officer attending;
- whether the client is aware of any pending prosecutions (eg whether he was warned that he may be prosecuted or that he may be needed as a witness in the prosecution of the other driver);
- whether he is comprehensively insured and the amount of excess he has to pay on his own insurance policy (his uninsured loss);
- whether he is the owner of the vehicle, and details of the owner if he is not.

If the client wrote anything down at the time of the incident, such as the name and address of the other driver(s), these should be retained. If he explains what happened, for example, by referring to the offside and nearside of his vehicle, the solicitor should check that he understands what is meant by those terms. Clients may believe that they have to speak to their solicitor using words which they would not normally use in everyday speech and, consequently, they may use words that they do not fully understand. For the avoidance of doubt, the solicitor should check with the client that when referring to a vehicle's 'offside' the client means the driver's side, and that 'nearside' refers to the side of the vehicle nearest the gutter.

In road traffic cases, it is vitally important to trace and interview witnesses as soon as possible. It is unlikely that the witnesses will be known to the client and they may prove difficult to trace if not contacted immediately, and in any event their memory of the events will fade quickly and will therefore be of less use evidentially. The question of whether there are any independent third party witnesses is of central importance because the case will be much easier to prove if an independent witness can be found who is prepared to give evidence to a court that he saw the incident and believes that the cause of the incident was the fault of the other driver. If the client does not have any details of witnesses, the police accident report may have statements from witnesses whom the solicitor can contact. The police should be notified of all incidents involving personal injury, and will prepare a report on the incident including witness statements (see Chapter 5).

Tripping/slipping incidents

Trips and slips make up a large proportion of incidents in the work-place, and the HSE has targeted this area in order to heighten awareness of the problem (see the HSE publication *Watch Your Step* (Stationery Office, 1985) and *Slips and Trips: Guidance for employers on identifying hazards and controlling risks* (Stationery Office, May 1996)).

Tripping incidents occurring other than at the work-place are governed by the Highways Act 1980, s 41, under which the highway authority (usually the local district council responsible for the area in which the fall or trip took place) has a duty to maintain the highway, which includes the pavements used by the public. It is for the claimant to show that the highway was not reasonably safe. Uneven paving stones or the sites of road improvements with poor temporary surfaces usually claim the most victims. Local authorities sometimes contract out such road works to independent contractors, in which case it may be advisable to sue both the contractor responsible for the safety of the site and the local authority which delegated the improvement work to them. If the client can show that the highway was not reasonably safe, the authority must show that it has taken such care as in all the circumstances was reasonably required to ensure that the highway was not dangerous.

Applying the above rule to the client's proof it will be necessary to ask the client:

- whether he was in a hurry or was running at the time of the incident;
- whether he was carrying anything which obscured his view;
- whether there was a warning sign to take care and, if so, what the sign said;
- whether there were any witnesses;
- what sort of shoes the client was wearing; and
- the exact location of the incident.

It will then be necessary to procure photographs of the locus without delay, as the local authority may act quickly to repair the relevant area as soon as it becomes aware of a possible claim, in order to show that it has taken such care as in all the circumstances was reasonably required.

Clinical negligence claims

In a clinical negligence claim, the client is likely to be in a more confused or uncertain position than in a personal injury matter. Whilst a client is normally able to explain, for example, what occurred during a road traffic incident, he may not understand the treatment and care he received from a medical practitioner. The terminology will be unfamiliar and, in the case of alleged negligence during hospital treatment, the client may not be able to recall or identify the doctors or nurses who treated him.

When obtaining a proof in a clinical negligence case, it is important that every detail is obtained, such as what exactly was said when the claimant attended at the hospital or when the client was asked to sign the consent form.

Unless the alleged negligent act arises out of an illness not previously suffered by the client, full details of any previous medical problems should be obtained. Other matters contained in the proof could be as follows:

- the symptoms which led the client to seek medical advice;
- the information given by the client to the doctor;

- any questions asked by the doctor (eg, where the client went to his GP complaining of headaches, whether the doctor asked the client if he had hit his head or whether the client had been sick – questions which would lead a competent GP to suspect a severe head injury);
- whether the client was given details of a diagnosis at that time;
- what form of treatment was prescribed;
- whether the treatment was explained to the client and whether he was warned of any potential risks and the likely consequences of not receiving treatment;
- the name of the doctor who treated the client and his status;
- whether the client was receiving treatment from different doctors;
- whether the client asked for a second opinion;
- whether any witnesses were present at the consultation;
- any previous medical problems which could have affected the client;
- whether the client has complained to the hospital/doctor;
- whether the client has received any reply or relevant correspondence;
- whether an apology has been received.

This should be followed by details of the injury in the normal fashion.

In certain cases, it can be useful to ask what prompted the client to contact a solicitor. In some cases, the client is advised by other medical professionals to seek legal advice as they believe that a mistake may have been made.

Example

A client injures his leg playing football and attends at the local accident and emergency department. The accident and emergency department is busy and, although the client is sent for an X-ray, the house officer fails to spot the fracture and discharges the client immediately. The client is in considerable pain for a number of weeks and eventually attends at his GP's surgery, who refers him back to the hospital for another X-ray. In such circumstances, the client may be told that in fact the leg is fractured and that it was missed when the client first attended. Such information is clearly of assistance in assessing liability.

4.7 WELFARE BENEFITS

It will be necessary to advise the client of the welfare benefits he may be entitled to receive because of the incident. It may be months or years before the claim is settled, and if the client is unfit for work, he may experience financial difficulties and feel pressured into accepting the first offer of compensation from the defendant. The client may not have had any previous experience of the Benefits Agency (an executive agency of the DSS) and may initially be sceptical or even unwilling to approach the Agency. The solicitor should give the client general advice on the types of benefits that may be available to him to cover payment in respect of his inability to work, assistance with mobility, assistance with household tasks and even assistance with child care. It should be stressed that if only general guidance is given, then the client should seek detailed advice from the Agency or from the firm's welfare rights adviser, if the solicitor is not fully familiar with the current benefits available. Regulations relating to particular benefits change frequently, and up-to-date information on benefits can be obtained from the Benefits Agency on free or low-cost telephone information lines. It should be stressed to the client that they act quickly when seeking benefits as it is not normally possible to back-date benefits and benefit may be lost due to delay.

4.7.1 Types of benefit

Non means-tested benefits

The relevant non means-tested benefits to be considered are as follows.

ATTENDANCE ALLOWANCE

Attendance Allowance is available only to people aged 65 or over. It covers help with personal care due to illness or disability. The amount payable depends on the person's care requirements. (See leaflet DS 702 Attendance Allowance.)

INDUSTRIAL INJURIES DISABLEMENT BENEFIT

Industrial Injuries Disablement Benefit is available for people disabled as a result of an accident at work or as a result of a prescribed industrial disease. They may also be entitled to Constant Attendance Allowance and Exceptionally Severe Disablement Allowance. Reduced Earning Allowance may be applicable if the accident occurred or the disease started before 1 October 1990, and as a result the person cannot return to his job or work to the same standard. (See leaflet NI 6 Industrial Injuries Disablement Benefit.)

DISABILITY LIVING ALLOWANCE

Disability Living Allowance is available for people who have difficulty with:

(1) personal care; or
(2) getting around/mobility;

or both, because of illness or disablement.

Normally, help is available only if it has been needed for at least 3 months and is likely to be needed for a further 6 months. People over 65 years old are not eligible, and should apply instead for attendance allowance. (See leaflet DS 704 Disability Living Allowance.)

DISABLED PERSON'S TAX CREDIT

Disabled Person's Tax Credit is available to people aged 16 or over who work at least 16 hours per week but whose disability limits their earning capacity. The claims process is via the Inland Revenue.

PNEUMOCONIOSIS, BYSSINOSIS AND MISCELLANEOUS DISEASE BENEFIT SCHEME

This benefit is intended only for people who contracted the above illnesses, and certain other diseases, as a result of employment which ended before 5 July 1948. (See leaflet PN 1.) If the illness was contracted from or after 5 July 1948, the relevant benefit will be Industrial Injuries Disablement Benefit (see above).

WORKMEN'S COMPENSATION (SUPPLEMENTATION) SCHEME

This scheme supplements weekly payments made under the Workmen's Compensation Acts. (See leaflet WS 1.)

SEVERE DISABLEMENT ALLOWANCE

Severe Disablement Allowance is available to persons aged between 16 and 65 who have been unable to work for at least 28 consecutive weeks because of illness or disablement, and are not eligible for incapacity benefit (see below) because they have not paid sufficient NI contributions. If incapacity began after the age of 20, they must also be assessed and, to qualify, be found to have been at least 80% disabled for at least 28 consecutive weeks. Extra benefit may be claimed for dependent children and adults. (See leaflets SD 1 Sick or Disabled, and HB 5 A Guide to Non-Contributory Benefits for Disabled People.)

INVALID CARE ALLOWANCE

Invalid Care Allowance is available to people aged between 16 and 65 who spend at least 35 hours per week caring for a severely disabled person who is in receipt of disability living allowance or attendance allowance. However, the claimant must not earn more than £50 per week after allowable expenses, or be in full-time education. (See leaflet SD 4 Caring for Someone?)

INCAPACITY BENEFIT

Incapacity benefit is available for people who are incapable of work and are employed, but who cannot get Statutory Sick Pay from their employer, or are self-employed. Unemployed people may get Incapacity Benefit if they have paid enough NI contributions. Extra benefit may be paid for dependent adults and children. (See leaflet SD 1 Sick or Disabled.)

STATUTORY SICK PAY

Statutory Sick Pay (SSP) is available for people who are employed and have been sick for at least 4 or more consecutive days; it is available for a maximum of 28 weeks. A self-certification form (SC 2) is produced by the DSS for employees to certify themselves as sick for the first 7 days of sickness for SSP purposes. SSP is paid in the same way as wages, and therefore the client may inform the solicitor that he has suffered no loss of wages as a result of the accident, believing this to be correct. It will be necessary to check the client's contract of employment to find the true position. It is often the case that the contract provides that the salary (above the level of SSP) must be repaid in the event of money being recovered from a third party (see leaflet N/245, An Employees Guide to SSP).

Means-tested benefits

The relevant means-tested benefits to consider are as follows.

INCOME SUPPORT

This is available to persons aged 16 or over who are on a low income, as long as they work less than 16 hours per week and have capital of less than £8,000. See leaflet IS20 A Guide to Income Support.

COUNCIL TAX BENEFIT

This is available to people on a low income and is administered by the local council to whom the Council Tax is paid. The amount is deducted from the person's Council Tax bill on a sliding scale depending on their financial circumstances. See leaflet GL17 Help Paying Council Tax.

HOUSING BENEFIT

This is paid by the local council to people who need help with paying their rent. The person must have less than £16,000 in savings. See leaflet GL16 Help Paying Rent and RR2 A Guide to Housing Benefit and Council Tax Benefit (available from local councils).

WORKING FAMILIES TAX CREDIT

This scheme replaced Family Credit from 5 October 1999. It is a tax credit scheme administered by the Inland Revenue to families with children. The claimant and/or their partner must be working at least 16 hours per week and have responsibility for at least one child and have a low income.

DISABLED PERSON'S TAX CREDIT

This scheme replaced Disability Working Allowance from 5 October 1999. It is a tax credit scheme administered by the Inland Revenue. The claimant must be aged 16 or over and have an illness or disability which puts them at a disadvantage in getting a job. They must also be working for at least 16 hours per week.

4.7.2 Responsibility for paying benefits

Most industrial injuries benefits can now be paid by the Benefits Agency direct into the claimant's bank account.

Claims for Disability Living Allowance and Attendance Allowance are dealt with by the Disability Benefits Directorate which is based at Blackpool and operates 11 disability benefits centres around the country, rather than the claimant's local office.

4.7.3 Eligibility for benefits

Clients who do not have an employer because they are self-employed or unemployed may claim incapacity benefit if they have paid sufficient NI contributions. If they have paid insufficient NI contributions, they may claim income support.

The client should be advised that, although he may qualify for any of the above benefits, if his claim is successful he will be subject to recoupment under the Social Security (Recovery of Benefits) Act 1997. This area is considered in detail in Chapter 12.

The client's eligibility for benefits will be assessed by the Benefits Agency. People who claim incapacity or disablement benefit are examined either by doctors who work for Benefits Agency Medical Services or by health service doctors who are paid a fee. The doctor tests whether the person claiming can perform a range of tasks, and reports his findings back to the Agency. The test the doctor applies when assessing people for incapacity benefit or severe disablement allowance is called the 'all work' test. (See leaflet IB 215 Incapacity Benefit: The All Work Test – Assuring Medical Quality.)

The fact that a claimant has been in receipt of the above benefits will mean that he falls within the criteria laid down by the DSS in the 'all work' test, and this may be something which the defendant's solicitors should note. Similarly, if the claimant is claiming continuing disability in his personal injury claim, but fails the 'all work' test, or is certified unfit but is later passed as fit, this will also be a factor to be borne in mind by the parties' advisers. However, the test is not designed to be based on a 'snapshot' of the person's capabilities, but is to assess the difficulties which the person has over a sustained period of time.

When considering eligibility to benefits, it is necessary to have regard to whether the receipt of compensation will take the claimant out of financial eligibility for means-tested benefits. In *Beattie v Secretary of State for Social Security* [2001] 1 WLR 1404, Charles Beattie was injured in a road traffic accident and rendered quadriplegic. He sued by his litigation friend and Court of Protection receiver, Stephen Beattie. The claimant appealed a decision of the Social Security Commissioner that he was not entitled to income support because payments 'falling to be treated as income' under a structured settlement took him beyond the limit on income for the purpose of claiming income support. This issue was appealed because guidance from the Public Trust Office suggested that, as long as the compensation was held on trust and payments were made on a discretionary basis and were not used to fund items that would normally be paid for using benefits, then those payments would not affect benefit entitlement. In *Beattie* the court ruled that the agreement, as part of the structured settlement, to make regular payments for a fixed number of years was in fact an annuity and was therefore 'capital treated as income' under reg 41(2) of the Income Support (General) Regulations 1987, SI 1987/1967. The essential difference in this case is that the compensation was paid to the Court of Protection who would hold the money for the benefit of the patient, rather than simply held on discretionary trust.

4.8 THE ROAD TRAFFIC (NHS CHARGES) ACT 1999

The Road Traffic (NHS Charges) Act 1999 (the 1999 Act) received Royal Assent on 10 March 1999. The Act replaces an existing provision in ss 157 and 158 of the Road Traffic Act 1988.

Under the 1999 Act, when a person makes a successful claim for compensation as a result of a road traffic accident, the NHS hospital where he receives treatment can also claim an amount to cover the costs of treatment from the relevant insurer (called the compensator). This includes Motor Insurers Bureau (MIB) cases.

The purpose of the 1999 Act is to provide a national administration system, the aim of which is to ensure that costs of treatment are, in fact, recovered in as many cases as is possible. The responsibility for collecting the NHS costs will be undertaken by the Compensation Recovery Unit (CRU) (see Chapter 12 for a detailed consideration of the CRU and benefit recovery). The CRU was given this task as they already have extensive knowledge of the insurance industry and will therefore keep collection costs to a minimum.

In many ways, the NHS costs recovery scheme will mirror the benefit recovery scheme considered at Chapter 12. However, unlike the benefit recovery scheme, the NHS costs recovery scheme will not affect the amount of damages recovered by the claimant. The compensator will apply to the CRU for a Certificate of NHS Charges. The certificate may have an expiry date, depending on whether or not NHS treatment is still continuing.

The Act allows for NHS charges to be calculated according to a tariff. The tariff will allow for:

(i) a set fee for patients treated in accident and emergency departments or out-patient clinics (the fee will be the same regardless of the number of out patient appointments);

(ii) a daily rate for patients admitted to hospital.

The appeal and review procedure for NHS costs recovery are designed to mirror the appeal and review provisions governing benefit recovery under the Social Security (Recovery of Benefits) Act 1997, as to which, see Chapter 12.

4.9 REHABILITATION, EARLY INTERVENTION AND MEDICAL TREATMENT

It has long been recognised that a claimant's long-term prognosis can be dramatically improved by the intervention of rehabilitative treatment at the earliest possible opportunity. Research by insurers has found that the UK lags behind much of Europe and North America in terms of our ability to provide restorative care for injured claimants. The result of early intervention strategies in other countries is that they have a far better rate of return to work at an earlier stage than is able to be achieved in the UK. Whilst it is recognised that the reasons for this are complex, insurers whose operations include much of Europe are starting to question why return to work rates are so poor in the UK.

The problem in the past has been that the claimant is not able to adequately fund the treatment until after his claim for damages for personal injuries is settled. Insurance companies are now recognising that early intervention in the form of extra sessions of physiotherapy, for example, can be in their own best interests as well as the claimant's if it assists the claimant to recover sufficiently to return to employment either earlier or at all. In the long term, insurers recognise that, if they fail to co-operate in paying for rehabilitative treatment in cases where liability is unlikely to be an issue, both they and the claimant will be the ultimate losers. The claimant will lose the opportunity of therapeutic medical treatment at the earliest opportunity and the insurer (if found liable) is likely to find an increased claim for future loss as the claimant is not fit to return to work.

To alleviate this problem, a voluntary code of practice on rehabilitation, early intervention and medical treatment has been drafted by insurers and lawyers with the aim of ensuring that both sides are aware of the rehabilitation issue and of their respective obligations under the code. The code places responsibilities on both claimants' solicitors and insurers to consider whether rehabilitation is appropriate and places a duty on both to contact the other to raise the issue if either of them thinks that the claimant could benefit.

Examples of such early treatment are: surgery, physiotherapy, counselling, occupational therapy and speech therapy. They may also include making adaptations to the claimant's home to make his life easier in the period prior to the settlement of the claim.

It is important to stress that the code is entirely voluntary and has no sanctions attached to it. It is, however, noteworthy that because of the benefits that are clear to both sides the code is likely to become a feature of the pre-litigation landscape in personal injury cases.

4.10 CONCLUSION

If the first interview is handled correctly, it should save the solicitor a great deal of time in the future. As personal injury litigation is 'front loaded', much of the essential work is covered during or shortly after the first interview. If essential matters have been missed, old ground will need to be covered again, which will lead to inevitable delay and upset for the client. If this is allowed to happen, the solicitor will have failed in one of his main objectives, that of avoiding delay, and thereby will allow the opposition to gain the advantage.

4.11 FURTHER READING

Slips and Trips: Guidance for employers on identifying hazards and controlling risks (Stationery Office).
Statutory Sick Pay Manual for Employers
Five Steps to Risk Assessment (HSE Publications).
A Guide to Risk Assessment Requirements (HSE Publications).
The Legal Services Commission Manual (Sweet & Maxwell)
Code of Best Practice on Rehabilitation, Early Intervention and Medical Treatment in Personal Injury Claims (BICMA)
www.justask.org.uk

4.12 OVERVIEW OF MATTERS TO BE CONSIDERED AT THE FIRST INTERVIEW

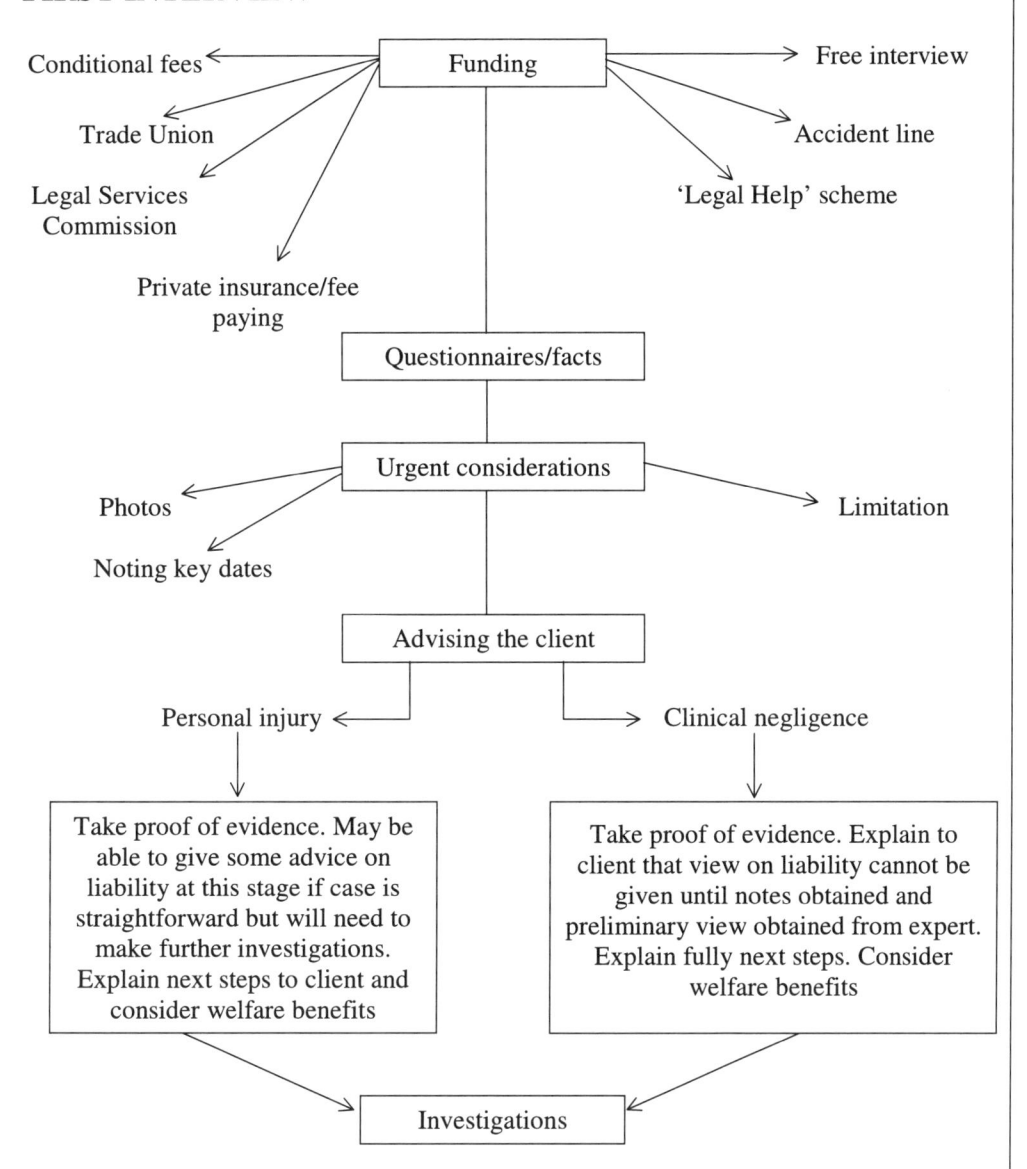

Funding
- Conditional fees
- Trade Union
- Legal Services Commission
- Private insurance/fee paying
- Free interview
- Accident line
- 'Legal Help' scheme

Questionnaires/facts

Urgent considerations
- Photos
- Noting key dates
- Limitation

Advising the client

Personal injury: Take proof of evidence. May be able to give some advice on liability at this stage if case is straightforward but will need to make further investigations. Explain next steps to client and consider welfare benefits

Clinical negligence: Take proof of evidence. Explain to client that view on liability cannot be given until notes obtained and preliminary view obtained from expert. Explain fully next steps. Consider welfare benefits

Investigations

Chapter 5

FACT GATHERING AND ANALYSIS

5.1 INTRODUCTION

Following the first interview, it will be necessary to gather evidence prior to advising the client whether he should commence the pre-action protocol. It is particularly important to ensure that evidence is gathered quickly as circumstances can change and important information may be lost. For example, in an incident at work involving a machine, the Health & Safety Executive (HSE) may recommend that the safety guards are upgraded. Unless a specific request is made to the employer to preserve the machine as it is, the employer may carry out the recommendations of the HSE or may even replace the machine with a new one. This can lead to enormous difficulties for the claimant later on, and therefore steps must be taken to avoid it taking place. In clinical negligence cases, it is equally important to act quickly, while events are fresh in the minds of clients and witnesses.

5.2 IDENTIFYING THE DEFENDANT

In many cases, the identity of the defendant will be obvious. Nevertheless, this question should always be addressed as things are often not as straightforward as they seem. It is crucial to issue proceedings within the primary limitation period against the correct defendant. Generally, there is little point in pursuing a claim against a defendant unless he has the means with which to pay the judgment or is insured. If the defendant is a health authority or trust, it will not carry insurance provided by an insurance company, but will settle the claims itself out of its own funds.

5.2.1 Road traffic incidents

In a road traffic incident claim, it is necessary to establish not only the name of the driver of the vehicle and his insurance position, but also the name of the owner of the vehicle and of his insurer. Frequently, the driver of a vehicle may be using a vehicle owned and insured by his employer. In such cases, it is usual to sue the employer (or vehicle operator in the case of commercial vehicles), and a clear indication in response to the letter of claim under the pre-action protocol will usually be given by the insurance company as to whether it is prepared to deal with the claim on behalf of the proposed defendant. If such an indication is not received, or there is any reason to doubt whether the driver was acting within the course of employment, or the pre-action protocol is otherwise exhausted, it is usual to sue both the driver and the employer. Similarly, if protective proceedings are necessary to avoid the claim being statute-barred by the Limitation Act 1980, it is best, initially, to sue all potential defendants if there is a degree of uncertainty.

Chapter 5 contents
Introduction
Identifying the defendant
Letter of claim
Notice in road traffic cases
The Motor Insurers Bureau
Acquiring evidence
Early access to documents and other items
Obtaining medical records in clinical negligence claims
Conclusion
Further reading
Overview of initial liability investigations

Example

Alice is a passenger in a car driven by her brother Peter. The car is registered in the name of their father, Harold, who also insured it in his name with Peter as a named driver on the policy. It was cheaper to insure the vehicle this way as Harold is over 50 years old and has a good driving record, whereas Peter is under 25 years old and has never insured a car before. Although the car is registered in Harold's name he has given it to Peter to use on a day-to-day basis. Peter crashes the car and is unhurt, but Alice suffers serious injuries. Alice will have to sue the driver of the car, her brother, who will seek to rely on his father's insurance. However, if Harold did not make it clear to his insurer that he was not the main driver of the vehicle, the insurance company is likely to avoid the policy because of non-disclosure by Harold and Peter. In that event, Alice will be left to sue Peter and will have to seek to rely on the provisions of ss 151–152 of the Road Traffic Act 1988 (see below) and to inform the Motor Insurers Bureau (see **5.5**).

5.2.2 Employers' liability

If an incident occurs at work, notwithstanding that the incident was caused by another employee or someone acting as agent for the employer, provided they were acting in the course of employment, it is usual to sue the employer only. Although the defendant will generally be the employer, a claim may also be made against the occupier of the premises or the person with control of the premises if different from the employer.

However, this is a complicated area and it will be necessary to analyse what has been agreed contractually between the parties. In *Breaveglen Ltd (t/a ANZAC Construction Co) v Sleeman Ltd* (1997) *The Times*, May 10, A had been defending the main action and claimed a contribution from S who was a third party to the proceedings in respect of damages claimed by an employee (M). S was the main contractor and subcontracted the supply of labour and materials to A. It was part of the agreement that A would insure and indemnify against employers' liability. M worked at S's site under the instruction of S's foreman and was injured. A claimed a contribution towards damages from S but the court found that A was under a statutory duty to insure against injury, and remained under a personal duty to M. A carried primary liability even if there was negligence on the part of S's foreman.

It will also be necessary to consider who is the appropriate defendant in cases where a business undertaking is transferred as a going concern from one owner to another. This is a common scenario, and it will be necessary to identify who is liable for the damages when an employee suffers injury prior to the transfer of the business but then sues the new employer after the transfer of the business. This was considered in *Taylor v Serviceteam Ltd and London Borough of Waltham Forest* [1998] PIQR P201. Mr Taylor was employed as a refuse collector by the council. In 1994, an incident occurred in the course of his employment. Subsequent to this, the refuse collection service was privatised to the first defendants, Serviceteam. As an employee, Mr Taylor's contract of employment was transferred to his new employer within the meaning of the Transfer of Undertakings (Protection of Employment) Regulations 1981, SI 1981/1794. Mr Taylor was then dismissed by Serviceteam on medical grounds. Mr Taylor sued Serviceteam, notwithstanding that they were not actually his employers at the date of the incident. Not surprisingly, Serviceteam said that the council was responsible and joined them as second defendant. As a matter of law, the court had to decide who was the appropriate defendant. It was held that the correct defendant was Serviceteam, despite the fact that they were not Mr Taylor's employers at the date of injury. The court construed the Transfer of Undertakings Regulations and decided that liability for personal injury did transfer to the new employer on a relevant transfer of an undertaking or a part thereof. Although this point may now appear to be settled, it will also be necessary to establish who is the relevant insurer. In the above scenario, the council would be on risk at the time of the accident, and unless there is a clearly defined indemnity clause included in the Transfer of Undertakings Agreement between the old employer and the new employer, the claimant may have difficulties recovering compensation.

This ruling accords with *Wilson v West Cumbria Health Care NHS Trust* (see below).

5.2.3 Cases involving negligence of doctors and medical staff

Actions arising out of NHS hospital treatment

If the action arises out of treatment by a health service employee (including hospital doctors), the defendant is the health authority at district level (pursuant to the National Health Service Act 1977, Sch 5, para 15, as amended by the Health Services Act 1980). Where the hospital has been granted trust status, the trust is named as the defendant. If the allegations cover the period pre- and post-trust status, it may be necessary to name both the health authority and the trust as defendants. Enquiries will need to be made as to whether liability for 'pre-trust' cases has also been transferred. It is not necessary to sue individual doctors or nurses in the direct employment of the NHS or trust.

When ascertaining the correct title of the health authority or hospital trust, it is necessary to check the Medical Register which lists all hospitals and their controlling authority/trust, or alternatively a telephone call to the 'quality control manager' at the hospital where the treatment was carried out will reveal the name of the authority. It is also necessary to check the date when the trust came into being to ensure that the correct authority is named as the defendant to the action. Where a recently created trust is involved, there may be some apportionment in respect of the funding of the damages between the old health authority and the newly created trust. In *Wilson, Holdham & Adams v West Cumbria Healthcare NHS Trust* (1995) PMILR, 3 August, it was held that, on the transfer of an undertaking from a health authority to an NHS trust created by the National Health Service and Community Care Act 1990, liability in tort is transferred together with the contract of employment.

It may be the case, notwithstanding the granting of trust status, that individual consultants' contracts may still be held by their former employers, the regional health authority or the district health authority. This is a transitional phase and legal responsibility for all consultants' contracts has passed to trusts from the date of trust status. Thus, the contractual relationship of an individual practitioner with a trust is irrelevant to the identification of the correct defendant.

General practitioner

The general practitioner is liable for his own acts, for the acts of his employees and (arguably) for the acts of anyone else whom he employs to look after his patients, for example nurses and allied staff.

Where the action arises following treatment by a general practitioner, the situation may be more complicated. The general practitioner has a contract of services with the family health service authority, ie he is an independent contractor. It is necessary to obtain the notes from a general practitioner to ascertain who supplied the treatment and whether it was one doctor, two, or more. It may be necessary to join in all the doctors in the group who were involved. This can cause some problems in that the individual general practitioners may be members of different medical defence or protection societies who may each instruct separate solicitors. This will affect the conduct of the case.

Private hospitals

A clinic or private hospital will take out its own insurance. It will employ the staff who run and administer the hospital. However, the medical staff (eg consultants or other allied doctors) are using the services of the clinic and are independent contractors and, therefore, proceedings must identify them as defendants. The clinic will advise on the position of the doctors who use their premises and, in almost all cases, the individual doctor is sued. The doctors will be indemnified by their own defence organisations.

If the action arises out of private treatment and is a clinical fault, then the doctor should be named as the defendant. Alternatively, if the treatment is a nursing fault, then the hospital/clinic should be named as the defendant.

Private treatment from dentists

A dentist treating private patients is not under any statutory or professional requirement to have insurance cover in respect of professional negligence – although the majority are insured.

Alternative/complementary health practitioners

An alternative health practitioner faces exactly the same risks as a general practitioner except that he is not involved in surgical intervention or, in some branches, medical prescription. The College of Osteopathy, for example, has prescribed a questionnaire which it invites its practitioners to complete before commencing any treatment and which recommends that, if the practitioner is in any doubt over the form or consequences of treatment, no treatment should be undertaken by the osteopath who should instead refer the prospective patient to a general practitioner.

5.3 LETTER OF CLAIM

5.3.1 Personal injury claims

The letter of claim is the first intimation that a claim is being made against the proposed defendant; two copies are forwarded to the proposed defendant with instructions to pass one copy to his insurer. It should be written to the proposed defendant before commencing proceedings as part of the pre-action protocol. The main function of the letter is to warn the proposed defendant of possible legal proceedings if it is ignored and to alert his insurance company to the proceedings. The letter should deal with matters in sufficient detail so that the proposed defendant (and his insurer) is left in no doubt as to the position. Tactically, it is important to bear in mind that the insurance company's normal response to the letter of claim will be to send a letter requesting further information 'to enable it to investigate the claim'. This is often seen as an attempt to get as much information as possible to use subsequently against the claimant if either his statement of case or evidence contradicts the letter of claim. The letter should be constructed in such a way that further information from the solicitor is unnecessary, and the insurance company letter can therefore be answered with a polite but firm response to contact its own insured who already has all the information that the insurer needs about the incident.

Full details of the personal injury claims pre-action protocol and contents of the letter of claim are contained in Chapter 9.

No attempt should be made to quantify the claim (in monetary terms) in the letter – an apparently simple injury worth a few hundred pounds at the outset may unexpectedly (and quickly) develop into a serious injury worth thousands of pounds.

If possible, the proposed defendant's insurance details should be obtained. In the case of an incident at work, the insurance certificate is required to be displayed on the premises in a suitably prominent position. In the case of a road traffic incident, the proposed defendant may have volunteered his insurance details or may have been obliged to produce the documentation to the police. In the latter case, it is possible for the solicitor to ask the police to disclose the full name, address and insurance details of the proposed defendant. Although any police accident report will not be released until after any criminal proceedings have been dealt with, these limited details will be released if requested. No fee is payable for this. If the client did not manage to get any details of the proposed defendant and the police were not called out to the accident, it is possible to obtain the name and address of the owner of the vehicle if the client has the registration number. The solicitor can write to the Vehicle Enquiry Unit at DVLA Swansea SA99 1AJ which, on payment of a fee, will disclose the name and address of the registered keeper of the vehicle. Because this enquiry is being made by someone other than the current registered keeper, the DVLA requires a letter of explanation to accompany the enquiry stating why the enquirer needs this information. It is also possible to write to the proposed defendant asking him to supply his insurance details. If he fails to do so, or makes a false statement, he will be guilty of an offence under s 154 of the Road Traffic Act 1988.

5.3.2 Clinical negligence claims

In clinical negligence cases, the contents of the letter of claim are dealt with in the pre-action protocol in relation to clinical negligence claims. This is dealt with in detail in Chapter 9.

5.4 NOTICE IN ROAD TRAFFIC CASES

Under ss 151 and 152 of the Road Traffic Act 1988, where the claimant has obtained judgment against a defendant he can enforce that judgment against the insurer notwithstanding that the insurer may be entitled to avoid or may have avoided or cancelled the policy.

5.4.1 Section 151

Section 151 applies only to a judgment obtained after insurance has been granted in respect of risks required to be compulsorily insured and either:

(1) the liability is covered by the terms of the policy and judgment is obtained against any person insured under the policy; or
(2) the liability would be covered if the policy covered all persons and the judgment is obtained against any person other than one who is insured by the policy (s 151(2)).

Matters required to be compulsorily insured are:

(1) personal injury or death of any other person;
(2) the cost of emergency hospital treatment; and
(3) damage to property (other than the insured vehicle) up to £250,000.

This means that, as long as there is an insurance certificate in respect of the vehicle and judgment is obtained against the driver, the insurer is obliged to pay damages to the claimant, even if the insurance did not cover the defendant. However, payment is only in respect of the matters required to be compulsorily insured by law.

5.4.2 Section 152

The only way in which the insurance company can avoid paying damages under the policy is under s 152 of the Road Traffic Act 1988. Nothing is payable by the insurer if:

(1) before or within 7 days after commencement of proceedings the insurer was not given notice of the proceedings; or
(2) before the event giving rise to the liability the policy was cancelled by mutual consent and before the event occurred the certificate was surrendered to the insurer, or (in certain circumstances) was declared lost or destroyed; or
(3) the insurer commences an action before or within 3 months of the commencement of (the claimant's) proceedings in which judgment was given, and the insurer obtains a declaration that he is entitled to avoid the policy on the ground that it was obtained by non-disclosure of a material fact, or by representation of a fact that was false in some material particular. To take advantage of this declaration, the insurer must also give the claimant notice of the proceedings against its own insured before or within 7 days of commencement of its action for a declaration, specifying the non-disclosure or false representation on which it proposes to rely (s 152(2)).

5.5 THE MOTOR INSURERS BUREAU

The Motor Insurers Bureau (MIB) Agreements are voluntary agreements by which all motor insurers (including Lloyd's) provide a fund for compensating the victims of road incidents caused by uninsured or untraced drivers. It is not usual to name the MIB as defendant unless a ruling on the construction of the agreement itself is sought.

5.5.1 The First MIB (Compensation of Victims of Uninsured Drivers) Agreement 1988

This Agreement requires the MIB to meet unsatisfied judgments against identified drivers who were not insured. The Agreement was first entered into in 1946, but was replaced in 1988 to reflect changes to compulsory insurance requirements brought about by the Road Traffic Act 1988, which requires that the user of a motor vehicle on a road must insure the vehicle against legal liability to third parties in respect of both bodily injury and property damage. The Agreement therefore covers damage to motor vehicles as well as walls, fences, gates and other roadside property damaged by uninsured motorists. **This Agreement has itself been replaced by an up-to-date First MIB Agreement for accidents that occur on or after 1 October 1999** (see **5.5.2**).

(1) The claimant should sue the driver and take proceedings up to and including entering judgment.
(2) Within 7 days after commencement of proceedings, notice in writing must be given to the MIB. Notice periods for the MIB and for the Road Traffic Act 1988, s 152 notice are different. A notice previously given by the claimant if given at the same time as the s 152 notice (see above) will not count unless given within 7 days after commencement of proceedings. The s 152 notice can safely be given with the letter of claim as the notice can be given before or within 7 days after commencement of proceedings. The MIB will, however, rely strictly on the time-limit and will apply to strike out the claim if notice is not given within the time-limit. See *Silverton v Goodall and MIB* (1997) PIQR P451, CA.
(3) The notice must be accompanied by official evidence of instigation of proceedings.
(4) If judgment remains unpaid after 7 days, the MIB will pay. In the case of bodily injury, there is no financial limit on the level of compensation. In the case of property damage the first £175 claimed is excluded and there is an upper limit of £250,000.
(5) In addition to damages, the MIB will also pay any sum awarded by the court in respect of taxed costs or any costs awarded without taxation.
(6) It is a condition of payment that the judgment is assigned to the MIB so that it can pursue the uninsured driver to recoup the payment if it wishes.
(7) The Agreement applies whether the driver is a British resident or a foreign visitor.
(8) The MIB's liability arises only when the claimant has successfully established his case against the driver in the usual way and judgment has been given in his favour.

Exceptions

The Agreement does not extend to:

(1) vehicles owned by the Crown;
(2) vehicles that are not required to be insured;
(3) judgments obtained by exercise of a right of subrogation (as the victim has already been compensated);
(4) claims for damage to vehicles which themselves were not insured and the claimant knew or ought to have known that this was the case;
(5) claims for injury or death or damage to property of a passenger who:

(a) knew or ought to have known that the vehicle was stolen or unlawfully taken; or

(b) knew or ought to have known that the vehicle was being driven without insurance.

However, exception (5) will apply only if the owner of the vehicle or the person using it (ie the driver) was at fault, ie incurred liability in respect of the compulsory risks and had judgment entered against him.

5.5.2 The new MIB (Compensation of Victims of Uninsured Drivers) Agreement 1999

This Agreement came into force on 1 October 1999 and replaces the First MIB Agreement in relation to accidents occurring on or after that date. The First MIB Agreement will therefore continue to be of significance for a number of years to come as claims relating to accidents which pre-date October 1999 are made.

5.5.3 Procedure under the new Agreement

The new Agreement sets out a far more complicated set of procedural steps than was required by the previous Agreement that it replaces. A summary of those steps is set out below, however, recourse should be had to a copy of the new Agreement itself as only the basic provisions are introduced below.

5.5.4 Notice to MIB

Claims should be made by completing the MIB's own application form. This should be completed and returned to the MIB or their nominated solicitors together with documents in support (as to which see below). The application form is currently available only from the MIB. It is important to note that the application must be signed by the claimant or his solicitor. If this is not complied with the MIB can refuse to accept the application.

(i) Notice of proceedings

The following notice provisions are at the heart of the new Agreement and are far more complex than those in the previous Agreement it replaces. The claimant must give the MIB notice in writing that he has commenced proceedings. This notice together with the completed application form and documents in support must be received by the MIB no later than 14 days after commencement of proceedings.

(ii) Service of notice

The notice and supporting documentation must be served either by facsimile transmission or by Registered or Recorded Delivery post to the MIB's registered office. Service by ordinary post and Document Exchange is not allowed. Service by facsimile is the preferred method.

(iii) Supporting documentation

The application must be supported by the following documents:

(a) notice in writing that proceedings have been commenced by Claim Form or other means;

(b) a copy of the sealed Claim Form or other document evidencing commencement;
(c) a copy of any relevant insurance policy;
(d) copies of all relevant correspondence in the possession of the claimant or his solicitor;
(e) a copy of any particulars of claim;
(f) a copy of all other documents required by the rules of procedure to be served on the defendant; and
(g) such other information relevant to the proceedings as the MIB may reasonably specify.

(iv) Requirements after the accident and prior to issue of proceedings – RTA 1988, s 154

Clause 13 of the new Agreement places a requirement on all would-be claimants to make full and timely use of their rights under s 154 of the RTA 1988. Clause 13 puts the onus on the claimant to ensure that he has as soon as reasonably practicable:

- demanded the particulars specified in s 154, and if the person fails to give the information;
- complained to a police officer in respect of this failure to give details following an accident; and
- used all reasonable endeavours to obtain the name, address and registered keeper of the vehicle.

(v) Notice requirements on service of proceedings

If proceedings are commenced, the claimant must inform the MIB of the date of service:

(a) if service is effected by the court, notice must be given within 7 days after the date that the claimant receives notice from the court or the defendant that service of the Claim Form has occurred; or
(b) if service is effected personally, notice must be given 7 days from the date of personal service; or
(c) if recourse to deemed service is appropriate, 7 days after the date when service is deemed to have occurred in accordance with the CPR 1998.

(vi) Notice requirements after service of proceedings

There are further notice requirements post service of proceedings which require notification to the MIB in writing within 7 days of the occurrence of any of the following:

(a) filing of a defence;
(b) amendment of particulars of claim;
(c) setting down for trial;
(d) notification of trial date received.

In the event that the claimant intends to enter judgment the claimant must, not less than 35 days before applying for judgment, give notice in writing to the MIB of their intention so to do.

Because of the onerous nature of the notice requirements, some commentators advocate joining the MIB as second defendants at the outset of proceedings. Once they are a party to the proceedings, the claimant's solicitor can then seek written confirmation from them that they will waive reliance on the further notice provisions.

(vii) Prosecution of proceedings and judgment

The claimant must take all reasonable steps to obtain judgment against every person who may be liable (including any person who may be vicariously liable). The obligation of the MIB to pay normally arises only if a judgment is not satisfied within 7 days after the claimant became entitled to enforce it.

However, the MIB is not obliged to satisfy a judgment unless the claimant has in return assigned the benefit of the unsatisfied judgment to the MIB or its nominee.

5.5.5 The Second MIB (Compensation of Victims of Untraced Drivers) Agreement

This Agreement requires the MIB to consider applications for compensation from victims of 'hit and run' cases where the owner or driver cannot be traced. The decision of the MIB can be appealed.

(1) This Agreement covers bodily injury or death only and not claims for property damage.
(2) Application must be made in writing within 3 years of the date of the accident (this includes claims by minors).
(3) The MIB will investigate the claim and may require the applicant to make a statutory declaration setting out the facts in support of the claim.
(4) If the applicant wishes to appeal against the decision he must notify the MIB of this within 6 weeks of being informed of its decision.
(5) There must be proof that the untraced driver was negligent.
(6) The death or injury must not have been caused deliberately by the untraced driver.
(7) The award made by the MIB is made in the same way as a court would assess damages payable by the untraced person if the applicant had been able to bring a successful claim against him.
(8) In cases where an untraced person and an identified person are both partly responsible, the MIB will make a contribution in respect of the responsibility of the untraced person.
(9) The MIB is not obliged to pay the claimant's costs. In practice, it will pay a standard fee plus certain disbursements.
(10) The MIB is not obliged to include an element of interest to an award. However, if the bureau has made an award which is subsequently deemed inappropriate by an arbitrator on the grounds that the amount is too small, interest may be awarded for the period between the date of the bureau's decision and the date of the arbitrator's decision. Further interest may be awarded where an arbitrator finds that the bureau has not acted with reasonable expedition, interest may be awarded from the time at which the sum ought to have been paid to the date of the actual award (see *Evans v Motor Insurers' Bureau* (1997) *The Times*, November 10).

Exceptions

The Agreement does not cover:

(1) cases where the death or injury is the result of a deliberate attempt to run the person down;
(2) Crown vehicles;
(3) cases where the applicant allowed himself to be carried in a vehicle when he knew or should have known that the vehicle had been taken without consent, unless:

   (a) he believed that he had authority to be carried or that he would have had the owner's consent if he knew of the circumstances; or
   (b) he learned of the circumstances of the taking of the vehicle after the journey commenced;

(4) cases where the owner or user of the vehicle was using or permitting use knowing that there was no insurance policy in force.

5.6 ACQUIRING EVIDENCE

5.6.1 Expert evidence

The majority of cases will involve some expert evidence. This area is dealt with fully in Chapter 8.

5.6.2 Proofing witnesses

Witnesses should be contacted and interviewed as soon after the incident as possible. If the witness is not interviewed at an early stage his memory of the events may fade or he may be untraceable. In the case of an accident at work, if the witness is a fellow employee of the client he may be concerned about his employer's reaction, and may therefore have second thoughts about making a statement. Witnesses to road incidents are often initially enthusiastic, but later decide that they have little to gain and would rather not get involved. For this reason, a proof or at least a letter in reply from the witness should be obtained from the witness confirming what he saw and/or heard and that he is prepared to make a statement to that effect.

In a straightforward case, it may not be necessary to interview the witness. If his letter of response is sufficiently clear, a proof can be prepared from it and from any questionnaire he may also have been sent. A copy of the proof should be forwarded for approval and signature by the witness. This should be accompanied by a stamped addressed envelope and covering letter requesting the witness to read the proof carefully, and make any amendments or additions that he feels to be necessary before signing and dating the document for return in the envelope provided. The witness is a volunteer to the client's cause and should be thanked accordingly for the time and trouble he has taken on the client's behalf.

Having prepared a full proof of evidence from each witness at this early stage, it will not be necessary to incur the expense of preparing witness statements for disclosure if the witness evidence is irrelevant, or simply repeats what other more reliable witnesses say.

If it becomes necessary to have a formal statement drawn up for the witness, it should be checked, signed and dated by the witness. This statement will form the basis of the witness's evidence to be relied on at trial and will stand as his evidence-in-chief. The statement must conclude with a declaration of truth incorporated as the last paragraph of the statement.

Furthermore, the statement may have to be used at the trial under the Civil Evidence Act 1995 if the witness subsequently becomes unavailable. It should therefore be the best statement that the witness can produce and should deal fully with any points of evidence that only this witness would be able to state.

5.6.3 Other statements

It may be advisable for the solicitor to obtain statements from other persons, such as shop stewards or co-workers who, although they may not have seen the accident, may know of other similar accidents in the past or be able to give background information on policy changes that may have taken place within the organisation. In road incident or tripping cases, people living or working adjacent to the area of the incident may be able to give useful information relating to similar incidents that have happened in the past and even the identities of past claimants in similar incidents.

5.6.4 Employment details

The client's loss of earnings is likely to form a significant part of his claim for special damages, but may be difficult to calculate if the client is self-employed or his earnings fluctuate for some other reason. See Chapter 13 for a detailed consideration of this point.

Obtaining details from employers

A letter to the client's employer should ask for details of earnings for 13 weeks prior to the incident and for a copy of the client's contract of employment so that the solicitor can check whether sick pay has been paid by the employer and whether it is recoverable in the event of the client recovering damages. The loss of earnings details should be set out to show weekly earnings both gross and net so as to reveal a pattern over 13 weeks.

Self-employed clients

Documentary evidence in the form of the previous year's trading accounts (or longer if appropriate) of the client should be obtained if possible, together with other evidence of contracts or offers of work that had to be turned down as a result of the incident. The client's accountant, business associates and colleagues in the same area of work should be approached to assist in this.

Unemployed clients

Even if the client is unemployed, evidence should be obtained of his last employer and of the likelihood of his obtaining suitable work which he could have undertaken but for the accident, as evidence of earning capacity. Colleagues in the same area of business and employment agencies should be approached for evidence of availability of work within the client's specialism and the level of possible earnings.

5.6.5 Obtaining a police accident report

In the case of a road traffic incident, a police accident report (PAR) should be obtained, if it exists. The following should be borne in mind.

(1) The solicitor should contact the accident records department at the police force headquarters for the area concerned (not the policeman assigned to the case). The letter should be addressed to the Chief Superintendent of the area in which the incident occurred and should include details of the date, time and place of accident, registration numbers of vehicles and full names of those involved.

(2) The PAR will contain statements from the parties, witness statements, a sketch plan, comments on condition of the vehicles, the road surface and weather conditions.

(3) The PAR will not be released until the conclusion of any criminal investigation and proceedings.

(4) A fee (which is reviewed periodically) is payable for the PAR. The Association of Chief Police Officers' Traffic Committee recommended fee is £50 per report, and £84 for interviews with police officers. The solicitor should ensure that funds are available to cover this. In the case of advice under the legal advice and assistance scheme, an extension should be obtained.

(5) In addition to the usual documents contained in the PAR, the police, particularly in the case of accidents which have led to serious injury or death, may have taken photographs, copies of which are usually obtainable on payment of a further fee.

(6) Again, on payment of a further fee, the police officer who prepared the PAR may be interviewed, and will be accompanied by a senior officer. Police officers will give evidence in civil proceedings, but must be witness summonsed.

(7) If there is no PAR, it is still possible to obtain copies of police notebooks and witness statements on payment of a fee. Because reports may be destroyed (in some cases after as little as one year) a request for a report should be made promptly, notwithstanding that the report will not actually be released until the conclusion of criminal investigations.

5.6.6 Obtaining a Health & Safety Executive report

HSE reports are the equivalent of police reports in the field of industrial incidents. Generally, the same rules apply as with police reports, although, because of lack of resources, in practice it may be that in certain areas it is unlikely that an HSE report will be available except in the case of very serious injury or death.

The HSE officer responsible for the factory or work-place concerned should be approached with a request for a copy of his report. As with the PAR, the HSE report will not be available until after any criminal prosecution has been dealt with. If the HSE is unwilling to provide a copy of its report voluntarily, it may be necessary to wait until after proceedings have been commenced and then make an application for non-party disclosure.

Employers are required to report certain classes of injury or disease sustained by people at work, and specified dangerous occurrences. The regulations are contained in the Reporting of Injuries, Diseases and Dangerous Occurrences Regulations 1995 (RIDDOR 1995), SI 1995/3163. RIDDOR 1995 require the responsible person (ie safety officer/manager) to inform HSE as soon as possible of the incident and follow it up with written confirmation within 10 days.

The reportable occurrences are:

(a) death of any person;
(b) any person suffering a specified major injury;
(c) any person not at work due to an injury resulting in evacuation of the person to a hospital for treatment;
(d) any person not at work due to an injury sustained due to working at a hospital;
(e) where there has been a dangerous occurrence. Dangerous occurrences are listed in Sch 2 to RIDDOR 1995 and include such things as dangerous occurrences involving overhead electric lines, biological agents and radiation generators, as well as occurrences in mines, at quarries, on the railways and at off-shore installations.

Documents to request from the HSE are:

– Form 2508 employer's report of a dangerous occurrence;
– Form 2508A report of a case of disease;
– Form 2508G report of a gas incident;
– Form 155 factory inspector's report;
– Form 142 health and safety inspector's report.

5.6.7 The accident book

An accident book must be kept by employers with premises to which the Factories Act 1961 applies, and premises where 10 or more persons are employed in trade or business. A copy of the relevant page of the accident book should be obtained, and consideration should be given to inspecting the book itself for evidence of similar incidents in the past.

5.6.8 Criminal prosecutions

If the proposed defendant is to be prosecuted, ideally the claimant's solicitor should attend the proceedings to note the evidence. The date of the proceedings may be obtained from the police or the HSE as appropriate.

Any resulting conviction of the defendant which is relevant to the issues in civil proceedings may be referred to in the civil proceedings.

5.6.9 Coroner's inquests

In certain circumstances, the coroner for the district will hold an inquest. The purpose of the inquest is not to determine civil or criminal liability of any particular person, but instead to determine how the death occurred and to ascertain the identity of the deceased. However, the inquest provides a valuable opportunity to gauge the strength of the evidence and observe a witness giving evidence. Inquests are dealt with in detail in Chapter 14.

5.7 EARLY ACCESS TO DOCUMENTS AND OTHER ITEMS

If documents or other items are in the possession of the client, clearly the solicitor will have no trouble obtaining access to those items. The same is true if the item is in the public domain, such as the scene of a road traffic incident on a public road.

5.7.1 Pre-action disclosure and inspection

An application for pre-action disclosure is governed in the High Court by the Supreme Court Act 1981, s 33(2); and in the county court by the County Courts Act 1984, s 52(2) and made under Part 35.16 of the Civil Procedure Rules 1998 (CPR 1998). This area is dealt with in detail in Chapter 9.

It may be necessary for the client's solicitor or other advisers to gain access to information which is held only by the defendant. If the solicitor is unable to advise his client as to whether or not he has a claim without this information, a claim for pre-action disclosure and/or inspection is appropriate. This is most likely to be necessary in cases alleging clinical negligence where the health authority or trust which will be the defendant holds the client's medical notes to which the solicitor needs access before he can instruct an expert to make any judgement on the suitability of the treatment received.

5.8 OBTAINING MEDICAL RECORDS IN CLINICAL NEGLIGENCE CLAIMS

5.8.1 Request for explanation and invitation to admit liability

Following *Naylor v Preston Area Health Authority* [1987] 1 WLR 958, claimants have been encouraged to request an explanation from the potential defendant. The advantage of this is that an early investigation may result in a prompt settlement in cases where liability is unlikely to be in issue, and this may save the necessity of issuing proceedings. The claimant's solicitor should be wary, however, of agreeing not to issue proceedings in order to see if a settlement can be reached, with the result that the matter then falls outside the limitation period. An explanation will also give an early indication of how the defendant views the case, which can then be considered with the claimant's expert. This letter often fills the role of the letter of claim in a personal injury claim, as it is the first intimation that the health authority/trust/doctor receives that there is a potential problem, and may invite an admission of liability.

5.8.2 Obtaining records

It is necessary to obtain a copy of the client's records from the general practitioner and from the hospital where he was treated to build up a full picture of the client's health records prior to the incident and of the treatment which he has received subsequently. The general practitioner's records will show a detailed record of all treatments, referrals to hospital, reports back from hospital doctors and referrals to other professionals such as occupational therapists, physiotherapists or community nurses. The hospital records will show details of the client's admission, his consents to treatment, nursing records and comments made by the doctors who were treating him. The Law Society has produced a Protocol for obtaining hospital medical records which recommends the use of standard forms (set out at Appendix 3) when making an application for hospital records. The solicitor who is requesting the records would normally be expected to give an undertaking to be responsible for the reasonable charges incurred in supplying copies of the records to him (see below).

Until all records have been traced and disclosed, the solicitor will not be in a position to instruct an expert to review the evidence (ie the notes) and form a view on liability/causation. Permission of the court is likely to be necessary prior to instruction of experts under the CPR 1998. Early and full disclosure is the key to successful clinical negligence litigation as, until this has been complied with, both solicitor and client are essentially in the dark as regards what actually happened.

5.8.3 Client's authority

The solicitor must obtain from his client a signed authority permitting the solicitor to make an application to the relevant doctor(s)/hospital for copies of the client's records. There is no standard form for this authority, and a short letter addressed to the solicitor and signed by the client will suffice.

5.8.4 Data Protection Act 1998

The Data Protection Act 1998 (DPA 1998) came into force on 1 March 2000. The Act gives the right to living individuals to access their health records. The Act allows individuals to gain access to personal data of which they are the subject, and therefore talks in terms of 'subject access'. A 'health record' is defined in the Act in s 68(2) as any record which:

(a) consists of information relevant to the physical or mental health or condition of an individual; and
(b) has been made by or on behalf of a health professional in connection with the care of that individual.

Both written records and also other types of records such as x-rays and scans will therefore come within the definition.

Section 7 of DPA 1998 provides that, subject to certain provisions, an individual is entitled to have communicated to him in an intelligible form information constituting any personal data of which that individual is the data subject.

Obtaining access to health records

Access to information is governed by s 7 of DPA 1998. A written request should be made to the 'data controller' (a personal body who decides the purpose for which data is being processed). It is likely to be doctors' surgeries, health authorities and NHS Trusts. The request should contain enough information to allow the data controller to identify the data subject (the individual) and to locate the information requested.

By s 8(2), the information must be conveyed by supplying a copy of it in permanent form unless either:

(a) that is not possible or would involve disproportionate effort; or
(b) the data subject agrees otherwise.

By s 7(2) a data controller is not obliged to supply any information unless he has received a request in writing and such a fee (not exceeding the prescribed maximum) as he may require. The maximum fee is prescribed in reg 6 of the Data Protection (Subject Access) (Fees and Miscellaneous Provisions) Regulations 2000, SI 2000/191.

'Personal data' is defined in s 1(1) as data which relates to a living individual.

In *Hubble v Peterborough Hospital NHS Trust* (2001) unreported, 16 March, it was held that an x-ray was an image and constituted a visual record of the state of a person's body at the particular time when it was recorded. It therefore did include information about an individual's physical health or condition and was therefore an accessible record for the purpose of s 68. The court found that information contained in and recorded by virtue of an x-ray was readily communicated in an 'intelligible' form as was required by s 7(1)(c)(i). X-rays were clearly information and clearly part of a health record and if Parliament had intended to exclude x-rays from the 1998 Act, this intention would have been made clear.

Fees for access

The maximum fee of £10 may be charged for granting access to health records that are automatically produced or are recorded with the intention that they be so processed.

The maximum fee of £50 may be charged for granting access to manual records or a mixture of manual and/or automated records where the request for access will be granted by supplying a copy of the information in permanent form. This provision relates to requests up to 24 October 2001. After that date, the maximum of £10 may be charged.

No fee is chargeable where the individual requests access to merely inspect their health records. This provision relates to requests for access to non-automated records where some of the records were made after the beginning of the period of 40 days immediately preceding the date of the request. This provision allows individuals access to recently created health records without charge.

Human Rights Act 1998

It is likely that the Human Rights Act 1998 may be used to encourage health authorities to interpret DPA 1998 liberally (see *Hubble v Peterborough NHS Trust* above).

The meaning of 'health professionals'

Section 69 of DPA 1998 sets out an exhaustive list of health professionals. Most of those listed will be employed within the NHS, such as registered medical practitioners, registered dentists, registered opticians, registered nurses and registered osteopaths. However, the list does not include alternative practitioners.

Correction of health records

Sections 12A and 14 of DPA 1998 allow individuals to request the correction of 'inaccurate' data defined in s 70(2) as 'incorrect or misleading as to a matter or fact'. The court can order the data controller to rectify, erase or destroy such data.

Unlike its predecessor (the Access to Health Records Act 1990), DPA 1998 is of retrospective effect. Subject to transitional provisions, it allows access to health records created before the Act was passed.

Access to health records of deceased individuals

The Access to Health Records Act 1990 continues to govern access to health records which relate to the physical or mental health of individuals who are now deceased. Access may only be requested by a personal representative or a person who may have a claim arising out of the death. A written request should be dealt with, within 40 days from the date of the request, or within 21 days if the record has been added to within 40 days preceding receipt of the written request.

5.8.5 Medical notes

Where the solicitor requires medical notes, he should ensure that he obtains all the notes, not just those which are supplied and marked relevant to the matter in hand. It is important to obtain the full set with a background history and disclosure should not be limited merely to the accident or the incident itself. In *Wickham v Dwyer* (1995) *Current Law Weekly*, 1 January, the court held that it was for the expert to determine whether or not there was any information of any irrelevance contained within the notes and, therefore, it was fair to allow the solicitors and experts access to the full notes.

5.8.6 Receipt of medical records

The following lists summarise the type of information the solicitor might expect to be supplied to him in response to a request for records or notes. The exact contents of the records or notes will vary from case to case, and the following lists are not exhaustive but are intended as a general guideline to the type of information which the solicitor can expect to receive.

Hospital records

(1) *Admission details/record sheet.* These should give the date and the time of admission, the record number, the name of the ward and the name of the consultant in charge of the case.
(2) *In-patient notes.* These include casualty notes (where appropriate), personal details of the patient, a detailed history of the patient and of the initial examination, daily progress and record notes, discharge notes, a copy of the letter to the GP giving details of the patient's treatment and general report to the GP.
(3) *Nursing records.* Nursing records are detailed notes made by nursing staff including temperature charts, vital signs, test results, results of all investigations carried out, and details of drugs prescribed and taken.
(4) *Letters of referral.* These include referrals from GPs, responses to GPs following consultation or complaint of a missed appointment and comments on the patient's demeanour and attitude.
(5) *Records of X-rays.* These include other films taken. Copies of the X-rays and films themselves are not supplied automatically (only the record of the fact that the X-ray was carried out) and copies of the films will have to be obtained separately.
(6) *Anaesthetic details.* These are details of the examination of the patient prior to an operation, a record of the drugs administered during pre-med and during the operation itself.

(7) *Patient consent forms*. These forms show what treatments the patient consented to have performed on him.
(8) *Internal inquiry reports*. Where an internal inquiry has been held and the dominant purpose of that inquiry was not in contemplation of litigation, the inquiry notes will be discoverable.
(9) *Obstetric cases*. The following documents should also be supplied:

   (a) progress of labour cards;
   (b) cardiotachograph (CTG) traces showing foetal heart rates and mother's contractions;
   (c) partogram (showing labour in chart form);
   (d) ante-natal records;
   (e) neo-natal records;
   (f) paediatric notes.

General practitioner notes

General practitioner notes are usually supplied in a cardboard FP5 envelope, with the patient's name, National Insurance number and date of his registration with the named doctor written on the outside. The records are usually contained on FP7 record cards and will include the doctor's notes. Additionally, the envelope may contain reports of investigations requested by the doctor, letters of referral to hospital or consultants, the hospital or consultant's responses, letters from the hospital including out-patient clinic attendances and treatment and in-patient discharge summaries. A request should be made to the GP to preserve his original records so that they are not inadvertently destroyed or microfiched before the trial.

5.8.7 Examining the records

The solicitor should ensure (as far as possible) that the notes or records supplied to him are complete and are in date order (beginning with the earliest in time), which will show the pattern of the disease or problem and its treatment and may also highlight missing documents or records. Missing documentation should be requested since an incomplete set of records may distort the overall picture and thus give a false impression of the client's claim. Badly copied or illegible documents should be noted and a further request for clear copies made. It may be advisable to make an appointment with the GP or hospital to inspect the original documents at this stage, which will confirm whether a document is really missing and/or whether a document contains a minor clerical error. It is also helpful for the solicitor to go through the records with the client to ensure that the treatment shown on the records accords with the client's recollection of what actually occurred. The records should be supplied to the solicitor and not direct to the expert so that the solicitor has an opportunity to check them through before instructing the expert to prepare his report.

5.9 CONCLUSION

The essential element when gathering evidence at the preliminary stage is to act quickly. A failure to act on the client's instructions as soon as they are received can have disastrous consequences for the subsequent conduct of the litigation. In extreme cases this can seriously prejudice the client's chances of success, and can amount to negligence on the part of the solicitor.

5.10 FURTHER READING

Hendy, Day, Buchan and Kennedy *Personal Injury Practice* 3rd edn (Butterworths).

5.11 OVERVIEW OF INITIAL LIABILITY INVESTIGATIONS

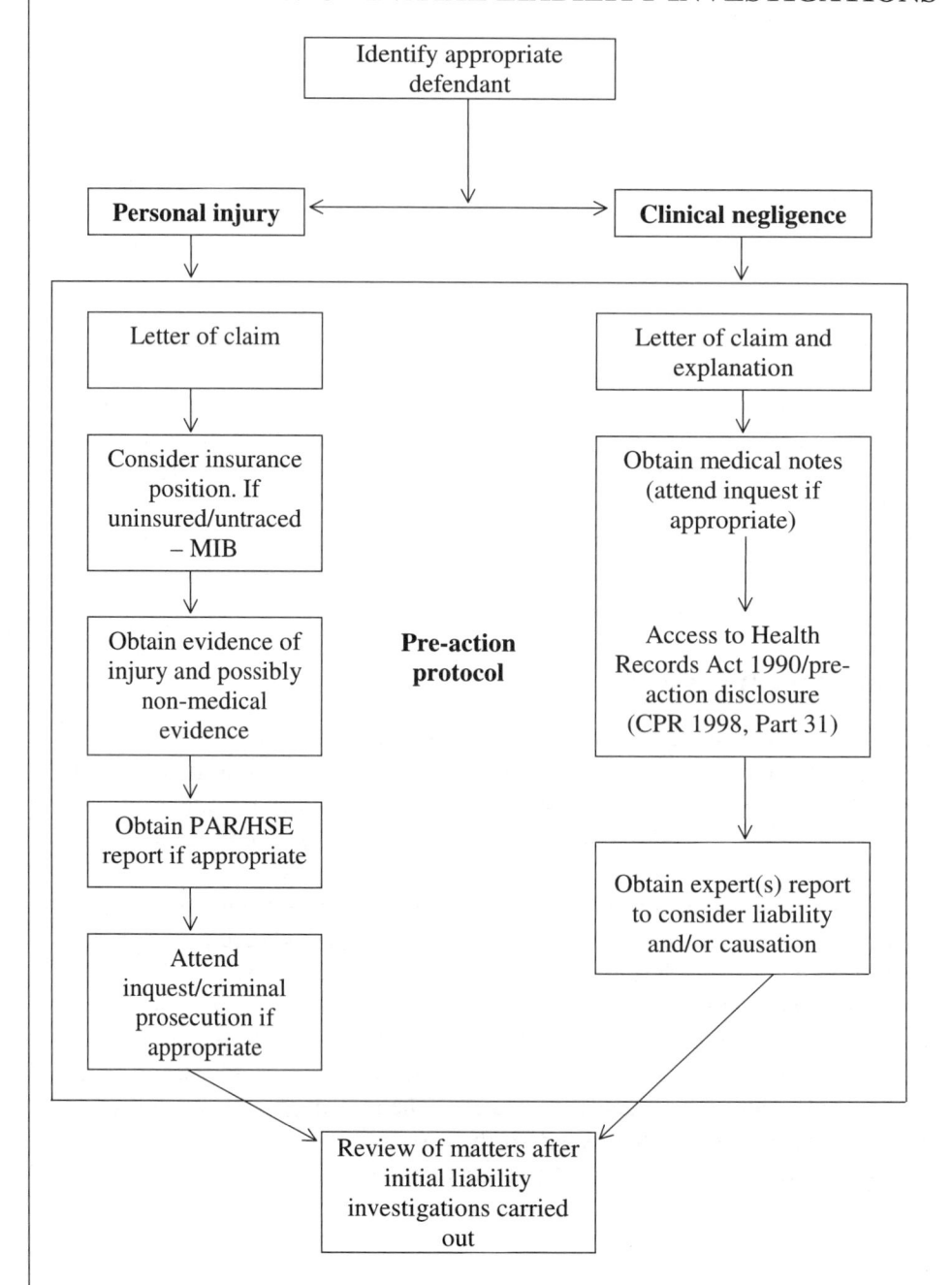

```
                    ┌──────────────────────┐
                    │ Identify appropriate │
                    │      defendant       │
                    └──────────┬───────────┘
                               │
         ┌─────────────────┐   ▼   ┌──────────────────┐
         │ Personal injury │◄─────►│Clinical negligence│
         └────────┬────────┘       └─────────┬────────┘
                  ▼                          ▼
         ┌─────────────────┐       ┌──────────────────┐
         │ Letter of claim │       │Letter of claim and│
         │                 │       │    explanation    │
         └────────┬────────┘       └─────────┬────────┘
                  ▼                          ▼
         ┌─────────────────┐       ┌──────────────────┐
         │Consider insurance│      │ Obtain medical   │
         │ position. If    │       │ notes (attend    │
         │uninsured/untraced│      │ inquest if       │
         │     – MIB       │       │ appropriate)     │
         └────────┬────────┘       └─────────┬────────┘
                  ▼    Pre-action            ▼
         ┌─────────────────┐ protocol ┌──────────────────┐
         │ Obtain evidence │       │ Access to Health │
         │injury and possibly│     │ Records Act 1990/pre-│
         │ non-medical     │       │ action disclosure│
         │   evidence      │       │ (CPR 1998, Part 31)│
         └────────┬────────┘       └─────────┬────────┘
                  ▼                          ▼
         ┌─────────────────┐       ┌──────────────────┐
         │ Obtain PAR/HSE  │       │Obtain expert(s) report│
         │report if appropriate│   │ to consider liability │
         └────────┬────────┘       │  and/or causation  │
                  ▼                └─────────┬────────┘
         ┌─────────────────┐                 │
         │     Attend      │                 │
         │inquest/criminal │                 │
         │ prosecution if  │                 │
         │   appropriate   │                 │
         └────────┬────────┘                 │
                  └──────────┐   ┌───────────┘
                             ▼   ▼
                    ┌──────────────────────┐
                    │ Review of matters after│
                    │    initial liability  │
                    │ investigations carried│
                    │         out          │
                    └──────────────────────┘
```

Chapter 6

LIMITATION OF ACTIONS

6.1 INTRODUCTION

The limitation period for actions can be a difficult area for the unwary, and the large number of negligence claims against solicitors who have allowed their clients' claims to expire by failing to issue proceedings within the limitation period is testament to this. Consequently, one of the first priorities for the claimant solicitor will be to identify when the limitation period ends and, having established this, to mark the file with that date, and enter it into the diary system.

The principal statute dealing with limitation issues is the Limitation Act 1980.

For the purpose of limitation in a personal injury claim, 'personal injury' includes any disease and any impairment of a person's physical or mental condition (s 38).

Chapter 6 contents
Introduction
The limitation period
Date of knowledge
Claims in fatal accidents
Persons under disability
The court's discretion to override the limitation period
Special periods of limitation
Avoiding limitation problems
Conclusion
Further reading

6.2 THE LIMITATION PERIOD

Under ss 11 and 12 of the Limitation Act 1980 (LA 1980), where a claimant claims damages either for negligence, nuisance or breach of duty, and that claim consists of or includes a claim for personal injuries, the claimant must normally commence his action within 3 years from:

(1) the date on which the cause of action accrued; or
(2) the date of knowledge (if later) of the person injured (s 11(4)).

When calculating the 3-year period (generally referred to as the 'primary' limitation period), the day on which the cause of action accrued is excluded (s 2). Therefore, in a simple road incident case, generally the claimant has 3 years from the incident (excluding the date of the incident) in which to commence the action. However, in more complex claims, the claimant may seek to rely on a subsequent date of knowledge, which may enable him to commence the action more than 3 years after the event complained of.

6.3 DATE OF KNOWLEDGE

6.3.1 Section 14 of the Limitation Act 1980

Section 14 of LA 1980 defines 'date of knowledge' for the purpose of ss 11 and 12 as the date on which the claimant first had knowledge of all of the following factors:

(1) that the injury was significant; and
(2) that the injury was attributable in whole or in part to the act or omission which is alleged to constitute negligence, nuisance or breach of duty; and
(3) the identity of the defendant; and

(4) if it is alleged that the act or omission was that of a person other than the defendant, the identity of that person and the additional facts supporting the bringing of an action against the defendant.

In *Nash v Eli Lilly* [1993] 1 WLR 782, CA, a number of patients who had taken the drug Opren brought actions against the pharmaceutical company. The Court of Appeal considered the meaning of 'knowledge' in s 14, and decided that a claimant had knowledge when he knew enough of the various matters specified in LA 1980 to justify taking legal advice. As regards the significance of the injury, the court held that the claimant must know of the act or omission to which the injury was attributable and, once he believed his symptoms were due to Opren, that was sufficient in terms of the 'act or omission'. Accordingly, the court refused to exercise the discretion to extend the limitation period.

According to s 14(2), an injury is significant if the person whose date of knowledge is in question would reasonably have considered it sufficiently serious to justify instituting proceedings against a defendant who did not dispute liability and was able to satisfy a judgment. In *Halford v Brookes* [1991] 3 All ER 559, it was stated that knowledge does not mean 'know for certain and beyond the possibility of contradiction' but meant 'know with sufficient confidence to justify embarking on the preliminaries to issue of proceedings, such as submitting a claim to the proposed defendant, taking legal advice and other advice and collecting evidence'. For example, a claimant may work in an environment which exposes him to excessive and injurious dust particles such as asbestos dust or coal dust. It may be many years before an injury deemed 'significant' manifests itself, and it may be some time later before the claimant realises what the cause of his illness is. Similarly, in a clinical negligence context, a patient may be fully aware of his pain and suffering, but assume that it is entirely due to an underlying illness, rather than caused by the negligence of a doctor (see *James v East Dorset HA* (1999) *The Times*, December 7).

In *Dobbie v Medway Health Authority* [1994] 1 WLR 1234, CA, Mrs Dobbie had surgery to remove a lump in her breast. It was only during the operation that the surgeon took the decision to perform a mastectomy (removal of the breast), as he believed the breast was cancerous. In fact, the lump was not cancerous and the mastectomy had not been necessary. Mrs Dobbie accepted at the time that the surgeon had acted reasonably and it was her good fortune that the lump was not cancerous. Some years later when she heard about a similar case, Mrs Dobbie took advice from a solicitor. It was argued that in this case the court ought to exercise its discretion because Mrs Dobbie had not been aware that anything had gone wrong, as she did not have sufficient knowledge that she had suffered an injury, but the application failed.

In *Forbes v Wandsworth Health Authority* [1997] QB 402, the Court of Appeal held by a majority that the claimant was deemed to have constructive knowledge as soon as he had time to overcome the shock of the injury, take stock of his disability and seek advice. The facts of the case were that the claimant, who suffered from poor circulation, underwent surgery for a by-pass operation; this was not a success and a further by-pass was performed the next day. Unfortunately, the second operation was too late to be successful and the claimant was told that it was necessary to amputate his leg to prevent gangrene, to which he agreed. The sole allegation was that the authority had been negligent not to perform the second operation sooner. The claimant did not seek advice until 7 years after the limitation period had expired. The court found that the amputation was a significant injury, but had to decide whether it could be attributed to some act or omission which constituted negligence. Having found that the claimant did have constructive knowledge, the court went on to decide whether to exercise its discretion under s 33 of LA 1980. The court took into account prejudice to the defendant in that insurance arrangements and medical standards had changed and medical records were missing. The court also considered the merits of the case. It was noted that the claimant was legally aided, that there was a substantial burden on the defendants and every likelihood that the claim would fail. The court therefore declined to exercise its discretion.

However, in *Penney v British Steel* (1997) unreported, 1 July, in a refinement to the objective test for constructive knowledge used in *Forbes*, the court held that the claimant had taken all reasonable steps to acquire the necessary knowledge, and, although he had known for 15 years that he had significant health problems, it was not reasonable for him to disregard his GP's view and insist on a consultation with an expert, as his GP had diagnosed his condition as not linked to any negligent act or omission.

According to *Roberts v Winslow* (1999) *The Times*, January 12 (a clinical negligence case), the date from which the claimant knows that the lesser part of his injuries is attributable to the defendant is the date when time starts to run for limitation purposes, not the date when he later discovers that the greater part of his injuries are attributable to the defendant.

In relation to the method of apportionment of damage where the court finds that the relevant date of knowledge actually occurs part way through the period when the damage is being done, see *Allen v British Rail Engineering Ltd* [2001] EWCA Civ 242, (2001) LTL, 23 February. In this case, the claimant suffered vibration white finger (VWF) injuries due to work with vibrating tools. The defendants contended that the state of knowledge as to the danger from such tools changed during the time the claimant was employed. Because of this, the defendants argued they were negligent only after they had knowledge of the problem but failed to advise the claimant of the problems and that the damage was already done by then in any event. The court decide it had to do its best to decide the correct level of apportionment and should not deny the claimant a remedy if it could not establish the proportion with accuracy. The judge was correct to try to decide how much damage was due to the defendants' negligence. Even though the figure would not be precisely accurate, that was preferable to awarding the claimant nothing because he failed to establish exactly the amount of damage that was attributable to the negligence.

6.3.2 Constructive knowledge

The claimant is expected to gain constructive knowledge by making reasonable enquiries. Under s 14(3) of LA 1980, a person's knowledge includes knowledge which he might reasonably have been expected to acquire:

(1) from facts observable or ascertainable by him; or
(2) from facts ascertainable by him with the help of medical or other appropriate expert advice which it is reasonable for him to seek,

but he shall not be fixed with knowledge of a fact ascertainable only with the help of expert advice as long as he has taken all reasonable steps to obtain (and, where appropriate, to act on) that advice.

In the example at **6.3.1**, the claimant's own doctor and his trade union representative (if any) may be people from whom he ought to seek advice.

When trying to establish the claimant's date of knowledge for the purposes of s 14(1)(b) of LA 1980, the court found, in *Spargo v North Essex District Health Authority* [1997] 8 Med LR 125, that to establish the date of knowledge, a subjective test was to be applied, ie 'what did the claimant know?' and not 'what would a reasonable layman realise?' The facts of the case were that the claimant had been diagnosed as suffering from selective brain damage and was compulsorily detained in hospital from 1975 until 1981. The damages proceedings were not issued until 1993, although the claimant had first consulted solicitors in 1986. At this time, she did not know whether she had a case but felt clear in her own mind that her suffering was attributable to a mistaken diagnosis. It was held on appeal that because the claimant was clear in her own mind that a connection existed between her suffering and the misdiagnosis when she first sought legal advice in 1986, it was not necessary for the court to enquire further whether a rational lay person would have been willing to say that they knew of a connection between the suffering and the misdiagnosis without first obtaining a medical confirmation.

Further, the Court of Appeal has held that the date of a claimant's knowledge was the date on which the claimant first knew enough to begin to investigate whether he had a claim against the defendant. Where a specialist told the claimant that he had an inhaled disease or industrial injury, and the only source for this could be his work for the defendants (*Corbin v Penfold Metalizing* (2000) *The Times*, May 2).

When considering whether the claimant had constructive knowledge in *Sniezek v Bundy (Letchworth) Ltd* (2000) LTL, 7 July the Court of Appeal found that a claimant could have the requisite knowledge even if medical experts advised him that this was not the case. The court ruled that the claimant had the knowledge from the date when he went to complain to his doctor of severe symptoms but was assured that there was no link between the illness and his work. The court decided that although this decision might appear harsh, the better view was that the Limitation Act 1980 was clear that time should run even when a claimant had taken reasonable steps to obtain expert advice to confirm his own belief in an injury but the advice was negative. Under such circumstances it was correct to rely on s 33. Here the claimant acted promptly and made reasonable efforts to instruct solicitors, such that the court was right to exercise its discretion under s 33 in these circumstances.

6.3.3 Knowledge of identity of defendant

The identity of the defendant may prove problematic in cases involving corporate groups. In *Simpson v Norwest Holst Southern Ltd* [1980] 2 All ER 471, the facts were that the claimant worked on a building site, and his contract of employment stated that he was employed by Norwest Holst Group. However, this did not identify his employer because at least four companies made up Norwest Holst Group, including Norwest Holst Ltd and Norwest Construction Co Ltd, and the claimant's payslips stated simply that his employer was 'Norwest Holst'. In the circumstances, the Court of Appeal found for the claimant, on the basis that neither the contract nor the payslips identified the employer and it was not reasonable to expect him to request further particulars of the identity of his employer prior to the expiry of his primary limitation period. For a case on similar facts, see *Rush v JNR (SMD) Ltd* (1999) unreported, 11 October, CA, where it was held that knowledge of a number of potential defendants was not sufficient knowledge for the purpose of s 14.

The issue of constructive knowledge of the identity of the defendant was considered in *Henderson v Temple Pier Co Ltd* (1998) unreported, 23 April, CA. In this case, it was held that, where a claimant instructed solicitors to bring a claim for damages, on the proper construction of s 14(3) of LA 1980 the claimant was fixed with constructive knowledge of facts which the solicitor ought to have acquired.

The above is also relevant where the possibility of vicarious liability exists. For example, if the claimant sues defendant A reasonably assuming him to be responsible (where A is driving the car that hits him) and the claimant subsequently finds out that A was acting in the course of his employment with B, any claim against B can be made within 3 years from the date of discovery that B was the employer, or the date that the claimant reasonably ought to have discovered that fact.

6.4 CLAIMS IN FATAL ACCIDENTS

6.4.1 Claims under the Law Reform (Miscellaneous Provisions) Act 1934 (LR(MP)A 1934)

Section 11(4) of LA 1980 states that the limitation period is 3 years from:

(1) the date the cause of action accrued; or
(2) the date of knowledge if later.

Section 11(5) of LA 1980 provides that if the injured person dies before expiration of the limitation period of 3 years then the limitation period shall be 3 years from:

(1) the date of death; or
(2) the date of the personal representative's knowledge,

whichever is the later. If there is more than one personal representative and they have differing dates of knowledge, time runs from the earliest date of knowledge (s 11(7)). Therefore, under s 11(4), the limitation period is 3 years from the date of accident or the date of knowledge. If a longer period elapses before death, the claim is statute-barred. If death occurs within 3 years, or having no knowledge, then s 11(5) applies a further 3 years from the date of death or date of knowledge of the personal representative. However, the court does have a general discretion to override the above provisions and disapply the limitation period, as to which, see LA 1980, s 33 (see **6.6**).

6.4.2 Claims under the Fatal Accidents Act 1976 (FAA 1976)

Section 12 of LA 1980 provides that an action under FAA 1976 cannot be brought if death occurred when the person injured could no longer maintain an action and recover damages in respect of the injury, whether because of a limitation problem or for any other reason. Therefore, the dependants of the deceased are in no better position than the deceased would have been, and, as such, if his claim would have been statute-barred under s 11 of LA 1980, the dependants are similarly barred.

Section 12(2) provides that the limitation period for the dependants under FAA 1976 is 3 years from:

(1) the date of death; or
(2) the date of knowledge of the person for whose benefit the action is brought,

whichever is the later (s 12(2)). Therefore, if the primary limitation period expires before the date of death, the dependant is statute-barred. If the primary limitation period has not expired at the date of death, s 12(2) applies and the relevant limitation period will be that of the dependants. Both LR(MP)A 1934 and FAA 1976 claims are also subject to the court's discretion under s 33 to disapply the limitation period of 3 years (s 28 of LA 1980), as long as the appropriate limitation period was set by the Limitation Act 1980 and not some other statute.

It should be noted that where an FAA 1976 claim is brought on behalf of minor dependants, if that action is dismissed for want of prosecution then even though as regards limitation, time has not run against the minor dependants, the dismissal of the action will preclude any second action being brought. See *Croft v Shavin & Co* (1995) unreported, 16 November, QBD.

6.5 PERSONS UNDER DISABILITY

A person is under a disability while he is a child (a person who has not attained the age of 18) or is of unsound mind within the meaning of the Mental Health Act 1983 and is therefore incapable of managing his property and affairs.

Under s 28 of LA 1980, whilst a person is under a disability, as defined above, he may bring an action at any time up to 3 years from when he ceased to be under a disability.

It is important to note that according to the wording of the section:

> 'If on the date when any right of action accrued ... the person to whom it accrued was under a disability, the action may be brought at any time before the expiration of 3 years from the date when he ceased to be under a disability or died (whichever first occurred).'

Therefore, the person must be under the disability when the cause of action first accrued. If a disability comes into existence after that date, time continues to run. However, under s 33(3) of LA 1980 (see **6.6**) the court will have regard to any period or periods of disability when it exercises its discretion. Similarly, there is no extension of time for a person under a disability claiming through a person who was not under a disability at the time the right of action accrued (s 28(2)). This was confirmed in *Thomas v Plaistow* (1997) *The Times*, May 19, CA. It was held that disability in s 33 of LA 1980 has the same meaning as in s 28, that is infancy or unsound mind. There is a mandatory extension of time where the claimant has an existing disability and a discretion if there is a supervening disability.

6.6 THE COURT'S DISCRETION TO OVERRIDE THE LIMITATION PERIOD

Section 33 of LA 1980 gives the court an unfettered discretion to disapply the 3-year limitation period. Section 33 provides that:

> 'If it appears to the court that it would be equitable to allow an action to proceed having regard to the degree to which:
>
> (a) the provisions of ss 11 and 12 of this Act prejudice the plaintiff or any person whom he represents; and

(b) any decision of the court under this subsection would prejudice the defendant or any person whom he represents;

the court may direct that those provisions shall not apply to the action, or shall not apply to any specified cause of action to which the action relates.'

When considering its discretion, the court is required to have regard to all the circumstances of the case, and in particular to:

'(a) the length of, and the reason for, the delay on the part of the plaintiff;

(b) the extent to which, having regard to the delay, the evidence adduced or likely to be adduced by the plaintiff or the defendant is or is likely to be less cogent than if the action had been brought within the time allowed by s 11 or s 12;

(c) the conduct of the defendant after the cause of action arose, including the extent (if any) to which he responded to requests reasonably made by the plaintiff for information or inspection for the purpose of ascertaining facts which were or might be relevant to the plaintiff's cause of action against the defendant;

(d) the duration of any disability of the plaintiff arising after the date of the accrual of the cause of action;

(e) the extent to which the plaintiff acted promptly and reasonably once he knew whether or not the act or omission of the defendant, to which the injury was attributable, might be capable at that time of giving rise to an action for damages;

(f) the steps, if any, taken by the plaintiff to obtain medical, legal or other expert advice and the nature of any such advice he may have received.'

The onus rests upon the claimant to show why the limitation period should be disapplied (*Halford v Brookes* [1991] 3 All ER 559).

In *Donovan v Gwentoys* [1990] 1 WLR 472, the House of Lords emphasised that s 33 gave the court an unfettered discretion to disapply the strict time-limits; the matters contained in s 33(3) are merely guidelines. For example, the time of notification of the claim to the defendant is of extreme importance in ascertaining prejudice, although there is no specific reference to this in s 33. Depriving the defendant of the limitation defence as such is of little importance; the matter of paramount importance is the effect of the delay on the defendant's ability to defend, as illustrated by *Hartley v Birmingham City District Council* [1992] 2 All ER 213, CA.

When considering s 33(3)(b), the extent to which evidence is less cogent, the Court of Appeal highlighted the importance of written evidence when memories of witnesses are unreliable due to the lapse of time see *Farthing v North East Essex Health Authority* [1998] Lloyd's Rep Med 37, CA. The claimant had had a hysterectomy which was negligently performed. Following her operation in 1981, she sued the defendants in 1995. When considering her application under s 33, the court found that due to the lapse of time a number of the witnesses had died or had moved abroad and could recall little of the events in question. However, the Court of Appeal further found that because there was considerable evidence available in the form of the medical records and a letter from the surgeon to the claimant's GP written shortly after the operation, their would be little need for reliance on memory alone and consequently the appeal should be allowed.

Further guidance was provided by the Court of Appeal in *Coad v Cornwall and Isles of Scilly Health Authority* [1997] 1 WLR 189, CA. The court found that s 33(3)(a) required the court to apply a subjective test to why the claimant had delayed, the length of the delay and whether the reason was good or bad. There was no requirement for the claimant to provide a 'reasonable' explanation. In relation to the conduct of the defendants, the judge is entitled to consider the conduct of the defendants, and if he establishes that the defendants have brought upon themselves the tragedies that they claim to suffer then that should be taken into account and the prejudice should be significantly discounted. In the case of *Hammond v West Lancashire Health Authority* [1998] Lloyd's Rep Med 146, CA, the defendants claimed prejudice to their case as they had destroyed the deceased's X-rays after 3 years had elapsed. The court held that the destruction of the X-rays was a policy implemented by the defendants, and which had no regard for the time-limits of LA 1980. Because of this prejudice to their case, it should still be taken into account, although it would be significantly discounted.

An example of what might amount to a reasonable delay can be found in *Whittaker v Westinghouse Brake and Signal Holdings* (1996) CLR, 9 August. In this case, a widow sought to bring a claim under s 33 of LA 1980 after a delay of 31 years. The court found that there were still witnesses available and that the defendant would not be seriously prejudiced. The court found that the widow was not blameworthy in respect of the delay.

It should be borne in mind that the limitation period is important not only to the claimant personally but also to the claimant's solicitor. Where the proceedings are brought against the defendant outside the limitation period as a result of the negligence of the claimant's solicitor, and the action is not allowed to proceed, the claimant may have a claim against his own solicitor. It has been argued that the fact that the claimant has a cast-iron claim against his own solicitor provides an overwhelming reason why the limitation period should not be disapplied; the claimant will not be prejudiced because he can pursue an alternative claim against his solicitor (rather than the defendant). However, although the ability to claim against the solicitor is a factor for the court to bear in mind, it is not an absolute bar against disapplying the limitation period (*Ramsden v Lee* [1992] 2 All ER 204; *Hartley v Birmingham City District Council* (above):

> 'if the [claimant] has to change from an action against a tortfeasor, who may know little or nothing of the weak points of his case, to an action against his solicitor, who will know a great deal about them, the prejudice may well be major rather than minor...')

The court considered the above issue in *Steeds v Peverel Management Services Ltd* (2001) *The Times*, May 16. In this case, solicitors failed to issue proceedings within the relevant limitation period. The court found that the proceedings were only 49 days outside of the limitation period. On appeal, the court found that the district judge at first instance was wrong to treat the claimant's good claim against his own solicitors as justification for refusing to exercise a discretion under s 33. The better view was that the existence of a claim against his own solicitors was a relevant factor in weighing the degree of prejudice suffered by the defendant in not being able to rely on the limitation period as a defence. To that end, it would always be relevant to consider when the defendant first had notification of the claim (see *Donovan v Gwentoys*). On the facts of the case, the judgment was set aside and the court exercised its discretion under s 33 as it was unlikely that the defendants were caused any appreciable prejudice as it was equitable to allow the claim to continue allowing for all of the circumstances of the case.

6.7 SPECIAL PERIODS OF LIMITATION

Although in the vast majority of personal injury cases the 3-year rule will apply, it is possible that a special rule applies, for example, in regard to claims relating to aircraft under the Carriage by Air Act 1961 or the Warsaw Convention, or relating to vessels used for navigation under the Maritime Conventions Act 1911 or the Merchant Shipping Act 1995. In those cases, the limitation period is generally 2 years.

The most common form of special rule is in respect of contributions between tortfeasors under the Civil Liability (Contribution) Act 1978, where no action to recover a contribution may be brought after the expiration of 2 years from the date on which the right accrued. This is generally the date on which judgment was given against the person who is seeking the contribution or the date when he pays or agrees to pay compensation.

6.8 AVOIDING LIMITATION PROBLEMS

If limitation appears to be a problem which the solicitor becomes aware of at the first interview, the following matters should be taken into account.

(1) The date of the incident should be checked and the limitation period calculated from this date.
(2) Consideration should be given as to whether any special rule applies (date of knowledge, disability etc).
(3) If limitation will shortly expire, the solicitor should consider issuing protective proceedings to safeguard his client's position. If limitation will expire imminently, application can be made ex parte and in a real emergency the court will accept oral statements, followed by an undertaking to verify them by affidavit (see *Phillips v Taunton and Somerset NHS Trust* (1996) 33 BMLR 154).
(4) If limitation expired recently, the solicitor should consider issuing proceedings as soon as possible in order to show the court that the very minimum of delay has occurred, when making an application for the court to use its discretion under s 33 to disapply the limitation period. *Carlton v Fulchers (a Firm)* [1997] PNLR 337, CA, is a good example of how a solicitor can be found to be negligent due to a failure to be aware of limitation problems. In this case, even though the claimant did not consult the solicitor until after the 3-year limitation period had expired, he was held liable due to his failure to advise of the possibility of an application under s 33.
(5) In clinical negligence cases, the solicitor should consider whether to apply for emergency assistance from the Legal Services Commission.
(6) If limitation expired a long time ago, it will be too late for protective proceedings to be of any use. Therefore, the solicitor should check whether date of knowledge may be relevant and, if not, consider the likelihood of success of

any application under s 33 having regard to the circumstances of the case and how they compare with the factors contained in s 33.

6.9 CONCLUSION

Failure to issue proceedings within the limitation period is a major source of negligence claims against solicitors. Although this chapter includes the law and procedure relevant to an application under s 33 to override the limitation period, prevention is better than cure. It is therefore essential that the solicitor establishes a routine of checking and rechecking the limitation period on the files for which he is responsible. There may also be many other files, for which he is not responsible, but which may pass through his hands on a regular basis. Such files are often the source of limitation problems, as one solicitor may assume (wrongly) that the responsibility for checking limitation resides with someone else, and the date of limitation may go unchecked. To avoid this, the solicitor should adopt a routine of checking for limitation on every file on which he is involved.

6.10 FURTHER READING

McGee *Limitation Periods* (Sweet & Maxwell).

Chapter 7

COMPLAINTS PROCEDURES AND DISCIPLINARY PROCEDURES OF HEALTHCARE PROVIDERS

7.1 INTRODUCTION

The Health Act 1999 imposes a 'duty of quality' on National Health Service (NHS) trusts and establishes a Commission for Health Improvement which has wide investigative powers. These measures are designed to alleviate concerns over quality of service in the NHS.

When advising a client about the right to complain in relation to NHS care, and how to go about it, there are a number of matters for the solicitor to consider. Whilst the complaint has the primary purpose of ensuring that the client's voice does not go unheard, it will also ensure that the matter is investigated quickly, whilst events are still fresh, and that detailed information is obtained. There are, however, two potential problems. The first is that the NHS formal complaints procedure makes it clear that the procedure will cease as soon as a firm indication is given by the complainant that legal proceedings are being contemplated. The second is that Community Legal Service funding is not available for any work done by a solicitor in making a complaint on behalf of a client.

7.2 THE NHS COMPLAINTS PROCEDURE

The complaints procedure was introduced on 1 April 1996. The procedure has two objectives: first, to simplify the method by which patients can complain about different members of the medical profession and, secondly, to separate complaints completely from disciplinary procedures. The aim is to deal with complaints simply and swiftly at local level, if possible.

The complaints procedure involves two stages:

(1) local resolution; and
(2) independent review.

The procedure is applicable to complaints concerning NHS staff in all areas, whether they are GPs, hospital doctors, nursing staff or ambulance crew, or any other relevant NHS employee. A complaint by a patient can encompass any expression of dissatisfaction, from a complaint about the food or politeness of staff to one about the ability of a doctor properly to diagnose or treat an illness or injury (ie a clinical complaint).

NHS staff are asked to be alert to the fact that a prompt and thorough response to a complaint as it arises, if handled correctly, may result in the complaint being nipped in the bud, before it has the chance to gain momentum. This 'local resolution' is seen by the NHS Executive as the main thrust of the procedure. Complaints are most

Chapter 7 contents
Introduction
The NHS complaints procedure
Local resolution
Convener of the independent review panel
The independent review panel
Complaints involving clinical matters
Role of the independent clinical assessors
The independent review panel report
Time-limit
Formal ending of complaints procedure
Changes implemented as a result of the report
The Health Service Commissioner (Ombudsman)
Access to Health Records Act 1990
Effect of coroner's inquest
Disciplinary proceedings against doctors
Disciplinary proceedings against the nursing profession
Conclusion
Further reading
NHS complaints procedure

likely to be voiced to staff on the spot, who are the people best placed to make the initial response. The aim is to resolve problems and answer concerns of patients immediately and informally if possible.

The procedure is aimed only at satisfying complaints, and will not apportion blame amongst staff. It is completely separate from disciplinary procedures. A complaint may bring a deficiency to the notice of management, which may then consider disciplinary action; however, this will involve the complainant only to the extent of possibly giving a statement to be used in the disciplinary process. Thereafter, the complainant should be informed of any outcome of any disciplinary procedure.

Assistance on how to make a complaint can be obtained from the community health council (in Scotland, the local health council). The Health Information Service gives information on the NHS complaints system.

7.3 LOCAL RESOLUTION

7.3.1 Local resolution and NHS hospitals

As part of its complaints procedure, the trust or health authority must have a clear local resolution process. If the complaint concerns a relatively minor matter, which can be resolved quickly, the person to whom the patient complains should either deal with it at the time or ensure that it is passed to an appropriate person who can respond to the complaint more fully. If the complaint is more serious and an investigation is required, it is likely that the staff member will refer the matter to the complaints manager for the hospital, who will then deal with the patient. A large number of complaints are dealt with in this way without the necessity for independent review.

However, as an alternative, under the Patients' Charter, the chief executive of the trust or health authority must respond in writing to all written complaints and all oral complaints subsequently put into writing and signed by the complainant. If the complaint is more serious, the patient may be invited to a meeting to discuss the circumstances of the incident together with those involved with it, or the hospital may hold a more formal enquiry involving examination of medical records, interviewing those involved and possibly seeking the opinion of senior doctors. The aim is to provide a full investigation within 20 working days, according to NHS targets, but there is no sanction in place if this target is not met.

If the patient remains dissatisfied, or is unwilling to voice a complaint to the person giving care, or the staff member is unable to deal with it, the complaint should be referred to the complaints manager.

7.3.2 Local resolution and GP or other family health service complaints

In the case of family health services (ie GP practices and NHS dentists), local resolution is the responsibility of the practitioner. From 1 April 1996, family health service practitioners are obliged to have a practice-based complaints procedure, which they must publicise.

If the complaint concerns a GP, an NHS dentist or any person employed by their practice, it will be necessary to seek clarification from the practice as to how it operates its local complaints procedure. If the complaint cannot be dealt with immediately, the matter should be referred to the complaints manager, who in this instance is likely to be one of the other doctors or dentists in the practice or the practice manager if there is one. If the complaint is not dealt with on the spot, and requires investigation, the complaint should be acknowledged within 2 working days and, if possible, a written response or a meeting to try to resolve the complaint should be undertaken within 10 working days.

If the patient does not wish to complain direct to the practice, the complaints leaflet provided by the practice should include details of the complaints manager at the local health authority who can mediate between the patient and the practice.

7.3.3 Time-limits

A complaint should be made within 6 months of the date of the matter complained of, or within 6 months of the date of discovering the problem, provided it is within 12 months of the incident.

Complaints outside the time-limit may be investigated at the discretion of the health service provider.

7.4 CONVENER OF THE INDEPENDENT REVIEW PANEL

If a complainant remains dissatisfied with local resolution by either a health authority or trust, or a family health services practitioner, the complainant then has 28 days within which to request the convener to set up an independent review panel.

However, an independent review panel is not an automatic right of the complainant. Whether such a panel ought to be held is first decided by the convener. The convener may decide that all that could be achieved has already been done at local level, in which case the complainant has the right to seek redress through the Ombudsman. Alternatively, he may refer the complaint back for further attempts at local resolution.

7.4.1 The role of the convener

As soon as the convener is contacted by the complainant he should immediately obtain a full written statement signed by the complainant setting out his grievances, and why he remains dissatisfied. The convener should then notify in writing those complained against, setting out what the complainant has stated as his grievance. The clarity and content of the statement is important as there is no automatic right to independent review, and the convener may require to be persuaded that it is appropriate, and that local resolution has been fully utilised.

In deciding whether to convene a panel, the convener will consider whether those complained against:

(1) can take any further action under local resolution procedure to satisfy the complainant and, if so, refer the complaint back and arrange conciliation to help resolve the complaint; or
(2) have already taken all practical action, and therefore establishing a review panel would add nothing further.

If either of the above applies, the convener should not convene a panel.

According to NHS guidance, conveners should not set up a review panel where legal proceedings have commenced or there is an explicit indication of an intention to make such a claim based on the same incident as that giving rise to the complaint.

The convener must inform the complainant in writing of his decision as to whether or not to convene a panel. If he decides that a panel should be convened, he must set out the terms of reference of the panel's investigations clearly. If he decides that it is not necessary to convene a panel he must set out his reasons for refusal to set up a panel. Where a panel is refused the complainant should be advised in writing within 20 working days of receipt of request and of his right to complain to the Ombudsman.

If the complainant remains dissatisfied following referral back to local resolution, he may refer the complaint once again to the convener.

7.4.2 Time-limit

The request to the covener should be made within 28 days from the conclusion of the local resolution process.

7.5 THE INDEPENDENT REVIEW PANEL

If the convener decides that the complaint should be investigated, he will appoint an independent review panel. The panel will consider the complaint according to the terms of reference given by the convener, and the written statement given by the complainant.

7.5.1 Composition of the panel

The panel comprises three people, with a majority of independent members, who will investigate the facts taking into account the views of all concerned.

The three panel members will usually be:

(1) an independent lay chairman (who is usually a non-executive director of the trust or health authority);
(2) the convener;
(3) an independent person (in the case of a health authority) or a representative of the purchaser (in the case of a trust).

In addition, if the convener decides that the complaint is a clinical complaint, the panel will be advised by at least two independent clinical assessors.

The chairman and third panel member (in the case of a health authority), should be seen as totally independent, and to this end practising or retired members of clinical professions should not be chosen.

7.5.2 Role of the panel

Once the convener has decided to set up an independent review panel, he must set out the terms of reference for the panel. At this point, the responsibility for leading the panel falls to the independent lay chairman.

The functions of the panel are:

(1) to investigate the complaint according to the terms of reference, having regard to the complainant's grievance; and
(2) to compile a report which will set out conclusions, appropriate comments and suggestions.

However, the panel has no executive authority to impose change, and may not make any suggestion that any person be subject to disciplinary action.

7.5.3 Procedure

The panel has considerable freedom in deciding how to conduct its investigation. It may investigate by interviewing both sides, separately or at a joint meeting. It should go about its business fostering an air of conciliation and goodwill, the key element being an ability to respond flexibly to different kinds of complaint, and avoid confrontation at all costs. As such, there is no form of formal hearing.

The panel must conduct its business within the following rules:

(1) proceedings must be held in private;
(2) both complainant and complained against must have an opportunity to express their views;
(3) any disagreement within the panel as to how it conducts its review will be decided by the chairman, whose decision is final;
(4) the complainant (and any other person interviewed) may be accompanied by a person of his choosing, who may, with the approval of the chairman, speak to the panel, except that if the person who accompanies the person is legally qualified, he may not act as an advocate.

7.6 COMPLAINTS INVOLVING CLINICAL MATTERS

The panel has access to all records relating to the handling of the complaint. In the case of a clinical complaint, the panel also has access to relevant parts of the patient's health records. The panel will produce a written report setting out its conclusions.

If the complaint relates wholly or partly to clinical matters, the panel must be advised by at least two independent clinical assessors, whose role is to advise and report to the panel on clinical aspects of complaints. At least one assessor should be present when the panel (or panel member) interviews either or both parties when matters relating to the exercise of clinical judgement are under discussion.

7.7 ROLE OF THE INDEPENDENT CLINICAL ASSESSORS

Assessors must have access to all the patient's health records, together with information about the handling of the complaint. They may interview/examine complainants and may interview any person complained against, but should not explain their findings at that stage before advising the panel of their views.

Assessors may produce individual or combined reports. These should not be disclosed to the complainant or the person complained against in advance of their being made available to panel members.

Assessors' reports must be attached to the panel's final report when it is issued. If the panel disagrees with the assessor's reports, it must state in its report the reason for doing so.

Assessors should not act independently to resolve a complaint. They should have no connection with any of the parties to the complaint, and therefore should be selected from outside the region concerned.

7.8 THE INDEPENDENT REVIEW PANEL REPORT

The panel may provide a draft of the report (but not necessarily the conclusions) to the complainant and the person complained against to check for factual accuracy.

The panel's final report must be sent to:

(1) the complainant;
(2) the patient, if different from the complainant and if competent to receive it;
(3) any person named in the complaint;
(4) the clinical assessors (if any);
(5) the trust/health authority chairman and chief executive; and
(6) in the case of complaint against family health services practitioners/GP fundholders, the practitioner concerned.

The panel may not make any recommendations or suggestions relating to disciplinary matters.

7.8.1 Confidentiality

The panel should not send its report to any other person. The panel chairman has the right to withhold any part of the panel's report and all or part of the assessors' reports to ensure confidentiality of clinical information.

If the complainant wishes to show the report to an appropriate adviser, the panel must protect the overall confidentiality of the report and, therefore, it will be necessary to seek permission from the chairman prior to showing the report to someone not previously involved in the complaint.

7.9 TIME-LIMIT

The first draft of the report should be available within 50 working days of the panel being established (or 30 working days in the case of family health service complaints).

7.10 FORMAL ENDING OF COMPLAINTS PROCEDURE

Following receipt of the panel's report, the chief executive must write to the complainant informing him of any action the trust or health authority is taking as a result of the panel's deliberations and of the right of the complainant to take his grievance to the Ombudsman if he remains dissatisfied.

This notification signifies the end of the complaints procedure and is important because it will not normally be possible to complain to the Ombudsman until a clear indication is received that the procedure is at an end. However, if the circumstances of the case make it clear that the complaints procedure itself is failing to operate, this failure will form part of the complaint and will be dealt with by the Ombudsman.

7.11 CHANGES IMPLEMENTED AS A RESULT OF THE REPORT

The health authority or trust may take some time to respond to the report because policy review changes will necessitate the board consulting with others prior to reaching a decision. If, subsequent to its final letter, the board takes any further decisions relating to the outcome of the case, the complainant should be informed by a further letter setting out any changes that have been decided on.

7.12 THE HEALTH SERVICE COMMISSIONER (OMBUDSMAN)

7.12.1 The role of the Ombudsman

The Ombudsman is entirely separate from the NHS. His role includes the following:

(1) investigation of clinical complaints; and
(2) complaints relating to family health services; and
(3) whether the complaints procedure itself is working; or
(4) complaints where the NHS body has refused to investigate the complaint on the basis that it is outside the time-limit; or
(5) complaints where the complaint has been dealt fully with by NHS complaints procedure and the complainant is still dissatisfied; or
(6) complaints where the complainant is dissatisfied with the local resolution and the convener has refused to hold an independent review.

The Ombudsman has power:

(1) to request the convener to reconsider the case; or
(2) to investigate the matter himself.

The Ombudsman can also investigate complaints from NHS staff if they feel that they have suffered hardship or injustice as a result of the procedure, provided that established grievance procedures have been followed and the persons remain dissatisfied.

7.12.2 Time-limit

The complaint should be made within one year of the event complained of.

If a client needs help to formulate a complaint, he can get help from the local community health council, which is independent and provides information and advice to the public on health care issues.

Investigations by the Ombudsman are published in a quarterly report, the text of which is available from the Ombudsman's Office or the Internet.

7.13 ACCESS TO HEALTH RECORDS ACT 1990

If a request for access to health records has not been complied with, under the Access to Health Records Act 1990, it is now possible to use the complaints procedure to complain about this as an alternative to making an application to the court.

7.14 EFFECT OF CORONER'S INQUEST

The fact that a death has been referred to a coroner does not mean that the investigation of any complaint must be suspended. The healthcare provider should initiate its own investigations, so as to be of assistance to the coroner's own enquiries, or to extend its own enquiries if the coroner so requests.

7.15 DISCIPLINARY PROCEEDINGS AGAINST DOCTORS

7.15.1 Statutory provisions

The General Medical Council (GMC) has jurisdiction in relation to professional misconduct and criminal offences. This power was first conferred on the GMC by the Medical Act 1858, and is now regulated by ss 36–45 of and Sch 4 to the Medical Act 1983, as amended by the Medical (Professional Performance) Act 1995.

The Act provides that if a registered practitioner is:

(i) found by the Professional Conduct Committee to have committed a criminal offence in the British Isles; or
(ii) is adjudged by the Professional Conduct Committee to have been guilty of serious professional misconduct,

then the Committee may direct that:

(i) the doctor's name be erased from the register; or
(ii) the doctor's registration be suspended for a period of not more than 12 months; or
(iii) that registration be conditional on the doctor's compliance for a period of not more than 3 years with such requirements as the Committee thinks fit to impose in order to protect the public or in the doctor's own interests.

The GMC has power given to it by the Medical (Professional Performance) Act 1995 which amended the Medical Act 1983 to deal with less serious cases falling short of serious professional misconduct, but constituting 'seriously deficient' performance.

Where the Committee on Professional Performance finds that a doctor's professional performance has been seriously deficient, the Committee must:

(a) direct that his registration be suspended for a period not exceeding 12 months (in the first instance, but can be extended to an indefinite period); or
(b) that his registration be made conditional.

Where registration is made conditional, the condition will often specify that he undertake re-training or that he refrain from a certain area of practice in future, for a period not exceeding 3 years. Failure to comply with conditions imposed can lead to a direction that the doctor be suspended from the register.

7.15.2 The meaning of 'conviction'

Conviction means a conviction by a criminal court in the British Isles. Any conviction in itself gives the Professional Conduct Committee jurisdiction, even if the offence does not involve professional misconduct. The Committee is, however, most concerned by convictions which affect a doctor's fitness to practice.

One of the key issues to advise a doctor about in relation to criminal offending is that, when considering convictions, the GMC is bound to accept the determination of the court as conclusive evidence of guilt of the offence for which he was convicted. Therefore, if a doctor is advised to plead guilty (eg in order to avoid publicity), he should also be advised that admission of guilt will be conclusive evidence when the matter falls to be considered by the GMC. A doctor who has been convicted on a plea of guilty cannot subsequently argue before the Professional Conduct Committee that he was in fact innocent.

7.15.3 The meaning of 'serious professional misconduct'

The phrase 'serious professional misconduct' means serious misconduct when judged according to the rules, written or unwritten, governing the medical profession.

7.15.4 The Professional Conduct Committee and the Preliminary Proceedings Committee

The Professional Conduct Committee is elected annually and consists of 30 members. Of those, 23 are medical members and seven are lay members. It normally sits in public and its procedures are similar to those of a court of law; for example witnesses may be witness summonsed to attend and will give their evidence on oath to the Committee. The Committee will be advised on questions of law by a legal adviser who is usually a barrister, advocate or solicitor of not less than 10 years' standing. Doctors appearing before the Committee are usually legally represented.

7.15.5 Function of the Preliminary Proceedings Committee

Cases coming before the Preliminary Proceedings Committee or Professional Conduct Committee may arise:
(i) from a conviction before the courts; or
(ii) where it is alleged that a doctor has done something which amounts to serious professional misconduct.

Convictions of doctors are normally reported to the GMC by the police, unless the conviction is for a minor motoring offence or other trivial matter.

Complaints which may amount to serious professional misconduct are reported to the GMC fall into two categories:

(i) matters which have been investigated by some other procedure for example the NHS complaints procedure;
(ii) complaints received from other doctors or members of the public direct to the GMC. Complaints must be supported by evidence of the facts complained of in the form of either affidavit or a statutory declaration. Having considered the allegation, if it appears that there is a question of serious professional misconduct but insufficient evidence has been put forward, the GMC's own solicitor can make further enquiries. A decision as to whether to proceed with an allegation of such serious professional misconduct will then be made by the President or other medical member of the GMC.

If a matter comes to the attention of the GMC via criminal, civil or family proceedings and an issue of disclosure of documents relied on in the case to the GMC arises, guidance on the procedure to be followed was given in *Re A (Disclosure of Medical Records to the GMC)* [1998] 2 FLR 641.

7.15.6 Procedure

Having had the matters outlined above referred to it, the Preliminary Proceedings Committee may:

(i) refer the case to the Professional Conduct Committee; or
(ii) contact the doctor concerned by letter; or
(iii) decide to take no further action.

Most cases being considered by the Preliminary Proceedings Committee are of a less serious nature and are therefore filtered out and disposed of by way of a warning letter or a letter giving advice to the doctor concerned, for example, where a doctor has been convicted for the first time of a driving offence involving excess alcohol. However, if the doctor's fitness to practise may be impaired, the Committee may refer the matter either to the Health Committee or to the Professional Conduct Committee.

If the Preliminary Proceedings Committee decides to forward the matter to the Professional Conduct Committee or the Health Committee, it may make an interim order suspending the doctor's registration to practise or make that registration conditional. The Committee has the power to do this if it is satisfied that it is necessary to protect members of the public or that it is in the doctor's own interests so to do. However, no order can be made until the doctor concerned has had the opportunity to appear before the Preliminary Proceedings Committee and make representations in relation to whether registration should be suspended or made conditional. At such a hearing, it is normal for the doctor to be legally represented. Any order that is made can run for up to a period of 6 months, and thereafter can be renewed for further periods of 3 months.

7.15.7 Function of the Professional Conduct Committee

The function of the Professional Conduct Committee is to protect the public and uphold the reputation of the medical profession. If, having had a matter referred to it, the Committee considers that the doctor's fitness to practice may be seriously impaired because of his physical or mental condition, it may refer that question to the Health Committee for determination. If the Health Committee does find that the doctor's fitness is seriously impaired, the Conduct Committee will then take no further action.

In relation to matters referred to it, arising out of a criminal conviction, the Professional Conduct Committee is bound to accept the fact of the conviction as conclusive evidence that the doctor was guilty of the offence of which he was convicted. As such, proceedings concerning convictions are concerned only to establish the gravity of the offence and take account of any mitigating circumstances. In cases relating to conduct allegations, unless they are actually admitted by the doctor, the allegation must be proved by evidence in the usual way. The function of the Committee is to determine whether, on the facts as presented to it by evidence, the doctor has been guilty of serious professional misconduct.

7.15.8 Powers of the Professional Conduct Committee

The Professional Conduct Committee may take any of the following courses:

(i) postpone determination of the case; or
(ii) direct that the doctor's registration be made conditional upon such matters as the Committee may think fit to impose in order to protect members of the public or in the doctor's own interests. Conditional registration may take effect for a period not exceeding 3 years; or
(iii) direct that the doctor's registration be suspended for a period not exceeding 12 months; or
(iv) direct that the doctor's name be erased from the register.

An example of conditional registration might be that the doctor should not engage in a specified branch of medical practice, or should only practise in that practice under supervision, or should not prescribe or possess certain drugs, or should take steps to remedy deficiencies in his knowledge or clinical skills. If a doctor's registration is suspended, he ceases to be entitled to practise as a registered medical practitioner for that period. Erasure from the register will remain effective until the doctor makes an application for restoration to the register. An application cannot be made until at least 10 months has elapsed since the order took place.

7.15.9 Appeals

In cases of erasure from the register, or suspension or subjection to conditions, the doctor has 28 days in which to give notice of appeal against that order to the Judicial Committee of the Privy Council. During the intervening period, the doctor's registration is not affected unless the Professional Conduct Committee makes a separate order that the doctor's registration should be suspended forthwith. The Committee will do this if satisfied that it is necessary to do so for the protection of members of the public or is in the interests of the doctor concerned. There is a right of appeal against this order for immediate suspension to the High Court. The doctor may make an application for restoration to the register at any time after 10 months has elapsed since the order took effect. If this is unsuccessful, a further 10 months must elapse before a further application can be made. Further information regarding disciplinary procedures can be obtained from the Fitness to Practise Directorate at the GMC.

7.16 DISCIPLINARY PROCEEDINGS AGAINST THE NURSING PROFESSION

7.16.1 Statutory provisions

The United Kingdom Central Council for Nursing, Midwifery and Health Visiting (UKCC) is the regulatory body for nurses, midwives and health visitors. The UKCC's jurisdiction in relation to professional misconduct is contained in the Nurses, Midwives and Health Visitors Act 1979.

7.16.2 What constitutes serious professional misconduct

The UKCC will consider only complaints which, if proven, would be serious enough to justify removal of the practitioner's name from the register in order to protect the public. The standard required by the UKCC is that registered nurses, midwives and health visitors should be judged against the standard which the public is entitled to expect from the average practitioner and not the highest possible standard of professional expertise. Examples of professional misconduct are:

(i) physical, sexual or verbal abuse of patients;
(ii) stealing from patients;
(iii) failure to care for patients properly;
(iv) failing to keep proper records;
(v) failing to administer medicines safely;
(vi) deliberately concealing unsafe practices; or
(vii) committing serious criminal offences.

Practitioners may also be found to be unfit to practice by reason of ill-health. An example of unfitness by reason of ill-health would include alcohol or drug dependency.

7.16.3 The Professional Conduct Committee and the Preliminary Proceedings Committee

These Committees are set up along very similar lines to the GMC Committees. In relation to criminal offences, for example, in the same way as doctors, the police are required to notify the UKCC of any registered nurse, midwife or health visitor who has been convicted of a criminal offence.

7.16.4 Function of Preliminary Proceedings Committee

The PPC comprises UKCC council members and is responsible for considering all complaints made against members in relation to professional misconduct or criminal conviction.

7.16.5 Powers of Preliminary Proceedings Committee

Once it has considered the available evidence before it, the PPC may deal with the matter as follows:

(i) it may close the case having taken no action;
(ii) it may refer the case to the UKCC Professional Conduct Committee;
(iii) it may issue a formal caution;
(iv) if the complaint refers to unfitness to practise by reason of ill-health, it may refer the matter to the Health Committee.

The PPC may issue a caution where the facts, although proven, are admitted by the practitioner and there are mitigating circumstances which mean that removal from the register would not be appropriate. The caution is retained on the practitioners' register for 5 years and is automatically disclosed to potential employers.

7.16.6 Function of Professional Conduct Committee

The PCC considers allegations of professional misconduct which are referred to it by the PPC. Each committee consists of five UKCC council members. PCC meetings are held in public, and the committee is advised by a lawyer who advises on points of law and admissibility of evidence. The practitioner is also usually represented, by his trade union or his nominated solicitor or barrister. The practitioner may apply for the hearing to be held in private, but this will be granted only if it is necessary to protect the anonymity of a patient whom, it is alleged, is the victim, or if disclosure of confidential medical information would be involved. The future reputation of the practitioner concerned will not justify the hearing being held in private.

7.16.7 Powers of Professional Conduct Committee

The PCC has the following powers. It may:

(i) declare the facts of the case not proven and take no further action;
(ii) declare the facts proven and go on to rule that the facts do not constitute professional misconduct and take no further action; or
(iii) impose an interim suspension of registration if the hearing is adjourned.

If the facts are proved and misconduct is proven, the committee may:

(i) issue a caution;
(ii) remove the practitioner from the register indefinitely;
(iii) remove the practitioner from the register for a specified period after which the practitioner may apply for his name to be restored to the register; or
(iv) refer the case to the UKCC Health Committee in cases of ill-health of the practitioner.

7.17 CONCLUSION

Healthcare providers are clearly making great efforts to ensure that complaints do not go unheard, and that patients are made aware of the relevant complaints and disciplinary procedures available. Solicitors have an important role to play, not only in ensuring that patients are aware of their rights, but also that healthcare professionals are adequately advised in relation to claims which may be made against them.

7.18 FURTHER READING

Complaints: Listening, Acting, Improving (Department of Health, March 1996)
Duties of a Doctor (GMC)
Complaints about Professional Conduct (UKCC)
www.gmc-uk.org

7.19 NHS COMPLAINTS PROCEDURE

PART I LOCAL RESOLUTION

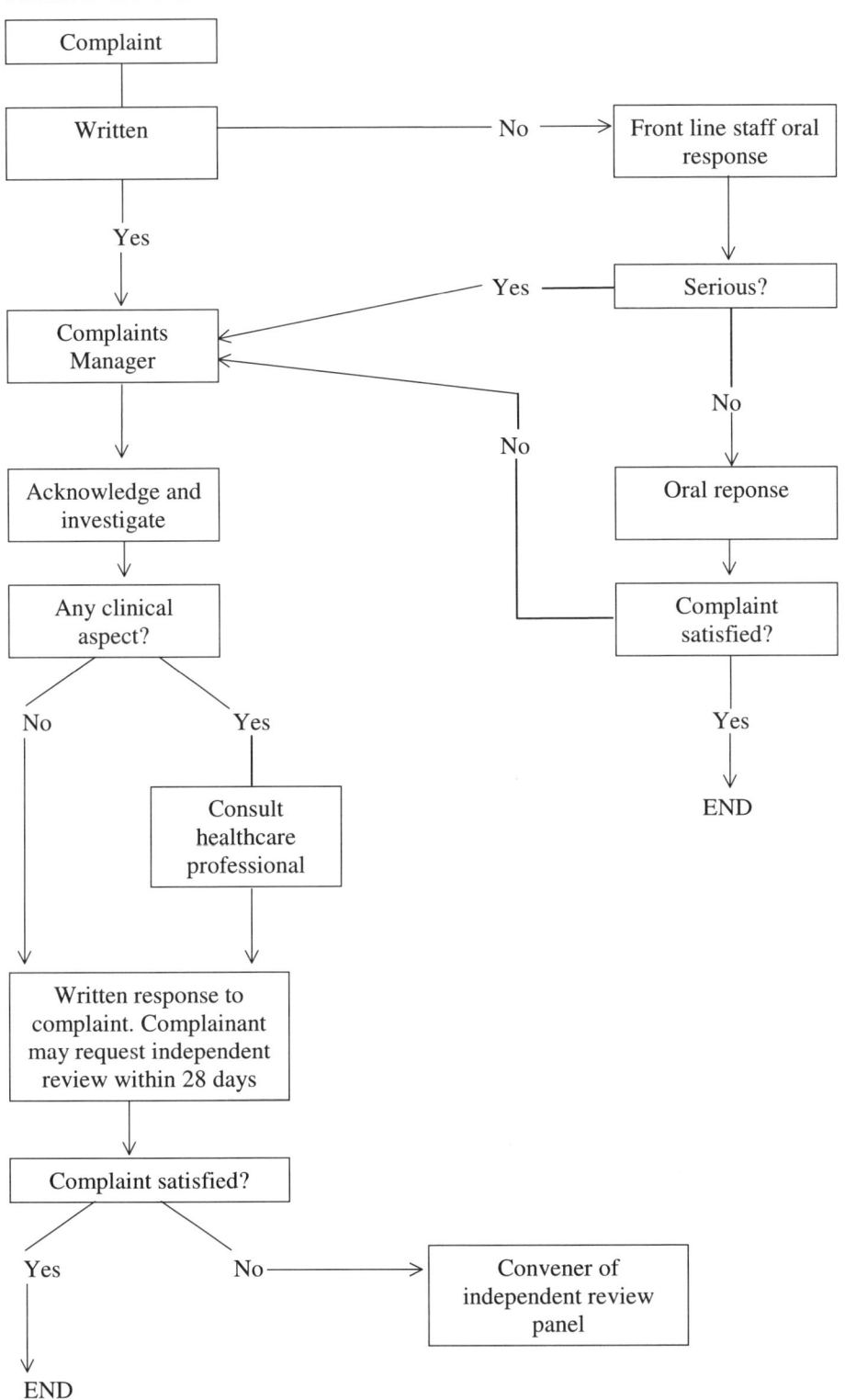

```
Complaint
    │
    ▼
 Written ─── No ──▶ Front line staff oral response
    │                      │
   Yes                     ▼
    │                  Serious? ── Yes ──▶ Complaints Manager
    ▼                      │
Complaints Manager ◀───── No
    │                      │
    ▼                      ▼
Acknowledge and        Oral response
investigate                │
    │                      ▼
    ▼                  Complaint satisfied?
Any clinical aspect?       │        │
    │        │            No       Yes
   No       Yes            │        │
    │        │             │        ▼
    │        ▼             │       END
    │   Consult healthcare │
    │   professional       │
    │        │             │
    ▼        ▼             │
Written response to complaint. Complainant may request independent review within 28 days
    │
    ▼
Complaint satisfied?
    │        │
   Yes       No ──▶ Convener of independent review panel
    │
    ▼
   END
```

PART II INDEPENDENT REVIEW

```
                    ┌─────────────────────┐
                    │ Complainant requests│
                    │ convener for        │
                    │ independent review  │
                    │ panel (IRP)         │
                    └──────────┬──────────┘
                               ↓
┌──────────────┐    ┌─────────────────────┐    ┌──────────────┐
│ Convener     │    │ Complainant         │───→│ Any specific │
│ writes to    │    │ provides statement  │    │ intent to make│
│ chief exec   │    │                     │    │ legal claim  │
│ to reactivate│    └─────────────────────┘    └──────┬───────┘
│ local        │                                      │
│ resolution   │                                      │ Yes
└──────▲───────┘                                      ↓
       │ No                                          END
┌──────┴───────┐    ┌─────────────────────┐
│ Has local    │←───│ Convener and lay    │←── No ──
│ resolution   │    │ chairman decide     │
│ been         │    │ whether IRP         │
│ exhausted?   │    │ necessary           │
└──────────────┘    └─────────────────────┘
        Yes               │    ↑No         ┌──────────────┐
                          ↓                │ Clinical     │
                    ┌─────────────┐        │ aspects?     │
                    │ Panel of:   │        └──────┬───────┘
                    │ – chairman  │               │ Yes
                    │ – convener  │               ↓
                    │ – other     │        ┌──────────────┐
                    │ independent │        │ IRP seek     │
                    │ person      │        │ advice from  │
                    │             │        │ at least 2   │
                    │ produce     │        │ clinical     │
                    │ report with │        │ assessors    │
                    │ conclusions │        └──────┬───────┘
                    └──────┬──────┘               ↓
                           │            ┌──────────────┐
                           │            │ Clinical     │
                           │←───────────│ assessors'   │
                           │            │ separate     │
                           │            │ report       │
                           ↓            └──────────────┘
            ┌─────────────────────────┐
            │ Complainant informed of │
            │ report and action being │
            │ taken                   │
            └────────────┬────────────┘
                         ↓
            ┌─────────────────────────┐
            │ Complainant satisfied?  │── Yes ──→ END
            └────────────┬────────────┘
                         │ No
                         ↓
            ┌─────────────────────────┐
            │ May refer complaint to  │
            │ Health Service          │
            │ Commissioner            │
            └─────────────────────────┘
```

Chapter 8

INSTRUCTING EXPERTS

8.1 INTRODUCTION

The personal injury or clinical negligence solicitor will usually instruct an expert in nearly every case. The obvious example of such an expert is a doctor who is instructed to prepare a report of the client's injuries suffered as a result of an accident at work. In a clinical negligence case, the appropriate doctors will provide a report not only on the injuries suffered as a result of the incident but also the standard of care provided/causation. The need to obtain expert medical evidence is highlighted in the professional negligence case of *May v Pettman Smith (a Firm) and Jacqueline Perry* (2001) Lawtel, 4 July where a failure to obtain the appropriate expert evidence resulted in the claimant accepting an undersettlement at the trial of his personal injury claim. The court held that the shortfall in damages was recoverable from the solicitors responsible for obtaining the evidence.

Whilst there are many different types of experts available to provide reports, the Civil Procedure Rules 1998 (CPR 1998) are clear that expert evidence should be restricted to that which is necessary (Part 35 of the CPR 1998) and the parties should, if at all possible, co-operate in the selection of the expert. The above philosophy can best be illustrated by the case of *Coker v Barkland Cleaning Co* (1999) unreported, 6 December, CA. In that case, the Court of Appeal upheld the trial judge's decision to refuse to allow the costs of instructing two experts and the court further held that the exercise of obtaining expert evidence in that case was a 'wholly fruitless exercise'.

It is clear that in each case a solicitor must consider if, and what type of, expert evidence is appropriate. In *Barings plc and Another v Coopers and Lybrand and Others* (2001) unreported, 9 February, the court held that expert evidence can be excluded if the court concludes that such evidence would not be helpful in resolving any issue in the case (see also *Regan v Chetwynd* (2001) JPIL 2/01).

8.2 WHO IS AN EXPERT?

An expert must be someone with an area of expertise and who can supply the court with objective criteria. This evidence should be presented in a clear and concise way so that the judge can use the information to reach his own conclusions.

8.3 HOW TO FIND AN EXPERT

In considering who to choose to deal with the case, the solicitor responsible must instruct the correct person. This is a vital point to note.

Many firms will have their own in-house directory of experts, which should be referred to in the first instance. Frequently, other fee earners will have inserted comments about

Chapter 8 contents
Introduction
Who is an expert?
How to find an expert
Key qualities to look for in an expert
Joint selection of experts
Particular matters relating to instructing experts in personal injury actions
Particular matters relating to instructing experts in clinical negligence actions
Use of experts' reports
Conference with experts and counsel where expert instructed by one party
Meeting of experts
Experts' costs
Types of experts
Conclusion
Key points
Further reading

the expert alongside the entry in the directory. Information, such as how well the expert gave evidence in court, can be vital.

8.3.1 Personal injury cases

If an in-house directory of experts is not available or is inappropriate then other sources can be used. The following sources may be of use.

(1) The Association of Personal Injury Lawyers. This organisation provides information to members on appropriate experts.
(2) A barrister who also practises in the personal injury/clinical negligence field may be able to assist in the choice of expert.
(3) *The Law Society Directory of Expert Witnesses.*
(4) A search through the appropriate law reports will often reveal the name of the person who appeared as a witness in a particular case. It may be possible to approach that person directly. As an alternative, the firm of solicitors named in the report can be contacted and may offer assistance in providing the name of the relevant expert.
(5) The Academy of Expert Witnesses.
(6) The Society of Expert Witnesses.
(7) Expert Witness Institute.
(8) The *New Law Journal* and *Solicitor's Journal* regularly issue expert witness supplements which carry advertisements from experts who are prepared to provide reports for the purposes of litigation.
(9) Many professional institutes also prepare a directory of expert witnesses, for example the Royal College of Nursing.
(10) The Medico-Legal Society publishes reports which may reveal the name of a suitable expert.

Whilst it is possible to select an expert from one of the sources referred to above, it is important to appreciate that it is the solicitor's responsibility to choose the correct expert for his client's case.

8.3.2 Clinical negligence cases

The above sources may be useful for clinical negligence claims but, in addition, the Association for Victims of Medical Accidents (AVMA) provides a very useful experts' database. The aim of this service is to provide solicitors with information for the assistance of victims of clinical negligence. Prior to any expert's name being entered upon the database, AVMA assesses the quality and impartiality of the expert. The organisation has a good reputation within the profession. The solicitor (whose firm must belong to AVMA) normally sends a letter of instruction setting out the nature of the potential claim, details of what advice is sought and confirmation that the notes from the hospital and medical practitioner have been obtained. AVMA will then, within 4 to 6 weeks, send the solicitor a list of experts who have provided reports in a similar case and include details of whether the reports are accurate and have been relied upon at court. AVMA has the advantage that it can use medically qualified workers, who can identify experts with specialist interests and those who have published papers in the particular field. AVMA can also provide information on the cost of the report.

When the solicitor approaches an expert doctor who has been recommended by AVMA, the solicitor should not inform the expert that AVMA has made the recommendation. AVMA expects its members to report back to it on the expert's performance. For that purpose, AVMA sends an 'expert report form' to the solicitor which asks the solicitor to comment on such matters as the expert's helpfulness, speed and costs. This enables AVMA to keep its list up to date.

8.4 KEY QUALITIES TO LOOK FOR IN AN EXPERT

A number of key qualities must be looked for when selecting an expert.

(1) Is the person appropriately qualified to deal with the matter and does he have the relevant practical experience in the area?
(2) Does the expert have experience in litigation of this type? Does he prepare reports and attend at trial regularly to give evidence? Only a small percentage of cases proceed to trial, and thus an expert may claim to have been involved in, say, 200 cases but may only have given evidence in a few of those cases (especially as, in the fast track, expert evidence is normally given in written form). It cannot be assumed that the case will settle and, however good the written report might be, convincing oral testimony and the ability to withstand tough cross-examination is essential. The expert's general reputation should be checked with his colleagues who practise in the same area.
(3) Does the expert have sufficient time to deal with the case properly? A good expert will refuse instructions when he has insufficient time, but this is not always the case. Whether the case is a personal injury or clinical negligence claim, the expert will have to spend considerable time examining the papers and the subject-matter of the claim.
(4) Can the doctor provide a clear and comprehensive report?
(5) Can the expert be regarded as impartial (see *Liverpool Roman Catholic Archdiocesan Trust v Goldberg* (2001) NLJ, 20 July).

8.5 JOINT SELECTION OF EXPERTS

The CPR 1998 and the pre-action protocols require the court to exert control over the use of experts in personal injury and clinical negligence cases. The aim is to try and create a less 'confrontational' approach between experts and joint selection by both parties is encouraged by the CPR 1998. In an attempt to do this, the personal injury pre-action protocol makes reference to:

(1) the claimant exchanging experts' names prior to instruction of the expert;
(2) the claimant's solicitor obtaining the medical notes;
(3) if the defendant objects to the suggested expert (which he should do within 14 days of receipt of the list of proposed experts from the claimant's solicitor), then attempts should be made to instruct an expert upon whom both parties can agree;
(4) if an expert cannot be agreed on, then, if the defendant instructs his own expert, the court will look at this decision with care to see if it was reasonable or otherwise upon the issuing of proceedings;
(5) if an expert is agreed upon, either party may send to the expert written questions, via the instructing solicitor. The expert should send answers to the questions to each party (see *Carlson v Townsend* [2001] All ER (D) 99 (April) concerning the

status of a medical report if the defendants do not object to the expert (it does not become a single joint expert's report)).

The clinical negligence pre-action protocol also emphasises the importance of the selection/instruction of experts and the need to balance each party's desire to obtain the appropriate expert evidence, with the 'overriding objective' of the CPR 1998. However, the clinical negligence protocol is less prescriptive in respect of experts than the PI protocol.

8.6 PARTICULAR MATTERS RELATING TO INSTRUCTING EXPERTS IN PERSONAL INJURY ACTIONS

In personal injury cases, the most frequently employed experts are doctors, who are employed to prepare reports on the claimant's injuries. Consulting engineers are also used in appropriate cases, to prepare reports on machinery or systems of work, and accident reconstruction experts are sometimes instructed in road traffic accidents.

8.6.1 The doctor

If acting for the claimant, there can be a temptation to instruct the doctor who has treated the client to prepare a report for the purposes of litigation, the reason being that this doctor will know the client's medical history and so will prepare a better report. However, this is often inappropriate. Whilst the doctor will be familiar with the patient, he may not have the qualities required of an expert witness, referred to above, and may never have given evidence before, or have no experience of cross-examination or of giving oral evidence at trial. He may also be unfamiliar to the defendant and thus objections may be raised when his identity is revealed in accordance with the pre-action protocol.

It should also be borne in mind that the doctor who treated the client may believe that his actions have resulted in the improvement of the patient's condition. Few doctors are likely to admit that their actions have not improved a client's condition or that, despite treatment, the client is still suffering a great deal of pain. The most senior form of doctor is a consultant, and in most cases a specialist consultant in the particular field should be instructed to prepare a report on the client's injuries. The consultant should possess the key qualities referred to above. The importance of instructing a doctor who works in the appropriate speciality that relates to the client's case should not be underestimated, and the trainee solicitor should seek assistance from a senior colleague where appropriate, if he is uncertain as to which doctor to instruct.

Letter of instruction

Reference should be made to the pre-action protocol which sets out a specimen letter of instruction to a medical expert in a personal injury case (see Appendix 3).

The heading of the letter should contain: the client's full name, address, date of birth, date of the accident, his telephone number (which will allow the doctor to contact the client quickly in case of a cancelled appointment) and, if considered appropriate, details of the hospital where the client was treated. It is important that the letter of instruction makes it clear on whose behalf the solicitor is acting, if the notice of appointment is to be sent directly to the client or if the appointment is to be sent via the solicitor. The doctor will need to obtain the notes from the hospital/GP where the client was treated and for this purpose a written authority for the release of his medical records will need to be obtained from the client and sent to the hospital/GP. It is not normally necessary to ask the doctor to examine all of the client's medical notes, but if there is any possibility that the injury could be due to pre-existing problems then such a request should be made.

A number of specific questions relating to the injury should be asked. For example, what is the prognosis, capacity for work, and what are the likely long-term effects of the injuries?

It may be thought appropriate to ask for the doctor's opinion as to whether any other medical opinion is needed from other specialists. For example, an orthopaedic surgeon may suggest that the opinion of a radiologist is required.

If medical notes are forwarded to the doctor, every attempt should be made by the solicitor to understand what they mean as they may be vital evidence. The doctor who has been instructed may be able to assist, but the personal injury solicitor must become fully familiar with the abbreviations and symbols used by the medical profession.

It can take many months for an appointment to be made with the client and for the report to be returned to the instructing solicitor and thus the letter of instruction should include the estimate as to when the solicitor might receive the report and an invitation for the expert to contact the solicitor if the expert cannot prepare the report in the appropriate time. Once the report has been received, it should be read (and understood) by the solicitor and sent to the client for his approval.

As noted above, it is possible to send to the expert written questions and, in the case of *Mutch v Allen* [2001] EWCA Civ 76, (2001) Lawtel, 24 January, the Court of Appeal held that further written questions could be put to an opponent's expert to enable clarification of points not included in the expert's report, provided the questions were within the area of expert's expertise.

8.6.2 Consulting engineers' reports

Many personal injury claims involve machinery or systems of work (especially employers' liability claims) and in such cases it may be thought appropriate for a consulting engineer to be instructed to prepare a report on the machinery involved or the system of work undertaken.

> *Example*
> A client is injured whilst driving a fork-lift truck and alleges that the steering wheel failed to respond whilst he was driving it. It is part of the client's case that the employer failed adequately to maintain the fork-lift truck. If the truck has not been modified prior to the solicitor being instructed, a consulting engineer may be instructed to examine the vehicle and its maintenance records. The solicitor will therefore obtain an expert's view as to whether the appropriate system of maintenance was adopted and attempt to identify the cause of the accident.

Once a choice of consulting engineer has been made, a letter of instruction should be sent to him. Clear instructions should be given as to who is instructing the engineer and what the engineer is being instructed to do, ie visit the premises, inspect the machinery and prepare a report for use in connection with court proceedings. If the solicitor is to attend the inspection, this should be made clear in the letter of instruction. Details of who the expert should contact to arrange a date for the inspection must also be given. Permission from the employers (who are normally the defendants in such cases) is required. If this is not granted then it will be necessary to apply to court for an order granting inspection facilities.

Frequently, even prior to the introduction of the CPR 1998, consulting engineers held joint inspections, where both the claimant's and defendant's engineers attended at the scene of the accident at the same time. This had the advantage of saving costs and time, as the engineers could agree on measurements and technical details. However, whilst it may, in certain cases, still be appropriate to instruct two engineers, the pre-action protocol also makes reference to the joint selection of and instruction of liability experts such as consulting engineers, and thus consideration must be given to this important point.

8.6.3 Accident reconstruction experts

In more complicated road traffic cases, an accident reconstruction expert may need to be instructed. Normally, the accident reconstruction expert will attend at the scene of the accident and examine any skid marks etc and will also consider such evidence as tachographs, if available. He will then provide an opinion as to the cause of the accident. Normally, such experts are instructed only in serious cases such as fatal road accidents and it is important that as much information as possible is obtained surrounding the events of the accident, so that the expert has full details available to him at the time the report is prepared. Frequently, the expert will want to see the police reconstruction report (if one has been prepared) and attempts must be made to obtain this as soon as possible, as in certain areas of the country the reports are being destroyed as little as a year after the incident. The appropriate police force should be contacted and a request made for the relevant documentation to be preserved.

In many cases, it is also appropriate for the expert to examine the vehicles involved in the accident and if the client has instructed the solicitor at an early stage, action must be taken to ensure that the vehicles are not disposed of or repaired prior to the expert carrying out his examination.

8.6.4 Joint instruction/ joint selection

The distinction should be noted between the joint selection of an expert (as detailed by the Protocol) and the joint instruction of an expert. As regards the latter, the expert can be regarded as instructed by both parties and any report would be sent to both parties once it had been prepared.

8.7 PARTICULAR MATTERS RELATING TO INSTRUCTING EXPERTS IN CLINICAL NEGLIGENCE ACTIONS

The choice of expert in a clinical negligence case can be more complex than in a personal injury case. In clinical negligence cases, experts' reports can be divided into three areas.

(1) Reports on liability. A doctor reviews the case and provides a report as to whether the appropriate standard of medical care has been achieved.

(2) Reports on causation. A doctor reviews the case and provides an opinion as to whether the failure to act with the appropriate standard of care (if established) caused the injury.

In certain clinical negligence cases, one doctor may be able to provide one report on both liability and causation, but whether this is appropriate will be dependent on the type of case concerned.
(3) Reports on quantum. A doctor provides a report on the claimant's current and future medical condition.

In most cases, the solicitor will have no idea as to whether there is a case to be pursued or otherwise until the first report on liability from the expert has been obtained.

It is necessary to instruct an expert in a similar speciality to that which is alleged to have given rise to the negligence. For example, if a doctor is working in accident and emergency and is alleged to have been negligent, then a consultant in accident and emergency should be instructed. In certain cases, there will be allegations relating to different specialities and an expert in each speciality will be required.

8.7.1 Choice of experts

Some doctors may be reluctant to provide reports for clinical negligence litigation and the views of the proposed expert must be obtained. Enquiries must also be made as to whether the doctor who is alleged to have been negligent is known to the expert preparing the report as, clearly, this may affect the contents of the report. It may also be appropriate to ensure that the expert is kept informed of who is continuing to treat the client, in case the expert knows any of the other doctors involved and does not believe that he is the appropriate person to report on the matter.

Even if the expert has been used by the solicitor before, in all clinical negligence cases it is good practice to send a preliminary letter of enquiry. Such a letter may have any of the following objectives:

(1) to obtain confirmation that the doctor deals with the appropriate speciality;
(2) to obtain confirmation that the expert is prepared to carry out the necessary post-initial report work such as attending conference with counsel and attending experts' meetings;
(3) to confirm that he would be willing to provide oral evidence to support his written report;
(4) to inform the expert of the identity of the potential defendant (to establish whether the doctor is known to the expert or has worked with him in the past);
(5) to confirm that the medical notes have been obtained (however, they must not be forwarded to the expert at this stage);
(6) to obtain details of the likely waiting time for the report;
(7) to obtain details of the expert's charging rate and/or to explain that the client has the benefit of public funding;
(8) to confirm on whose behalf the solicitor is acting (but without giving any view on liability).

To avoid instructing an expert who knows the potential defendant, it is appropriate to instruct an expert out of the locality where the alleged negligent act took place.

If the expert is prepared to act in response to an initial letter of enquiry, then a full letter of instruction should be sent. It is vital that the expert has access to all medical notes prior to preparing his report (indeed, one of the points that should be raised with the expert is whether all of the necessary medical reports have been disclosed by the relevant hospital or GP). The medical notes must not be sent to the doctor without first being checked by the solicitor to ensure that they are complete and in order. Identical ring binders should be prepared, with copies of paginated medical notes included, in date order, indexed and divided into relevant sections. A ring binder of notes should be prepared for each expert, counsel and the solicitor.

The full letter of instruction should deal with the following matters (to be amended if an expert is jointly instructed/selected):

(1) a chronology of the events/factual resumé to which the doctor can refer. A concise overview of the events should be available for the doctor to consider;
(2) a brief explanation of the relevant standard of care;
(3) liability/causation – it will be necessary to remind the doctor that there is a need to establish a causational link between the identified negligence and injury;
(4) to provide an offer to meet the claimant, which may not be necessary but the facility should be made available;
(5) the date by which the report is needed;
(6) who is responsible for the fee;
(7) a request that the doctor consider whether all the relevant medical notes have been disclosed and, if not, what further notes should be obtained;
(8) to obtain the expert's confirmation as to whether any other type of expert evidence is required in addition to his own;
(9) the doctor should be asked to make reference to medical publications to support his case. It is important to remember that the doctor who is alleged to have been negligent would not have had access to textbooks published in the year 2002, if the alleged incident occurred, for example, in 1990. The expert should be asked to refer to texts and authoritative works that were available at the time of the incident;
(10) specific questions that the expert is required to answer should be included in the letter of instruction. The expert should also be informed that he may be required to attend a conference with counsel at the appropriate time;
(11) specify how the doctor should structure the report.

In the case of *Sharpe v Southend Health Authority* [1997] 8 Med LR 299, the Court of Appeal stated that an expert in a clinical negligence case should make it clear in his report that, even if the expert would have adopted a different approach, he should state whether the approach adopted by the defendant was in accordance with a responsible body of medical practitioners. If it is not known that the expert is aware of this point, then this must also be mentioned in the letter of instruction.

8.7.2 Joint instruction/ joint selection

In a clinical negligence case, solicitors may be more willing to jointly instruct/select an expert in relation to quantum matters, such as future care costs, rather than in relation to liability and/or causation (see *S (A Minor) v Birmingham Health Authority* (1999) CTL, 23 November and *Daniels v Walker* [2000] 1 WLR 1382 concerning difficulties in agreeing instructions to joint experts). However, each case must be considered on its own merits. For example, in the case of *Oxley v Penwarden* (2000) MLC 0250, the Court of Appeal, in dealing with a clinical negligence claim, held:

> 'This was eminently a case where it was necessary for the parties to have the opportunity of investigating causation through an expert of his own choice ...'

Thus, the joint instruction of an expert can be challenged where appropriate. Similarly, on occasions, despite a single joint expert being appointed under r 35.7 of the CPR 1998, the court may grant an application by a litigant to call his own expert witness (see *Cosgrove and Another v Pattison and Another* (2001) *The Times*, February 13 and *Alderson and Another v Skillorgan Sales Ltd and Another* [2001] All ER (D) 104 (June).

8.8 USE OF EXPERTS' REPORTS

As noted earlier, a key aim of the CPR 1998 is to attempt to encourage a less confrontational approach by the parties (especially as regards experts) and to reinforce the principle that the expert's primary duty is to the court (see also *National Justice Compania Naviera SA v Prudential Assurance Co (Ikerian Reefer)* [1993] 2 Lloyd's Rep 68, which is a pre-CPR 1998 case subsequently referred to, setting out the responsibilities of an expert).

In order to achieve these aims, the CPR 1998 (Part 35 and the accompanying Practice Directions) make reference to several requirements regarding expert evidence, including the following:

(1) The duty to the court is the primary duty with which the expert should be concerned.
(2) No expert evidence shall be used without leave of the court and details of the speciality and, if possible, the name of the expert should be provided.
(3) In fast-track cases, expert evidence will normally be given in written form and it will not be necessary for the expert to attend.
(4) The expert's report must contain a statement that he understands and has complied with his primary duty to the court.
(5) The expert's report must contain a statement of the substance of the instructions given to the expert. It should be noted that r 35.10(4) specifically states that the instructions are not privileged, but the court will not normally allow cross-examination of the expert on the instructions, unless it believes the statement is inaccurate.
(6) The expert may apply to the court himself for directions without reference to the parties.
(7) The report should give details of the expert's qualifications.
(8) The report should give details of any literature relied upon.
(9) The report must be verified by a statement of truth.

In addition to the specific points set out above, there is also a general power (see CPR 1998, r 32.1) which allows the court to indentify the key issues and detail what evidence is required, and in what form (see also *Daniels v Walker* [2000] 1 WLR 1382 in relation to difficulties which may be encountered with jointly instructed experts).

8.9 CONFERENCE WITH EXPERTS AND COUNSEL WHERE EXPERT INSTRUCTED BY ONE PARTY

8.9.1 The initial conference prior to proceedings being issued

Personal injury

An initial conference prior to proceedings being issued is not normally necessary in personal injury cases, but consideration should be given to this approach if the claimant is resistant to the solicitor's advice that the claim is likely to fail or if the matter is unusually complicated.

Clinical negligence

In clinical negligence cases, because the issues involved are likely to be complex, it may be appropriate to arrange a conference with the expert, counsel and the client after the initial medical report has been obtained. By this stage, full details of the claimant's claim should be available, together with the medical records and the expert's report. This will give the parties the opportunity to examine fully all the issues, and for the solicitor and counsel to test the expert's evidence and to ensure that he is the appropriate person to be instructed. It also provides an opportunity to assess the merits of the claim to see if proceedings should be issued. An initial conference at this stage is also appropriate when the medical report is unfavourable and it appears that the claim should not proceed.

The conference provides a valuable opportunity to satisfy the client that every possibility has been investigated and that he is not being ignored and there is no medical conspiracy against him. Consideration should be given to instructing counsel to produce a written advice following the conference, to ensure that all matters have been dealt with. During the conference, a detailed note should be taken of matters covered.

If the case is going to proceed, the next stage is the drafting of the letter of claim which is to be sent to the potential defendant.

8.9.2 Conference with counsel after proceedings issued

Personal injury

In the majority of personal injury cases, proceedings will be issued without the need for a conference with counsel, and many low-value cases proceed to trial without such a conference, save for a meeting on the day of the trial (in cases where expert evidence is going to be given orally). In more complex personal injury cases, there may be a conference which will allow an assessment of the expert's knowledge of the case. The solicitor and counsel will want to be sure that the expert has studied all the papers sent to him, has understood the facts of the case, and that he has excellent communication skills. These and other matters can be assessed at the conference.

Clinical negligence

In addition to the conference prior to the issue of proceedings in a clinical negligence case, it is common to have a further conference after the exchange of lay witness statements to check whether all the experts can still support the case. A further conference is normally arranged prior to the trial to review matters.

8.10 MEETING OF EXPERTS

Under the CPR 1998, the court has the power to order a meeting of the experts involved in the case and, where both parties have their own experts, this of often ordered by the court. The aim is to identify the issues that are truly in dispute and, where appropriate, to prepare a joint statement which highlights the evidence which is and that which is not disputed. Certain commentators believe that these meetings (they can be done by telephone) can be of significant benefit in attempting to either resolve the case or at least identify the true issues in dispute.

8.11 EXPERTS' COSTS

Experts will charge a fee for which the solicitor is ultimately responsible. The solicitor should therefore ensure that, as far as possible, he will be reimbursed for the payment of those fees at every stage of the case. As much detail as possible about an expert's fees should be obtained prior to instruction. This information must then be put before the client, and his instructions taken. Many solicitors ask for costs on account for experts' fees. It should be noted that the court may restrict the level of the experts' fees.

8.12 TYPES OF EXPERTS

The number and variety of experts available to prepare reports is often a surprise to those unfamiliar with this area. The following are examples of experts who provide reports.

(1) Liability – employer/public liability cases:
  – general consulting engineers to provide reports on machinery, systems of work, slipping accidents;
  – mining engineers;
  – ergonomics experts;
  – bio-engineers;
  – pharmacologists.
(2) Liability – road traffic accidents:
  – accident investigators to reconstruct the events leading up to the road traffic accident;
  – mechanical engineers to examine the vehicles involved in the accident, to identify damage or to investigate if any mechanical defects were present in the vehicle.
(3) Liability/causation in clinical negligence cases and condition and prognosis in both clinical negligence and personal injury cases – medical specialities:
  – orthopaedic surgeons;
  – neurologists;
  – psychiatrists;
  – plastic surgeons;
  – dental surgeons;
  – psychologists;
  – neuro-surgeons;
  – oncologists;

- urologists;
- obstetricians;
- otorhinolaryngologists.

(4) Quantum – condition and prognosis and costs of living with a particular injury:
- occupational therapists;
- behaviourial therapists;
- speech therapists;
- physiotherapists;
- architects;
- employment consultants;
- doctors;
- nurses.

(5) Quantum – financial loss and investment of damages:
- employment consultants;
- accountants;
- actuaries.

8.13 CONCLUSION

The role that the expert has in a personal injury or clinical negligence case is a significant one. The importance of the selection of the correct individual cannot be underestimated. At the time of writing, a Draft Code of Guidance on Expert Evidence has been published, and reference should be made to the Code of Guidance (when appropriate) as it is intended to help those who instruct experts and experts themselves where the CPR 1998 applies. It is anticipated that the Code of Guidance will become incorporated into PD35.

8.14 KEY POINTS

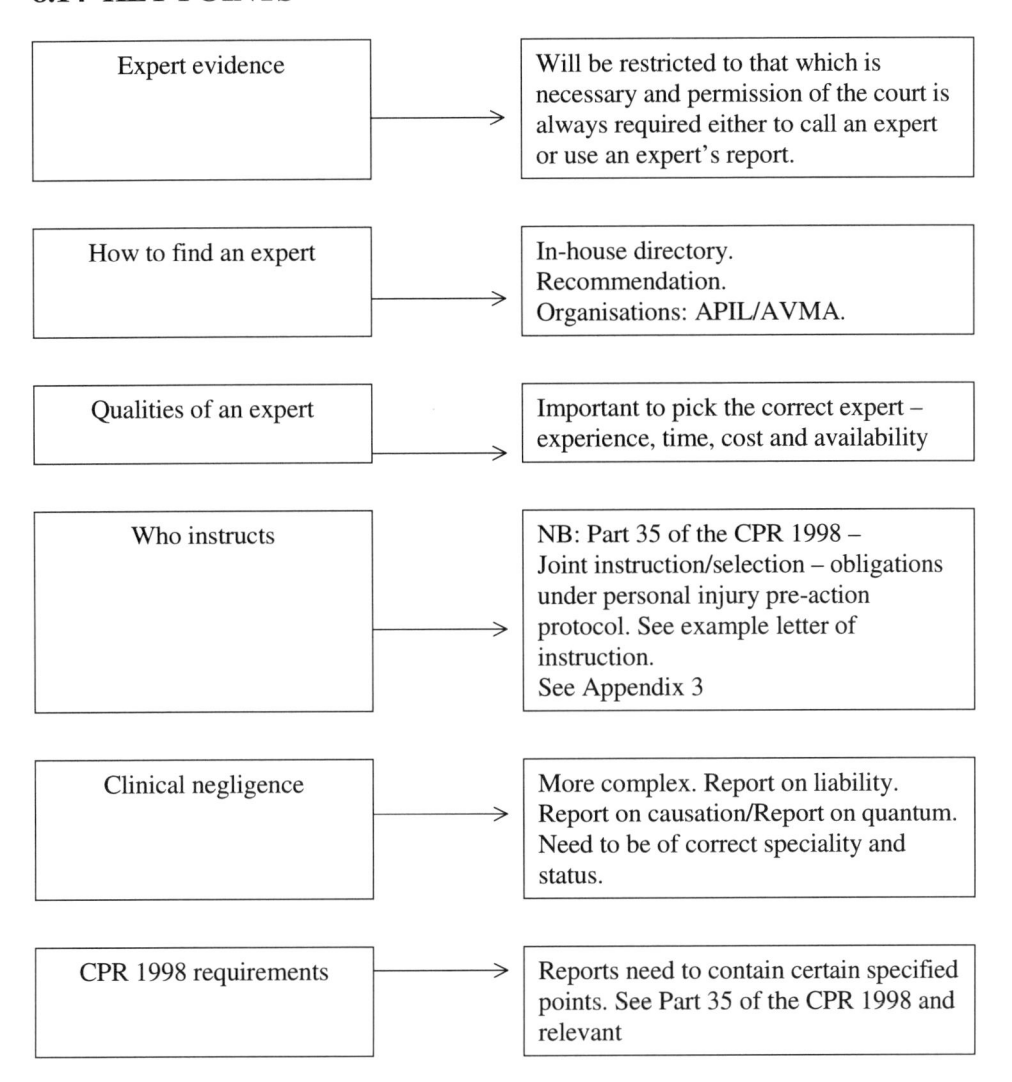

Expert evidence	→ Will be restricted to that which is necessary and permission of the court is always required either to call an expert or use an expert's report.
How to find an expert	→ In-house directory. Recommendation. Organisations: APIL/AVMA.
Qualities of an expert	→ Important to pick the correct expert – experience, time, cost and availability
Who instructs	→ NB: Part 35 of the CPR 1998 – Joint instruction/selection – obligations under personal injury pre-action protocol. See example letter of instruction. See Appendix 3
Clinical negligence	→ More complex. Report on liability. Report on causation/Report on quantum. Need to be of correct speciality and status.
CPR 1998 requirements	→ Reports need to contain certain specified points. See Part 35 of the CPR 1998 and relevant

8.15 FURTHER READING

Kemp and Kemp *The Quantum of Damages* (Sweet & Maxwell).
Hendy, Day, Buchan and Kennedy *Personal Injury Practice* (Butterworths).
Pre-action Protocol for Personal Injury Claims (see Appendix 3).
Pre-action Protocol for Clinical Disputes (see Appendix 3).

Chapter 9

PRE-COMMENCEMENT AND COMMENCEMENT STEPS

9.1 INTRODUCTION

9.1.1 Reasons for and against commencing proceedings early

It is usually to the claimant's advantage to begin proceedings early for the following reasons.

(1) Once the claimant has complied with the provisions of the relevant pre-action protocol (normally 3 months from the date of acknowledgment of the letter of claim), he is free to issue and serve the proceedings without sanctions being applied at a later date by the court on the basis that proceedings have been issued prematurely.

(2) To avoid problems with the limitation period. In personal injury litigation, proceedings must normally be commenced within 3 years of the accident occurring; ongoing negotiations with the proposed defendant/defendant's insurers do not have the automatic effect of extending the limitation period and, in any event, negotiations may continue after proceedings have been commenced.

(3) It will put pressure on the defendant/defendant's insurers to act in relation to the claim. In personal injury cases, it will often precipitate the defendant's file moving from the insurance company claims department to the insurer's nominated solicitors who may be more willing to negotiate.

(4) In practice, judgment usually carries entitlement to interest and costs. A settlement achieved prior to the commencement of proceedings does not carry such an entitlement (although the claimant's solicitor will always include in any such settlement an element in respect of interest and costs). After proceedings have been issued, if there is any argument by the defendant as to how much of the claimant's costs he should pay on settlement, the claimant's solicitor can have his costs assessed by the court.

(5) Commencing proceedings enables the claimant to apply to the court for an interim payment in the event that a voluntary payment cannot be negotiated.

It may not be advisable to commence proceedings in the following circumstances, which are usually beyond the control of the solicitor.

(1) The claimant is obliged to comply with the relevant pre-action protocol requiring that a detailed letter of claim be forwarded to the proposed defendant, followed by a waiting period of not less than 3 months.

(2) The solicitor may not be in a position to issue proceedings because of a restriction on the client's legal aid certificate, or because of a similar restriction in relation to the client's private legal expenses insurance requiring specific authority to be granted prior to issue of proceedings.

Chapter 9 contents
Introduction
Pre-action protocol to be used in personal injury claims
Pre-action protocol to be used in clinical disputes (medical negligence)
Pre-action disclosure
Issuing proceedings
Conclusion
Further reading

(3) The client may be waiting for an appointment to be medically examined in order to provide the medical report which must be filed at court on issue of proceedings.

(4) If the amount of claim for pain, suffering and loss of amenity is not more than £1,000 and the overall value of the claim is not more than £5,000, it will be allocated to the small claims track, in which case only very limited costs can be recovered.

9.2 PRE-ACTION PROTOCOL TO BE USED IN PERSONAL INJURY CLAIMS

9.2.1 Introduction

In his final report on *Access to Justice*, Lord Woolf placed emphasis on the development of what he termed pre-action protocols. He wished to 'increase the benefits of early but well informed settlement'. The aim of the protocols in both personal injury and clinical negligence claims is that it will help the parties to make an informed decision on the merits of the case and lead to an increased number of pre-action settlements. This will be achieved by encouraging pre-action dialogue between the parties, exchanging better quality information and by better pre-action investigation. The net result of this will be two-fold; either a reduction in the need for recourse to litigation, or that subsequent proceedings will run more smoothly.

In order to ensure that the protocols have their desired effect, it is necessary that they be supported by sanctions for non-compliance. The Lord Chancellor has intimated his support for strict adherence by all parties to the protocols and that strong sanctions should be imposed by the judiciary in the event of non-compliance. The courts will treat the standards set down in the protocols as the reasonable approach to be expected in pre-action conduct. The court has power to ensure compliance with the protocol by means of costs penalties. If the court decides that non-compliance has led to commencement of proceedings which could have been avoided with use of the protocol, or costs have been incurred needlessly, the court may penalise the party at fault in costs. The party at fault may be ordered to:

(a) pay the costs/part costs of the other party;
(b) pay costs on the indemnity basis;
(c) if he is a claimant he may be penalised by not being awarded interest on all or part of the award, or interest at a lower rate;
(d) if the party at fault is a defendant, an order for interest on damages may be awarded at a higher rate (not exceeding 10% above base rate).

The following protocols have been included in the Practice Directions under the CPR 1998.

9.2.2 The protocol for use in personal injury claims

This protocol is designed for use in:

(i) road traffic cases;
(ii) tripping and slipping cases; and
(iii) employers' liability cases.

Because most of these cases are very likely to be allocated to the fast-track, it is important that as many preliminary issues as possible are dealt with at the pre-commencement stage. This will be especially important for the defendant, who traditionally has had less time to prepare his case. However, the court will expect that in multi-track cases, the spirit if not the letter of the protocol should be adhered to as the standard of reasonable pre-action behaviour (see *Carlson v Townsend* [2001] EWCA Civ 511, [2001] All ER (D) 99 (April)). If one or both parties consider that the protocol is not appropriate to their case, the court will expect an explanation as to why the protocol has not been followed.

9.2.3 The letter of claim

The letter of claim is most commonly sent to the proposed defendant, who will be an individual. The function of the letter of claim is to ensure that the insurer is involved at the earliest possible date and therefore stresses the importance of passing on the letter of claim to the relevant insurer. If the claimant's solicitor is not yet able to formulate a letter of claim, he may still notify the defendant or his insurer of the claim before sending a detailed letter of claim. This may be used where the defendant is unaware, or has little knowledge of the incident.

The letter of claim should contain the following:

(i) a clear summary of the facts on which the claim is based;
(ii) an indication of the nature of all of the injuries that have been sustained; and
(iii) an indication of other financial losses.

The letter should contain enough information to enable the defendant or his solicitor to investigate the proposed claim, and put a broad valuation on the claim.

The letter should also ask the defendant to pass a copy of the letter of claim to his insurer. However, if the insurer is known, a copy of the letter of claim should also be sent to the insurer direct.

The pre-action protocol does not currently require information about how the claim is being funded to be included in the letter of claim. It is, however, recommended that this information be given at the earliest opportunity as it is required to be given by notice with the Claim Form on issue of proceedings. The sooner the opposition is on notice that there is a CFA with a success fee in place, the more likely it is that there will not be a problem arguing for recovery of the success fee when an assessment of costs and success fee takes place at the conclusion of the proceedings.

Such a letter of claim is reproduced at Appendix 3, marked 'Annex A'.

9.2.4 The response by the defendant

The defendant should be asked to reply to the letter of claim within 21 calendar days of the date of posting, confirming the identity of his insurer, if he has one. If the defendant fails to reply within 21 days and there is no response from his insurer within the same period, then the claimant may commence proceedings.

If the defendant or his insurers do respond to the letter of claim within 21 days, they have a maximum of 3 months from the date of acknowledgment of claim to investigate the claim. Within that time, they must reply to the claimant, confirming whether or not they admit liability. If liability is denied, then they must give reasons for the denial. If liability is admitted, the defendant is bound by that admission for all claims up to a value of £15,000.

9.2.5 Early disclosure of documents

Disclosure of documents by the defendant is designed to clarify and resolve the issues in dispute. Either within the letter of claim, or appended to it, the claimant's solicitor can forward a list of possible documents which he considers to be relevant and which he considers the defendant ought to have in his possession. If the defendant responds to the letter of claim with a denial of liability, he should include in his reply all documents which are material to the issues between the parties and which would be likely to be ordered to be disclosed by the court. Lists of likely documents to be disclosed are reproduced at Annex B of Appendix 3.

If the defendant admits liability but alleges contributory negligence on the part of the claimant, the defendant should disclose documents which are still relevant to the issue of contributory negligence.

9.2.6 Documents to be produced by the claimant

A schedule of special damages with supporting documents should be produced by the claimant for use by the defendant.

9.2.7 Selection of experts

Because, at this stage, there are no proceedings, the protocol does not require joint instruction of experts as set out in Part 35 of CPR 1998. At this stage, the instructing party only will be sent the report. The instructing party will then decide whether or not to disclose the report. If he wishes to rely on it, he discloses it to the defendant who, if he agrees with it, will not then obtain his own report. It should be noted that, in *Carlson v Townsend* [2001] EWCA Civ 511, [2001] All ER (D) 99 (April), the Court of Appeal confirmed that the protocol encouraged voluntary disclosure of claimant's expert reports. However, the protocol did not require disclosure and therefore the claimant's withholding the report did not constitute non-compliance with the protocol. The defendant's non-objection to the claimant's choice of expert did not transform that expert into a single joint expert. Therefore, the report subsequently produced would not be available to the defendant as of right and the claimant could claim privilege for it.

The defendant may, after proceedings have been commenced, if he thinks that it is necessary, obtain his own report, with permission of the court. It should be borne in mind that if more than one report is prepared, the court will have to decide whether or not to allow the cost of more than one report.

Prior to instructing an expert, the claimant should give the defendant a list of names of one, or preferably more, experts within the same speciality, any of whom he considers suitable to instruct.

Within 14 days, the defendant may object to one or more of the experts proposed by the claimant. The claimant will then instruct one of the mutually acceptable experts.

If the claimant nominates his expert in the letter of claim, the defendant has 14 days to object *after* the period of 21 days within which he has to reply to the letter of claim.

If the defendant objects to all of the experts proposed by the claimant, both parties are then at liberty to instruct the expert of their own choice. If more than one expert is instructed in this way, the court must decide subsequently whether either party has acted unreasonably as to the question of recovering the costs of more than one report.

The reason for seeking the defendant's approval to the claimant's expert is that if the defendant does not object to the claimant's nominated expert he is not entitled to rely on his own evidence in the same speciality unless:

(i) the claimant agrees;
(ii) the court so directs; or
(iii) the claimant's expert's report has been amended and the claimant is not prepared to disclose the original report.

The same reasoning will apply where it is the defendant who wishes to instruct an expert of a particular specialism and provides a list of experts to the claimant for him to agree or disagree as the case may be.

Subsequent to the expert's report having been received, either party may ask the expert to answer written questions on relevant issues via the instructing party's solicitors. The expert should then send written answers to those questions both separately and directly to each of the parties.

9.2.8 Part 36 offers

The protocol advises (para 3.21) that both parties should always bear in mind whether it is appropriate to make a Part 36 offer prior to investigating proceedings.

If a claim is not resolved at protocol stage, the parties are encouraged to 'stocktake' by considering the issues in dispute and the evidence necessary before the court will be able to decide those issues. If the defendant is insured, the insurer will normally be expected to nominate solicitors at that stage, and should do so 7–14 days prior to the intended issue date.

9.3 PRE-ACTION PROTOCOL TO BE USED IN CLINICAL DISPUTES (CLINICAL NEGLIGENCE)

9.3.1 Introduction

The pre-action protocol for resolution of clinical disputes is aimed at improving the pre-action communication between the parties at the earliest possible date. The protocol itself establishes a timetable for exchange of key information relevant to the dispute and provides templates for the documents to be used by both sides. The protocol has been prepared by the Clinical Disputes Forum. The Forum includes healthcare professionals, NHS management, lawyers specialising in clinical claims working for both claimant and defendant and experts. In relation to penalties for non-compliance with a protocol, the court may refuse to grant extensions of time for filing statements of case or evidence, or award or disallow costs where proceedings have been issued prematurely.

The protocol encourages a climate of openness when something has 'gone wrong' with a patient's treatment. It recommends a timed sequence of steps for claimants and healthcare providers to follow if a dispute arises. The trend in relation to healthcare disputes is that the number of complaints and subsequent litigation is on the increase, and that this trend is likely to continue as more and more patients become likely to complain about treatment and to subsequently embark on litigation. Currently, the period of delay between a suspicion by the patient that 'something has gone wrong' and receiving a response from the healthcare provider merely serves for those suspicions to take root, and for there to be reluctance of healthcare providers to reveal details to patients, especially if there has been an adverse outcome (but not necessarily as a result of negligence).

9.3.2 The protocol for use in clinical disputes

In his report on *Access to Justice*, Lord Woolf recommended that patients, their advisers and healthcare providers should work towards resolution of disputes without recourse to litigation if possible. The clinical disputes protocol works towards this by standardising not only the timetable for, but also the content of, the disclosure of information prior to litigation. Although the protocol sets strict time-limits, its aim is to be flexible enough so that it may apply to all aspects of health service care, both public and private. For example, access to GP records may prove relatively easy to accomplish, whereas it may be rather more complicated and therefore slow to obtain records concerning events which may have happened many years ago from a large hospital.

9.3.3 Good practice commitments

The commitments section of the protocol summarises guiding principles that healthcare providers, patients and advisers should consider at the point where they are dealing with patient dissatisfaction.

Healthcare providers should:

(1) ensure that key staff are appropriately trained and have some knowledge of healthcare law and the complaints procedures;
(2) develop a system of clinical risk management;
(3) set up 'adverse outcome reporting systems' in all specialities to record and investigate unexpected and serious adverse outcomes as soon as possible;
(4) use the results of adverse incidents and subsequent complaints in a positive way (as a guide to how to improve service);
(5) ensure that all patients receive a clear and comprehensible response to their complaints or concerns;
(6) establish efficient and effective systems of recording and storing patient records, notes, diagnostic reports and x-rays and retain these in accordance with Department of Health guidance. The current minimum period for storage in the case of adults is 8 years, and in the case of obstetric and paediatric notes for children, until they reach the age of 25;
(7) advise patients of a serious adverse outcome and on request provide the patient with an oral or written explanation.

According to the protocol, it is incumbent on the claimant and his advisers to:

(1) report any concerns and dissatisfactions which he may have to his healthcare provider as soon as possible;
(2) consider all of the options available to him if he is dissatisfied, including seeking clarification, and negotiation but not only to consider litigation;

(3) inform the healthcare provider when the patient is satisfied that the matter has been concluded.

9.3.4 The steps in the protocol

The following steps in the protocol should be followed once non-litigation options have been considered and litigation is proposed.

Obtaining the health records

Requests for patient records should:

(1) provide sufficient information to tell the healthcare provider where an adverse outcome has been serious or has had serious consequences;
(2) be as specific as possible about the nature of the records that are required to be disclosed.

Form of request for records

Requests for copies of patient records should be made using The Law Society and Department of Health-approved standard forms. According to the protocol, copy records should be provided within 40 days of request. The cost of copies should not exceed the charge permissible under the Access to Health Records Act 1990, as amended by the Data Protection Act 1998 (currently a maximum of £50 for hard copies and £10 for electronic copies). If the healthcare provider is not able to comply with the 40-day time-limit, they should inform the person requesting the copies quickly, as well as explaining what they are doing to resolve the situation. If the healthcare provider fails to provide the copy records within 40 days, the patient or his adviser may apply to the court for pre-action disclosure.

9.3.5 The letter of claim

The protocol provides a template for the recommended contents for the letter of claim as follows.

If, following receipt and analysis of records, the patient or his adviser decide that there are grounds for claim, they should, as soon as practicable, send to the healthcare provider a letter of claim.

The letter should contain the following information:

(1) a clear summary of the facts on which the claim is based, including details of the alleged adverse outcome and main allegations of negligence;
(2) it should describe the patient's injuries, present condition and prognosis;
(3) it should describe the financial loss incurred by the claimant and indicate the heads of damage to be claimed.

If the letter of claim refers to relevant documents, and it is envisaged that normally it will, it should, if possible, enclose copies of all of those documents which would not already be in the potential defendant's possession, for example, any relevant general practitioner records if the claimant is making a claim against a hospital.

In complex cases, a chronology of relevant events should be provided (eg where a patient has been treated by a number of different healthcare professionals, and/or has been referred to a number of different hospitals and clinics).

Sufficient information must be given to enable the healthcare provider to:

(i) commence investigations and;
(ii) put an initial value onto the claim.

Proceedings should not be issued until after 3 months from the letter of claim, unless there is:

(i) a limitation problem or;
(ii) the patient's position needs protecting by early issue of proceedings.

9.3.6 Claimant's offer to settle

The claimant can make an offer to settle the claim at this stage by putting forward an amount of compensation which he would be prepared to accept in settlement of the claim. An offer to settle at this stage should be supported by:

(i) a medical report confirming the injuries, condition and prognosis of the claimant; and
(ii) a schedule of loss, together with supporting documentation.

9.3.7 The proposed defendant's response

The proposed defendant should acknowledge the letter of claim within 14 days of receipt and should identify who is dealing with the claim. Within 3 months of the date of the letter of claim, the proposed defendant should provide a substantive response in the following terms.

(1) If the claim is admitted in full, the proposed defendant should say so in clear terms.
(2) If part is admitted, the proposed defendant should make this clear, stating which issues of breach of duty and/or causation are admitted and which issues are denied.
(3) Admissions made at this stage will be binding only if the healthcare provider has indicated that they be binding.
(4) If the claim is denied, the response should make specific comments relating to the allegations of negligence that have been made. If a chronology of events was provided by the claimant, details in rebuttal of this should be provided.
(5) Where additional documents are referred to and relied upon, copies should be provided with the response.
(6) If the claimant has made an offer to settle, the proposed defendant should respond to that offer in the response.

9.3.8 Proposed defendant's offer to settle

The proposed defendant may make his own offer to settle at this stage, either as a counter-offer to the claimant's offer to settle or not. Any offer of settlement should be supported by medical evidence and/or other evidence relevant to the value of the claim which the proposed defendant has in his possession.

9.3.9 Quantification of claim

If both the claimant and the proposed defendant are in agreement on liability, but, as often happens, it is necessary to wait before a clear prognosis on the injuries can be arrived at, the parties should try to agree a reasonable time-scale within which to reach agreement in relation to the value of claim.

9.4 PRE-ACTION DISCLOSURE

An application for disclosure prior to the start of proceedings is permitted under s 33 of the Supreme Court Act 1981 or s 52 of the County Courts Act 1984. The application must be supported by appropriate evidence, and the procedure is the same in both the High Court and county court. (This procedure is dealt with in r 31.16 of the CPR 1998.) The court may make an order for disclosure only where:

(1) the respondent is likely to be a party to subsequent proceedings;
(2) the applicant is also likely to be a party to the proceedings;
(3) if proceedings had started, the respondent's duty by way of standard disclosure set out in the rules would extend to the documents or classes of documents of which the applicant seeks disclosure; and
(4) disclosure before proceedings have started is desirable in order to:

   (i) dispose fairly of the anticipated proceedings; or
   (ii) assist the dispute to be resolved without proceedings; or
   (iii) save costs.

An order under this rule must specify the documents or class of documents which the respondent must disclose and require him, when making such disclosure, to specify any of those documents which he no longer has or which he claims the right or duty to withhold from inspection. The order may also specify the time and place for disclosure and inspection to take place.

9.4.1 Orders for disclosure against a person who is a non-party

Where application is made to the court, under any Act, for disclosure by a person who is not a party (but is likely to become so) to the proceedings, the application must be supported by suitable evidence.

The court may make an order under this rule only where:

(1) the documents of which disclosure is sought are likely to support the case of the applicant or adversely affect the case of one or other of the parties to the proceedings; and
(2) disclosure is necessary to dispose fairly of the claim or save costs.

An order under this rule must specify the documents or class of documents which the respondent must disclose, and require the respondent to make disclosure or specify any of those documents for which he no longer has or for which he claims the right or duty to withhold from inspection. Once again, the order may specify a time and place for such disclosure and inspection.

An order for an interim remedy can be made at any time prior to the proceedings being started unless there is a rule or a specific practice direction which says otherwise. The court may grant an interim remedy before a claim has been made only if:

(i) the matter is urgent; or
(ii) it is otherwise necessary to do so in the interests of justice.

9.4.2 Procedure

The court may grant an interim remedy on application without notice if it appears to the court that there are good reasons for not giving notice to the proposed defendant. Such an application must be supported by evidence, unless the court orders otherwise. If the applicant makes an application without giving notice, the evidence in support of his application must state the reasons why no notice was given.

9.4.3 Rules in relation to inspection of property before commencement or against a non-party

The evidence in support of such an application must show, if practicable, by reference to any statement of case that has been prepared in relation to the proceedings or anticipated proceedings, that the property:

(a) is or may become the subject matter of the proceedings; or
(b) is relevant to the issue that will arise in relation to those proceedings.

A copy of the application and a copy of the evidence in support must be served on the person against whom the order is sought; and every party to proceedings other than the applicant (CPR 1998, r 25.5).

9.4.4 Offers to settle prior to commencement of proceedings under CPR 1998, Part 36

Offers to settle and payments into court are dealt with in detail in Chapter 10. An offer of settlement can be made at any time by either party.

9.5 ISSUING PROCEEDINGS

Issuing proceedings in both the High Court and the county court uses the same procedure and the same terminology. However, cases of higher value and/or greater complexity may be issued only in the High Court.

When issuing proceedings in a case being funded by a CFA, regard must be had to the requirement to give notice that the matter is being funded in this way, as to which see **4.3**.

The procedure for issuing proceedings is dealt with in the LPC Resource Book *Civil Litigation* (Jordans).

9.5.1 Statements of value

In a claim for personal injuries, the claimant must state on the claim form whether the amount which he reasonably expects to recover in general damages for pain, suffering and loss of amenity is:

(1) not more than £1,000; or
(2) more than £1,000.

If a claim is to be issued in the High Court, it must state that the claimant reasonably expects to recover £50,000 or more; or must state that some other enactment provides that the claim may be commenced in the High Court and specify that enactment.

When calculating how much he expects to recover, the claimant must disregard any possibility:

(1) that he may recover interest and costs;
(2) that the court may make a finding of contributory negligence against him;
(3) that the defendant may make a counterclaim or that the defence may include a set-off; or
(4) that the defendant may be required to pay money which the court awards to the claimant by way of compensation recoupment under s 6 of the Social Security (Recovery of Benefits) Act 1997.

9.5.2 Particulars of claim

The particulars of claim must be contained in or served with the claim form, or be served on the defendant by the claimant within 14 days after service of the claim form. In any event, particulars of claim must be served on the defendant no later than the latest time for serving a claim form (ie within 4 months after date of issue of the claim form).

The particulars of claim must include:

(1) a concise statement of the facts on which the claimant relies;
(2) if the claimant seeks interest, a statement detailing the interest claimed.
(3) if the claimant is seeking aggravated damages or exemplary damages, a statement confirming the grounds on which that claim is made; and
(4) such other matters as may be set out in the relevant practice direction.

PD 16 states that the following matters must be contained in the particulars of claim:

(a) the claimant's date of birth;
(b) brief details of the claimant's injuries; and
(c) details of past and future expenses and losses.

If the claimant wishes to rely on medical evidence of a medical practitioner, such a report must be served with or attached to the particulars of claim detailing the injuries.

There are further provisions in the Practice Direction relevant to provisional damages claims.

If the claim relates to a fatal accident, the claimant must state in his particulars of claim:

(a) that it is brought under the Fatal Accidents Act 1976;
(b) the dependants on whose behalf the claim is made;
(c) the date of birth of each dependant; and
(d) details of the nature of the dependency claim.

If the claimant seeks interest, he must state whether he is doing so under the terms of a contract or under an Act and, if so, which Act.

Both the claim form and the particulars of claim must contain a statement that the claimant (and if the claimant is acting as a litigation friend, the litigation friend) believes that the facts stated in the document are true.

9.5.3 Service of proceedings

After the claim form has been issued, it must be served within 4 months after the date of issue. If the claim form is to be served out of the jurisdiction, the period is 6 months.

9.5.4 Acknowledgment of service

The defendant may respond to the claim by either:

(1) defending the claim; or
(2) admitting the claim; or
(3) acknowledging service of the claim form.

If the defendant makes no response to the claim, the claimant may enter default judgment.

The defendant may acknowledge service if he is unable to file a defence in time, or if he contests the court's jurisdiction.

The time for acknowledgment of service is 14 days from the service of the claim form, unless the claim form indicates that the particulars of claim are to follow separately, in which case the defendant does not have to acknowledge service until 14 days after service of those particulars of claim.

The acknowledgment of service form must be signed by the defendant or his legal representative and must include an address for service for the defendant which must be within the jurisdiction.

On receipt of such an acknowledgment of service, the court must notify the claimant in writing of this.

9.5.5 The defence

The defendant must file a defence within 14 days of service of the particulars of claim, or, if the defendant has filed an acknowledgment of service, within 28 days after service of the particulars of claim.

9.5.6 Extension of time for filing defence

The parties may agree an extension of time for filing of the defence of up to 28 days. The defendant must give the court written notice of any such agreement.

9.5.7 Contents of the defence

The defence must contain the following information:

(1) the allegations made in the claim which are admitted;
(2) the allegations made in the claim which are denied; and
(3) the allegations made in the claim which are neither admitted nor denied but which the claimant is required to prove.

If the claimant has attached a schedule of past and future expenses and losses to his particulars of claim, the defendant must include with his defence a counter-schedule stating which items he agrees, disputes or neither agrees nor disputes but has no knowledge of. If items are disputed, an alternative figure must be supplied.

Where allegations are denied, the defendant must give reasons for that denial and, where relevant, give his own version of the facts. If the defendant disputes the claimant's statement of value, he must give reasons for doing so and, if possible, give his own estimate of value.

Unless the defendant has already acknowledged service, the defendant must give an address for service which is within the jurisdiction.

The defence must contain a statement that the defendant, or, if the defendant is conducting proceedings with a litigation friend, the litigation friend, believes the facts stated in it are true.

The defence must contain a statement of truth and should be signed either by the defendant or by his legal adviser.

The defence should make clear the defendant's version of the facts, insofar as it is different from that stated in the claim.

The basic function of the statements of case is to state, for the benefit of the court, the facts which are relied upon by the parties. Once the claim and defence have been filed, they will be considered by the procedural judge and, if the factual issues cannot be identified from them, directions should be given to the parties in order to rectify this. In cases where there is a case management conference (see Chapter 10), one of the items to be concluded either prior to or after that conference, will be to produce a comprehensive statement of the issues which are currently in dispute.

9.5.8 The counterclaim

Counterclaims and third-party claims are simply known as Part 20 claims. The person seeking to make the further claim is known as the Part 20 claimant.

In the case of a counterclaim, the original claimant does not need to acknowledge service of the counterclaim, but he must, however, file his defence when he files his allocation questionnaire.

Where there are co-defendants, if one of them wishes to seek a contribution of an indemnity from the other, then, once he has filed his acknowledgment of service or defence, he may proceed with his claim against the co-defendant. To proceed with a claim against the co-defendant, the Part 20 claimant must:

(1) file a notice stating the nature and grounds of his claim; and
(2) serve that notice on the co-defendant.

A defendant does not need leave to make a Part 20 claim if it is issued before or at the same time as he files his defence. In all other cases, he does need leave to make a Part 20 claim. The application for leave can be made without notice, unless the court otherwise directs. The defendant does not need leave to make a Part 20 claim if he serves the claim within 14 days of filing his defence.

9.5.9 The reply to defence

The claimant may file a reply to the defence, but, if he does not do so, he will not be deemed to admit the matters raised in the defence.

The claimant may file a reply and a certificate of reply when he files his allocation questionnaire (see Chapter 10). If he does serve a reply, he must also serve it on all other parties.

9.5.10 Contents of the reply

The reply must respond to any matters in the defence which have not been dealt with in the particulars of the claim and must also contain a statement that the maker believes the contents of the document are true.

The particulars of claim, defence and reply are said to be the statements of case. No subsequent statements of case may be filed without the court's leave.

9.6 CONCLUSION

Because of the positive need to state a case in simple terms, solicitors acting for claimants and defendants spend more time gathering and analysing evidence in order to establish what the issues in the case are as early as possible. It should also be borne in mind that, because the statements of case are considered by the procedural judge when he makes his decision as to which track the matter should be allocated, they will be scrutinised at a much earlier date than under the old system as they will be used as the basis for a statement of issues in the case. Therefore, if the statements of case are not sufficiently clear the procedural judge will give directions to remedy this, with poorly drafted statements of case being struck out.

9.7 FURTHER READING

Pre-action Protocol for Personal Injury Claims (see Appendix 3).
Pre-action Protocol for Clinical Disputes (see Appendix 3).

Chapter 10

CASE TRACKING AND CASE MANAGEMENT

10.1 INTRODUCTION

Interlocutory matters can be categorised as all of the stages of the litigation process, subsequent to the issue of the proceedings and prior to the trial. The interlocutory stage is taken up mainly with obtaining and then complying with the directions issued by the court, either under the fast-track procedure or under the multi-track procedure, following the case management conference to ensure that the case is properly prepared for trial. The following paragraphs deal with this stage as it relates to personal injury and clinical negligence claims. A detailed consideration of this area is dealt with in the LPC Resource Book *Civil Litigation* (Jordans).

10.2 CASE MANAGEMENT

Under the CPR 1998, cases are allocated within a three-tier system as follows:

(1) small claims track – for claims of not more than £5,000 (£1,000 in personal injury claims);
(2) fast track – for claims of more than £5,000 but less than £15,000 (more than £1,000 in personal injury cases);
(3) multi-track – for claims of more than £15,000 and claims where the remedy is other than damages.

Where a claim is defended, on receipt of defence the court will serve each party with an allocation questionnaire. Each party must return the allocation questionnaire within 14 days. The parties must complete the allocation questionnaire indicating where they consider the case should be allocated. When allocating a case, the court may take into account the following factors:

(1) financial value of the claim (or amount in dispute if different);
(2) the nature of remedy sought;
(3) the likely complexity of the facts, law or evidence;
(4) the number of parties or likely parties;
(5) the value of any counterclaim or other claim and the complexity of any matters relating to it;
(6) the amount of oral evidence that may be required;
(7) the importance of the claim to persons who are not parties to the proceedings;
(8) the views expressed by the parties;
(9) the circumstances of the parties.

Although the court will have regard to the above factors, it may allocate a case into an alternative track if it thinks it appropriate in the circumstances. For example, the multi-track rather than the fast track may be appropriate if either the trial is likely to last for more than one day or there will be expert evidence in more than two fields or

Chapter 10 contents
Introduction
Case management
Allocation to track
The case management conference and pre-trial review
Group litigation
Interim payments
Disclosure and inspection of documents
Witness evidence
Use of plans, photographs and models as evidence at trial
Expert evidence
Offers to settle and payments into court
Conclusion
Further reading

more than one expert in any one field. This is likely to be the case in clinical negligence cases, even though the value of the claim may be quite modest.

Once the court has allocated a claim to a track, it will notify all parties and it will also serve them with:

(1) copies of the allocation questionnaire provided by all other parties;
(2) a copy of any further information provided by a party about his case.

10.2.1 Stay to allow settlement of case

A party returning his allocation questionnaire may request a stay of up to one month while the parties try to settle the case. Where all parties request a stay, or where the court, of its own initiative, considers such a stay would be appropriate, the court will direct a stay for one month. The court may also extend the period of the stay until such a date or such a period as it considers appropriate. Having stayed proceedings, if proceedings are settled, the claimant must inform the court of this.

10.3 ALLOCATION TO TRACK

Once every party has filed an allocation questionnaire, or once the period for filing the questionnaire has expired, the court will allocate the claim to a track. Before deciding which track to allocate the proceedings, the court may make an order for a party to provide further information (eg if their statement of case is at all unclear). The court may also hold an allocation hearing if it thinks that this is necessary.

10.3.1 The small-claims track

In relation to personal injury claims, the small-claims track is the appropriate track where the financial value of the claim does not exceed £5,000 and the claim for damages for personal injuries is not more than £1,000. Rule 2.3 defines a 'claim for personal injuries' as proceedings in which there is a claim for damages in respect of personal injuries to the claimant or any other person or in respect of a person's death.

10.3.2 The fast track

The fast track is the usual track for claims for personal injuries where the financial value of the claim is not more than £15,000 but is more than £5,000 and where the claim for damages for personal injuries is more than £1,000. However, although the above is the normal rule, this assumes that:

(1) the trial is likely to last for no longer than one day;
(2) oral expert evidence at the trial will be limited to:

    (i) one expert per party in relation to any expert field,
    (ii) expert evidence in two expert fields.

According to the CPR 1998, 'damages for personal injuries' means damages claimed as compensation for pain, suffering and loss of amenity and does not include any other damages which are claimed.

When assessing the financial value of a claim the court will disregard:

(1) any claim for interest;

(2) costs;
(3) any claim for contributory negligence.

Notice of allocation

Once it has allocated a claim to a track, the court will serve notice on every other party, together with a copy of the allocation questionnaire filed by all other parties and a copy of any further information provided by any other party about his case.

If the statements of case are later amended and it becomes clear that the case has been allocated to an inappropriate track, the court may subsequently re-allocate a claim to a different track.

When it allocates a claim to the fast track, the court will give directions for management of the case and a timetable of steps to be taken between the giving of directions and the end of the trial. When it gives directions, the court will, at that point, fix a trial date; or fix a period not exceeding 3 weeks in which the trial will take place. The standard period between giving directions and trial will be not more than 30 weeks.

Directions in the fast track

Matters to be dealt with by way of directions include:

(1) disclosure of documents;
(2) service of witness statements;
(3) expert evidence.

Listing questionnaire

The court will send each party a listing questionnaire for completion and return to the court by the date specified in the notice of allocation. The date specified for filing a listing questionnaire is not more than 8 weeks before the trial date.

If a party fails to file a completed listing questionnaire within the time-limit or fails to give all of the information, or the court thinks it is necessary, the court may fix a listing hearing or give such other directions as it thinks appropriate.

Fixing trial date

As soon as practicable after filing of the completed listing questionnaires, the court will fix a date for trial, give any directions for trial and specify further steps that need to be taken by the parties prior to the trial.

The court will give each party at least 3 weeks' notice of the trial date. Only in exceptional circumstances will the notice period be shorter than this.

10.3.3 The multi-track

When allocating a case to the multi-track, the court will either:

(1) give directions for case management and set a timetable; or
(2) fix a case management conference and/or a pre-trial review, or both,

and may give such other directions relating to management of the case as it thinks fit.

10.4 THE CASE MANAGEMENT CONFERENCE AND PRE-TRIAL REVIEW

The court may fix a case management conference and pre-trial review at any time after the defence has been filed. Where a party is legally represented, any case management conference or pre-trial review called by the court must be attended by a legal representative who is familiar with the case.

10.4.1 The case management conference

The parties may agree their own proposals for case management of the proceedings and, if the court is satisfied with these proposals, it may give directions in accordance with the proposals without the need for a court hearing.

Variation of case management timetable

If a party wishes to apply to vary any of the dates which the court has fixed for:

(1) the case management conference;
(2) the pre-trial review;
(3) the return of listing questionnaires;
(4) the trial,

he may do so only with leave of the court. However, a party cannot vary the timetable in such a way as will result in an alteration of the overall timetable mentioned above.

The listing questionnaire

The court will send each party a listing questionnaire for completion and return. The procedure and consequences of failure to return the questionnaire are the same as for the fast track listed above.

10.4.2 Pre-trial review

On receipt of the parties' listing questionnaires, the court may decide to hold a pre-trial review or cancel a pre-trial review if it has already decided to hold one, having regard to the circumstances of the case.

After filing of listing questionnaires, the court will set a timetable for the trial (unless this has already been done or is impracticable) and will notify the parties of that timetable. If it is able to do so the court, will fix or confirm the trial date and will notify the parties of it.

10.5 GROUP LITIGATION

Engaging in group litigation is time-consuming, difficult and, therefore, costly. Group litigation results when there are a number of prospective claimants who have a common interest or common defendant arising out of a common incident. An example of group litigation is the litigation brought by a number of families following the *Marchioness* disaster.

The relevant rule of the CPR 1998 governing group litigation can be found at Part 19, with its accompanying PD 19B. Part 19 makes provision for the making of a Group Litigation Order (GLO) at the request of the parties where there are, or are likely to be, a number of similar claims. The aim of the GLO is to 'steer' the group litigation by ensuring that the case is managed to suit the needs of multi-party litigation. The aim of the GLO is to ensure that all cases that are eligible to join the group do so and are then all treated in like manner to ensure consistency of result. The GLO must include specific directions for the maintenance of a group register, specify the GLO issues and appoint a particular court and particular judge to oversee the case management process. By giving one court/ judge 'ownership' of the management process, the case can be more effectively managed than if all potential claimants were allowed to issue and deal with their case at any court of their choosing. The managing judge appointed to the group litigation will quickly amass specialist knowledge in relation to that particular group litigation and will therefore be able to deal with matters as they arise more quickly and effectively.

The details of group litigation are beyond the scope of this book but recourse should be had, as a starting point, to CPR 1998, PD 19B and to consult with the Law Society's multi-party action information service.

10.6 INTERIM PAYMENTS

A claimant may not seek an interim payment until after the time for acknowledging service has expired. More than one application for an interim payment may be made by a claimant.

An application for an interim payment must be supported by evidence and be served at least 14 days before the return date for the application. If a party wants to rely on a witness statement in an application for an interim payment, he must file and serve a copy of that witness statement:

(1) at least 7 days before the hearing, in the case of the respondent; or
(2) at least 3 days before the hearing, in the case of an applicant who wishes to use the witness statement in reply to a respondent's submissions.

The court may order payment of an interim payment, and the court may order that such payment be by instalments.

The court may order an interim payment only if:

(1) the defendant admits liability; or
(2) the claimant has a judgment for damages to be assessed; or
(3) the claimant would obtain judgment for a substantial amount of money.

In personal injury cases, the court may order an interim payment only if:

(1) the defendant is covered by insurance in respect of the claim; or
(2) the defendant's liability will be met by:

    (i) an insurer under s 151 of the Road Traffic Act 1988; or
    (ii) an insurer concerned under the MIB agreement; or

(3) the defendant is a public body.

Further, in a claim for personal injuries where there are two or more defendants, the court may make an order for interim payment against any of them if it is satisfied that, if the claim went to trial, the claimant would obtain judgment for substantial damages against at least one of the defendants and the conditions specified above in relation to insurers are satisfied.

The amount of the interim payment must not exceed a reasonable proportion of the likely amount of the final judgment taking into account:

(i) contributory negligence; and
(ii) any relevant set-off or counterclaim.

If a defendant has made an interim payment, the court may order that that sum be repaid or that another defendant reimburse that defendant.

If a defendant makes an interim payment which it transpires exceeds his liability under the final judgment, the court may award interest on the overpaid amount from the date the interim payment was made.

10.7 DISCLOSURE AND INSPECTION OF DOCUMENTS

A party is not required to give more than standard disclosure unless the court otherwise orders.

Standard disclosure means that a party is required to disclose only:

(1) the documents on which he relies;
(2) the documents which could adversely affect his own case, adversely affect another's case or support another party's case; and
(3) all documents which he is required to disclose by any practice direction.

The court may dispense with or limit standard disclosure, and the parties can agree in writing to dispense with or limit any part of standard disclosure. As under the old rules the duty of standard disclosure continues throughout the proceedings and, if a document comes to a party's notice at any time, that party must immediately notify every other party.

10.7.1 Procedure

Each party must make and serve a list of documents in accordance with the practice form which must identify the documents 'in a convenient order and manner as concisely as possible'. A detailed consideration of the procedure on disclosure can be found in the LPC Resource Book *Civil Litigation* (Jordans).

The list must indicate documents which are no longer in the parties' control and state what has happened to those documents.

The list must include a disclosure statement by the party:

(1) setting out the extent of the search made to locate the documents;
(2) certifying that he understands the duty of disclosure and that, to the best of his knowledge, he has carried out that duty.

10.7.2 Specific disclosure

An order for specific disclosure can require a party to disclose specified documents or classes of documents, or carry out a search for specified documents and disclose any documents located as a result of that search.

An application for specific disclosure must be supported by evidence. The court will order specific disclosure only if necessary to fairly dispose of the claim or save costs.

The party has a right to inspect a document mentioned in another party's:

(1) statement of case;
(2) witness statement or summary;
(3) affidavit;
(4) expert's report.

10.8 WITNESS EVIDENCE

As part of its management powers, the court will decide the issues on which it requires evidence, the nature of that evidence and the way in which the evidence should be placed before the court.

10.8.1 Witnesses

Facts should normally be proved at the trial by oral evidence of witnesses, and at any other hearing by the written evidence of witnesses. The court may allow a witness to give evidence by any means, which includes by means of a video link.

10.8.2 Procedure

The court may order a party to serve on any other party a witness statement containing the evidence which that party intends to rely on.

According to the CPR 1998:

> 'A witness statement is a written statement which contains the evidence, and only the evidence, which a person would be allowed to give orally at trial.'

The court will normally order each party to serve the witness statements of the oral evidence on which they intend to rely at the trial. The court may give directions as to the order in which such witness statements are to be served and whether or not the statements are to be filed.

10.8.3 Use at trial of witness statements

If a witness statement has been served and a party wishes to rely on that evidence at trial, the party must call the witness to give oral evidence unless the court otherwise orders.

10.8.4 Statements to stand as evidence-in-chief

Where a witness is called to give oral evidence, his statement shall stand as evidence-in-chief, unless the court otherwise orders.

The witness giving the oral evidence may amplify the witness statement, and give evidence in relation to new matters that have arisen since the statement was served. However, he may do this only if the court considers there is a good reason not to confine his evidence to the contents of the statement that has been served.

Evidence in proceedings other than at the trial should be by witness statement, unless the court or a particular practice direction otherwise directs.

10.8.5 Witness summary

Where a party is required to serve a witness statement, if he is not able to obtain a witness statement, he may apply to the court for permission to serve only a witness summary instead. This application should be made without notice. The witness summary is a summary of the evidence which would otherwise go into a witness statement; or if the evidence is not known, matters about which the party serving the witness summary will question the witness.

Where a witness statement or a witness summary is not served, the party will not be able to call that witness to give oral evidence unless the court allows it.

10.9 USE OF PLANS, PHOTOGRAPHS AND MODELS AS EVIDENCE AT TRIAL

Where a party wishes to use evidence such as plans, photographs or models or other evidence:

(i) which is not contained in a witness statement, affidavit or expert's report;
(ii) which is not given orally at trial;
(iii) which has already been disclosed in relation to hearsay evidence,

the party wishing to use the evidence must disclose his intention to do so not later than the latest date for serving witness statements.

If the evidence forms part of expert evidence, it must be disclosed when the expert's report is itself served on the other party. Having disclosed such evidence, the party must give every other party an opportunity to inspect it and agree its admission without further proof.

10.10 EXPERT EVIDENCE

The duties of experts in relation to court proceedings, and the contents of their report are dealt with in Chapter 8.

10.11 OFFERS TO SETTLE AND PAYMENTS INTO COURT

Under CPR 1998, Part 36, either party may make an 'offer to settle' to the other before the commencement of proceedings. If a party receiving the offer fails to accept it, and the offer is not beaten at trial, that party will have a costs penalty to pay for refusing to accept the offer. Once proceedings have commenced, when a defendant pays money into court in an attempt to settle a claim, he will make a

Part 36 payment. When a claimant intimates an amount of money which he is prepared to accept to settle the claim, he will make a Part 36 offer. The key feature of this procedure is that it is both open to claimants as well as defendants. However, cases proceeding in the small claims track are not eligible for a Part 36 offer procedure.

It is important to note the difference between a Part 36 offer and a Part 36 payment. In relation to the effect of recovery of social security benefit, the rules operate differently, depending on whether there has been a payment into court or merely an offer to settle. A defendant can only claim costs protection if he makes a payment into court. Although he may make an 'offer' before proceedings are commenced, once he receives formal notice of proceedings he must make a payment into court within 14 days of an amount at least equal to the amount of the offer. If he fails to do so, the costs protection of making the offer prior to issue of proceedings will be lost. In contrast, a claimant can make an offer prior to commencement of proceedings, or at any time during proceedings but cannot make a payment into court.

10.11.1 Contents of Part 36 offers

A Part 36 offer must:

(1) be in writing;
(2) state whether it relates to all or part of the claim;
(3) state whether it takes account of any counterclaim;
(4) confirm details of interest claimed (if expressed not to be inclusive of interest, give details of interest);
(5) be expressed to be open for not less than 21 days;
(6) state that it can be accepted after 21 days if the parties agree liability for costs or the court so permits.

Any such offer made will be treated as being made 'without prejudice save as to costs'.

10.11.2 Contents of Part 36 payments

A Part 36 payment may relate to the whole claim or part of it.

In order to make a Part 36 payment, the defendant must file with the court and serve on all other parties a notice (a Part 36 payment notice) which states:

(1) the amount of the payment (or increased payment);
(2) whether the payment relates to the whole claim or part of it;
(3) whether it takes into account any counterclaims;
(4) details of interest (unless expressed not to be inclusive of interest).

In the terms of the above notice, the claimant can apply for an order that the defendant clarifies his notice.

Care must be taken when considering whether or not to make a Part 36 payment. It is not enough to simply make a written offer instead of a Part 36 payment into court (see *Amber v Stacey* [2001] 2 All ER 88). Here, the Court of Appeal found that in order for an offer of payment to have the costs consequences outlined in Part 36 it was necessary for the defendant to maker a Part 36 payment into court. A written offer by letter would not do.

The rules on acceptance of Part 36 payments and the costs consequences are the same as for Part 36 offers as outlined above.

10.11.3 Effect of acceptance of Part 36 offer or Part 36 payment

The effect of acceptance of an offer or payment, if it relates to the whole of the claim, is that the claim will be stayed. Where the offer relates to the whole claim, the stay will be upon the terms of the offer, and either party can apply to enforce those terms without the need for a new claim. If the offer or payment relates to only part of a claim and is accepted, the claim is stayed as to that part only; and unless the parties have agreed costs, costs shall be assessed by the court.

In the case of a minor, where court approval is required, the settlement is final, and any stay arising on acceptance of an offer or payment will take effect only when such approval has been obtained.

10.11.4 Acceptance by a defendant of a claimant's Part 36 offer

A defendant can accept a Part 36 offer made not less than 21 days before trial without need for the court's permission, if he gives the claimant written notice of acceptance not later than 21 days after the offer was made. If the claimant's offer was made less than 21 days before trial or the defendant does not accept it within 21 days of the offer being made, the court's permission will only be needed if the parties do not agree liability for costs. If the trial has not yet started, permission is sought by making an application under Part 23; if the trial has started, application is made to the trial judge.

10.11.5 Consequences where the claimant fails to match the defendant's Part 36 offer or payment

Where at the trial the claimant fails to better a Part 36 payment or fails to obtain a judgment which is more advantageous than a defendant's Part 36 offer, the court will order that claimant to pay any costs incurred by the defendant after the latest date on which the payment or offer could have been accepted without the need for the court's permission unless it considers it unjust to do so (CPR 1998, r 36.20).

The phrase 'unless the court considers it unjust to do so' has been considered in *Ford v GKR Construction* [2000] 1 All ER 802. Here, the court considered that it was unjust to make the usual costs order against a claimant who had failed to beat the defendant's payment into court. The relevant facts of the case are that the defendants made a payment into court well in advance of the trial. Once the trial had commenced, the defendants employed video surveillance on the claimant and sought to use this evidence at the trial as it was clear that the claimant's injuries were not as severe as her evidence suggested. When giving judgment, the court made the following observations.

- When exercising his discretion as to costs, the judge was required to consider the matter of late disclosure of evidence.
- The guiding principle that the judge should have in mind was that the parties should conduct litigation by making full disclosure.
- The parties had to be provided with the necessary information to assess whether to make or accept payments under Part 36.

- Where a party failed to provide that information the court should take that into account when considering what costs order to make.
- The normal costs consequences should not apply when the claimant has not been furnished with the necessary information to gauge whether to accept or reject the Part 36 payment as it would be unjust to do so.

10.11.6 Defendant's failure to obtain more than offered in a Part 36 offer

Where at trial a defendant is held liable for more than the offer, or the judgment against him is more advantageous to the claimant, the court may order interest on the whole or any part of the award not exceeding 10% above base rate from the period starting with the latest date the defendant could have accepted the offer without permission of the court.

The court may also order the claimant his entitlement to the costs on the indemnity basis from the latest date the defendant could have accepted the offer without permission of the court. The court may also grant interest on those costs at a rate not exceeding 10% above base rate.

10.11.7 Compensation recovery and Part 36 offers to settle

Benefit recovery (which is dealt with in detail at Chapter 12) must be taken into account when considering payments into court. A Part 36 payment, but not an offer, is treated as making a compensation payment for the purpose of reg 8 of the Social Security (Recovery of Benefit) Regulations 1997. PD 36 requires benefit recovery to be taken into account when giving notice of a Part 36 payment into court. The notice must state:

(a) the total amount represented by the Part 36 payment (the gross compensation);
(b) that the defendant has reduced the payment in by the amount of recoverable benefit in accordance with s 8 of the Social Security (Recovery of Benefits) Act 1997; and
(c) that the amount paid into court is the net amount after the deduction of the amount of benefit.

The Practice Direction also requires the compensator (defendant) to file with the court a certificate of recoverable benefit with the notice of payment in.

The Part 36 payment should be made on court form N242A.

There are no such requirements in respect of Part 36 offers in relation to benefit recovery. However, it is advisable to set out such offers in the same way as the above in order to avoid confusion.

When seeking to establish whether or not the claimant has bettered, or obtained a judgment more advantageous than, a Part 36 payment, the court will base its decision on the gross sum specified in the Part 36 notice.

10.12 CONCLUSION

The above statements in relation to the CPR 1998 are correct at time of writing. However, the CPR 1998 are subject to continuing amendment. Accordingly, it will be essential to check that the version of the Rules and Practice Directions being consulted is current.

10.13 FURTHER READING

The Civil Procedure Rules (Lord Chancellor's Department, 1998).
The Civil Court Practice (Butterworths).
Civil Procedure (Sweet & Maxwell).

Chapter 11

NEGOTIATIONS, ADR AND TRIAL

11.1 INTRODUCTION

Over 90% of personal injury claims and many clinical negligence claims settle without trial. It is usually the case that the solicitor's skill in arguing his client's claim with the defendant's insurer or solicitor rather than his ability to argue the case at trial will determine the level of damages. For this reason, the personal injury solicitor is more likely to become a skilled negotiator than a trial advocate.

11.2 PROFESSIONAL CONDUCT

As a matter of conduct, a solicitor does not have ostensible authority to settle a client's claim until after proceedings have been issued. It is imperative for the solicitor to seek the client's specific instructions prior to settling a claim. For example, even if the client instructs his solicitor that he can settle his claim as long as the client receives at least £1,000 the solicitor should, when negotiating with the defence, stipulate that any agreement is 'subject to his client's instructions'. In this way, if the client should change his mind (which he may do at any time) the solicitor will not have committed the client to the settlement irrevocably.

Negotiations should always be entered into on an expressly 'without prejudice' basis. When talking to an insurer in person or on the telephone it is advisable for the solicitor to preface anything he says by stating expressly at the outset that the entire conversation is without prejudice to his client's claim.

11.3 NEGOTIATING WITH INSURANCE COMPANIES AND DEFENCE SOLICITORS

Claims can be settled by agreement being reached between the parties at any stage. The pre-action protocols encourage early disclosure of information to facilitate this. Claimant solicitors have in the past considered that defendant insurers will not make reasonable offers for settlement prior to issue of proceedings. For this reason, many claimant solicitors have tended to issue proceedings first and negotiate second. This strategy is not encouraged by the CPR 1998. The pre-action protocols require that attempts be made to settle disputes. For a detailed consideration of the protocols, see Chapter 9. If the claim is being funded by a conditional fee agreement (CFA), there is also the further requirement to disclose to the insurer that the matter is being funded in this way, and the identity of any After The Event insurer, it is not necessary to give any further details. In particular, it is not required or desirable to disclose the level of the success fee, as this would give the insurer a good indication of how confident the claimant's solicitor was about winning the case at trial.

Chapter 11 contents
Introduction
Professional conduct
Negotiating with insurance companies and defence solicitors
Conducting the negotiation
Negotiating in clinical negligence claims
Alternative dispute resolution (ADR)
Funding any settlement
Court orders
Preparation for trial
The trial
Conclusion
Further reading

When negotiating with the defendant's insurer or its solicitor, a firm approach should be taken by the claimant's solicitor. He must be alert to the fact that the insurer is in business to make money for its shareholders and its employees are employed to ensure that as little money as possible is paid out in damages. Therefore, the claimant's solicitor should not delay in issuing proceedings, after the pre-action protocol has been complied with if the defendant has failed or refused to make an acceptable response. Failure to do so is likely to be a failure to act in the best interests of the client.

The technique of negotiation is contained in the LPC Resource Book *Skills for Lawyers* (Jordans). Prior to any negotiation the claimant's solicitor should first familiarise himself with the file, noting specifically any matters likely to increase the level of damages, such as the risk of osteoarthritis or permanent scarring. There is a risk that the solicitor will fail to remember the file adequately because he may be running many very similar claims at any one time. When reviewing the file it is good practice to build up a profile of the severity of the injuries by reading the medical reports and client's statement. Matters relevant to each head of loss should be noted so that the solicitor has a list of areas of loss without having to make reference to the specifics of the claim itself.

Example

Client, A, is aged 56 and has suffered injuries to her left shoulder and abrasions to both arms and legs when she tripped over a loose paving stone in her local high street. She is a keen gardener and likes to attend aerobics once a week, and enjoys walking her dog in the countryside near her home. Her husband took early retirement due to ill-health and is not able to assist her much, but he has been driving her to the doctor and for physiotherapy and has been helping her bathe and dress herself. Day-to-day cleaning of the house and gardening has been undertaken by friends and relations.

The profile in such a case would be:

General damages claim:

- female aged 56, therefore likely to take some time for injuries to mend, danger of osteoarthritis revealed in medical report;
- report revealed split fracture to the clavicle (collar bone) together with a tear to the *latissimus dorsi* (muscle beneath the shoulder) and associated soft tissue damage;
- medical intervention involved substantial and uncomfortable strapping to render the injury immobile followed by light physiotherapy. Physiotherapy continued for 20 weeks;
- reasonably fit, unable to undertake pastimes such as aerobics and walking in countryside for X weeks;

Special damages:

- clothes and personal items lost or damaged in the accident;
- taxi fares to hospital/physiotherapy;
- prescription charges;
- daily care necessary;
- husband unable to care on his own due to his own ill-health;
- cleaning of house and garden maintenance undertaken by others.

Having built up such a profile, the next stage is for the solicitor to become familiar with the likely level of damages to be awarded in such a claim. Such familiarity comes with experience. The method of approach to calculation of damages is considered in detail in Chapter 13.

The client should be aware that any form of litigation carries with it a certain amount of risk that the claim will fail because the evidence may not come up to proof at trial. Because of this 'litigation risk', it is likely that the defence solicitor will seek some reduction in damages because the claimant is being spared the upset and risk of failure at trial.

11.4 CONDUCTING THE NEGOTIATION

When conducting negotiations, it is worth bearing in mind the following.

(1) Settlement should not be entered into prematurely. If proceedings are never issued and the defendant's insurers make clear that they do not contest the case, argument will centre on quantum, and it will be fairly safe to negotiate. If, however, the matter is contested, it is unwise to negotiate prior to disclosure of each side's evidence. For this reason, many solicitors believe that settlement should not be contemplated prior to the exchange of witness evidence. Once the claimant's solicitor has considered the evidence, he can then assist the client to make an informed decision as to whether he should accept a settlement.

(2) The solicitor must never negotiate when unprepared. The file must be considered thoroughly prior to proceeding with negotiations. If the solicitor receives a surprise telephone call from a defendant insurer seeking a settlement, it is better for the solicitor to call back later after having considered the case afresh.

(3) The defence should be invited to put forward its settlement figure with supporting argument as to why that figure is correct. Comments should be kept to a minimum and further negotiations postponed while the offer is considered. This is easiest to do if negotiating over the telephone, as negotiation can be cut short and re-established later with minimum difficulty. The telephone has the added advantage that the person making an offer cannot see the reaction of the recipient of the call, and will be unable to gauge how well or how badly the offer is received. The claimant's solicitor should never disclose his valuation of the claim first in negotiations and should not put forward any figures until he believes the defendant is putting forward a realistic amount.

(4) The defence opening offer is unlikely to be the best it is prepared to come up with. All offers must, however, be put to the client. A solicitor has a duty to act in the best interests of his client, and this includes obtaining the best possible settlement figure.

(5) An offer by the defence to pay the claimant's costs to date should not sway the solicitor into advising his client to accept an offer. If the defence is offering to settle, it is effectively admitting (albeit without prejudice) that there is merit in the claim and would normally be obliged to pay the claimant's reasonable costs if the case went to trial.

(6) Often the solicitor has specific instructions to try to settle the case on the client's behalf. In such a case, he may seek confirmation that a settlement will be agreed as long as the client will receive at least £X. If this is the case, the solicitor must be careful not to jump at the first offer simply because it will secure for the

client the minimum that he requires and will usually also secure payment of the solicitor's costs.

(7) Consideration of the defendant's offer should not be rushed. Any attempt to force an agreement quickly should be regarded as spurious. The defence would not have made an offer if it was happy to take the case to trial. Therefore, regardless of whether a time-limit is placed on the offer, it is likely that unless fresh evidence comes to light strengthening the defence case, an offer once made will remain open. By making an offer at all the defence is saying that it would far rather pay than fight.

(8) When negotiating, defendant insurers will often offer to 'split the difference' if agreement cannot be reached on a particular head of loss. This is a favourite tactic that the claimant solicitor should consider carefully before accepting. On the face of it, it may appear to be a generous offer, bringing negotiations to a speedy conclusion. On closer scrutiny, it may be a ploy which results in the loss of a substantial portion of the client's legitimate expectation in a particular head of damages.

11.5 NEGOTIATING IN CLINICAL NEGLIGENCE CLAIMS

When considering negotiation in the context of clinical negligence claims, the following should be borne in mind.

(1) In many cases, the NHS complaints procedure will already have been put to use and there may therefore be greater clarity as regards what the issues of the claim are.

(2) It is unlikely that any negotiations with a view to settlement will be made prior to full recourse to the clinical disputes pre-action protocol. Only after both sides have had access to full disclosure and expert opinion will it be possible for any meaningful negotiation to take place.

(3) In straightforward claims of low value, negotiating tactics as outlined above may be appropriate. In relation to more complex claims, it is more likely that there would be a meeting of the parties' solicitors with or without experts to try to narrow as many issues as possible. In appropriate cases, counsel for both sides may be asked to discuss the case informally to try to narrow areas in dispute.

11.6 ALTERNATIVE DISPUTE RESOLUTION (ADR)

The use of alternative dispute resolution (ADR) is likely to become more important in the resolution of disputes, as the overriding objective (stated in Part 1 of the CPR 1998) encourages the prompt use of ADR as a way of furthering the overriding objective, and to aid prompt settlement. Most disputes are capable of resolution either by discussion and negotiation or by trial on the issues. The rules encourage the use of alternatives to litigation as a first resort and litigation as a last resort. ADR is explained in detail in the LPC Resource Book *Civil Litigation* (Jordans).

11.6.1 Different types of ADR

The main types of ADR available today are as follows.

(1) *Mediation*

In mediation, a neutral third party is chosen by the parties as their intermediary (mediator). The mediator is likely to meet the opposing parties separately to try to establish some common ground before finally bringing the parties together to try to reach an agreement.

(2) *Conciliation*

Conciliation is a similar process to mediation. However, the conciliator is likely to take a more interventionist approach by taking a more central role. He will often consider the case as put forward by both sides and then suggest terms of settlement which he feels to be most appropriate.

(3) *The mini-trial*

The format and content of a mini-trial is much more like a trial. It will be chaired by a neutral mediator who will sit with a representative from each party.

All of these three methods of ADR are mechanisms which aim to bring the parties together to obtain a consensual agreement rather than a ruling which is forced upon them.

11.6.2 Case management conference

At the case management conference/pre-trial review, the parties will be told to confirm whether the question of ADR has been considered and also to confirm that, if it has not, why this is the case.

When considering the conduct of the parties, the judge is entitled to consider the parties' unreasonable refusal to use ADR, as this is central to the ethos of how to deal with disputes in accordance with Part 1 of the CPR 1998. Where ADR has been refused or where a party has later failed to co-operate with ADR, the court is entitled to take that into account when considering what costs order to make or whether to make any costs order at all.

11.6.3 ADR and personal injury claims

Use of the pre-action protocol will ensure that the parties are better able to obtain a greater depth of knowledge about the case against them than has been the case in the past. Full use of pre-action disclosure, and preliminary disclosure of key documents will enable each side to obtain a far better view on the issues of the case in relation to liability, and will therefore allow them to make a far better and earlier assessment of their client's case.

At the stage where the parties complete their allocation questionnaire, they will be asked whether they would like their proceedings to be stayed while they try to settle the case (by way of ADR).

Because the court is very likely to ask whether the parties are interested in attempting ADR, and whether the possibility of ADR has been discussed with the client prior to the case management conference, it follows that the solicitor will need to ask his client at an early stage whether he would be interested in pursuing the matter by way of ADR, and must explain to the client what this will entail.

11.6.4 The timing of ADR

It is likely that in complicated cases ADR will not be appropriate until such time as statements of case and disclosure of documents by both sides have been dealt with. Only then will ADR be a practical alternative to a trial. It is therefore likely that cases which were initially felt to be unsuitable for ADR may find that ADR is a possibility once the case is at the case management conference stage.

11.6.5 Procedure following failed ADR

Where the parties have attempted ADR and this has failed to produce a settlement, the parties are likely to wish to fall back on their original court proceedings or intended court proceedings.

At this stage, if proceedings have already been issued, the solicitor for the claimant will need to apply promptly for further directions in the case so that the matter may proceed swiftly to trial.

However, although ADR may fail to produce a settlement, it may produce a degree of information about the other side's case which prior to ADR had not been clear. If this is the case, it may be that an offer to settle or payment should be considered by either or both parties.

11.6.6 ADR in clinical negligence cases

The Legal Services Commission (LSC) Manual recommends the use of ADR techniques to resolve clinical negligence disputes. Guidance Notes make the point that although most successful claims settle, they do so at a very late stage. Because many clinical negligence claims are very complex, lengthy and very costly, a settlement reached earlier would have the effect of saving significant amounts of CLS funding. The NHS Litigation Authority which handles large clinical negligence claims also encourages the use of ADR. The Clinical Disputes Forum has also produced a guide on the use of mediation in clinical negligence disputes. The guidance applies both to legal aid certificates issued under the Legal Aid Act 1988 and certificates issued under the Funding Code and applies with effect from 1 June 2001.

The guidance aims to:

(a) ensure the use of ADR is considered by clients and solicitors at key points in clinical negligence claims;
(b) require solicitors to report to their regional office at various stages in the litigation, explaining why ADR has not been pursued if appropriate;
(c) explain the approach regional offices should take in deciding whether to limit a certificate to work necessary to progress ADR;
(d) help the parties set up mediation.

When should ADR be considered in clinical negligence claims?
The parties should keep the possibilities of ADR in mind at all times. However, at the outset of litigation ADR is not likely to be appropriate until the pre-action

protocol for use in clinical negligence claims has been complied with because the client and his solicitor are unlikely to have information available to enter into a fair settlement of the claim.

According to the LSC Manual, once the clinical negligence pre-action protocol has been complied with, solicitors should consider with their clients the use of ADR at the following stages:

(a) prior to issue of proceedings;
(b) before and immediately after case management conference;
(c) before and immediately after pre-trial review;
(d) whenever the other side offer ADR;
(e) whenever the new parties are specifically asked to consider ADR by the court or the LSC.

If at any of the above points it is decided by the client or solicitor not to pursue ADR, the reason for that decision should be recorded on the solicitor's file. Following on from this, where application is made by the solicitor for the certificate to be extended, the reason for not pursuing ADR must be reported to the regional office when submitting Form APP 8 for amendment of certificate.

Cases where ADR may not be appropriate

The LSC Manual gives the following specific guidance and examples of types of claim that may not be suitable for ADR:

(a) where essential basic information (such as relevant medical records, key expert evidence on liability and causation) is not available;
(b) where there is no clear prognosis for the condition of the client and time is needed to see how the client progresses before settlement can be considered;
(c) ADR is unnecessary as all parties are already negotiating effectively;
(d) proceedings need to be issued urgently in order for the claim to be within the relevant limitation period;
(e) the claim includes future cost of care claim and information is needed as to quantum before any settlement can be discussed;
(f) the case is a 'test case' and requires a ruling from a court in order to lay down a precedent for future claims;
(g) ADR would not be a cost effective way of dealing with the claim because there is no reason to believe that the claim will be resolved more quickly or cheaply by using it.

Although the LSC in their Manual state that they do not wish to impose ADR as a condition of funding, they do make it clear that they will consider limiting a certificate so that it only covers participation in ADR in the following circumstances:

(a) when they receive a report that ADR has been refused;
(b) where the opponent or the NHS Litigation Authority suggests ADR has been unreasonably refused;
(c) where an application is made to extend the scope of a clinical negligence certificate to full representation or to cover the costs of a trial.

In any of the above cases, the regional office will consider the reason given for not pursuing ADR. In the guidance notes, the LSC state that the following reasons are not good reasons for refusing ADR:

(a) the client refuses ADR and still wishes to have their day in court;

(b) that there are important, outstanding facts or legal issues between the parties;
(c) the parties feel that their positions are so far apart that they cannot foresee settling;
(d) further information or exchange of evidence is required but this information is not sent forward to the clients case.

Once ADR has been attempted, the LSC will lift restrictions on the certificate if the ADR having been attempted in good faith, breaks down.

In cases where ADR is not successful the LSC expect both sides to be able to put forward their most realistic Part 36 offers as a result of having taken part in the ADR.

11.6.7 NHS complaints procedure

The complaints procedure (which is dealt with in detail in Chapter 7) is designed specifically to provide an explanation to patients in cases where they have felt sufficiently concerned about the healthcare received to make a complaint. The procedure is not designed or able to give compensation to patients. It is useful if the only or main issue at stake is for an explanation or an apology to be obtained, or simply to find more information to help the patient to come to terms with an event, or to help him decide whether he should take further action, and, if so, what form this should take.

11.6.8 Mediation

Mediation may be appropriate in some cases where the parties agree. This may be seen as particularly useful when there are allegations of clinical negligence, as ADR will be conducted in private, and this is something which is likely to appeal to medical practitioners who may not wish the allegations to be made public and reportable, as would be the case if the matter were to proceed in open court to a trial.

11.7 FUNDING ANY SETTLEMENT

In nearly all personal injury cases, there will not be a problem with the financing of any settlement, as the defendant will have been required to be insured in respect of the potential liability. Thus a commercial insurer will normally meet any settlement.

In clinical negligence cases, also, the defendant will normally not have a problem with the financing of any settlement but the administration of the settlement can be rather more complicated in certain cases. The NHS Litigation Authority (NHSLA) administers the Existing Liability Scheme and Clinical Negligence Scheme for Trusts (CNST). The CNST came into force on 1 April 1995 as a result of concern over the financing of damages claims and the object of the scheme is to protect NHS trusts and improve the quality of risk management. The CNST is not an insurance scheme but a mutual fund.

The administration of any settlement is normally of little concern to claimant solicitors, but many practitioners become frustrated by the delays which can arise with insurance companies in personal injury cases and also the NHSLA, as they operate a system whereby certain levels of claims have to be given specific approval.

11.8 COURT ORDERS

It is good practice to obtain a court order formally stating the terms of the settlement. A settlement on behalf of a minor should always be contained in a court order (see Chapter 16).

11.8.1 Advantages of obtaining a court order

The advantages of obtaining an order are:

(1) payment of interest and costs can be specifically dealt with;
(2) if the amount stated in the order is not paid the order can be enforced in the same way as any other judgment;
(3) if costs cannot be agreed they can be assessed by the court if there is provision in the order;
(4) if the client has Community Legal Service (CLS) funding, he will need an order for CLS assessment.

The order should contain a provision that the action be stayed rather than dismissed, and the stay should contain provision for return to court in the event that the terms of the stay are not complied with.

11.8.2 Drawing up the consent order

The procedure for drawing up a consent order is:

(1) it must be drawn up in the agreed terms;
(2) it must be expressed as being 'by consent';
(3) it must be signed by solicitors or counsel for the parties;
(4) it must be presented to the court for entry and sealing.

An order takes effect from the date given, unless the court orders otherwise. An order for payment of money (including costs) must be complied with within 14 days unless the order or any of the CPR 1998 specifies otherwise. When drafting a consent order, the guiding principle is that the order shows where the money is to come from to satisfy the order and where that money will go.

> *Example*
> In a case where there has been a payment in of £2,000 which was not accepted, and later a settlement is achieved by which the defendant agrees to pay £3,000 plus costs to be assessed if not agreed, the order should state:
>
> (1) that the action is stayed on payment of £3,000;
> (2) where that £3,000 is to come from, ie partly from money already in court and the balance to be paid by the defendant within a given time-scale (usually 14 days);
> (3) that an order for payment out will be needed because the money in court was not accepted;
> (4) who is to have the interest earned on the money whilst in court (normally the defendant);
> (5) where the money is to go (in this case to the claimant). In a case involving a minor the money will usually be ordered to be invested by the court;

(6) who is to bear the costs. If this has been agreed the figures should be stated with a time-limit for payment. Usually, the provision will be for costs to be assessed if not agreed;
(7) whether CLS assessment is needed; and
(8) liberty to apply – which simply allows the parties to return to the court if there is subsequently a disagreement as to what the terms of the order mean or because the terms have not been complied with.

If there had been an interim payment in the above example, this should also be reflected in the terms of the order. The order should state that the amount agreed in full and final settlement takes into account the interim payment, specifying the amount and the date it was given or the date of the court order so ordering it to be paid.

11.9 PREPARATION FOR TRIAL

11.9.1 Outstanding orders

Once it becomes apparent that the case will proceed to trial as no Part 36 payment has been made nor any satisfactory Part 36 offer received, the claimant's solicitor should undertake a thorough stocktaking of the file to ensure that all directions or other orders of the court have been complied with. Any outstanding matters in the claimant's own file should be attended to without further delay, and any outstanding matters for the defendant to attend to should be chased by issuing an interlocutory application for judgment in default of compliance with the direction/other order if necessary.

11.9.2 Experts

Experts' reports will usually have been exchanged in accordance with directions. Provision of joint experts and agreed expert evidence is dealt with in Chapter 8.

11.9.3 Use of counsel

The solicitor may not have instructed counsel before this stage if the action has been straightforward. If the case has been complex, as is likely in a clinical negligence case, counsel will probably have been involved at an early stage from drafting documents to advising on evidence. It is usual for the barrister who drafted the statements of case also to be briefed for the trial. As counsel will be handling the witnesses at trial, it may be thought to be appropriate to send the witness statements to counsel for approval before exchange to ensure that an important area concerning the conduct of the case at trial is not overlooked. It may be more cost-efficient to brief counsel for the trial than for the solicitor himself to attend. However, with trial on the fast track limited to one day, and with fixed costs of trial, it may be that many more solicitor-advocates will undertake the advocacy of this type of claim. If the case involves complex elements, such as clinical negligence, catastrophic injuries or difficult questions of fact or law, consideration should be given to whether it would be appropriate to instruct leading counsel; junior counsel will usually advise the solicitor if he thinks that this would be appropriate. The solicitor should advise the client accordingly of the extra cost involved and, if the client is CLS funded, seek authority from the CLS to instruct leading counsel. The client should also be advised that if leading counsel is instructed, and this is disallowed on assessment, the cost will ultimately be borne by the client in the form of the statutory charge on the client's damages.

11.9.4 Narrowing the issues

When preparing for trial the solicitor should ask himself, 'what do I have to prove?'. A review should be made of the case file to ascertain areas of agreement, which are no longer in issue. One useful device may be a list comprising two columns: the left-hand column listing the facts which have to be proved (eg that the claimant was driving the car; that an accident occurred; the date of the accident; the place of the accident; an itemised list of the losses, etc); and the right-hand column indicating whether the fact is admitted by the opponent.

Admissions will normally be found in the statements of case or in open correspondence.

11.9.5 Schedule of special damages

The claimant's solicitor must check that the schedule of special damages is up to date and, if necessary, serve an updated schedule of special damages. Ideally, this should be the final schedule (although it may have to be revised again if there is a significant delay before the trial), the purpose of which is to identify the areas of agreement and disagreement between the parties. With this in mind, the following format could be usefully employed (the figures are merely for illustration):

Item of claim	Claimant's figure	Defendant's figure	Discrepancy
Purchase of wheelchair	£350	£350	Nil
Loss of future earnings	£50,000 (multiplicand = £5,000, multiplier = 10)	£32,000 (multiplicand = £4,000, multiplier = 8)	£18,000

The defendant's solicitor should be sent the updated schedule of special damages, with a covering letter requesting that he agrees it or specifies the items he is not prepared to agree, and giving a time-limit for the reply. It should be pointed out that, if he fails to reply, the claimant's solicitors will have to issue a witness summons for any persons necessary to prove the amounts claimed, and the claimant will ask for the costs of this exercise be paid by the defendant in any event.

In clinical negligence claims, where special damages claims are likely to involve substantial amounts of money, it is more likely that the defence will seek to query items claimed as special damages. For this reason the directions will normally require that the defendant also provide a counter-schedule of special damages itemising the areas of disagreement.

11.9.6 Trial bundles

In both the High Court and the county court, bundles of documents upon which the parties intend to rely must be lodged within the appropriate time, for use by the trial judge.

The bundle must be paginated and indexed. The medical records must be complete and in good order to enable medical experts to study them easily. X-rays or scans included in the bundle should be clearly identified. Scans may be several feet long, and should be professionally copied if possible.

The quality of preparation of bundles varies enormously, and this can have serious implications for the client's case if preparation is not undertaken properly. Although there are rules governing the content of the bundles, there is very little guidance on how the documents should be presented. When preparing the bundle the aim should be to enable whoever is conducting the trial to turn to any document at any time with the minimum of fuss or delay, and that all others concerned with the case can do likewise. The more documents there are in the bundle, the more difficult this task becomes. In a straightforward road traffic claim, there will be few documents and, as such, the bundle should be relatively easy to prepare. In serious cases involving multiple injuries or in clinical negligence cases, however, the documents are likely to extend to many hundreds of pages. In such cases, it is even more important that the court is not hindered by trying to find documents that should be readily to hand. Poor preparation of the case will not impress the judge, nor will it go unnoticed. Documents will need to be split into a number of smaller bundles which are easier to handle. Using colour-coded lever arch files is often a good method, with a separate file for each class of document. As a matter of courtesy, if counsel has been instructed, the solicitor may wish to send the proposed index to the core bundle of documents to counsel in advance of the trial, so that counsel has the opportunity to ask for further items to be included if necessary.

11.9.7 Use of visual aids

Plans, photographs and models can be of enormous value at the trial as an aid to clarity, thereby shortening the length of the trial (avoiding long testimony of a witness) and saving costs. A judge may more readily understand the testimony of a witness if that witness is allowed to refer to a plan or photograph. Medical experts can often supply good quality colour diagrams, anatomical illustrations or models to make their testimony more comprehensible. In clinical negligence cases, it is worth the extra time and effort to find good visual aids. A judge is unlikely to have in-depth medical knowledge, and attempts to help the judge fully comprehend the circumstances giving rise to the alleged negligence are likely to be gratefully received.

Visual aids must be disclosed to the opponent in advance. No plan, photograph or model shall be receivable in evidence at trial unless the party wishing to use the evidence discloses it no later than the latest date for serving witness statements.

A video-recording is more useful than photographs in the case of 'movement'. Two common examples are:

(1) a video-recording of an industrial process;
(2) a video-recording showing the difficulties of the claimant in coping with his injuries (a 'day in the life'). Although the claimant should call, in addition to his own evidence, members of his family or friends to give evidence as to how the plaintiff manages with his injuries (evidence of his bodily and mental condition before and after the accident), a video film (eg showing the medical assistance required, such as physiotherapy or even surgery) may illustrate the situation more graphically.

If the photographs or other visual aids are agreed, they are admissible in the absence of the maker. If the aids are not agreed, the maker must be called to prove their authenticity.

The solicitor should ensure at the trial that there are enough copies of photographs for the use of the judge, advocates and witnesses.

11.10 THE TRIAL

11.10.1 The morning of the trial

The solicitor should arrive early to ensure that he has time:

(1) to check with the clerk to the court that the court has the trial bundles, and place a bundle in the witness-box;
(2) to ensure that counsel has arrived and consider any last minute questions he may have;
(3) to meet the client on his arrival and attempt to put him at his ease;
(4) to introduce counsel to the client (if they have not already met in conference);
(5) to ensure that an interview room is reserved for the pre-trial conference with counsel.

11.10.2 Advice to clients and witnesses

The case will usually turn on how well or how badly the witnesses give their evidence and how they are perceived by the judge. The client and other witnesses should be reminded that they will not be able to take their statements into the witness-box. The solicitor should run through the procedure to be adopted when giving oral evidence with the witnesses, as follows:

(1) explain the procedure on taking the oath, and whether the client wishes to affirm;
(2) remind the witness that all responses should be addressed to the judge regardless of who asked the question; and
(3) that the judge must be addressed in the appropriate manner; and
(4) go through the order in which the witnesses will be examined.

Each witness's statement will normally stand as evidence-in-chief, in which case the witness's evidence will move to being cross-examined almost immediately.

It is important to allay the client's fears about giving oral evidence. The solicitor should advise the client to speak slowly and directly to the judge, just as if there was no one else in the room. The judge will be writing notes and therefore the witness should watch the judge's pen and only resume speaking when the judge has finished writing.

It is unlikely that the client and lay witnesses will have given evidence before. They should be advised that if they do not understand the question they should say so, and to take their evidence slowly, answer only the question put to them and not to engage in questioning opposing counsel or offer unsolicited opinions of their own. It is up to the solicitor to keep his witnesses in check and ensure that they do not embarrass the client or harm his case.

11.10.3 Conduct of the trial

Counsel (if instructed) will have the conduct of the trial, and the solicitor's function will be to sit behind counsel and take full notes of evidence. For the purpose of costing, a note should be made of the start time, any adjournments and the time the trial finishes. The questions asked by counsel should be noted, as well as the responses given, as counsel will not be able to make any notes himself whilst on his feet.

11.10.4 Order of evidence

Although evidence is usually given by the claimant first, followed by the defence, in clinical negligence cases all witnesses of fact may be called first, followed by witnesses giving evidence of opinion. This is because the facts themselves are often complex and it assists the judge greatly if the facts are laid out clearly by hearing evidence from the witnesses of fact for the claimant, followed directly by those of the defence. The object is to clarify the areas of disagreement so that experts can concentrate their efforts there, and shorten the length of trial. However, the parties must apply to the trial judge on the first day of the trial to use this procedure, as the order of evidence in the judge's court will be decided by the individual judge as a matter of discretion.

11.10.5 Judgment

The solicitor should take a careful note of the judgment delivered by the judge at the end of the case, as it may be crucial if the client decides to appeal.

Counsel must be made aware of any specific orders which may be necessary.

The solicitor should also check the pre-trial orders to see if costs were reserved in any interlocutory proceedings, and, if so, that this is brought to the attention of the judge so that a costs order can be made in relation to that application.

The judgment should be fully explained to the client, which can be undertaken by counsel.

11.10.6 The order

Following trial in the county court, the court will draw up the order, which should be checked carefully to ensure that it reflects the judge's decision, as mistakes are sometimes made by the court staff.

11.11 CONCLUSION

Taking a case to trial will be the exception rather than the rule in personal injury litigation. Nevertheless, every case must be approached from the standpoint that it will go to trial, and must be prepared accordingly.

11.12 FURTHER READING

The Civil Procedure Rules (Lord Chancellor's Department, 1998).
Civil Court Practice (Butterworths).
Civil Procedure (Sweet & Maxwell).

Chapter 12

CLAWBACK OF BENEFITS – SOCIAL SECURITY (RECOVERY OF BENEFITS) ACT 1997

12.1 INTRODUCTION

Certain sums of money received by the claimant (eg sums received from his employer under a contract of employment which are not refundable) will be deducted when calculating the claimant's loss of earnings. The claimant may receive other sums of money as a result of the accident, such as State benefits. The purpose of this chapter is to examine how the receipt of such sums affects the claimant's damages.

12.2 THE LEGISLATION

The legislation is predominantly contained in the Social Security (Recovery of Benefits) Act 1997 (the 1997 Act). This received Royal Assent on 19 March 1997, and was brought into force on 6 October 1997. The key features of the 1997 Act are as follows.

(1) Recoupment is not allowed against general damages for pain, suffering and loss of amenity.
(2) Recoupment is allowed only against certain special damages, ie those for loss of earnings, damages for costs of care and damages for loss of mobility.
(3) Certain benefits can only be recouped against the above and only on a 'like-for-like basis' (ie benefits paid as a result of loss of earnings can only be recouped out of damages awarded in respect of past loss of earnings).
(4) The burden of recoupment is shifted onto the 'compensator' (usually the defendant's insurer). The compensator is responsible for repayment of all relevant benefits paid to the injured person even if they are unable to recoup the full amount out of that person's damages.
(5) There is no deduction from damages for future loss.
(6) There is no deduction from damages in respect of medical expenses (not included in cost of respite or nursing care and attendance).

The main Regulations relevant to the Scheme are found in the Social Security (Recovery of Benefits) Regulations 1997, as amended by paras 148–152 of Sch 7 to the Social Security Act 1998.

Chapter 12 contents
Introduction
The legislation
Definitions
Compensation subject to recoupment
'Like-for-like' recoupment
The role of the compensator
The meaning of 'recoverable benefits'
Exempt payments
Contributory negligence
Multiple defendants ('compensators')
Clinical negligence
Structured settlements
Part 36 payments
Interim payments
Appeals system
The Compensation Recovery Unit and the Road Traffic (NHS Charges) Act 1999
Conclusion
Further reading

12.3 DEFINITIONS

12.3.1 The meaning of 'compensation payment'

A compensation payment is a payment made by a person (whether on his own behalf or not) to or in respect of any other person in consequence of any accident, injury or disease suffered by the other (s 1 of the 1997 Act). This is a very wide definition and is designed to cover payments whether made by the tortfeasor or his insurer. The 1997 Act also applies to all claims settled or judgments given on or after 6 October 1997, regardless of whether proceedings were issued prior to that date.

12.3.2 The meaning of 'compensator'

The compensator means the person, company or agent who is paying the compensation, usually an insurance company, on behalf of their insured.

12.3.3 The meaning of 'recoverable benefit'

A recoverable benefit is any listed benefit which has been or is likely to be paid in respect of an accident, injury or disease (s 1 of the 1997 Act).

'Recoverable benefits' are listed in Sch 2 to the 1997 Act and are reproduced at **12.7** below.

12.4 COMPENSATION SUBJECT TO RECOUPMENT

The reforms introduced by the 1997 Act are designed to spread the burden evenly between claimants and compensators.

Further safeguards in respect of recoupment out of special damages are also provided by the 1997 Act. Recoupment is allowed only against specified areas of loss (see below).

The three specified areas subject to recoupment are:

(1) compensation for loss of earnings;
(2) compensation for cost of care; and
(3) compensation for loss of mobility.

Scope for recoupment is further limited by the fact that recoupment out of the above three types of compensation is allowed only on a 'like-for-like' basis.

In relation to all three of the above, recoupment can occur only in respect of losses during what the 1997 Act terms 'the relevant period'.

The relevant period is defined in s 3 as:

(1) 5 years from the date of the accident or injury; or
(2) in the case of a disease, 5 years beginning with the date on which a listed benefit was first claimed; or
(3) the period ending with a compensation payment in final discharge of the claim (if less than 5 years).

Therefore, the overall effect of the legislation is that:

(1) it allows recoupment against certain items of special damage; and
(2) it should ensure that general damages are protected from recoupment.

Note that claims for future loss including cost of care and mobility *beyond* the above 5-year period are *not* subject to recoupment.

12.5 'LIKE-FOR-LIKE' RECOUPMENT

Having established that only special damages can be the subject of recoupment, Sch 2 to the 1997 Act further safeguards special damages as it allows only 'like-for-like' recoupment. This means that only benefits which closely correspond to the relevant head of loss can be recouped from damages awarded in respect of that head of loss.

For example, if you consider the schedule at **12.7**, you will see that attendance allowance can be recouped only from compensation for cost of care, and not from compensation for loss of earnings.

If compensation for cost of care is less than the amount actually paid out in listed benefits during the relevant period, the claimant will receive nothing in respect of that head of loss; *however*, any excess in benefits for cost of care which has not so far been recouped, cannot be recouped from any other head of compensation. In this instance, the burden of paying off the excess falls on the compensator (usually the insurance company), and will be refunded to the DSS, so that the State will always achieve 100% recoupment, the only question being how much will be out of compensation, and how much will be paid by the compensator.

For example, due to an accident at work 6 years ago, John (who is aged below 65) has received severe disablement allowance and reduced earnings allowance over the entire 6-year period. He has also received disability living allowance.

Severe disablement allowance and reduced earnings allowance are both recoupable in full, but only for the first 5 years and only from compensation paid in respect of lost earnings. Similarly, disability living allowance will be recoupable, as regards the care component only, from compensation paid in respect of cost of care.

12.6 THE ROLE OF THE COMPENSATOR

(1) In most cases, the claimant's solicitor will supply to the compensator the necessary Compensatory Recovery Unit (CRU) information.
(2) Within 14 days, the compensator informs the CRU on Form CRU 1 giving required particulars.
(3) The CRU acknowledges receipt of the notification and issues Form CRU 4 to the compensator. Form CRU 4R is sent to the claimant's solicitors.
(4) The claim then progresses to the settlement stage.
(5) When ready to make an offer of compensation, the compensator submits Form CRU 4 to obtain a Certificate of Recoverable Benefit.
(6) The CRU acknowledges receipt of Form CRU 4 (within 10 days).
(7) Within 4 weeks, the CRU sends the Certificate of Recoverable Benefit to the compensator. A copy will also be sent to the claimant's solicitor. The

compensator will then settle the compensation claim and then pay the relevant amount to the CRU within 14 days of the settlement.

12.6.1 Notifying the CRU

Section 4 of the 1997 Act requires the the compensator inform the CRU not later than 14 days after receiving the claim. The notification is made on Form CRU 1 which is sent to the CRU.

The information required by the compensator to complete Form CRU 1 is:

(1) the name and address of the claimant;
(2) (if known) the date of birth and national insurance number of that person;
(3) the date of the accident or injury (or in the case of disease the date of diagnosis);
(4) the nature of the accident, injury or disease (as alleged by the claimant);
(5) (if known) the name and address of the claimant's employer and his payroll number at the relevant time.

On receipt of Form CRU 1, the CRU will send Form CRU 4 to the defendant. This has a twofold function:

(1) it acknowledges receipt of the notification of claim; and
(2) the compensator should retain it safely on the file as it will be needed later to obtain the Certificate of Recoverable Benefit (ie the details of the benefit paid or to be paid to the claimant).

Despite the requirement that the CRU be informed of the claim within 14 days of notification of the claim, this is sometimes overlooked by insurance companies. If proceedings are issued and the insurer instructs solicitors, Form CRU 1 should be completed immediately, if this has not already been done. In such circumstances, it may be appropriate for the address of the compensator given on Form CRU 1 to be care of the solicitors, to ensure that the certificate of recoverable benefit is forwarded to the solicitors, who are likely to make the compensation payment to the claimant.

When the matter is lodged with the CRU, the claimant's solicitor will be notified and a Form CRU 4R will also be sent to the claimant's representative, which can be used to obtain benefit information (the claimant's solicitor can also obtain benefit details by writing to the CRU). It is important that, prior to negotiating any settlement or accepting any payment into court, the claimant himself examines the benefit details to ensure that they are correct.

12.6.2 The Certificate of Recoverable Benefit

The provision central to the whole system is that no compensation is to be paid until the defendant has obtained a 'Certificate of Recoverable Benefit'. If compensation is paid without obtaining a certificate, the DSS can still take steps against the defendant to recover the benefits.

The defendant obtains the certificate by completing and returning Form CRU 4 to the CRU. The defendant must ensure that all the information required by Forms CRU 1 and CRU 4 is given, after which the CRU will acknowledge the form in writing and, within 4 weeks, send a certificate to the defendant and a copy to the claimant.

The certificate details:

(1) the amount of relevant benefits paid or likely to be paid by a specified date;

(2) the details of any continuing benefit; and

(3) the amount to be recouped in the event of a compensation payment being made.

12.7 THE MEANING OF 'RECOVERABLE BENEFITS'

A schedule of recoverable benefits and the heads of damage to which they are recoverable against on a like-for-like basis (see **12.5**, above for explanation of 'like-for-like' recoupment) is contained in Sch 2 to the 1997 Act as:

Head of compensation	Benefit
(1) Compensation for earnings lost during relevant period	Disablement pension payable under s 103 of the 1992 Act
	Incapacity benefit
	Income support
	Invalidity pension and allowance
	Jobseeker's allowance
	Reduced earnings allowance
	Severe disablement allowance
	Sickness benefit
	Statutory sick pay paid before 6 April 1994
	Unemployability supplement
	Unemployment benefit
(2) Compensation for cost of care incurred during the relevant period	Attendance allowance
	Care component of disability living allowance
	Disablement pension increase payable under s 104 or s 105 of the 1992 Act
(3) Compensation for loss of mobility during the relevant period	Mobility allowance
	Mobility component of disability living allowance

NOTE: References to incapacity benefit, invalidity pension and allowance, severe disablement allowance, sickness benefit and unemployment benefit also include any income support paid with each of those benefits.

Any reference to statutory sick pay:

(1) includes only 80% of payments made between 6 April 1991 and 5 April 1994; and

(2) does not include payments made on or after 6 April 1994.

In the case of *Griffiths and Others v British Coal Corporation and the Department of Trade and Industry* [2001] 1 WLR 1493, it was held that an award of interest on damages for past loss of earnings fell within the expression 'compensation for earnings lost' in Sch 2 to the 1997 Act and was therefore subject to reduction on account of payments by the tortfeasor to the CRU. In the same case, it was also held that any compensation for services in the nature of care, gratuitously rendered, fell within the term 'compensation for cost of care incurred during the relevant period', and allowed the tortfeasor to set off the benefits paid against the damages.

12.8 EXEMPT PAYMENTS

Schedule 1, Part 1 of the 1997 Act contains the payments which are exempt from recoupment under the Act. These include payments by or under the following.

(1) Fatal Accidents Act 1976.
(2) Criminal Injuries Compensation Authority payments.
(3) Vaccine damage payments.
(4) The Macfarlane Trust (established partly under funds from the Secretary of State to the Haemophilia Society) and the Eileen Trust.
(5) British Coal, in accordance with the NCB Pneumoconiosis Compensation Scheme.
(6) Cases of hearing loss, where the loss is less than 50db in one or both ears.
(7) The National Health Service (Injury Benefits) Regulations 1974, SI 1975/1547.
(8) Criminal Court Compensation Orders, s 35 of the Powers of Criminal Courts Act 1973.
(9) Certain trust funds (in particular 'disaster funds', where more than half of the fund is raised by public subscription).
(10) Certain private insurance contracts between the victim and his insurer entered into before the contract.
(11) Any redundancy payment already accounted for in the assessment of damages.
(12) Any amount which is referable to costs.
(13) Any contractual amount paid to an employee by an employer in respect of incapacity for work (eg occupational sick pay).

12.9 CONTRIBUTORY NEGLIGENCE

Since 'compensation payment' is defined as the sum falling to be paid to the claimant, it follows that the relevant sum is that which is paid to the claimant after any deduction for contributory negligence by the claimant. However, the amount of the benefits to be deducted is unaffected by the contributory negligence.

Example
Assume that on a full liability basis the value of the claimant's loss of earnings claim is £10,000, but he is 60% contributorily negligent. He has received relevant benefits of £3,000. The calculation is as follows:

	£
£10,000 – 60% contributory negligence	4,000
Recoverable benefits	3,000
Defendant pays to claimant	1,000
Defendant pays to CRU	3,000
Total payment by defendant	4,000

Thus, although the compensation payment was reduced by contributory negligence, the amount of benefits to be recouped remains the same.

12.10 MULTIPLE DEFENDANTS ('COMPENSATORS')

In certain cases, the claimant will sue two or more defendants, and, as such, all defendants are jointly and severally liable to reimburse the CRU. However, in practice, it is usual for a sharing agreement as between defendants to be made, whereby the defendants reach an agreement as to how they are to pay the claimant and the CRU.

12.11 CLINICAL NEGLIGENCE

The rules relating to the clawback of benefit apply to clinical negligence claims and, due to their complexity, especially with regard to causation, the CRU has set up a specialist group to deal with the claims and makes a special request that compensators inform the CRU about clinical negligence claims as soon as the pre-action correspondence is received.

12.12 STRUCTURED SETTLEMENTS

The provisions of the clawback of benefits will also apply to structured settlements (see Chapter 16). Benefits are recoverable from the lump sum figure but not from the periodic payments made under the structured settlement agreement. In a structured settlement case the 'date of settlement' is regarded as the date the agreement is approved by the court or the date the agreement is entered into. The relevant cheque should be sent to the CRU within 14 days.

12.13 PART 36 PAYMENTS

If the defendant wishes to place pressure on the claimant to settle the case and proceedings have been commenced, the defendant will make a Part 36 payment into court. PD 36 requires the notice of payment into court to state:

(1) the amount of the gross compensation;
(2) that the gross amount has been reduced by the amount of benefits in accordance with s 8 of and Sch 2 to the Social Security (Recovery of Benefits) Act 1997, specifying the name of the benefit and the amount; and
(3) the net amount paid in after the reduction.

Form N424A should be used for the Part 36 payment and the compensator should file with the court a certificate of recoverable benefit (see also *Campion v Bradley* (1999) 8 CL 203 concerning clarification of a Part 36 notice).

12.14 INTERIM PAYMENTS

It should be noted that if an interim payment is made, then the compensator is liable to repay any relevant recoverable benefits at that stage.

12.15 APPEALS SYSTEM

The grounds for appeal include:

(1) that any amount, rate or period in the Certificate of Recoverable Benefits is incorrect;
(2) against the calculations in the certificate of recoverable benefits relating to benefits not paid in consequence of accident, injury or disease.

An appeal can be made only after final settlement of the compensation claim and payment of the recoverable benefits has been made. The basic time-limit for the appeal is 1 month from the date on which the compensator makes the full payment of recoverable benefits and is dealt with by an independent tribunal administered by the Appeals Service.

Appeal can be made by:

(1) the person who applied for the certificate, ie the compensator; or
(2) the injured person whose compensation payment has been reduced.

If the appeal is unsuccessful, there is then a possible appeal on a point of law from the Appeals Service to the Social Security and Child Support Commissioners.

There is a less formal procedure that can be adopted and that is known as a 'review'. This can be requested at any time and as a result the CRU will look at the matter again and clear the benefits that are listed as recoverable.

12.16 THE COMPENSATION RECOVERY UNIT AND THE ROAD TRAFFIC (NHS CHARGES) ACT 1999

The CRU also acts as the collector of hospital charges under the Road Traffic (NHS Charges) Act 1999 (see Chapter 4). It should be noted that the CRU can accept cheques from compensators for NHS charges only once the case is settled.

12.17 CONCLUSION

Solicitors should exercise care when dealing with this area to ensure that it is clear whether any offer put forward is net or gross of benefits, and that the benefit figures are correct. In *Hilton International v Martin-Smith* (2001) LTL, 12 February, it was held that, where a party made an error of judgment (in this case, in relation to the amount stated on the Certificate of Recoverable Benefit), it did not follow that the court would permit that party to escape its consequences. Similarly, defendant solicitors also need to ensure that benefits listed as recoverable benefits are as a consequence of the accident (see *Eagle Star Insurance v Department of Social Development (Northern Ireland)* (only persuasive) (2001) NICE, 12 February) and the unreported case of *Secretary of State for Social Security v Oldham MBC and Others* (2001) unreported, 15 May.

12.18 FURTHER READING

Leaflet Z1 *Deduction from Compensation – A Guide for Companies* (the Benefits Agency).
Kemp and Kemp *The Quantum of Damages* (Sweet & Maxwell).

Chapter 13

QUANTIFICATION OF DAMAGES

13.1 INTRODUCTION

The claimant's solicitor has as his aim the achievement of the highest possible level of damages for his client. This chapter explains how these damages are calculated.

In tort, the aim of the award of damages in a personal injury claim is to restore the claimant to the position that he was in prior to the accident. In practice, for a personal injury claim this clearly cannot be achieved. For many clients, the award of damages is recompense not only for the injuries that they have suffered but compensation for the stress and inconvenience of being involved in a litigation process which can take many years. Many victims of clinical negligence complain that the difficulties that they have encountered in pursuing their investigation of the potential negligence can result in continued illness or failure to recover within the expected period of time. However, the award of monetary compensation is the only available remedy to the court.

Many claimant's solicitors believe that the level of damages awarded in personal injury cases does not adequately compensate the injured claimant, and organisations such as the Association of Personal Injury Lawyers (APIL) campaign on this issue.

The court can make true recompense for the financial losses which the claimant has incurred prior to trial, as these can be calculated precisely. Such losses are referred to as 'special damages'. (The phrase 'past pecuniary loss' is also used but the meaning is the same.) The element of the compensation award that cannot be calculated specifically, for example the pain and suffering which the claimant suffered, are referred to as 'general damages'. The distinction is significant not only in the method of calculation but also with regard to the level of interest awarded by the court (see **13.4**). Although the claimant regards his compensation payment as one lump sum, the personal injury solicitor must fully understand on what basis the court will award damages, to ensure that he can maximise the level of damages awarded to his client, where appropriate.

The claimant's damages are assessed as at the date of the trial, and it is therefore important that sufficient and up-to-date evidence is available in respect of special and general damages. For example, an up-to-date loss of earnings calculation must be put before the court, together with up-to-date medical evidence on the client's condition, where appropriate.

The following guidance applies to both personal injury and clinical negligence claims.

Chapter 13 contents
Introduction
Special damages
General damages
Interest
The award of damages at trial
Further reading

13.2 SPECIAL DAMAGES

Special damages are the items of loss that can be specifically calculated, and represent the claimant's financial loss from the date of the accident until the date of trial.

The main heads of special damages are:

(1) items of specific loss;
(2) loss of earnings to the date of trial;
(3) medical expenses prior to trial;
(4) cost of services provided by a third party prior to the trial;
(5) expenses relating to the cost of living with disabilities prior to trial.

13.2.1 Items of specific loss

In the majority of personal injury cases, there will be certain one-off losses incurred by the claimant. In a road traffic accident, the claimant will normally have several items of specific loss, for example:

(1) the cost of repair of the vehicle;
(2) policy excess if the car was comprehensively insured;
(3) hire car charges;
(4) bus fares;
(5) damage to clothing;
(6) taxi fares;
(7) prescription charges;
(8) recovery or storage charges relating to the car;
(9) damaged items in the vehicle;
(10) pre-accident value of the car (less salvage if the car is written off);
(11) loss of petrol if the car is written off.

It is for the claimant to prove the items of loss, and he should be reminded at the outset of the case that he should retain documentary evidence (such as receipts) in support of as many items as possible. Insurance companies often deny payment for items that cannot be supported by documentary evidence, but it is open to the claimant to attempt to prove the loss by evidence at trial (see *Hughes v Addis* (2000) LTL, 23 March).

All of the above items are frequently claimed for in a road traffic case and many are uncontroversial. However, there can be difficulties in advising as regards to hire charge claims, especially where the claimant wishes to hire a different type of vehicle than that involved in the accident (compare *Mattocks v Mann* [1993] RTR 13, with *Coyne v Cawley* [1995] CLY 1624) or the hire charges are for a long period of time. In such cases, reference should be made to the relevant case-law and *Current Law* is a useful source of information. It is clear that hire car charges can be claimed while the claimant's vehicle is being repaired but the claimant must show that he has acted reasonably. For example, if the hire car is being hired by the claimant at a daily rate (which is frequently the most expensive charging rate) rather than at a weekly rate (which is often cheaper), then the court may take the view that only the weekly rate should be recoverable, unless the claimant can show a good reason for using the daily rate (see *Usher v Crowder* [1994] CLY 1494).

It appears that the claimant is able to claim for losses from the defendant that were due to the claimant's lack of money. For example, the defendants admit liability for a road traffic accident but the claimant cannot afford to pay for the repairs out of his own funds. As a result, the claimant hires a car until the defendants pay for the repairs to the claimant's car. Following *Mattocks v Mann* (see above), such a claim is recoverable. However, in certain circumstances, the claimant may use a vehicle supplied by a 'credit hire' company. However, for any such agreement to be enforceable, it must comply with the Consumer Credit Act 1974 (or be exempt) and the amount recoverable should be the 'market rate'; see *Dimond v Lovell* [2000] 2 WLR 1121.

If a claim for hire charges is made then, generally, a claim for loss of use (see **13.3.7**) will not be made as the claimant has not been without a vehicle.

It may also be possible to recover as special damages the loss of any non-recoupable benefits which are no longer being paid to the client as a result of the injury (see *Neal v Bingle* [1998] 2 All ER 58, CA).

13.2.2 Loss of earnings up to the date of the trial

This is the most common example of special damages. Only in the most simple of personal injury cases will there be no claim for lost earnings. The claimant is allowed to recover his net loss of earnings; this represents the figure which he would have earned after tax, national insurance and contractual pension payments (if his pension is left unaffected – *Dews v National Coal Board* [1988] AC 1, HL).

The claimant's solicitor should contact his client's employer and ask for details of the client's wages prior to the accident (providing the employer is not the defendant, in which case such detail will be provided via the defendant's insurance company). It is common to obtain the details for the period of 13 weeks prior to the accident and a standard form is often used for such a purpose. However, if there is any evidence that the average of the 13 weeks prior to the accident is not representative of the claimant's average pre-accident wage then further enquiries should be made and a longer period of pre-accident wage details should be obtained, for example 6 months. In particular, it must be ensured that any overtime, bonus payments or commission that the claimant would have earned if he had been at work are included in the net loss of earnings figure. Enquiries also need to be made as to whether the client would have received any pay increase, promotion, or obtained any other benefits such as a company car had he not been absent from work.

In appropriate cases, it is good practice to obtain details of a comparative earner when calculating the loss of earnings figure. This involves obtaining the wages details of another employee of the client's employer who is on the same wages as the client. For example, where a solicitor represents a factory operative who is paid a basic wage of £200 net per week, but the client can also earn additional overtime, details can be obtained of another employee who is on the same pay scale and who has the same opportunity for overtime work as the client, and the amount that the comparative employee has earned whilst the client has been absent from work can be put to the defendants as the figure that the client would have earned had he not been involved in the accident. This can be particularly useful in cases where the claimant has only recently obtained a job and a clear pattern of pre-accident earnings cannot be established. The comparative figures must be shown to the client for confirmation that they represent a true comparison.

Very few employees receive no income whatsoever whilst absent from work and so the calculation of the claimant's lost earnings is not simply: weekly net loss of earnings × period of absence = net loss. A detailed examination of what income the claimant received whilst absent from work is required as certain types of income have to be credited in calculating the net loss figure, for example:

Net pre-accident earnings × 10 weeks' absence from work	£100
	£1,000
Claimant received £50 per week from his employer whilst absent, in accordance with his contract of employment. The contract does not make any provision for the money paid whilst absent to be repaid to the employer.	£500
TOTAL NET LOSS OF EARNINGS	£500

Most common items dealt with in net loss of earnings calculation

The following are the most common items which must be accounted for in the net loss of earnings figure (for both past and future loss of earnings calculations).

(1) TAX REFUNDS RECEIVED DUE TO ABSENCE FROM WORK AS A RESULT OF THE ACCIDENT

A claimant who is an employee will generally pay income tax on the Pay As You Earn (PAYE) system. To a certain extent, this system is a payment of tax in advance as it assumes that the claimant's earnings will continue throughout the whole of the forthcoming year. In the event of the claimant's absence from work, he may then have paid too much tax. In this case, the claimant may receive a tax rebate via his employer. An amount equivalent to the whole of the rebate has to be given credit for in the calculation of wage loss (*Hartley v Sandholme Iron Co Ltd* [1975] QB 600). Occasionally, instead of a 'cash-in-hand' tax rebate the claimant may receive a tax credit against future tax liability so that on his return to work he pays no tax for a period (a 'tax holiday'). A sum equivalent to this tax credit also has to be given credit for in the calculation of the wage loss (*Brayson v Wilmot-Breedon* [1976] CLY 682).

(2) SUMS PAID TO THE CLAIMANT BY HIS EMPLOYER

Whether sums equivalent to such payments fall to be deducted from the damages depends on:

(1) the basis of the payment; and
(2) who is the tortfeasor.

The following are the most common situations.

(1) The sum is paid under a legal obligation (eg under the claimant's contract of employment) and is not refundable by the claimant to his employer. An amount equivalent to the whole of the payment should be deducted from the damages.
(2) The sum is paid under a legal obligation (eg under the contract of employment) and must be repaid by the claimant to his employer out of any damages the

claimant receives from the defendant. Such a payment is effectively a loan and, as such, is not deducted when assessing the damages.

(3) The sum is paid ex gratia by the employer who is not the tortfeasor. Such a payment is effectively a 'charitable' payment and is not to be deducted when assessing the damages (*Cunningham v Harrison* [1973] 3 All ER 463).

(4) The sum is paid ex gratia by the employer who is the tortfeasor. An amount equivalent to the whole of the payment may (in certain circumstances) be deducted from the damages (*Hussain v New Taplow Paper Mills Ltd* [1988] AC 514).

(5) The claimant receives statutory sick pay from his employer. This is not a recoverable benefit to the CRU (see Chapter 12) and therefore an amount equivalent to the whole payment should be deducted (see also **4.7.1** for further details of SSP).

(3) ANY SAVING TO AN INJURED PERSON ATTRIBUTABLE TO HIS MAINTENANCE WHOLLY OR PARTLY AT PUBLIC EXPENSE

This would apply where the claimant was, for example, admitted into a National Health Service hospital, nursing home or other institution. The savings must be calculated and set off against any claim for income lost as a result of the injuries (Administration of Justice Act 1982, s 5). In practice, this deduction is overlooked because in most cases the sums saved are *de minimis* (while in hospital the claimant will generally have to meet the same household expenses such as rent, mortgage and council tax; any saving will usually only be in regard to the cost of food. This saving is then so small as to be ignored). For private medical expenses, see **13.2.3**.

(4) REDUNDANCY PAYMENTS

An equivalent amount is to be deducted in full from the damages calculation when redundancy occurs as a result of the injury caused by the accident (*Colledge v Bass Mitchells & Butlers* [1988] 1 All ER 536).

Most common items excluded from net loss of earnings

The following items are the most common payments to be left out of account in assessing an award for loss of past (and future) earnings.

(1) STATE RETIREMENT PENSION

The State retirement pension is ignored in assessing an award for loss of past and future earnings (*Hewson v Downs* [1970] 1 QB 73).

(2) PENSIONS RECEIVED

If the claimant receives a pension, this cannot be set against the claim for loss of earnings. However, if there is a separate claim for loss of pension rights, for example since the claimant is unable to work he will receive less pension in the future, any pension he does receive may be offset against the claim for loss of pension rights (*Parry v Cleaver* [1970] AC 1; *Smoker v London Fire and Civil Defence Authority* [1991] 2 All ER 449; see also **13.3.6**; *Longden v British Coal Corporation* [1997] 3 WLR 1336).

(3) INSURANCE MONEYS

The claimant may have the benefit of an insurance policy under which he is entitled to receive payment in the event of his sustaining injury. The claimant may have taken out the policy specifically to cover such eventualities or the personal injury cover may be an 'incidental' benefit (eg to a comprehensive motor insurance policy). In such cases, the payment is usually a fixed sum according to the type of injury; for example, in the event of a loss of a limb the insurance company will pay the insured the sum of £5,000. The claimant need not give credit for moneys received under such a policy against the damages payable by the defendant. The justification is that the defendant should not benefit from the fact that the claimant had the foresight to take out the cover and pay the premium (*Bradburn v Great Western Railway Co* (1874) LR 10 Exch 1; *McCamley v Cammell Laird Shipbuilders Ltd* [1990] 1 All ER 854). The claimant, however, should check the terms of his insurance policy. It is often the case (particularly in motor insurance) that there is a provision that if the claimant recovers damages in respect of a loss for which the claimant's insurance company has paid the claimant compensation, the claimant must reimburse his insurance company. In this case, although the claimant may claim for the losses from the defendant, he will receive no personal benefit if he does so.

(4) CHARITABLE PAYMENTS

If money is received by the claimant as a charitable payment (even if it is on an informal basis such as the proceeds of a collection taken amongst his friends) then the claimant is not required to give credit for such payments against the damages received. The justification is that as a matter of policy people should not be discouraged from making such payments to the victims of accidents (*Parry v Cleaver* (above)). However, the exact circumstances and sources of the ex gratia payment must be considered. In *Williams v BOC Gases Ltd* [2000] PIQR Q253, the Court of Appeal held that, where an employer (who was the tortfeasor) made an ex gratia payment on termination of his employment and 'it is to be treated as an advance against damages that may be awarded ... in respect of any claim ...', credit had to be given for that amount in a subsequent personal injury claim.

Clients with unusual employment histories

Not all claimants are employees; nor have they all had stable employment backgrounds. In such circumstances, further enquiries must be made in an attempt to provide evidence of pre-accident income. Self-employed claimants should be asked to supply copies of their accounts for the year prior to the accident, or a longer period if one year's figures are not representative. Unfortunately, this information can be difficult to obtain from the client, and the defendants will argue the validity of the claim. In certain cases, it will be necessary to obtain a report from an accountant (the term 'forensic accountant' is often used for those who specialise in this area; see **13.3.3**. It may also be necessary to contact the claimant's tax office to obtain copies of his tax returns. In an attempt to establish details of how much the claimant would have earned between the accident and trial in cases where an erratic employment history is presented (eg this can often be the situation with building labourers who had just commenced employment at the time of the accident), reference can be made to the New Earnings Survey produced by the Office for National Statistics, which is a statistical analysis of earnings throughout the country. The Survey can provide details of average earnings for particular industries or occupations on a national or regional basis and can be useful in attempting to persuade the defendant to accept that the claimant would have received a particular wage. (The Survey is also of particular use in connection with future loss claims.) The claimant must adduce as much evidence as possible to establish what he would have earned if it had not been for the accident.

It is still possible for an accident victim who was, prior to the accident, receiving earnings from a lawful source but failing to pay tax or National Insurance, to bring a claim for past and future loss of earnings (although adjustments will have to be made to the past and future loss of earnings calculation) (see *Newman v Marshall and Dunlop Tyres Ltd* (2001) LTL, 19 June and *Duller v South East Lincs Engineers* (1985) CLY 585).

13.2.3 Medical expenses prior to trial

In certain cases, where there are long waiting lists under the NHS, the claimant solicitor should suggest that the client undergo private medical treatment in an attempt to speed the recovery period. Indeed, the defendant's solicitors in serious cases will suggest further medical treatment in an attempt to reduce the level of damages payable if the claimant establishes liability.

> *Example*
> A 10-year-old girl is injured and has to undergo major abdominal surgery at the local hospital, which leaves her with a large surgical incision. As part of her general damages award she will claim for pain and suffering relating to the scarring. It is also likely that she will claim that she will suffer psychological problems in relation to the embarrassment of wearing swimming costumes throughout her teenage years and perhaps in later life. In such a case, it is likely that the defendant's solicitors will suggest that the claimant undergo specialist plastic surgery in an attempt to reduce the significance of the scarring and the potential psychological problems, which, in turn, will reduce the level of damages that the defendant will pay.

A claimant may claim for the reasonable cost of private medical care actually incurred. The availability of free NHS treatment is ignored (Law Reform (Personal Injuries) Act 1948, s 2(4)). However, the claimant cannot be treated free under the NHS system and then claim what it would have cost to have been treated privately. Future private medical care may also be claimed (if long term, on a multiplicand and multiplier system – see **13.3.3**) provided it is reasonably likely to be incurred (*Hodgson v Trapp* [1988] 3 WLR 1281). However, only the cost of the medical care may be claimed; the claimant cannot claim for the 'hotel' element in the expenses, for example the proportion of the fees that relate to the provision of meals, heating and lighting (*Lim Poh Choo v Camden and Islington Area Health Authority* [1979] 2 All ER 910).

Medical expenses incurred pre-trial are claimed as special damages; those incurred post-trial are claimed as general damages.

13.2.4 Losses incurred and services rendered by third parties as a result of the claimant's injuries

General principle
The general principle is that a third party cannot claim against the defendant for losses incurred by a third party as a result of injury to the claimant.

Example 1
An employer cannot claim for the loss of services of the claimant who is a 'non-menial servant', ie an employee who is not part of the employer's household, for example a butler (*IRC v Hambrook* [1956] 3 All ER 338). Therefore, if Fred employed Tom in his factory and Tom is injured in a road traffic accident as a result of Eric's negligence, Fred has no right of action against Eric.

Example 2
An employee cannot sue for loss of lucrative employment caused by injury to his employer (*Best v Samuel Fox & Co Ltd* [1952] 2 All ER 394). For example, Tom is employed by Fred. Fred is seriously injured in an accident as a result of Eric's negligence and subsequently Tom loses his job when Fred's firm ceases to trade. Tom has no right of action against Eric for the loss of his job.

Value of services rendered

The claimant (but not the third party) may recover the value of services provided to him by a third party, provided such services were rendered necessary by the act of the tortfeasor (*Kirkham v Boughey* [1958] 2 QB 338; *Schneider v Eisovitch* [1960] 2 QB 430).

In practice, a common example of such services is nursing (or quasi-nursing) services rendered to the claimant by his relatives or friends.

Example
Tom is injured in an accident caused by Eric's negligence. Tom is admitted to hospital for 6 weeks. Tom's wife, Ann, visits Tom each day that he is in hospital. Tom is discharged from hospital and spends 3 months convalescing at home. During that time, Ann cares for Tom by cooking his meals, giving him his medication and generally seeing to his personal needs. Ann cannot claim against Eric for the value of the services rendered to Tom. However, as part of his claim against Eric, Tom can claim for the value of the services rendered to him by Ann in respect of the visits to hospital (on the basis that the visits speeded his recovery) and the nursing care after his discharge from hospital.

The following should be noted.

(1) The value of the services may be claimed by the claimant irrespective of whether the third party has been put to actual expense in rendering those services, for example, by incurring loss of earnings (*Cunningham v Harrison* [1973] 3 All ER 463; *Daly v General Steam Navigation Co* [1980] 3 All ER 696; *Roberts v Johnstone* [1988] 3 WLR 1247).
(2) It is unnecessary (and undesirable) for there to be any agreement between the claimant and the third party as to the reimbursement of the third party for the services (*Cunningham v Harrison* (above)).
(3) The claim for the value of the services is made by the claimant, not by the third party. Similarly, the award is to the claimant, not to the third party, as it is the claimant's loss which is being compensated. This was explained by Megaw LJ in *Donnelly v Joyce* [1973] 3 All ER 475 in the following terms: 'The plaintiff's loss is not the expenditure of money to buy the special boots or to pay for the nursing attention. This loss is the existence of the need for those special boots or for those nursing services'.

(4) Although the claimant claims the value of the services, the damages awarded to him in respect of those services are held by the claimant in trust for the person who provided those services (the carer). Therefore, where the carer is also the defendant (eg where a wife is injured as a result of her husband's negligent driving and the husband provides quasi-nursing services to the wife during her convalescence) the claimant cannot recover the value of those services from the defendant/carer, since otherwise the claimant would have to repay the damages to the defendant/carer (*Hunt v Severs* [1994] 2 All ER 385, HL).

(5) If, for example, a mother (who is severely injured) and child (only minor injury) are involved in a road traffic accident, then it is not possible for the child to claim damages for the care element from the defendant. The appropriate course is for the mother to claim, as part of the case, the costs of care of the child (see *Buckley v Farrow and Buckley* [1997] PIQR Q78).

(6) It is not normally possible to recover damages for a spouse of an accident victim who does work for the victim's business on a 'gratuitous' basis. See *Harwick v Hindson and Another* (1999) NLJ 28 May.

VALUING THE SERVICES RENDERED

Megaw LJ, in *Donnelly v Joyce* (above), stated that 'the value of [the services] for the purposes of damages – for the purpose of the ascertainment of the amount of his loss – is the proper and reasonable costs of supplying those needs'.

In the case of professional services (eg professional nursing care), the claimant is entitled to the reasonable fee for those services. In the case of the services rendered by non-professionals (eg nursing care rendered by the claimant's spouse), where there is no fee incurred, the valuation may be more problematical. O'Connor LJ, in *Housecroft v Burnett* [1986] 1 All ER 332, stated:

> 'Where the needs of an injured plaintiff are and will be supplied by a relative or friend out of love and affection (and, in cases of little children where the provider is a parent, duty) freely and without regard to monetary reward, how should the court assess "the proper and reasonable cost"? There are two extreme solutions:
>
> (i) assess the full commercial rate for supplying the needs by employing someone to do what the relative does;
>
> (ii) assess the cost at nil, just as it is assessed at nil where the plaintiff is cared for under the National Health Scheme;
>
> "each" case must be considered on its own facts ... the court should look at it as a whole and consider whether, on the facts of the case, it is sufficient to enable the plaintiff, among other things, to make reasonable recompense to the relative.'

In some cases, the relative or spouse may have given up work in order to look after the claimant and therefore incurred an actual loss of earnings. In *Housecroft v Burnett*, O'Connor LJ went on to say that 'in [such] cases ... I would regard it as natural that the plaintiff would not wish the relative to be the loser so that the court would award sufficient to enable the plaintiff to achieve that result'.

Where there is no actual loss by the third party the court may take as the value of the services that which it would have cost to employ professional help (*Roberts v Johnstone* (above); but contrast *Daly v General Steam Navigation Company* (above), where there was no actual loss and the value of the services was awarded as part of the claimant's loss of amenity). It should also be noted that the defendant's solicitor will also argue that it is inappropriate to put forward a commercial rate as a figure representing the loss in these circumstances, because that rate includes an element of profit for the care organiser, such as a nursing agency. However, the ceiling for the value of the services would normally be the commercial rate (*Housecroft v Burnett*). If the claimant is claiming that the value of the services should exceed the commercial rate then the claimant has the onus of proving the higher value (*Rialas v Mitchell* (1984) *The Times*, July 17 where the claimant justified care at home which was approximately twice the cost of care in an institution) (see also *Fitzgerald v Ford* [1996] PIQR Q72).

Subject to the comments in *Daly* set out above, the value of services claimed pre-trial are special damages, and post-trial are general damages (and, where the services are likely to be necessary over a long period of time, a multiplicand and multiplier system will be used – see **13.3.5**).

LOCAL AUTHORITIES

Section 17 of the Health and Social Services Adjudication Act 1983 provides for local authorities to recover the cost of care services supplied, in certain circumstances, from those to whom such services have been supplied. If a local authority has provided such care to a client then an indemnity must be obtained from the defendant in respect of any such claim by the authority, or the local authority's claim should be paid by the defendant prior to the settlement of the action (see *Avon County Council v Hooper* [1997] 1 WLR 1605 and *Thrul v Ray* (2000) PIQR Q44).

13.2.5 Expenses relating to cost of living with disabilities prior to trial

In more serious cases, the claimant will incur specific items of cost relating to the disabilities resulting from the accident. These may be only one-off payments, but if these items are frequently required throughout the claimant's life the replacement cost must be included within any future loss calculation. It may be necessary to use an occupational therapist to provide a rehabilitation cost report. This will involve the occupational therapist assessing the claimant in his own home to see whether the client can carry out 'the activities of daily living'. Where someone has suffered extensive injuries the expenses relating the costs of living with a disability can be significant. Few clients will be able to afford the necessary equipment and the possibility of making an application for an interim payment must be considered throughout the case.

The following are examples of the types of items which may have to be purchased after an accident by a seriously injured client:

(1) adaptation of the family car to allow the claimant to drive;
(2) the cost of a wheelchair (defendants will argue that this can be provided free by the State but this may not be suitable for the client);
(3) beds ruined due to incontinence;
(4) incontinence pads;
(5) extra costs of laundry;
(6) odour control in the house due to incontinence;
(7) additional fuel costs due to the claimant being at home all day;
(8) installation of a stairlift;
(9) installation of a shower if clients are unable to use the bath;
(10) installation of a downstairs toilet;
(11) adapted furniture;
(12) therapy ball – to help with mobility.

In respect of adaptations to the claimant's home (eg ramp access for a wheelchair or the purchase of a vehicle to help cope with his disability), the claimant will have to give credit for any enhanced value of the house or vehicle as a result of the adaptation. Calculating the loss resulting from alternative accommodation to cope with the claimant's disability may be problematical. If the claimant buys alternative (more expensive) property he has, to a certain extent, acquired an investment, ie a valuable item that can be eventually sold. In such circumstances, the claimant can claim only a proportion of the amount of capital spent, see *Roberts v Johnston* [1988] 3 WLR 1247 and *Page v Sheerness Steel Co Ltd, Wells v Wells; Thomas v Brighton Health Authority* [1998] 3 WLR 329.

13.2.6 Evidence of special damages

Details of the client's special damages and evidence in connection with them must be included in the appropriate witness statement(s) prepared for exchange.

13.3 GENERAL DAMAGES

General damages are those which are not capable of precise mathematical calculation. The main heads of general damages are:

(1) pain, suffering and loss of amenity;
(2) handicap in the labour market;
(3) loss of earnings post-trial;
(4) loss of congenial employment;
(5) future cost of care/future cost of specialist equipment;
(6) lost pension;
(7) loss of use of a motor vehicle.

13.3.1 Pain, suffering and loss of amenity

Awards of damages under this head are designed to compensate the claimant for the pain and suffering attributable to the injury both immediately after the accident and in the future if the injury is serious. It will cover not only physical injury but also psychological illness. It is important to remember that most personal injury cases are settled on a full and final basis, and it is not, therefore, open to the claimant to obtain further compensation once the case has been settled (note the exception to this being provisional damages; see Chapter 16), and it must be ensured that damages negotiated under this head reflect sufficient compensation for the client.

The award is made on the basis of a subjective test, ie 'what was the pain and suffering of this particular claimant?'. If there is no evidence that the claimant actually experienced pain then no award will be made – there must be evidence. If the claimant's expectation of life has been reduced by the injuries, he will be compensated under this head of general damages.

When the court comes to assess damages, it will examine the claimant's position as at the date of trial. The relevant compensation payment compensation payment will include a sum for past and future pain (if applicable).

Damages for loss of amenity

Strictly speaking, there is a separate head of damages known as 'loss of amenity', but compensation for this loss is usually included with compensation for pain and suffering. This element is designed to compensate the claimant for the loss of enjoyment of life which has resulted from the accident. Examples under this head include interference with the claimant's sex life, or the loss or impairment of enjoyment of holidays, sports, pursuits and hobbies, as a result of injuries.

The award for loss of amenity is based on an objective test (in contrast to pain and suffering) and thus may be awarded irrespective of whether the claimant is personally aware of his loss, for example if he is unconscious (*West v Shephard* [1964] AC 326).

Although the test is primarily objective, it does have subjective overtones insofar as the court will have regard to the claimant's former lifestyle. This may be particularly pertinent where the claimant was formerly a very active person (eg a keen sportsman) and can no longer pursue his sport. Although his pain and suffering may be the same as another person with a similar disability, his loss of amenity may be greater and, as such, the total award for pain and suffering and loss of amenity may be greater.

Damages for loss of congenial employment (see **13.3.4**) may also be argued under this head, but, increasingly, the courts are making separate reference to these types of damages.

Quantification of damages for pain and suffering and loss of amenity

It is impossible to give a precise figure of what an injury is worth in regard to pain, suffering and loss of amenity. General damages are incapable of precise mathematical calculation. Even the most experienced personal injury lawyer would probably quantify the damages only approximately.

It should be remembered that there is no minimum award of damages which must be made (however, only exceptionally would an injury not be worth, for example, £500 or £750); nor is there any maximum.

In attempting to value the claim, reference should be made to specialist texts. Few cases are reported in general law reports such as the All England or Weekly Law Reports, and the following are the most likely sources:

(1) Kemp and Kemp *The Quantum of Damages* (Sweet & Maxwell);
(2) *Butterworths Personal Injury Service*;
(3) *Personal Injuries and Quantum Reports* (Sweet & Maxwell);
(4) *Guidelines for the assessment of damages in personal injury cases* (Judicial Studies Board) (Blackstone);
(5) *Current Law* (Sweet & Maxwell);
(6) *Halsbury's Laws Current Service* (Butterworths);
(7) *Personal and Medical Injuries Law Letter* (IBC);
(8) *New Law Journal* (Butterworths).

Increasingly, information technology is also being used in the valuation of general damages by means of CD-ROM packages such as the Kemp and Kemp CD-ROM (Sweet & Maxwell), *Current Legal Information* and Butterworths PI on-line service.

A useful starting point is the Judicial Studies Board guidelines which is an analysis of previous judgments and provides an easy reference to broad bands of damages awards. However, reference should be made to previous cases where the court has made an award for similar injuries to those suffered by the client. In *Dureau v Evans* [1996] PIQR Q18, the Court of Appeal commented that in relation to claimants who have suffered multiple injuries then the guidelines are of limited assistance as it is necessary to take an overall view of all the injuries and, if at all possible, the court should consider a comparable case. The court should also decide which was the most serious injury (to try to find a comparable award) and build on the other heads of injury from there. Similarly, in *Reed v Sunderland Health Authority* (1998) *The Times*, October 16, it was held that whilst the guidelines were an important source of information, they did not have the force of law and the Court of Appeal is unlikely to overturn a decision if the Guidelines are not followed precisely (see *Davis v Inman* [1999] PIQR Q26).

It should be remembered when looking at previous cases that it is the general damages figure which is significant and it must then be inflated to present-day values. The inflation table in Kemp and Kemp *The Quantum of Damages*, can be used for that purpose. It is important to note, when examining the previous cases reported in Kemp and Kemp or other such practitioner works, that the phrase 'general damages' is sometimes given a restricted meaning of general damages 'for pain and suffering and loss of amenity' (and occasionally an element is identified for a *Smith v Manchester* award – see **13.3.2**); it does not normally include the figure awarded in the case for future loss of earnings (if appropriate) as this will differ in each case.

The following points should be considered when examining the medical report obtained in support of the case prior to attempting to identify analogous cases in the sources referred to above.

(1) Identify the date of the accident and calculate how many years post-accident the report has been prepared. It is clearly a more significant injury if the doctor reports that the claimant is still in considerable pain 2 years after the accident, as opposed to merely 6 months afterwards.
(2) Calculate for how long the client was in hospital and how many operations (if any) he had to undergo.
(3) Calculate how long the client will suffer a major disability.
(4) Calculate how long the client will suffer with residual problems.
(5) Identify any future degeneration (eg osteoporosis).

When attempting to value the award, the following points should be considered when examining the previous cases.

(1) *Sex* – for example scarring (especially scars on the face) on a female carries a higher award than on a male (see Judicial Studies Board guidelines).
(2) *Age of the victim* – in cases of permanent disability, younger victims tend to get more compensation than older victims as the young will suffer longer.
(3) *Loss of amenity* – is heavily influenced by whether the victim had a previously active lifestyle.
(4) *Limb injuries* – injuries to dominant limbs attract higher awards than injuries to non-dominant limbs.
(5) Consideration must be given to the case of *Heil v Rankin and Another* [2000] 2 WLR 1173. In this case, the Court of Appeal considered the level of damages for pain and suffering. Also, in this case, the court held that, in cases where the level of damages for pain and suffering was in excess of £10,000, there should be a gradual increase of up to one-third in value for serious injuries. It is

important to consider this landmark decision when considering any earlier decision on damages for pain and suffering in law reports or legal texts. The decision has been incorporated into the 5th edition of the JSB Guidelines. It is important to note that an earlier case is to be relied on, then a conversion table (such as that found in *Quantum* 2/2000, 18 April 2000 (Sweet & Maxwell)) should be used.

When valuing pain and suffering, a solicitor should, if at all possible, rely on recent cases, not only because of *Heil v Rankin* (see above), but if older reports are relied upon, the level of damages may not be analogous. It is unlikely that an identical case will be found, and a number of cases will need to be examined. The approach that should be taken is to focus on the most significant injury and then look at the overall position. The court will not adopt a strictly mathematical approach of adding up the value of the different injuries sustained by the client.

Although each case must be considered individually, the following broad bands may be identified.

(1) Up to £1,000. It is likely that even the most minor injury, having no permanent effect but worth litigating, has a value of at least £500. Minor injuries such as bruising, uncomplicated cuts, grazes and loss of or damage to a back tooth are likely to fall into this category.

(2) £1,000 to £5,000. This band encompasses injuries which are more serious than minor, but have symptoms which should be resolved within a relatively short period. For example, the majority of simple whiplash awards and simple limb fractures would fall within this category.

(3) £6,000 to £25,000. This band encompasses injuries which leave a significant (but not great) degree of disablement. Awards in this bracket may include, for example, whiplash injuries leaving permanent disability; loss of smell, taste, or hearing in one ear.

(4) £25,000 to £45,000. Awards in this band occur where the claimant has suffered a serious injury resulting in serious disablement, such as minor brain damage, or loss of sight in one eye.

(5) £45,000 to £200,000. In this band, the claimant will have suffered a serious injury causing a crippling loss of function, resulting in permanent impairment in the quality of life. In this category, injuries include serious brain damage and quadriplegia.

Evidence

Although the medical evidence will be the primary matter which the court will have regard to in determining the award for pain, suffering and loss of amenity, the claimant will also give evidence of his injuries at trial. It is important that details are contained within the client's witness statement. It is surprising how many clients forget the exact details of the difficulties they had immediately post-accident, and it is good practice for the claimant's solicitor to suggest that a diary is kept by the client detailing the pain and practical difficulties that were suffered. In serious cases, it may also be necessary to obtain evidence from the claimant's spouse and family of the effect of the injuries on the claimant.

13.3.2 Handicap in the labour market

The purpose of this award is to compensate the claimant for the potential difficulties he may suffer in obtaining another job due to the injuries that he sustained in the accident, if he loses his current job. In practice, this is referred to as a *Smith v Manchester* claim (see *Smith v Manchester Corporation* [1974] 17 KIR 1).

For the court to award such damages, the claimant should have suffered a 'weakening' of his competitive position in the open labour market – or, in other words, what are his chances are of obtaining comparable employment in the open labour market if he should lose his job?

The case of *Moeliker v A Reyrolle & Co Ltd* [1977] 1 WLR 132 considered the award of damages under this head, where it was stated that:

'The consideration of this head of damages should be made in two stages:

(1) Is there a "substantial" or "real" risk that the plaintiff will lose his present job at some time before the estimated end of his working life?

(2) If there is (but not otherwise), the court must assess and quantify the present value of the risk of the financial damage which the plaintiff will suffer if that risk materialises, having regard to the degree of risk, the time when it may materialise, and the factors, both favourable and unfavourable, which in a particular case will, or may, affect the plaintiff's chance of getting a job at all or an equally well paid job.

It is impossible to suggest any formula for solving the extremely difficult problems involved in stage 2 of the assessment. A judge must look at all the factors which are relevant in a particular case and do the best he can ...'

The claimant must establish first that there is a risk that he will lose his job. However, the courts have given the words 'substantial or real' a liberal interpretation and what is required to be shown is that the risk is 'real' rather than 'speculative'. Evidence is required to support the contention that the claimant may lose his job, and a useful source of information may be the client's trade union, which will have details of any redundancies that have been made by the employer in recent years. It may also be able to provide information about the employer's future plans, of which the client may not have been aware. If the client does not belong to a trade union, evidence should be obtained from the client's workmates or managers. (If the defendant is the claimant's employer, such information should be obtained from the defendant's insurers or solicitor.) The solicitor representing the defendant must obtain clear evidence concerning the claimant's job security in an attempt to refute the *Smith v Manchester* claim.

Once the first test has been satisfied, the court attempts to quantify the risk and calculate the appropriate damages. The court has to anticipate what would be the claimant's chances of getting an equally well paid job if he was forced onto the labour market. This head of damages is notoriously hard to quantify as the court will consider each individual case on its own facts; but a common approach is to award between 0 to 2 years' net loss of earnings as at the date of trial. However, the Court of Appeal in *Foster v Tyne and Wear County Council* [1986] 1 All ER 567 stated that there was no 'conventional' figure for damages under this head, and awarded a sum equivalent to 4 years' net salary. This is, therefore, a particularly difficult element to value.

The fact that the claimant is suffering a handicap on the labour market should normally be put in the particulars of claim (*Chan Wai Tong v Li Ping Sum* [1985] AC 446).

Examples of cases where a *Smith v Manchester* award may be considered appropriate include the following.

(1) The claimant has returned to work after the accident and thus he has no continuing loss of earnings claim. However, if there is a risk that the claimant will lose his job in the future and he will have difficulty in obtaining a job as equally well paid due to his injuries, then a *Smith v Manchester* award will be claimed for.

(2) The claimant has returned to work and is earning, say, 20% less than he did prior to the accident. As a result, the claimant will have a continuing partial loss of earnings claim that could be calculated by using the multiplier/ multiplicand approach. In addition, if the court is satisfied that the claimant will lose his job and he will have difficulty in obtaining a job equally well paid due to his injuries, then a *Smith v Manchester* award will be claimed for.

(3) The claimant is still absent from work at the time of the trial as a result of the injuries suffered in the accident but he expects to return to his job in a few years, when he has recovered further from his injuries. The medical evidence suggests that he may still have problems in obtaining equally well paid work due to his injuries should he lose his job. In these circumstances, a *Smith v Manchester* award will be claimed.

The above are only a few illustrations as to when a *Smith v Manchester* award may be claimed. The medical evidence in every case must be examined to see whether a *Smith v Manchester* award can be justified. Although a *Smith v Manchester* claim should normally be claimed in the particulars of claim, the Court of Appeal in *Thorn v Powergen* [1997] PIQR Q71 upheld a decision allowing a *Smith v Manchester* award in a case where it had not been claimed specifically but was found by the trial judge to be implied due to the nature of the injuries revealed by the medical evidence.

This type of award is not normally appropriate where the claimant will never be able to return to work, as he will be compensated by his claim for lost earnings. However, the number of cases where the claimant is unable to work at all in the future will be small.

Evidence

Evidence must be obtained concerning the claimant's future job prospects including any skills he possesses (eg a labourer of 50 years of age with no qualifications will find it difficult to retrain if he loses his job), the prospects of the industry in which the claimant works and any unusual local problems that may be relevant to the claimant. It may be necessary to instruct an employment consultant to provide information about these matters, or obtain relevant information from other sources, ie New Earnings Survey. If an employment consultant is instructed, this will normally involve the expert considering the client's injuries, personal qualifications and forming an analysis of employment statistics and local press advertisements to provide a report to assist the court in determining the severity of the handicap on the labour market. In other cases, the trial judge will be aware of the employment situation in his area and be able to formulate the appropriate award (see

Goldborough v Thompson and Crowther [1996] PIQR Q86) – see also Chapter 8 on experts.

Any evidence relating to handicap on the labour market claim must be included within the witness statements for exchange.

13.3.3 Future loss of earnings

Damages for loss of earnings after the trial will be general damages.

Under this head, a lump sum is awarded which is arrived at by means of a 'multiplicand' and 'multiplier' system, which allows for:

(1) the contingencies of life; and
(2) the accelerated receipt of a sum which is available for investment.

No allowance is made for inflation (*Auty v National Coal Board* [1985] 1 All ER 930).

The same principles apply as to pre-trial lost earnings – they must be proved, necessary and reasonable. The object in assessing future earnings loss is to assess the amount of money which can be invested today to represent a fund which should last for precisely the period of the lost earnings. The compensation payment which the claimant receives at trial for future loss involves the court awarding today what the claimant would have earned in the future and is, therefore, extremely difficult.

The multiplicand

The multiplicand is the claimant's net annual earnings that he would have been receiving at the date of the trial. No increase is allowed for inflation, but allowance may be made for likely increased earning capacity as a result, for example, of the acquisition of greater skills or promotion. Conversely, a likely decrease in earning capacity may be taken into account. The items to be included or ignored in the calculation of the multiplicand are the same as for pre-trial earnings, as identified at **13.2.2**.

The multiplier

The multiplier is based on the period of likely future loss. This will depend on the facts of the case. For example, in the case of a male claimant who will never work again, the period of loss will normally extend until his likely retirement age (normally 60 or 65, or longer in the case of a professional person). The multiplier is therefore taken from the date of trial.

The period of loss is then converted into a multiplier. Following the House of Lords' decision in the joint appeals of *Page v Sheerness Steel Co Ltd, Wells v Wells; Thomas v Brighton Health Authority* [1998] 3 WLR 329, it can now be assumed that the starting point when attempting to identify the multiplier is to use the Government's actuarial tables (the Ogden tables).

For example, a male claimant is aged 45 at trial and is to retire at 65. He earns £10,000 net per annum. Using the Ogden tables (fourth edition, Table 25) (see also *Worrall v Powergen plc* (1999) *The Times*, February 10, concerning which set of tables are to be used in the Ogden tables), a multiplier of 15.22 is identified (using the 2.5% column). Future loss = 15.22 × £10,000 = £152,200. However, actuarial multipliers are, in certain circumstances, discounted by, for example, 10%, so the correct multiplier would be 13.7% giving a net loss of £137,000. The precise amount of the discount depends upon the exact circumstances of the case.

The House of Lords' decision confirmed that it may still be appropriate to discount multipliers for future loss of earnings calculations in certain circumstances, but that if the tables are used to identify a 'whole life multiplier' (which may be relevant in identifying a multiplier for the cost of care – see later at **13.3.5**), there is no reason to discount.

In June 2001, the Lord Chancellor set the 'discount rate' that should be referred to when using the Ogden Tables at 2.5%. The term 'discount rate' is identified in each set of the tables and it represents the real rate of return (ie after tax and making allowance for inflation) calculated over the appropriate period of time. As the Lord Chancellor has now set the 'discount rate' to be used, he should have eliminated scope for uncertainty and argument about the applicable rate (although the Lord Chancellor does acknowledge it is open to the courts under s 1(2) of the Damages Act 1996 to adopt a different rate if there are exceptional circumstances).

Reduced life-expectancy

The period of loss is assessed on the basis of the claimant's expectation of life as it was before the accident, not on the expectation of life as shortened by the accident. Therefore, if the claimant (aged 40), as at the date of the accident, was expected to die at the age of 55 (whereas formerly the claimant would have been expected to work until the age of 65), the period of loss would remain 25 years. However, in respect of the period actually lost from his life (the 'lost years') the claimant must give credit for the amounts which would have been spent on his own maintenance (*Pickett v British Rail Engineering Ltd* [1980] AC 136, overruling *Oliver v Ashman* [1962] 2 QBD 210). Thus, a simplified calculation will be divided into two periods.

> *Example*
> Tom, the claimant, is 40 years old at the date of the trial. The evidence is that he will never work again. His net annual earnings (gross salary less tax and National Insurance) at the date of the trial have been calculated at £10,000. The medical evidence indicates that as a result of the accident he will die at the age of 55, whereas prior to the accident he would have been expected to work until the age of 65. It is estimated that he spends £6,000 per annum upon his own maintenance.
>
> *Overall multiplier*
> - Period of loss: 65 (retirement age) less 40 (actual age) = 25 years
> - Overall multiplier = 16
> - Multiplicand period 1: age 40 to 55
> - Net annual loss = £10,000
> - Multiplicand period 2: age 55 to 65 ('lost years')
> - Net annual loss (£10,000) less sums expected to be spent on own maintenance (£6,000) = £4,000
>
> *Calculation: Period 1*
> Multiplicand (£10,000) × appropriate proportion of overall multiplier (say 11)
> = £110,000

Calculation: Period 2
Multiplicand (£4,000) × remainder of overall multiplier (5) = £20,000

Award
Total award for loss of future earnings: £110,000 + £20,000 = £130,000

In the case of *Phipps v Brookes Dry Cleaning Services Limited* [1996] PIQR Q100, it was held that in assessing a claim over the 'lost years' by a claimant, the correct approach in calculating expenses during the lost years was to divide the common expenses equally between the claimant and his partner. If there were any children, the division should be pro rata. The value of the claimant's DIY and gardening skills were not recoverable for the lost years, as they were amenities falling to be assessed in general damages.

Future loss of earnings in practice

The multipliers in the above sources are averages, and careful consideration must be given to each client's circumstances. Mustill LJ in *Cunningham v Camberwell Health Authority* [1989] 2 Med LR 49 stated:

> 'an intuitive process buttressed by reference to previously decided cases ... a rough and ready approach ... at least the start of a just system for computing damages.'

In only relatively few cases will the claimant be physically unfit to carry out any type of work in the future. In the majority of cases, the claimant will have to give credit for potential future earnings that he may receive against his future loss of earnings.

Example
The claimant has suffered an amputation to his non-dominant hand as a result of an accident at work. He is 45 years of age at the date of the trial and was previously employed as a manual worker in the steel industry. The court may consider taking the following approaches.

(1) That the claimant is totally unemployable and should be given his net annual earnings × a multiplier of, say (just as an example), 13.
(2) That the claimant should have a period of full loss of earnings, say 2 years' post-trial but from that time it is likely that the claimant will obtain some form of work, say as a car park attendant, and the claimant must give credit therefore for this income, and a reduced multiplicand should be calculated.

Although much would depend on the medical evidence, if the claimant was otherwise healthy it is likely that the court will adopt the second approach. The enormous difficulties in quantifying such a claim can be appreciated, as the court has to pick a date by which time it considers it reasonable for the claimant to have obtained work. Assistance can be provided by an employment consultant's report, but trade unions can also be of assistance in respect of employment prospects within a particular region. It will also be necessary to refer to the New Earnings Survey which will provide details of earnings for particular occupations, such as car park attendants (as an example of work that can be undertaken by an amputee) so as to provide a figure which has to be credited against the net loss of earnings from the original employer.

The method of calculating the claimant's future loss of earnings set out above is the method that is 'normally' adopted. However, it is an imprecise science and, in certain cases, the court has held that the multiplier/multiplicand approach is inappropriate because there are 'too many imponderables' (see *Hannon v Pearce* (2001) LTL, 25 June).

Evidence

The importance of expert evidence in such a case is vital. Medical evidence can provide an indication as to what work the claimant will be capable of undertaking both at present and in the future. This, together with evidence of the claimant's employment prospects, will assist the court in determining what will happen to the claimant in the future, which, whilst often appearing unsatisfactory to many clients, is usually the approach that the court will take.

13.3.4 Loss of congenial employment

Traditionally, an element for loss of job satisfaction was included under the head of pain, suffering and loss of amenity. However, the courts in certain cases are now prepared to make a separate award under this heading. In *Morris v Johnson Matthey & Co Ltd* (1967) 112 SJ 326, Edmund Davies LJ stated:

> 'the joy of the craftsman in his craft is beyond price. But the court had to give some monetary value to the loss of craft. The court should give consideration to the fact that a craftsman had to replace his craft with humdrum work.'

In that case, a precious metal worker, aged 52, sustained a serious injury to his left hand, which left him incapable of continuing his craft. His employers found him alternative employment as a storeman.

The leading case in this area is *Blamey* (1988) unreported, 16 December, in which a fireman was awarded £3,250. This case increased awareness of awards for loss of congenial employment. The court felt that there was an advantage in identifying such loss as a separate head of damages, to ensure that it was properly compensated. A table of awards under this heading is referred to in Kemp and Kemp *The Quantum of Damages* (Sweet & Maxwell), where it will be seen that the majority of the more recent awards are in the range of £5,000 to £10,000, once they have been updated for inflation. It can be seen in the case reports that the courts are more likely to make such an award where the claimant's job at the time of the accident involved a vocational element, ie nurse, actor, firefighter, etc.

Evidence

Any evidence relating to a loss of congenial employment claim must be included within the witness statements for exchange, together with details of the loss of job satisfaction.

13.3.5 Future cost of care/specialist equipment

In many cases, the cost of future expenses will exceed the multiplier used for loss of earnings, because the need for care will often exceed the claimant's normal retirement age. It must be remembered that the cost and type of care may change in the future.

For example, a severely injured child's costs of care will increase as he becomes older because it is unlikely that his parents will be able to look after him when they are elderly and, as such, increased professional help will be required.

The cost of care can normally be worked out on an annual basis and can be dealt with in a similar manner to the loss of earnings multiplicand. The cost of specialist equipment must be dealt with differently. For example, the claimant may include the cost of a wheelchair as part of his special damages claim. That wheelchair will not last the claimant for the rest of his life and, therefore, the replacement cost will need to be annualised. For example, where the cost of a wheelchair is £1,000 and it would have a life span of, say, 5 years, it is therefore necessary to include the annual cost of £200 within the multiplicand figure (£1,000/5).

In respect of the cost of care and other expenses (if lifelong), the multiplier is based on life-expectancy and, when examining the actuarial tables, care must be taken to refer to the 'Multipliers for pecuniary loss for life male/female' referred to in the Ogden tables, rather than 'Multipliers for the loss of earnings to pension age males/females' tables, to ensure that the correct multiplier is obtained. Medical evidence on life expectancy is vital if it is not a 'normal life expectancy' case. Following the House of Lords' decision in *Wells v Wells* (above), it is not appropriate to discount whole life multipliers.

13.3.6 Loss of pension

In more serious cases, where the claimant does not return to work or returns on a lower wage, consideration must be given for a claim for lost pension. The claimant's pension is normally based upon his period of service with the company and the salary that he would have earned at retirement age. In Kemp and Kemp, it is suggested that an appropriate compensation figure under this head can be calculated by obtaining quotations from insurance companies for the cost of an alternate pension that would cover the client's loss (see *Longden v British Coal Corporation* [1997] 3 WLR 1336 as regards to what receipts should be set against a claim for loss of retirement pension). A full discussion of this complex area is beyond the scope of this text.

13.3.7 Loss of use of a motor car

Loss of use of a motor car is included in damages claims in connection with road traffic accidents (with or without a personal injury), for example, where the client's vehicle is damaged and is off the road for 4 weeks whilst being repaired, and the client uses an alternative method of transport and claims compensation for the 'loss of use' of his vehicle. On occasions, solicitors can include this item in the schedule of special damages and claim a weekly figure, but it is for the court to decide on the exact level of compensation, which will depend upon the facts of the case and the claimant's actions whilst he was without the car.

The monthly editions of *Current Law* refer frequently to the latest 'loss of use' awards, and reference should be made to the latest case reports. However, it is now established that the claimant's inability to pay for repairs does not necessarily provide the defendant with a defence to a long loss of use or hire charges claim (see *Mattocks v Mann* [1993] RTR 13, CA – hire charges, and **13.2.1**.

13.4 INTEREST

A claim for interest should be included in the court proceedings. In the majority of personal injury cases, the court will award interest in addition to the basic damages. The purpose of an interest award is to compensate the claimant for having to wait to receive his compensation. Interest in a personal injury action is generally awarded in accordance with the following guidelines.

(1) Special damages carry interest at half the short-term investment/special account rate from the date of the accident to the date of trial (as from 1 August 1999, the full rate was set at 7%). In *Roberts v Johnstone* [1989] QB 878, it was held that damages for unpaid past services of care and attendance should be awarded in a similar manner to any other items of special damages.

It should also be noted that following the case of *Wadley v Surrey County Council* (2000) *The Times*, April 7, the House of Lords confirmed that, when calculating interest on special damages, the court should disregard deductible State benefits and interest is claimed on the gross amount (see Chapter 12).

(2) Damages for pain and suffering and loss of amenities carry interest from date of service of proceedings to the date of trial at 2% per annum following the case of *Felmai Lawrence v Chief Constable of Staffordshire* (2000) *The Times*, July 25.

(3) Damages for future losses carry no interest (as, by definition, the losses have not yet been incurred).

(4) General damages for a handicap on the labour market carry no interest.

It should be noted that these are general guidelines, but the court does have a discretion to depart from them in exceptional cases. In Kemp and Kemp *The Quantum of Damages*, it is argued that whilst the general approach for special damages stated above is appropriate for regular losses between the accident and trial (eg weekly wage loss), it is not satisfactory where there has been a one-off significant payment by the claimant just after the accident as the claimant is being under-compensated and, therefore, interest should be awarded at the full rate (see *Prokop v Department of Health and Social Security and Cleaners Ltd* (1983) unreported, 5 July).

Interest is awarded to mitigate the effects of delay. However, if the delay is the fault of the claimant, this may be a 'special reason' not to award full interest (*Birkett v Hayes* [1982] 2 All ER 70). This point was raised in the case of *Beahan v Stoneham* (2001) LTL, 16 May, where an appeal from an assessment of damages in a claim for personal injuries was allowed in part where the trial judge failed to reduce interest on damages. The matter concerned a case where there was a significant delay in proceeding with the action (see also *Spittle v Bunney* [1988] 1 WLR 847). The court held that the judiciary should be more ready to mark their disapproval of delay in this matter.

13.4.1 Calculation of interest

The calculation of interest on general damages should not present any problem. However, the calculation of interest on special damages can be more difficult. In practice, solicitors use the Nelson–Jones table which is printed annually in the *Law Society's Gazette* and reference should be made to the latest table when calculating interest on special damages.

The inclusion of interest on the settlement of a case must not be forgotten by the claimant's solicitor.

13.5 THE AWARD OF DAMAGES AT TRIAL

In conclusion, at the trial of a personal injury case the judge will award a lump sum figure to the claimant, but each head will be identified as separately appealable (*Jefford v Gee* [1970] 2 QBD 130). The Court of Appeal also held in *Coates v Curry* (1998) *The Times*, August 22 that it was necessary to identify past and future loss of earnings as specific figures for the purpose of the calculation of interest.

Personal injury damages are not chargeable gains and therefore the damages themselves are not subject to tax (however, the returns from the investment of those damages are subject to tax). If substantial damages are awarded, the client should be advised to seek professional assistance on this point and consideration should be given to obtaining a structured settlement (see Chapter 16).

It must be remembered that the general rule is that the award of damages by the court (or the negotiated settlement of the case) is in full and final settlement and it is not normally possible to re-open the case once it has been settled. It is therefore important that the claimant's solicitor includes all of the losses to which the client is entitled in the claim. (See *Wain v F Sherwood and Sons Transport Limited* (1998) *The Times*, July 16.)

Whilst this chapter has examined special damages, general damages and interest separately, there are certain circumstances where payments received by the claimant have to be given credit from the total amount of damages. For example, in the case of *Ballantine v Newalls Insulation Co Ltd* (2000) *The Times*, June 22, it was held that in an action brought by a claimant who suffered malignant mesothelioma (and subsequently died), the estate had to give credit for the payment of an award under the Pneumoconiosis etc (Workers' Compensation) Act 1979.

Finally, in a small number of personal injury cases the court finds that the claimant has been dishonest and has attempted to inflate the level of damages by lying or deliberately exaggerating his injuries. In these cases, the court is likely to take a dim view. One illustration of this is the case of *Molloy v Shell UK Ltd* (2001) LTL, 6 July, where the claimant was ordered to pay the defendants' costs in full.

13.6 FURTHER READING

Kemp and Kemp *The Quantum of Damages* (Sweet & Maxwell).

Chapter 14

POST-DEATH INVESTIGATIONS

14.1 INTRODUCTION

The personal injury/clinical negligence solicitor must, on occasion, advise either the family of an accident victim who has died or, alternatively, the person who it is claimed is responsible for the death. This can be very demanding work for the solicitor as the client is likely to make considerable demands both professionally and emotionally. There are three main processes in which the solicitor may become involved:

(1) the coroner's inquest;
(2) criminal prosecution for manslaughter or prosecution under the Health and Safety at Work etc Act 1974;
(3) criminal prosecution for death by dangerous driving.

Although each process has its own purpose, post-death investigations offer an important opportunity to gain evidence on liability for the civil claim.

Chapter 14 contents
Introduction
The coroner's court
Prosecution for manslaughter or prosecutions under the Health and Safety at Work etc Act 1974
Criminal prosecution for causing death by dangerous driving
Conclusion
Key points
Further reading and information

14.2 THE CORONER'S COURT

If acting for the claimant, the solicitor is likely to be instructed by a relative who may be upset and in a state of complete despair. The relative may also be looking to identify the person responsible for the death. It is important that the solicitor explains the post-death process thoroughly to the client, who, although he may recognise the phrases 'coroner's court' and 'inquest', may not understand the purpose of the process.

Whilst the claimant's solicitor may wish to use the inquest to examine the evidence surrounding the accident and to obtain full details of the circumstances leading to the death, the coroner is concerned only with how the death occurred (see **14.2.6**) and this should be made clear to the client.

Prior to advising a client on this area, reference must be made to the Coroners Act 1988 and the Coroners Rules 1984, SI 1984/552.

If acting for the defendant, the solicitor is likely to have been instructed by the defendant's insurance company, or, in the case of clinical negligence, by the hospital or defence union. In these circumstances, the solicitor's aim is:

(1) to protect the interests of the client (eg by making sure he does not incriminate himself); and
(2) to obtain as much evidence as possible relating to the issue of liability.

A fatal accident which leads to an inquest is one of the few occasions where a defendant's solicitor is instructed close to the time of the accident. He can therefore obtain details of any potential claims so that the insurance company can establish a reserve in its accounts for any potential liability.

Normally, the coroner will formally open the inquest and then immediately adjourn for enquiries to be made. The inquest will take place at the coroner's court (if the district has a specific court) or in the magistrates' court, council offices or at another public building. The inquest will be held in public unless matters of national security are being considered.

In Spring 2001, the Government announced that it would initiate a review of the inquest system but, as at the date of writing, no further information is available.

14.2.1 Personnel involved at an inquest

The coroner

The coroner is responsible for the inquest procedure and, although appointed by the local government body responsible for the area where the coroner sits, he is an independent judicial officer. The coroner must normally be a solicitor or barrister of not less than 5 years' experience, or a doctor of similar experience. A number of coroners are qualified both as doctors and (normally) as barristers, although this is not a strict requirement of obtaining the post. Those who are legally qualified only, normally have significant knowledge of medical matters.

In certain cases, the coroner may sit with an 'assessor' who is a person with specialist knowledge of the matters being considered, for example, a consultant anaesthetist in a case where a patient died due to an airway not being maintained. However, the assessor must remain under the control of the coroner and cannot give expert evidence (see *R v Surrey Coroner ex parte Wright* [1997] 2 WLR 16).

The coroner's officer

The coroner will be assisted by the coroner's officer, who is usually a serving or ex-police officer and will often be the first person with whom the personal injury solicitor will communicate about the case. The coroner's officer will obtain evidence relating to the accident or liaise with the police if they are carrying out investigations. His role is important to the solicitor as he can provide information regarding the investigations which are being carried out, details of the incident and may provide details of any witnesses the coroner intends to call. As noted below (see **14.2.5**), solicitors normally have little information prior to the commencement of the hearing, and a good relationship with the coroner's officer can go some way to help relieve that problem.

The coroner's officer will notify the relevant parties, and/or their solicitors of the inquest date. In certain specified circumstances, the deceased's trade union and the HSE will also be notified.

The deputy coroner

A coroner will appoint a deputy coroner, who will normally stand in when the coroner is absent. Provided specific requirements for allowing a deputy to act are fulfilled, the deputy has all the powers of the coroner.

14.2.2 Circumstances which lead to an inquest

The circumstances where a coroner will become involved in a death are set down in s 8(1) of the Coroners Act 1988.

If the coroner is informed that a dead body is within his jurisdiction (it is the fact that there is a body in his jurisdiction and not where the death occurred that is important), the coroner will hold an inquest as soon as practicable, where it is reasonable to suspect that a person has died:

(1) a violent or unnatural death; or
(2) a sudden death of which the cause is unknown; or
(3) in prison; or
(4) in such place or such circumstances as to require an inquest in pursuance of any Act.

Normally, the police, the GP or the hospital will contact the coroner's officer and inform the coroner of the death. However, there is a wider duty to report the matter (see below) and, on occasions, the relatives of the deceased will contact the coroner's officer if they believe that there has been an act of clinical negligence.

In addition to the criteria set down in s 8(1), there is an obligation on a GP to inform the Registrar of Births and Deaths stating the cause of the death if the GP was treating the 'last illness' or the hospital doctor if a patient dies undergoing surgery.

Once the coroner has been informed of the death, the coroner's officer will make preliminary enquiries and the coroner may then require a post-mortem examination to be made.

Post-mortem examinations

Although no absolute obligation is placed upon the coroner, usually he will request that a post-mortem takes place (see *R v HM Coroner for Greater Manchester Northern District ex parte Worch and Another* [1988] QB 513). Local standing orders specify which pathologist should carry out the post-mortem (usually the consultant pathologist at the local district hospital). Care should be taken to ensure that if the death occurred in hospital, the pathologist should not be connected with the hospital where the death occurred. There are detailed provisions contained in the Coroners Rules 1984, r 6 on this point. The claimant's solicitor must make strong representations on this point if there is any possibility of a clinical negligence claim and, in certain circumstances (if the first report is unsatisfactory), consideration should be given to having a second post-mortem carried out.

Consideration should be given to making a request that blood and tissue samples taken at the post-mortem are preserved, as they may provide important information.

Section 21(3) of the Coroners Act 1988 provides:

> 'Where a person states upon oath before the coroner that in his belief the death of the deceased was caused partly by or entirely by the improper or negligent treatment of a medical practitioner or other person, that medical practitioner or other person shall not be allowed to perform or assist at the post-mortem examination of the deceased.'

The coroner must inform the relatives of the deceased, the GP and the hospital (if the deceased died in hospital) of the arrangements of the post-mortem. These are normally referred to as the 'interested parties' and can be represented at the post-mortem by a doctor. The coroner can, in his discretion, also allow any other person to attend at the post-mortem (Coroners Rules 1984, r 7(4)).

The post-mortem report is vital evidence and an immediate request should be made to the coroner for a copy (but see **14.2.5**). The report can contain evidence which will assist in establishing civil liability. For example, if the death resulted from a road traffic accident the pathologist will give a detailed description of the injuries, and photographs will be taken of the body. The pathologist's investigations in respect of this may be vital evidence in indicating the events prior to the accident, for example whether the deceased was wearing a seat-belt. In fatal accident at work cases, the pathologist's report may also be of use in identifying whether the cause of the death resulted from exposure to dangerous materials at work, such as coal dust or asbestos. Whilst the Coroners Rules 1984, r 57(1) makes provision for a copy of the post-mortem report to be provided to 'interested parties', it is unclear if the right relates to any request prior to the inquest, but many coroners do provide a copy of the post-mortem prior to the inquest.

If acting for the defendant, the post-mortem may reveal whether there are any intervening illnesses from which the deceased may have died. This may then be used in negotiations in an attempt to reduce the multiplier in the future loss calculation. In addition, in a road traffic case, it is important to check the blood alcohol levels to see if the deceased had been drinking at the time of the accident. Such evidence can provide important arguments regarding liability and quantum.

14.2.3 The criteria for an inquest

As noted above, the coroner will hold an inquest only if the criteria in s 8(1) of the Coroners Act 1988 are satisfied. The personal injury/clinical negligence solicitor will be concerned only with the first two criteria.

The first limb of s 8(1) requires that there must have been a violent or unnatural death. What exactly is meant by this term?

(1) A violent death is normally regarded as one where an injury has occurred and will normally be apparent. For example, when a factory operative falls into machinery and dies.
(2) An unnatural death is not legally defined and it will be a question for the coroner to decide. Certain coroners believe that the phrase should be given its 'ordinary meaning'.

The coroner decides whether the death is natural or unnatural at his discretion, and this decision may need to be challenged. For example, in *R v Poplar Coroner ex parte Thomas* [1993] 2 WLR 547, a woman died following an asthma attack after there had been a considerable delay in an ambulance reaching her. There was evidence that if she had reached hospital earlier she might have survived. Was this an unnatural death? The Court of Appeal overturned the decision of the Divisional Court that it was an unnatural death and stated that 'unnatural' was an ordinary word whose meaning should be left to the coroner (unless his decision was unreasonable). If a solicitor believes that the death was unnatural, the coroner's officer must be contacted immediately and informed of the solicitor's interest. See also *R v Inner London North Coroner ex parte Touche* [2001] 3 WLR 148, and *R v HM Coroner for Avon ex parte Smith* (1998) 162 JP 403.

The second limb of s 8(1) requires that there must have been a sudden death of which the cause is unknown. In the context of a personal injury claim, this is less likely to be a significant cause, but may be appropriate in certain circumstances.

If the coroner refuses to call an inquest, the following two options are available:

(1) to make an application to the Divisional Court of the High Court;

(2) to make an application for judicial review.

By virtue of s 71 of the Access to Justice Act 1999 (introducing a new s 17A into the Coroners Act 1988), if a coroner is informed by the Lord Chancellor that a public inquiry chaired by a judge is to be held into the events surrounding a death and that inquiry is likely to be a sufficient investigation into the death, then it will not normally be necessary to hold a full inquest in addition to the public inquiry.

14.2.4 Funding representation at the inquest

It may be possible for a solicitor (with an appropriate contract) to provide assistance under the 'Legal Help' scheme for the initial preparations for an inquest. However, a solicitor may not represent the family at the inquest under the scheme using this method of funding. Nor is 'Legal Representation' usually available for attending cases at the coroners court. The Lord Chancellor's Department can grant 'exceptional legal aid' if, for example, the inquest is of 'wider public interest', but this is exceedingly rare.

All possible alternative sources of finance should be considered (eg in a fatal road traffic accident, the deceased's legal expense insurance may cover the cost of representation for the estate). Immediate enquiries must be made in respect of any claim on any insurance policy and, if appropriate, prior authorisation should be obtained from the insurer. Enquiries should also be made in the case of deaths in the work-place as to whether a trade union will fund representation at the inquest.

If there is a possibility of a clinical negligence claim being brought, any doctor who is required to give evidence will be represented by the hospital's solicitors or his defence union. Similarly, in a personal injury case, if a civil claim is likely to follow as a result of the death, the employers (eg in a factory accident) or the driver of the other vehicle (in a road traffic accident) will be represented by solicitors instructed by their respective insurers. This may appear to be unfair to the deceased's family, if they are not represented due to the unavailability of financial help from the Community Legal Service.

14.2.5 Preparation for the hearing

It is often not possible in the coroner's court for solicitors to obtain copies of the witness statements or reports prepared in advance. Only the coroner can decide which documents should be placed before the court. This makes preparation for the inquest difficult for the solicitor as he has little idea of what evidence will be called. The coroner's officer may be able to assist informally and he should be contacted to see what view the coroner may be taking in respect of the evidence. The coroner may decide to release documents before the inquest and a request should be made in each case.

The above practice came under review in the case of *R v Lincolnshire Coroner ex parte Hay* (1999) 163 JP 666, in which it was held that whilst the court would not lay down guidelines as to what procedures should be adopted by a coroner prior to an inquest, it did believe it would be helpful if the Coroners Society were to give guidance about pre-hearing techniques, such as circulation of a list of witnesses the coroner intended to call, together with a short summary of the witness evidence. In the case of *R v HM Coroner for Avon ex parte Bentley* [2001] EWHC Admin 170, (2001) LTL, 23 March, it was held that, on the facts, the request for advanced disclosure was reasonable and, since straightforward disclosure was requested by a party who would, in the end, be entitled to see it, the document should be disclosed.

In certain complicated matters, the coroner may be willing to hold a 'pre-inquest review' to allow the parties and the coroner to consider matters prior to the actual inquest, and this point needs to be considered.

Normally, statements have been taken from the proposed witnesses by the coroner's officer or police and it can be of considerable advantage if these can be obtained beforehand. At the hearing of the inquest, further evidence or information can become available. If such information leads the solicitor to believe that he cannot represent his client adequately, he should request an adjournment.

In an attempt to overcome the above difficulties, prior to the hearing detailed enquiries must be made of such bodies as the police, trade union or HSE, which may be able to provide background information. The more information that is obtained prior to the hearing the better.

In a clinical negligence case, the deceased's medical records should be obtained (see *Stobart v Nottingham Health Authority* [1992] 3 Med LR 284). Once received, they should be placed in an ordered, paginated file, and legible copies made. If the solicitor is instructed by an insurance company on behalf of the deceased's estate, in-depth research should be carried out into the nature of the illness, the usual treatment which is prescribed for the illness, and the usual consequences and recovery time of the illness. This research will include relevant medical literature, and copies should be taken of any appropriate material. Medical school libraries are generally very helpful with this form of research and can provide assistance and copying facilities. Research may reveal whether the treatment fell below the level which can be expected and required of the medical staff.

In addition, a solicitor may seek assistance from an expert who can advise him on how to examine any medical experts giving evidence on behalf of the doctor. Informed examination will test a witness's evidence, and may be useful if civil proceedings are later issued. It is important for the claimant's solicitor to make such detailed preparation, because solicitors acting for a doctor will be experienced in this field and have access to a wide range of sources, including many experts.

14.2.6 Procedure at the inquest

The inquest is formally opened without any significant evidence being given, and the formalities are carried out by the coroner sitting alone (who, eg, will take initial evidence, evidence of identification of the body, issue an order for disposal of the body and adjourn until a more suitable time). Evidence will be called concerning the death at the resumed hearing, with legal representatives for both sides attending. If appropriate, a jury (see below) will also be in attendance at that time.

The coroner will not proceed with the inquest until the relevant authority has been contacted (see the Coroners Rules 1984, r 26(3) – eg, in the case of industrial diseases) or after certain criminal proceedings have been brought (in the case of death by dangerous driving). In the latter case, the claimant's solicitor should attend the criminal proceedings and take notes of the trial (see later), as useful evidence may be obtained which can assist in identifying any civil liability for the death.

The majority of evidence at the resumed inquest will usually be given orally by witnesses on oath, but the coroner has power to admit documentary evidence if he believes that the evidence is unlikely to be disputed. However, it is possible to object to such a decision, and a solicitor should do this where he believes that a witness should be called to answer questions (see also *R v HM Coroner for Avon ex parte Bentley* [2001] EWHC Admin 170, (2001) LTL, 23 March).

The actual order of calling the witnesses lies entirely within the discretion of the coroner. However, the pathologist may be the first substantive witness to give evidence (see *R v HM Coroner for Kent (Maidstone District) ex parte Johnstone* (1994) 158 JP 1115). When the pathologist gives evidence, he will undoubtedly use medical language and it is important that the solicitor is able to understand the evidence which is given. Thus, research should be carried out prior to the inquest, so as to become familiar with the potential medical terms that may be used. The solicitor should not be afraid to ask the doctor to explain himself fully.

The coroner will normally then examine each witness so that the evidence is heard in the same order as the events leading to the death occurred. The solicitor should make careful notes of addresses etc, as these witnesses may need to be contacted in relation to a potential civil claim. If the witness does not give evidence in accordance with his previous written statement to the coroner, and the interested party is not aware of this, then the coroner must deal with this point (see *R v HM Coroner for Inner London North District ex parte Cohen* (1994) 158 JP 644, DC). Once the coroner has dealt with the witness, each interested party (or their legal representatives) will be allowed to question them.

Juries

A jury will be used at the coroner's court if the death:

(1) occurred in prison;
(2) occurred while the deceased was in police custody or resulted from injury caused by a police officer in the execution of his duty;
(3) was caused by an accident, poisoning or disease, notice of which is required to be given under any Act to a government department or to any inspector or other officer of a government department, or to an inspector appointed under s 19 of the Health and Safety at Work etc Act 1974; and
(4) occurred in circumstances the continuance or possible reoccurrence of which is prejudicial to the health and safety of the public or any section of the public.

A personal injury solicitor is most likely to be involved in cases coming within heads (3) and (4) above.

The jury will consist of between 7 and 11 people.

Witnesses

The coroner is the only person who has the power to call witnesses (the interested parties cannot), but if a solicitor believes that a particular witness should be called, representation can be made to the coroner. Enquiries need to be made of the coroner's officer (prior to the hearing) as to which witnesses the coroner intends to call. On occasion, the solicitor will make representations that other witnesses should be called. For example, the coroner may not have intended to call a nurse manager who may have been responsible for the system of work adopted on a hospital ward, because she was not present at the time of death, but she may have vital evidence. There is the possibility of having the inquest quashed if the coroner refuses to call a particular witness and certain specified circumstances occur.

In addition to instructing an independent pathologist to attend at the post-mortem or examine the post-mortem report, consideration should also be given to using non-medical experts, in order to get another view of the cause of the accident. The coroner may need to be persuaded that these expert witnesses are relevant to his fundamental role in determining how the deceased died and should thus be called.

Persons entitled to examine witnesses at an inquest are as follows:

(1) the parent, child, spouse or any personal representative of the deceased;
(2) any beneficiary under a policy of insurance issued on the life of the deceased;
(3) the insurer who issued such a policy of insurance;
(4) any person whose act or omission or that of his agent or servant may, in the opinion of the coroner, have caused, or contributed to, the death of the deceased;
(5) any person appointed by a trade union to which the deceased belonged at the time of his death, if the death of the deceased may have been caused by an injury received in the course of his employment or by an industrial disease;
(6) an inspector appointed by, or a representative of, an enforcing authority, or any person appointed by a government department to attend the inquest;
(7) the chief officer of police;
(8) any other person who, in the opinion of the coroner, is a properly interested person.

The Coroners Rules 1984 provide that the above persons can either examine witnesses in person or through counsel or solicitors. In *R v Portsmouth City Coroner ex parte Keane* (1993) 153 JP 658, the coroner refused leave to a brother of the deceased to examine certain witnesses through counsel on the basis that the brother was not a properly interested person within r 20(2) of the Coroners Rules 1984. It was held that the coroner was entitled by use of his discretion to come to that decision.

The questioning of witnesses at the inquest can be a difficult matter as the strict purpose of the inquest is limited to finding:

(1) who the deceased was;
(2) how, when and where the deceased came by his death;
(3) the particulars required by the Registration Acts to be registered concerning the death.

The Divisional Court has repeatedly reaffirmed that these are the only matters that the coroner's court is concerned with and the coroner will wish to concentrate on these fundamental points. However, there can be no doubt that many solicitors attend the inquest with a slightly wider agenda, that of trying to identify who was liable for the death and to examine the evidence surrounding the case. Much will depend upon the individual coroner as to the types of questions which are allowed, but the coroner will always limit questions concerned with civil liability.

To prevent the inquest apportioning blame, the Coroners Rules 1984, r 22 specifically provides that a witness is not obliged to answer any questions tending to incriminate himself. The witness may be called to the witness box and asked merely to give his name and address. On occasion, no further questions will be put to him. However, practice varies widely on this point and, in *R v Lincolnshire Coroner ex parte Hay* (1999) 163 JP 666, it was held that the privilege against self-incrimination did not give the witness complete immunity against further questioning. The privilege against self-incrimination is against criminal proceedings (and not civil proceedings) and this should be borne in mind when the coroner is deciding if the witness is entitled to claim self-incrimination. The solicitor may have to remind the coroner about this point. If the coroner allows the witness to be questioned, it is for the witness's representative to make the objection if a question is put which might lead to self-incrimination. If the witness answers the question, he will waive the privilege.

In certain cases, it is desirable for a witness's identity to be protected, as in the case of *R v Newcastle-upon-Tyne Coroner ex parte A* (1998) 162 JP 387, where a police officer was allowed to give evidence from behind a screen.

Doctors are not permitted to claim that matters are confidential or covered by the doctor/client relationship in answering questions put to them.

Summation

If a jury is present, the coroner will sum up the evidence to the jury after the witnesses have given evidence and will direct the jury on points of law. In *R v HM Coroner for Inner London South District ex parte Douglas-Williams* (1998) 162 JP 751, it was held that in complex cases, it would be good practice for the coroner to prepare a written statement of matters which the law requires in relation to possible verdicts. If such a policy is followed, a solicitor should request to inspect the statement prior to summing up. The jury may wish to make other comments outside its terms of reference (normally with the motive of trying to prevent another death occurring), but the coroner will not allow this.

If no jury is present the coroner normally sums up by means of a revision of the evidence and states his conclusions.

Submission on the law for the coroner

A submission on the law will not be required at every inquest, and is usually appropriate only where there are grounds for submitting that the death was 'aggravated' or 'caused' by neglect (see below). In a clinical negligence case, it is not in the hospital's interest that a verdict of death 'caused' or 'aggravated' by neglect is recorded. However, the family of the deceased may be keen to obtain such a verdict since, although it is not equivalent to civil negligence, it is often considered a stepping stone to a successful civil claim.

The law is now contained in *R v North Humberside and Scunthorpe Coroner ex parte Jamieson* [1995] QB 1, CA. This case states that, in the context of an inquest, the words 'lack of care' have no connection with the common law of negligence. Rather, 'lack of care' is the obverse of self-neglect. The term 'lack of care' has now been replaced by 'neglect'.

'Neglect', in this context, means a gross failure by others to provide adequate nourishment or liquid, or provide or procure basic medical attention for someone in a dependent position (because of youth, age, illness or incarceration) who cannot provide it for himself. Failure to provide medical attention (normally, over a period of time) for a dependent person whose physical condition is such as to show that he obviously needs it, may amount to neglect (see *R v HM Coroner for Inner West London ex parte Cleo Scott* [2001] EWHC Admin 105, (2001) LTL, 13 February and *R v HM Coroner for Coventry ex parte Chief Constable of Staffordshire Police* (2000) LTL, 28 September).

Expressing an opinion

Rule 43 of the Coroners Rules 1984 allows a coroner who believes that action should be taken to prevent the recurrence of fatalities similar to that in respect of which the inquest was held, to announce at the inquest that he is reporting the matter in writing to whoever has power to take such action.

Verdicts

Strictly, a verdict is not given by the coroner, who, instead, gives a summary of the results of the inquisition (see below).

If a jury is present, it will retire to consider its verdict. No communication is permitted with the jury once it has retired. A majority verdict is allowed where the minority is not more than two. The coroner may accept a majority verdict, but is not bound to do so.

A document called an 'inquisition' is completed by the coroner at the end of the inquest, and is signed by the coroner and jury members who concur with it. The form requires five matters to be dealt with:

(1) the name of the deceased;
(2) the injury or disease causing death;
(3) the time, place and circumstances at or in which the injury was sustained;
(4) the conclusion of the jury/coroner as to the death; and
(5) the particulars under the Registration Acts.

(The above vary depending on the particular type of case – see the Coroners Rules 1984, Sch 2, Form 22.)

The standard inquisition form gives a comprehensive list of suggested verdicts, of which the most significant in personal injury/clinical negligence cases are:

(1) industrial disease (this is given no defined meaning);
(2) want of attention at birth;
(3) accident/misadventure (the courts have taken the view that any distinction between the two words is undesirable (see below));
(4) unlawful killing;
(5) open verdict;
(6) suicide;
(7) natural causes.

(The notes to Form 22 have no binding effect whatsoever and are merely advisory.)

The following points should be noted in relation to four possible verdicts.

(1) ACCIDENT/MISADVENTURE

It may be pointed out to the coroner (especially if the submission is on behalf of a health authority, a trust or a doctor) that no distinction is drawn between accident and misadventure and that therefore the coroner should consider only the verdict of accident. Although nothing of importance rides on the distinction between the two, it is often considered that a verdict of misadventure is favoured by the family of the deceased following an accident. A finding of accidental death or death by misadventure will be returned where the treatment or a consequence of the treatment has caused the death (even if the standard of treatment was of an unquestionable quality) in a clinical negligence case (see *R v Birmingham and Solihull Coroner ex parte Benton* [1997] 8 Med LR 362 for a further explanation of the distinction between a verdict of accident and one of misadventure. See also the fourth supplement to *Jervis on Coroners* (Sweet & Maxwell, 1998)).

(2) AN OPEN VERDICT

This means simply that there is insufficient evidence to reach a conclusion.

(3) NEGLECT

This is a controversial verdict and, following the case of *R v Surrey Coroner ex parte Wright* [1997] 2 WLR 16, it appears that a coroner cannot return a verdict of 'lack of care', but the term 'neglect' may be used to describe a situation where there has been a period of neglect which resulted in the death. In this context, neglect means continuous, or at least 'non-transient' neglect (see also *R v HM Coroner for North Humberside and Scunthorpe ex parte Jamieson* [1995] QB 1, CA). This verdict does not necessarily mean that negligence can be established as it does not necessarily mean that the three elements of negligence required to be proved in a civil court can be established (see also *R v HM Coroner for Swansea and Gower ex parte Tristram* (2000) 164 JP 191 and *R v HM Coroner for Coventry ex parte Chief Constable of Staffordshire Constabulary* (2000) LTL, 28 September).

Some commentators state that neglect can rarely, if ever, be a verdict on its own. Rather, it is ancillary to any verdict where there is a link between the relevant conduct and the cause of death. In *R v HM Coroner for Inner West London ex parte Cleo Scott* [2001] EWHC Admin 105, (2001) LTL 13 February, a fresh inquest was allowed due to the fact that the coroner had not left a verdict incorporating an element of neglect to the jury.

(4) SUICIDE OR UNLAWFUL KILLING

The standard of proof required for a suicide or unlawful killing verdict to be returned is that of beyond reasonable doubt.

All other verdicts require a burden of proof based on the balance of probabilities.

The Divisional Court (and the Coroners Rules 1984 themselves) have made it clear that the coroner's court does not decide the responsibility for the death. Therefore, verdicts in the coroner's court are framed so as not to identify any individual as being responsible (see also *R v HM Coroner for Derby and South Derbyshire ex parte John Henry Hart Jnr* (2000) 164 JP 429 and *R v Director of Public Prosecutions ex parte Manning and Another* [2000] 3 WLR 463).

Transcripts

At the conclusion of the inquest, the coroner's officer will collect any documents or copy statements which were used during the hearing. A copy of the transcript of the case can be obtained on payment of a fee. It is possible for this transcript to be used for limited purposes at the civil trial if the appropriate procedure is used in the civil proceedings.

14.2.7 Representing the family

The inquest can be difficult for lay persons to understand. They will be unfamiliar with the role of the coroner and may expect that the purpose of the inquest is not to establish how the deceased died but to establish fault. Because of the lack of advance disclosure of evidence, the family of the deceased will not be aware in advance what evidence will be given and may be upset by the evidence disclosed at the inquest.

The procedure that the coroner will follow during the inquest must be explained to the family of the deceased. It will be necessary to discuss the evidence with them and, in particular, to discuss the verdict. The verdict should be explained thoroughly and the deceased's family reminded that the purpose of the inquest and the verdict is not to apportion blame, but to establish by what means the deceased came by his death.

14.2.8 Representing the potential defendant

Clinical negligence cases

The hospital will be asked by the coroner's officer to produce statements from all those directly involved in the incident.

REQUESTING RECORDS AND TAKING STATEMENTS

The solicitor for the health authority or health trust should obtain all relevant records and provide access to them to any medical and nursing staff who have been called by the coroner to give evidence at the inquest. The solicitor should then obtain statements from such staff.

The solicitor should help the staff by reviewing their statements prior to submission to the coroner. The solicitor should ensure that the statements contain only relevant facts and do not offer any opinion which the witness is not competent to give. For example, a house officer should not give an opinion on whether specific parts of the treatment contributed to the death, but should restrict his statement to the facts alone.

If it appears from the statements that disciplinary action might be taken against a member of the medical staff (eg because a mistake in treatment has been made), that person should be advised to seek his own representation from his defence organisation as his interests will conflict with those of the hospital.

The solicitor should advise the medical and nursing staff that the original records will be available at the inquest and that they are permitted to refer to these.

PURPOSE, FORM AND LIMITS OF INQUEST

The solicitor should advise the medical and nursing staff about the purpose and form of an inquest and encourage an attitude of openness and co-operation at the inquest.

EXPERT EVIDENCE

The solicitor may consider obtaining the specialist opinion on the issues arising at the inquest from a hospital consultant (but not from a consultant who is directly involved in the case).

Personal injury cases

In a personal injury case, as soon as the solicitor is instructed, he will make contact with the insured and attempt to investigate the matter further. This will normally involve attending at the insured's premises, if the accident was work-based, or at the scene of the accident with the insured, in the case of a road traffic accident. The defendant's solicitor will be under strict instructions from the insurer to formulate a view on liability and attempt to find out as much as possible about the deceased, so that some idea can be obtained about quantum. In a road traffic accident, the inquest will provide early access to the police investigation report (which may have involved a partial reconstruction) and useful information, such as whether a seat-belt was worn, may become apparent. In the case of an industrial accident, the solicitor investigating the case will normally be concerned with the system of work used or the employment history of the deceased. This may be particularly useful in asbestosis claims where it may become apparent that the deceased's main exposure to asbestos was during his employment with another employer.

14.2.9 Publicity at the inquest

There is often publicity attached to inquests. Reporters may request an interview with the key witnesses and, in particular, the family. The appropriate advice to witnesses is at the discretion of the solicitors acting for the parties. Usually, the solicitor representing the hospital or doctors will decline to say anything to the press to avoid saying anything amounting to an admission in subsequent proceedings, or which may be upsetting to the family. The solicitor should also advise the doctors and nursing staff not to make any comments to the media. In some cases, it may be appropriate, from a public relations point of view, for the hospital to issue a brief statement offering sympathy to the family following the death of the deceased.

If the family wishes to express its anger in a more public forum, the press is usually happy to provide this opportunity. If there are any concerns to which the inquest gave rise, these could be expressed to the press. It is important, however, that the family's solicitor does not get carried away on the tide of emotion and risk slandering any of the individuals concerned. If the solicitor gives a statement to the press on behalf of his clients, he should observe the guidelines set out in *The Law Society's Guide to Professional Conduct* and *The Law Society's Code for Advocacy*.

14.3 PROSECUTION FOR MANSLAUGHTER OR PROSECUTIONS UNDER THE HEALTH AND SAFETY AT WORK ETC ACT 1974

Personal injury solicitors will need to be familiar with the law surrounding prosecutions under criminal law, and the health and safety legislation concerning accidents that result in death. The defendant personal injury solicitor may be instructed by the insurers to represent the insured in criminal proceedings at a very early stage, to enable investigations to take place quickly and to take a view on the case. The insurers will be concerned not only with obtaining details on civil liability but also that a successful defence of the criminal case, and the absence of any criminal conviction, may assist in the defence of the civil claim.

The prosecution of employers for deaths resulting from workplace fatal accidents is normally under the Health and Safety at Work etc Act 1974. The relevant sections are:

(1) s 2(1): 'It shall be the duty of every employer to ensure, so far as is reasonably practicable, the health, safety and welfare at work of all its employees';
(2) s 3(1): 'It shall be the duty of every employer to conduct his undertaking in such a way as to ensure, so far as is reasonably practicable, that persons not in his

employment who may be affected thereby are not thereby exposed to risks in their health or safety';
(3) s 37(1): 'Where an offence under any of the relevant statutory provisions committed by a body corporate is proved to have been committed with the consent or connivance of, or to have been attributable to any neglect on the part of, any director, manager, secretary or other similar officer of the body corporate or a person who was purporting to act in any such capacity, he as well as the body corporate shall be guilty of that offence and should be liable to be proceeded against and punished accordingly'.

The other possible prosecution is for manslaughter. In April 1998, a protocol was agreed between the HSE and the Crown Prosecution Service (CPS), setting out procedures as to how to deal with workplace deaths. Normally, the police will investigate where there is evidence of manslaughter, and the HSE will be concerned with possible offences under the Health and Safety at Work etc Act 1974. The protocol also deals with liaison arrangements between the police and the HSE. A few significant prosecutions have been brought and show the approach that the courts are taking. In *R v British Steel plc* (1995) ICR 586, the company wanted to move certain heavy machinery and, in so doing, and contrary to the instructions from a British Steel supervising engineer, the sub-contractors cut most of the supports from the platform which, as a result, collapsed, killing one of the workers. The Court of Appeal held that, subject to a defence of reasonable practicability, s 3(1) of the Health and Safety at Work etc Act 1974 imposed absolute criminal liability.

Prosecutions of a company for manslaughter have been difficult. The most famous prosecution for corporate manslaughter was in *R v P & O European Ferries (Dover) Ltd* (1991) 93 Cr App R 72, following the *Herald of Free Enterprise* disaster when the ship capsized with the loss of 188 passengers and crew. The Sheen Enquiry found management failure and directed criticism at various personnel on and off the ferry. However, when the test of *Caldwell* recklessness was applied, the prosecution was not able to prove that the risk was 'obvious'. The prosecution against the individuals concerned and the company failed.

However, in December 1994 a prosecution was brought against OLL Ltd for manslaughter. In that case, four teenagers drowned while taking part in a canoeing exercise and evidence was given of exceedingly poor safety provisions. Convictions were successful against the company, which was fined £60,000, and the managing director, who was imprisoned for 3 years.

In *R v Adomako* [1995] 1 AC 171, an anaesthetist was convicted of manslaughter. The facts concerned an eye operation, which left the patient paralysed when the supply of oxygen to the patient ceased which resulted in a cardiac arrest. The doctor had not noticed the disconnection of the tube supplying the oxygen. Approximately 4½ minutes after the disconnection, an alarm sounded on one of the machines in the operating theatre, which prompted the doctor into action but at no stage did he check the tube. The prosecution alleged that the doctor failed to notice other clinical signs that the patient was displaying. The House of Lords held that in cases of manslaughter involving breach of duty, the ordinary principles of the law of negligence apply to ascertain whether the defendant had been in breach of duty of care to the victim. If so, the next question was whether it had caused the death and could be characterised as gross negligence and therefore a crime. Lord MacKay held:

'The essence of the matter which is supremely a jury question is whether, having regard to the risk of death involved, the conduct of the defendant was so bad in all the circumstances as to amount in their judgment to a criminal act or omission.'

Although such prosecutions are rare, the above cases should be borne in mind when considering responsibility for fatal accidents.

14.3.1 Future proposals

This is an area where the Government and commentators have called for changes to the current law but, at the date of writing, no further details are available.

14.4 CRIMINAL PROSECUTION FOR CAUSING DEATH BY DANGEROUS DRIVING

Causing death by dangerous driving is an indictable offence. The maximum penalty in the Crown Court is 10 years' imprisonment and/or an unlimited fine. The offence carries obligatory disqualification from driving for 2 years or obligatory endorsement on the driving licence of 3–11 points (if disqualification is avoided but not endorsement) and compulsory re-testing before recommencement of driving (see s 1 of the Road Traffic Act 1988 (as amended)). Forfeiture of the motor vehicle may be ordered.

The definition of dangerous driving is found in s 2A of the Road Traffic Act 1988:

'(1) For the purpose ... of section ... 2 above a person is to be regarded as driving dangerously if (and subject to subsection 2 below, only if) –

(a) the way he drives falls far below what would be expected of a competent and careful driver; and
(b) it would be obvious to a competent and careful driver that driving in that way would be dangerous.

(2) A person is also to be regarded as driving dangerously for the purpose ... of section ... 2 above if it would be obvious to a competent and careful driver that driving the vehicle in its current state would be dangerous.'

The procedure adopted in the magistrates' courts and Crown Court for such a prosecution is dealt with in the LPC Resource Book *Criminal Litigation* (Jordans). If such a prosecution occurs following a fatal road accident, the claimant's solicitor should attend at court to obtain details of the circumstances of the accident and take notes of the evidence. If a conviction is obtained, this will be very useful for the civil proceedings, and in these circumstances the relevant insurance company will often settle any claim.

Many motor insurance policies provide for the cost of defending such an offence, and the insurance company will nominate solicitors to act on the insured's behalf. The defendant's insurers will use the proceedings to establish a view on criminal, as well as civil liability. In such circumstances, the defendant's solicitor will usually instruct an accident reconstruction expert to assist in the investigations.

14.5 CONCLUSION

Evidence must be gathered as quickly as possible in all fatal accident claims and it is important that the above processes are used to protect the client's interests at all times.

14.6 KEY POINTS

Criminal prosecution
(1) Health and Safety at Work etc Act 1974
(2) Manslaughter

↓

Health and Safety at Work etc Act 1974, s 2(1), s 3(1), s 37(1). Role of HSE, CPS.

Coroner's inquest

↓

Coroner involved if Coroners Act 1988, s 8(1) applies, including:
(1) violent or unnatural death;
(2) sudden death of which cause unknown;
(3) death in prison.

↓

Purpose of inquest:
(1) who deseased was;
(2) how, when and where the deseased came by his death;
(3) particulars required by the Registration Acts.

↓

Other matters:
Post mortem
Obtain evidence/medical notes
Contact Coroner's Officer
Explain role of inquest to client

↓

Verdict:
Purpose *not* to express blame.

Criminal prosecution for dangerous driving

↓

10 years' imprisonment.
Obligatory disqualification.
Obligatory 3–11 points.
Compulsory re-testing.

14.7 FURTHER READING AND INFORMATION

Matthews and Foreman *Jervis on Coroners* 11th edn and supplement (Sweet & Maxwell).

Advice can be obtained from the organisation 'Inquest', which can be contacted at Alexandra National House, 330 Seven Sisters Road, Finsbury Park, London N4 2PJ.

Chapter 15

FATAL ACCIDENT CLAIMS – PROCEDURE AND QUANTIFICATION

15.1 INTRODUCTION

This chapter sets out the principles involved in assessing damages in personal injury and clinical negligence cases where the victim has died before trial.

There are two main causes of action in such circumstances:

(1) the Law Reform (Miscellaneous Provisions) Act 1934, which allows a claim for the benefit of the deceased's estate; and
(2) the Fatal Accidents Act 1976, which allows a claim for the benefit of the dependants and those entitled to an award of bereavement damages.

It will be assumed that the death occurred on or after 1 January 1983 as the above Acts were amended substantially relating to deaths after that date. Whilst the Acts provide two separate causes of action they are commonly brought together.

In certain cases, specific statutes provide for recompense for the deceased's family, such as the Carriage by Air Act 1961 in cases of death arising out of civil aviation accidents (these are not dealt with in this text).

15.2 LIMITATION PERIOD

The main limitation time-limits are as follows.

(1) If a claim is brought under the Law Reform (Miscellaneous Provisions) Act 1934, the action should be commenced 3 years from: (a) the date of death; or (b) the date of knowledge of the deceased's personal representative, whichever is the later, or if there is more than one personal representative and their dates of knowledge are different, from the earliest date of knowledge of any of them. It should be noted, however, that if the injured person dies after the period in which he could have brought the action, the case will be prima facie statute-barred (although the court has a power to override this time-limit under s 33 of the Limitation Act 1980).
(2) If a claim is brought under the Fatal Accidents Act 1976, the limitation period is: (a) 3 years from the date of death; or (b) the date of knowledge of the persons for whose benefit the action is brought. If an action brought under the Fatal Accidents Act 1976 is out of time by virtue of this provision, the court can use its discretion under s 33 of the Limitation Act 1980. It must be remembered, however, that an action under the Fatal Accidents Act 1976 cannot be brought if at the time of the injured person's death he could not have brought his own action for damages for the injuries that he sustained because, for example, he had failed to comply with the time-limit under the Carriage by Air Act 1961. The power to extend the limitation period will apply only where there has been

Chapter 15 contents
Introduction
Limitation period
Cause of action
The appointment of personal representatives
Damages under the Law Reform (Miscellaneous Provisions) Act 1934
Damages under the Fatal Accidents Act 1976
Interest
Pension loss
Establishing the case
Conduct
Simplified example of a schedule of loss in a fatal accident case – traditional method
Conclusion
Further reading

a failure to comply with the initial limitation period set by the Limitation Act 1980.

15.3 CAUSE OF ACTION

The Law Reform (Miscellaneous Provisons) Act 1934 (LR(MP)A 1934) provides (for the benefit of the deceased's estate) for the continuation of the cause of action to which the deceased was entitled the instant before he died (LR(MP)A 1934, s 1(2)). It does not create a separate cause of action.

The Fatal Accidents Act 1976 (FAA 1976) does create a separate cause of action for the dependants (and those entitled to the award of bereavement damages), but it is based on the pre-condition that the deceased, had he lived, would have been able to sue successfully (FAA 1976, s 1).

Three things follow from this, namely:

(1) if the deceased had no cause of action then the estate and the dependants have no cause of action;
(2) any defence that could have been used against the deceased can be used against the estate and the dependants;
(3) if the deceased was contributorily negligent then the damages of the estate and the dependants are reduced accordingly.

Example 1
Tom is driving his car when it collides with a car driven by Sharon. Tom dies as a result of his injuries. He is survived by his widow, Elaine, and his son, Christopher. The accident is entirely the fault of Tom. As a result, neither Tom's estate, Elaine nor Christopher have any right of action against Sharon.

Example 2
Lucy is killed in an accident at work. She is survived by her husband, Michael, and daughter, Patricia. Lucy and her employers are equally to blame for the accident. Although Lucy's estate, Michael and Patricia may claim against the employers, the damages awarded to each will be reduced by 50%.

In the case of *Jameson and Another v Central Electricity Generating Board and Another* [2000] AC 455, the House of Lords held that in a case where the second co-defendant had paid a compensation payment to the injured person when he was still alive (on a less than full liability basis), this did prevent the dependants bringing a claim under FAA 1976 against the first co-defendant (who was a concurrent tortfeaser) and did amount to a settlement of claim.

15.4 THE APPOINTMENT OF PERSONAL REPRESENTATIVES

Fatal accident claims are normally representative actions. This means that the personal representative normally brings an action simultaneously on behalf of the estate under LR(MP)A 1934 and on behalf of the dependants under FAA 1976. The grant of probate or letters of administration should therefore be obtained before the action is commenced.

A dependant may commence the action himself if either there is no personal representative appointed, or the personal representative does not bring an action within 6 months after the death (FAA 1976, s 2(2)) (see *Holleran v Bagnell* [1879] 4 LR Ir 940).

15.5 DAMAGES UNDER THE LAW REFORM (MISCELLANEOUS PROVISIONS) ACT 1934

Generally, the damages awarded to the estate under LR(MP)A 1934 are based on the losses for which the deceased could have claimed at the instant before he died. In essence, the estate inherits the deceased's right to sue in respect of the death. Any head of damages that is duplicated between LR(MP)A 1934 and FAA 1976 is only recoverable once.

The following heads of damages may be appropriate.

15.5.1 Pain, suffering and loss of amenity

There must be evidence that there was suffering. This will mean, in practice, that there must be a period of survival. If there is no significant period of survival (eg in the case of instantaneous death) an award will not be made (*Hicks v Wright* [1992] 2 All ER 65). If the victim enters an immediate coma after the accident and subsequently dies without regaining consciousness then, again, no damages for pain and suffering will be awarded under this head. However, if there is a period of survival and, during that period, the victim becomes aware of impending death, the award for pain and suffering will be increased. The most common example of a case where the deceased has a long and painful death is that of mesothelioma (lung cancer by asbestosis). In such a case, the victim will suffer haemoptysis (coughing up blood), shortness of breath, loss of weight and loss of appetite. In the case of lingering death (eg a protracted death as a result of disease), the amount of the award for pain and suffering and loss of amenity will depend upon the actual level of pain and the length of time over which the pain was experienced.

15.5.2 Loss of income

The estate is entitled to claim the lost net earnings of the deceased from the time of the accident until death, calculated in the same way as for a living claimant (see Chapter 13). No claim can be made for loss of income in respect of any period after that person's death (LR(MP)A 1934, s 1(2)(a)(ii), as amended by the Administration of Justice Act 1982).

15.5.3 Funeral expenses

Funeral expenses are specifically provided for in s 1(2)(c) of LR(MP)A 1934. The expenses may be claimed provided they are:

(1) reasonable; and
(2) incurred by the estate.

If the expenses are incurred by a dependant of the deceased rather than by the deceased's estate, the dependant may claim the expenses as part of the fatal accidents claim.

15.5.4 Value of services rendered by third parties

Services rendered by third parties may include, for example: nursing services rendered by a relative to the deceased up to the time of death; expenses incurred by a third party in assisting in bringing the deceased's body home from abroad; or the costs incurred by relatives in visiting the hospital. The quantum is the proper and reasonable cost of supplying the need (for the general principles involved, see Chapter 13).

15.5.5 Other losses

Other losses may include, for example, damage to chattels such as the car the deceased was driving at the time of the incident, or the clothing which he was wearing.

15.5.6 Distribution of damages

Damages under LR(MP)A 1934 pass to the deceased's estate, and from there to the deceased's beneficiaries according to the deceased's will or the rules of intestacy.

Damages under LR(MP)A 1934 are, in appropriate cases (eg where there was a long interval between the accident and the death, and the deceased had been in receipt of recoverable benefits), subject to the Social Security (Recovery of Benefits) Act 1997 (see Chapter 12) but are not subject to any other loss or gains to the estate, such as the receipt of insurance money (LR(MP)A 1934, s 1(2)).

15.5.7 Conclusion

In the case of instantaneous death, damages under LR(MP)A 1934 will normally be limited to damages for funeral expenses and damage to chattels. Where there is a period of survival, the damages may be more extensive but will normally still be severely curtailed by the inability of the estate to claim the lost future income of the deceased.

15.6 DAMAGES UNDER THE FATAL ACCIDENTS ACT 1976

In general terms, there are three possible heads of damages, namely:

(1) a dependency claim for the financial losses suffered by the dependants of the deceased;
(2) an award of bereavement damages; and
(3) a claim for the funeral expenses if paid by the dependants.

15.6.1 Loss of dependency

The broad requirements under the loss of dependency head are that the claimant must be a 'dependant', as defined by FAA 1976, who suffers financial loss as a result of the deceased's death which is referable to a personal family relationship with the deceased.

The statutory meaning of 'dependant'

The definition of 'dependant' at FAA 1976, s 1(3) is as follows:

'(a) the wife or husband or former wife or husband of the deceased;
(b) any person who:

    (i) was living with the deceased in the same household immediately before the date of the death; and

    (ii) had been living with the deceased in the same household for at least two years before that date; and

    (iii) was living during the whole of that period as the husband or wife of the deceased;

(c) any parent or other ascendant of the deceased;
(d) any person who was treated by the deceased as his parent;
(e) any child or other descendant of the deceased (including an infant born after the death but who was en ventre sa mere at the time of the injury that caused the death);
(f) any person (not being a child of the deceased) who, in the case of any marriage to which the deceased was at any time a party, was treated by the deceased as a child of the family in relation to that marriage;
(g) any person who is, or is the issue of, a brother, sister, uncle or aunt of the deceased.'

The requirement to come within the statutory definition of 'dependant' has resulted in adverse judicial comment (see *Shepherd v Post Office* (1995) *The Times*, June 15), and the introduction of the cohabitee ((b) above) by the Administration of Justice Act 1982 as a possible claimant was controversial.

In an unreported case, *Fretwell v Willi Betz* (2001), the definition of a 'dependant' was challenged, by virtue of the Human Rights Act 1998. The case was settled without any admission as regards the claimant's status as a 'dependant' (the argument concerned a child of the girlfriend who was living with the deceased prior to the accident), but it does illustrate the possibility of using the Human Rights Act 1998 to challenge the narrow statutory definition of a 'dependant'.

The requirement to have been living together for 2 years prior to the death should be noted, and evidence should be obtained on this point if it is anticipated that the defendant will challenge this. FAA 1976 contains a provision that the cohabitee's lack of enforceable right to support is to be taken into account (FAA 1976, s 3(4)). This may mean that a cohabitee will receive less compensation than a lawful spouse, as the court may use a lower multiplier in determining the dependency claim. For example, a multiplier of 13 was used for a cohabiting couple, instead of 15 which would have been used if they were married.

Further provisions with regard to the meaning of 'dependant'

Section 1(4) of FAA 1976 (as amended by the Administration of Justice Act 1982) provides:

'... former wife or husband ... includes a reference to a person whose marriage to the deceased has been annulled or declared void as well as a person whose marriage to the deceased has been dissolved.'

Section 1(5) of FAA 1976 (as amended by the Administration of Justice Act 1982) provides:

> 'any relationship by affinity shall be treated as a relationship by consanguinity; any relationship of the half blood shall be treated as a relationship of the whole blood;
>
> the stepchild of any person shall be treated as his child and an illegitimate person shall be treated as the legitimate child of his mother and reputed father.'

Thus, for example, the stepbrother of the deceased is treated as his true brother; the uncle of a wife is treated as the husband's uncle.

The Adoption Act 1976 provides that, generally, an adopted child is treated as the natural child of the adopters.

Identifying the dependants

It is important to identify all prospective dependants as s 2(3) of FAA 1976 provides that 'only one action may lie' and, as a result, only one action will be brought. A defendant is entitled to full particulars of all those on whose behalf the action is being brought. In practice, the particulars of the dependants are set out in the court documentation and generally include details of:

(1) the age of the dependants;
(2) their relationship with the deceased;
(3) the nature of the dependency (eg the dependant was a minor son wholly supported by the deceased father who was the family breadwinner and who had good promotion prospects).

In the case of *Cachia and Others v Francis Ola Faluyi* (2001) *The Times*, July 11, the Court of Appeal held that it was possible to interpret FAA 1976, s 2(3) under the European Convention on Human Rights, so as to prevent a dependent child's claim from becoming statute-barred for limitation purposes.

On occasions, the defendants will argue that a claimant is not a true 'dependant' under FAA 1976, and this is often resolved by the court ordering a trial of the point as a preliminary issue.

The requirement of 'financial loss'

It is not sufficient that the claimant merely satisfies the statutory meaning of 'dependant'. It must be shown in addition that there is a reasonable likelihood that the claimant has or will suffer financial loss as a result of the death of the deceased. In the case of *Thomas v Kwik Save Stores Ltd* (2000) *The Times*, June 27, the Court of Appeal reaffirmed the principle that, when awarding damages under FAA 1976, the court was concerned with the financial loss and not the emotional dependency of the claimant on the deceased.

In many cases, the dependants will have a clear and immediate financial loss. For example, where a husband before his death was maintaining his wife and children, the fact that they will suffer financial loss as a result of the husband's death is obvious.

The loss may still be regarded as 'financial' even if there was no expenditure by the deceased, provided the support can be quantified in monetary terms (eg where the deceased's elderly mother was allowed to live rent-free in the deceased's house before his death, the mother would be able to claim a quantifiable financial loss).

In the case of *Cox v Hockenhill* (1999) *Law Society Gazette*, 30 June, the Court of Appeal held that the important point in assessing the dependancy was to identify the loss the claimant has suffered as a result of a death. In that case, the deceased's income had been certain State benefits which she and her husband had relied upon. The court allowed the husband's claim for dependancy on the basis that he was dependent on certain benefits that had been received prior to the death and which he no longer obtained after his wife was killed in a road traffic accident.

The loss must be as a result of a personal family relationship with the deceased

If the loss to the dependant is, in reality, a loss attributable to a business relationship with the deceased, then the claim for loss of dependency will fail (*Burgess v Florence Nightingale Hospital for Gentlewomen* [1955] 1 QB 349).

> *Example*
> Tom is killed in a car accident as a result of the negligent driving of Keith. Tom is survived by his widow, Sally, and his 6-month-old son, Brian. Tom was the sole financial support of Sally and Brian. Tom worked in business with his brother, Joe. As a result of Tom's death, the business fails and Joe suffers heavy financial losses. Tom's married sister, Edwina, is very upset at the news of her brother's death.
>
> Sally and Brian may claim as defined dependants who suffer financial losses as a result of a family relationship with Tom.
>
> Joe cannot claim because, although he is a defined dependant, his financial losses are as a result of a business relationship with Tom.
>
> Edwina cannot claim because although she is a defined dependant, she has suffered no financial losses (merely grief and sorrow).

15.6.2 Assessing loss of dependency – the traditional method

The award for loss of dependency is ascertained by a multiplicand and multiplier system. The multiplicand is the net annual loss of the dependants; the multiplier is based on the number of years' loss of dependency (ie the length of time that the claimant would have been dependent on the deceased). The approach taken by the court is similar to that adopted by the court in determining the living claimant's loss of future earnings.

The multiplicand – the net annual loss to the dependants

THE DECEASED WAGE EARNER

The starting point is to calculate the amount of the deceased's earnings and deduct the estimated amount of how much was required or spent by the deceased on his own personal and living expenses (*Davies v Powell Duffryn Associated Collieries* [1942] AC 601 at 617).

(1) The deceased's net annual earnings

The deceased's net annual earnings must be calculated as at the date of the trial (*Cookson v Knowles* [1979] AC 556). In order to ascertain that sum, it may be necessary to adjust the deceased's earnings at the date of death.

(2) Sums spent on the deceased's own maintenance

A figure must be ascertained for sums spent exclusively on the maintenance of dependants or on items which benefited both the deceased and the dependants jointly (eg mortgage or rent payments are left out of account) (*Harris v Empress Motors* [1984] 1 WLR 212).

(3) Calculating the dependency figure

There are two approaches that the courts have considered:

(1) The 'old' system for calculating the dependency figure is to add up all the financial benefits received by the dependants from the deceased. It is necessary to produce a list of the items which contributed to the annual value of dependency and for the claimant to provide documentary evidence, bills etc for the year prior to the death. A proportion is then deducted for the deceased's own expenses. For example, the following items have been considered: how much housekeeping money was paid to the wife?; how much was spent on the deceased's food?; how much was spent on the food for the rest of the family?; who paid how much for the children's shoes, etc?.

(2) The modern practice is to deduct a percentage from the net income figure to represent what the deceased would have spent exclusively on himself. Conventional percentages are adopted. Where the family unit was husband and wife, the usual figure is one-third. Where the family unit was husband, wife and children the usual figure is one-quarter. However, it is important to note that each case must be judged on its own facts. The court is willing to depart from the conventional figures where there is evidence that they are inappropriate (*Owen v Martin* [1992] PIQR Q151), for example where the deceased was particularly frugal or a spendthrift. In such circumstances, less or more than the conventional figure should be deducted (see also *Coward v Comex Houlder Diving Ltd* (1988) unreported, 18 July and *Dhaliwal v Personal Representatives of Hunt (Deceased)* [1995] PIQR Q56, CA.

Furthermore, it is quite possible that different multiplicands may have to be selected according to different times in the period of dependency. Had he lived, the deceased's financial affairs would not have remained constant throughout his life. Similarly, therefore, the multiplicand will not remain constant either. For example, in the case of a husband with wife and children, 75% of the husband's earnings may be the appropriate initial multiplicand while his children are likely to be dependent. However, from the point where the children can be expected to become independent the multiplicand may be merely two-thirds of the husband's earnings (see also *Coward v Comex Houlder Diving Ltd* (above)).

Frequently, both husband and wife would have been earning at the time of death, and in such circumstances the approach adopted is to calculate the dependency as two-thirds or 75% (as the case may be) of the total joint net income less the continuing earnings (see also *Coward v Comex Houlder Diving Ltd* (above)).

(4) Other relevant factors

(a) Change in earning capacity

No allowance is made for inflation (*Auty v National Coal Board* [1985] 1 All ER 930), but allowance is made for a likely increase in the deceased's earning capacity (eg as result of promotion). Evidence will be needed in support of this, and the best evidence may be from a comparative employee or employees who have gone, or who are going through, the same career structure as the deceased would have done. This evidence could be obtained, for example, from the deceased's trade union or employer.

Conversely, there may be evidence of likely loss of earning capacity, for example because of redundancy.

(b) Services rendered by the deceased

The deceased may have been contributing to the support of the family not only in terms of a percentage of his earnings but also by rendering services to the family free of charge. Examples of such services include:

(1) do-it-yourself jobs (eg painting the house annually);
(2) vegetable gardening (therefore saving on grocery bills);
(3) nursing services to a sick member of the family;
(4) 'perks' of employment (eg the deceased was provided with a company car which was also used by the family, saving the family the capital cost of the car and the expense of maintenance and insurance, or coalminers who obtained free or cheap coal, which perk may have continued beyond retirement age).

On the deceased's death, such free services will be lost. The family will have to pay for the services (eg by employing a decorator) and thus incur a loss. The value of these services can add considerably to the multiplicand. Evidence must be obtained, for example, by quotations from the appropriate source.

The multiplier – the period of loss

Having calculated the multiplicand, the other side of the equation is to calculate the number of years' loss of dependency.

(1) COMMENCEMENT OF PERIOD OF LOSS

The starting point for the number of years' loss is the date of death (not the date of trial – *Graham v Dodds* [1983] 2 All ER 953).

(2) END OF THE PERIOD OF LOSS

In the case of a deceased wage earner, prima facie the number of years' loss will extend to the end of the deceased's working life (ie usually up to what would have been the deceased's retiring age). Direct evidence should be called on this point. (It must be remembered that certain items of loss such as the claim for the cost of DIY may extend beyond retirement age as the deceased would not necessarily have stopped doing DIY when he retired from work.)

However, each case will turn upon its own facts and the period of dependency may end before or after what would have been the normal date of the deceased's retirement. For example, where the deceased was a professional person, he may have been expected to work and support his dependants beyond normal retirement age. Equally, if the deceased would have enjoyed a pension, it may be argued that he would have continued to provide for his dependants beyond normal retirement age (although evidence would be needed to substantiate this – *Auty v National Coal Board* [1985] 1 All ER 930; see Chapter 13).

Conversely, the period of dependency may stop before what would have been the normally expected retirement age of the deceased. For example, if the deceased was already in a poor state of health, he may not have been expected to work until normal retirement age, and the financial support for the dependants would therefore have ended earlier. Similarly, if the dependant himself is in a poor state of health and has a short life-expectancy, the period of dependency will be shorter.

Where there is a claim by a widow as dependant, the likelihood that the marriage would have ended in divorce may be taken into account in assessing the period of dependency. In *Owen v Martin* [1992] PIQR Q151, the judge adopted a multiplier of 15, but the Court of Appeal reduced this to 11 on the basis that the widow's attitude towards her marriage vows as shown by her personal history led the court to believe that the marriage may not have lasted the whole of the natural life of the deceased. The court should take this approach only provided there is some evidence of likelihood of divorce (*Wheatley v Cunningham* [1992] PIQR Q100). See *also Dalziel and Dalziel v Donald* (2001) JPIL Issue 2/01, p 190, concerning an extra-marital affair. In *Cape Distribution Ltd v O'Loughlin* (2001) JPIL, Issue 2/01, p 191, the court confirmed that there is no prescribed method by which damages for loss of dependency had to be identified. The key factor was showing economic loss. However, the widow's prospects of remarriage or actual remarriage is to be ignored (FAA 1976, s 3(3)). Therefore, the period of the widow's dependency on her deceased husband is calculated without regard to the fact that she is or may be financially supported by a new husband.

Conversion of the period of loss to a multiplier

Once the number of years' loss of dependency has been ascertained, this is then converted to a multiplier (for the general principles on the selection of the multiplier, see Chapter 13).

The deceased non-wage earner

Where the deceased was a wage earner, the valuation of the multiplicand in the dependency claim is predominantly based on a proportion of the deceased's earnings (see above). This is so whether the deceased was male or female (eg whether husband, father, wife or mother). It is not uncommon, however, that the deceased was not in paid employment. In this case, the value of the services rendered to the family becomes the vital issue. For example, if the deceased was the wife and mother of the family and was not a wage earner at the date of her death, the services rendered by her to the family might be quantified in the terms of employing a housekeeper to provide the same services. In *Regan v Williamson* [1976] 1 WLR 305, Watkins J said that in this context 'the word "services" [has] been too narrowly construed. It should at least include an acknowledgement that a wife and mother does not work to set hours, and, still less, to rule'. Accordingly, a value in excess of a housekeeper was awarded in that case. In *Mehmet v Perry* [1977] 2 All ER 529, the claimant widower, on the death of his wife, reasonably gave up his job in order to look after his young children. The starting-point for the value of the services of the deceased wife was taken as the husband's loss of earnings.

Claims by parents, if children unmarried

A claim can be made by a parent (who is often unemployed or ill) who was dependent on the support from his unmarried child. When the court considers this type of case, it will have regard to the fact that the child may have married and the financial assistance provided by the child may have ceased.

Claims by child dependants

Where a claim is made by a surviving spouse and child, the court's approach is often to assess the claim for dependency of the widow alone, and then to apportion a small amount ('pocket money') to the child. This approach may be justified on the basis that:

(1) the surviving spouse will be expected to provide for the child out of her damages;
(2) compared to the surviving spouse, the period of dependency of the child will often be short (ending probably between the ages of 16 to 21 depending on whether the child is expected to go on to higher education); and
(3) it avoids repeated applications to the court for the release of invested funds for the benefit of the child.

However, the court is keen to protect the child's interest, and this approach may not be followed in every case. For example, if the surviving spouse is a known spendthrift and cannot be trusted to provide for the child, the court may assess the claims of the surviving spouse and child separately.

If the claim is brought by a child alone (eg if the death of a parent has left a child orphaned), the court may assess the child's dependency by the use of the 'nanny formula', that is to quantify the loss in the terms of employing a professional (a nanny) to care for the child or to have regard to the cost of employing a housekeeper. (See also *R v Criminal Injuries Compensation Board ex parte K* [1998] 2 FLR 1071, which held that while the child had the benefit of new parental sources after the death of the mother, for example by an aunt or uncle, it was not the case that the child had suffered 'no loss' for the purposes of FAA 1976; see also *Stanley v Saddique* [1992] 1 QB 1.)

Where the claim involves a minor dependant, the court's approval of any settlement should be sought as it will be necessary to satisfy the court that the child's interests are protected (see *M v S* (2001) CLI, May, concerning the payment of the award of damages to the dependants and not to their carer).

The multiplication

Having established the appropriate multiplicand and the overall multiplier. One method of calculating the award for loss of dependency is as follows:

(1) special damages: calculate the actual number of years' loss from the date of death until the trial;
(2) deduct the number of pre-trial years from the overall multiplier;
(3) apply the balance of the multiplier to the multiplicand (or multiplicands).

Example

Tom is killed in a road traffic accident. At the time of his death, Tom was 30 years old. Tom has left a widow, Lucy, aged 29, and twin boys, Mark and James, both aged 9. Tom was a do-it-yourself enthusiast and performed many decorating and maintenance tasks in the family home. The value of the services to the family was £750 per year. Prior to the accident, Tom was in good health and was expected to work until he was 65. His net annual earnings at trial have been calculated as £10,000. At the age of 40, Tom would have been promoted and would have been earning £15,000 net per year. At the age of 50, Tom would have been further promoted and would have been earning £20,000 net per year until his retirement. Mark and James will become independent at the age of 18. The case comes to trial 3 years after the accident.

The significant factors in the calculation are as follows.

(1) The length of dependency is likely to be based on Tom's age of 30 and his retirement age of 65, that is a period of 35 years. This is likely to produce an overall multiplier of, say, 21.
(2) There will be 3 years' special damages (pre-trial). This will leave 18 as the balance of the overall multiplier for post-trial losses.
(3) The multiplicand is likely to be based not only on the net annual earnings but also on the value of the services.
(4) The calculation may be split into various sub-calculations to reflect, for example, that for the first 9 years after the accident (but for his death) Tom would have been supporting a wife and children (therefore he might have been expected to spend one quarter of his net earnings on his own maintenance), but for the remaining 26 years of his working life (after the children became independent) he would have been supporting only a wife (and therefore he might be expected to spend one-third of his net earnings on his own maintenance). Another reason for splitting the calculation may be to reflect his increased earnings because of promotion 10 years and 20 years after the accident.

The above example is given merely to illustrate the general principles of quantifying a claim. It will be appreciated that, in practice, it will be rare that a person's working and family life can be predicted with such certainty and other methods of calculating the loss of dependency (eg nil discount tables issued by the Government's Actuary's Department) have been advocated.

It should also be remembered that different multipliers must be applied to items that would not have ceased at the age of 65. Detailed instructions need to be obtained from the client on this point. In practice, therefore, the facts of a particular case are usually such as to defy precise mathematical calculation. The assessment of dependency damages is a difficult matter and the court has to anticipate what would have occurred in the future. To assist the court, as much evidence as possible should be obtained.

15.6.3 Assessing loss of dependency – the Ogden Tables

The above paragraphs set out the 'traditional method' of calculating the dependency figure in a FAA 1976 case. However, in the fourth edition of the Ogden Tables, an alternative method is adopted and recommended for the calculation of the dependency claim. In the introduction to the Ogden Tables, Sir Michael Ogden states that the cases prior to *Wells v Wells* [1998] 3 WLR 329 (see Chapter 13) do not preclude the use of the new method suggested in the Ogden Tables.

For details of the method suggested, readers are referred to the fourth edition of the Ogden Tables, p 15.

As at May 2001, the author is not aware of any FAA 1976 cases in which the court has been asked to assess the damages on the basis suggested by the Ogden Tables.

15.6.4 Bereavement

The claimants

The claim for bereavement is open only to a limited class (not just 'dependants' generally: see **15.6.1**). The possible claimants are:

(1) the spouse of the deceased; or
(2) the parents of a legitimate unmarried deceased minor;
(3) the mother of an illegitimate unmarried deceased minor.

It should be noted therefore that, for example, a child is not entitled to the award of bereavement on the death of his parent, and in a case where both parents can claim, the damages are divided equally between them (FAA 1976, s 1A(4)). However, in *Navaei v Navaei* (1995) *Halsburys Laws* June 1995/1784, the mother was negligent and this resulted in the death of her daughter. The father claimed all of the bereavement damages and stated that they should not be shared with the mother. He argued that if he were to be paid only half of the damages, the mother/tortfeasor would be benefiting contrary to public policy. The court held that in bringing an action under FAA 1976, a claimant is under a duty to act on behalf of all dependants and was allowed only half the damages.

In the case of *Griffiths and Others v British Coal Corporation* (1998) unreported, 23 February, QBD, it was held that FAA 1976 did not require an apportionment of damages for bereavement where there were two causes of death (in this case, smoking and exposure to mine dust), and therefore the claimant recovered the full statutory sum.

The claim for the bereavement award by parents depends on the deceased being a minor at the date of death, not at the date of the accident (*Doleman v Deakin* (1990) *The Times*, January 30).

In the case of *Martin and Browne v Grey* (1998) unreported, 13 May, QBD, the court held that it is still possible for a spouse to bring a bereavement damages claim, despite a decree nisi.

The amount of the bereavement award

The award is a fixed amount of £7,500 in respect of causes of action arising on or after 1 April 1991. Many people have criticised the level of award. It should be noted that a cohabitee is excluded from the definition, despite the fact that a cohabitee can pursue a dependency claim as noted above. In certain cases, especially those with a media interest, defendants have offered a higher figure than the statutory minimum, so as to avoid allegations by the press that they have undervalued a life.

15.6.5 Funeral expenses (FAA 1976, s 3(5))

Funeral expenses can be claimed if reasonable and paid by a dependant. The question of reasonableness will be a decision on the facts of each case. Reference should be made to previous case-law in circumstances where the client puts forward an unusual claim so as to determine whether the court will regard the claim as reasonable or otherwise.

If the funeral expenses are paid by the estate then they are claimed as part of a LR(MP)A 1934 claim (see **15.5.3**). Clearly, funeral expenses cannot be claimed under both LR(MP)A 1934 and FAA 1976.

15.6.6 Disregarding benefits

Section 4 of FAA 1976 provides:

> 'In assessing damages in respect of a person's death in an action under this Act, benefits which have accrued or will or may accrue to any person from his estate or otherwise as a result of his death shall be disregarded.'

For example, if a dependant receives insurance money as a result of the deceased's death, the dependant does not have to give credit for that money against FAA 1976 damages. Similarly, if damages awarded to the estate under a LR(MP)A 1934 claim end up in the hands of a dependant by reason of the deceased's will or rules of intestacy, those damages do not necessarily reduce any FAA 1976 damages which may be awarded to that dependant.

15.6.7 Recoupment and offsetting of benefits

Any payment made in consequence of an action under FAA 1976 is not subject to recoupment under the Social Security (Recovery of Benefits) Act 1997 (see Chapter 12).

15.7 INTEREST

Interest on the bereavement damages may be awarded at the full short-term investment rate (*Sharman v Sheppard* [1989] CLY 1190) from the date of death.

The pecuniary losses to the date of the trial are treated as special damages in a fatal injury claim and therefore are awarded interest at half the short-term investment rate. Future pecuniary loss attracts no interest.

15.8 PENSION LOSS

Investigations should be made as to whether there will be a reduced pension fund available to the deceased's dependants due to the early death, and this should be included within the claim if appropriate (see also **13.3.6**).

15.9 ESTABLISHING THE CASE

A fatal accident case will be dealt with in essentially the same way as any other personal injury or clinical negligence claim. Evidence is needed to establish liability and the highest level of damages. The claimant's solicitor must remember to obtain a signed proof of evidence or statement from a client as soon as possible in every case, as this will be of considerable assistance if the client dies either due to the injuries sustained in the accident or otherwise. If the solicitor has failed to take this precaution he will make proving the case more difficult. Under the Civil Evidence Act 1995, the client's statement or proof can now be put before the court and it should be regarded by the court as important evidence.

It should also be remembered that the inquest will be an important source of information (see Chapter 14), and as much information as possible should be obtained.

15.10 CONDUCT

To avoid conflicts of interest arising, it is good practice to ensure that none of the dependants who could be to blame in whole or part for the accident that resulted in the death are appointed as personal representatives.

The conduct of a fatal accident claim clearly requires sympathy and diplomacy on the part of the solicitor. There are frequently conflicts of personality between the dependants and personal representatives and this is compounded by the fact that only one action can be brought in respect of the claim. If, after the fatal accident, it comes to light that the deceased had more than one dependent family, it can be anticipated that any interviews with the deceased's wife may be difficult!

15.11 SIMPLIFIED EXAMPLE OF A SCHEDULE OF LOSS IN A FATAL ACCIDENT CASE – TRADITIONAL METHOD (see 15.6.2)

COLLAWS SOLICITORS

SCHEDULE OF LOSS AS AT TRIAL IN THE CASE OF LUCY BROWN

Date of birth	1 January 1955
Date of accident/death	1 January 2000
Net pre-accident wage	£133.33 per week
Date of schedule/trial	1 January 2002

Reduction for deceased own needs: 25% so initial multiplicand = £100

Loss of earnings to date of schedule:

1 January 2000 to 4 April 2000	14 weeks × £100	£1,400.00
Thereafter annual payrise having the effect of a 5% rise on net pay effective from 5 April each year		
5 April 2000 to 4 April 2001	52 weeks at £105	£5,460.00
5 April 2001 to 1 January 2002	38 weeks at £110.25	£4,189.50
TOTAL		£11,049.50
Other services to family per annum (eg gardening, housework, DIY)	2 × £800	£1,600.00
TOTAL		£12,649.50
Bereavement	£7,500	
Funeral expenses	£1,390.50	

Loss of dependency
Earnings

At a weekly rate of	£110.25	
Annual rate of		£5,733.00
Other services to the family		
Annual rate of		£800.00
TOTAL		£6,533.00

A multiplier of, say, 12 from the date of death is used on the basis that the deceased would have worked until the age of 65. The multiplier from the date of trial 2 years post-accident is 10.

Total future loss of dependency: 10 × £6,533 = £65,330

SUMMARY

Pre-trial loss	£12,649.50
Future loss	£65,330.00
Bereavement damages	£7,500.00
Funeral expenses	£1,390.50
TOTAL	£86,870.00

In addition, interest is claimed on the items of loss to the date of trial at half the short-term rate and on bereavement damages at the full short-term investment account rate.

15.12 CONCLUSION

It should be noted that, at the time of writing, the Law Commission has published proposals to extend the definition of 'dependants' and to increase the level of bereavement damages, but the proposals have not been taken further at this point.

Finally, acting on behalf of the relatives in a fatal accident claim requires the personal injury/clinical negligence solicitor to have tact, sympathy and a detailed understanding of the law involved. It should be appreciated that each case will be dealt with on its own facts, and only broad principles have been established by the case-law in this area. In fatal accident cases, the court is required to anticipate what would have occurred in the future, which will be different in every case.

15.13 FURTHER READING

Kemp and Kemp *The Quantum of Damages* (Sweet & Maxwell).

Chapter 16

CLAIMS INVOLVING UNUSUAL ELEMENTS

16.1 CRIMINAL INJURIES COMPENSATION AUTHORITY

Victims of crimes of violence who have suffered injuries can apply for compensation from the Criminal Injuries Compensation Authority (CICA). The Criminal Injuries Compensation Scheme (2001) (the scheme) was made pursuant to ss 1 to 6 and s 12 of the Criminal Injuries Compensation Act 1995 and deals with all claims received on or after 1 April 2001.

To be eligible to make an application under the scheme, an applicant must have sustained a criminal injury on or after 1 August 1964 (in the case of a victim and assailant living in the same household, the injury must have been sustained on or after 1 October 1979). The personal injury must be directly attributable to a crime of violence that occurred in Great Britain. The applicant must have an injury serious enough to qualify for at least the minimum award (see below) available under the scheme for the application to be considered.

The CICA also requires that, unless good reasons can be shown, the incident should have been reported to the police as soon as possible after it occurred and any application should be received within 2 years from the date of the incident. (The CICA has a discretion to waive this time-limit, if appropriate.)

If an application is to be made, the appropriate form should be obtained from the CICA. The correct form must be used as different application forms are required for personal injury and fatal accident claims.

The procedure adopted by the CICA is that once the application has been received at its offices, it will acknowledge receipt of the application and send out routine enquiry forms to the police and medical authorities. The CICA retains the right to withhold or reduce an award if the applicant persistently fails to assist the CICA in its requests for information, fails to attend medical examinations or otherwise fails to give reasonable assistance. The CICA also has the power to withhold or reduce an award if the applicant has failed to take all reasonable steps to inform or co-operate with the police or, more significantly, if the conduct of the applicant makes it inappropriate for a full award to be made.

The CICA will have regard not only to the applicant's behaviour connected with the incident, but also the applicant's character as shown by his criminal convictions even if they are unrelated to the incident. In assessing an applicant's character, the CICA adopts a scheme of awarding 'penalty points' for any convictions of the applicant.

Chapter 16 contents
Criminal Injuries Compensation Authority
Claims on behalf of child claimants
Claims on behalf of mental patients
Provisional damages
Structured settlements
Choice of jurisdiction
Conclusion
Key points
Further reading

Table A

Examples of penalty points system adopted by the CICA

Sentence of the court	Period between date of sentence and receipt of application by CICA	Penalty points
Imprisonment for more than 30 months	Period of sentence or less	10
Fine Community service order	(a) less than 2 years (b) 2 years or more	2 1

Once the appropriate penalty points have been identified, a reduction in the damages is made on a sliding scale.

Penalty points	Percentage reduction
0–2	0%
3–5	25%
6–7	50%
8–9	75%
10 or more	100%

The CICA is concerned with the applicant's conduct before, during and after the event which resulted in the injury. The CICA guide to the scheme makes it clear that if, for example, the victim was injured in a fight, compensation will not be paid to the applicant if he had voluntarily agreed to take part in it, struck the first blow or the incident formed part of a pattern of violence in which the applicant was a voluntary participant.

16.1.1 Level of compensation for injuries

The scheme operates a standard level of compensation for certain injuries. A tariff identifies particular injuries and attaches a 'level' which determines the amount payable. Level 1 (£1,000) represents the minimum amount payable under the scheme and Level 25 (£250,000) represents the maximum amount payable for any single description of any injury.

In cases where the applicant has suffered separate multiple injuries, he is awarded the tariff amount for the highest rated description of injury, plus 30% of the tariff amount for the second highest rated description of injury, plus, where there are three or more injuries, 15% of the tariff amount for the third highest rated description of injury.

16.1.2 Compensation for loss of earnings

The scheme does not provide compensation for lost earnings for the first 28 weeks post-accident. After that point, the scheme sets out what will be taken into account in calculating the net loss of earnings (see para 31 of the scheme). The CICA has power to award compensation for future loss of earnings, if appropriate, and will adopt the normal multiplicand/multiplier approach. The losses must be directly as a result of the injury complained of.

The scheme also provides that any net loss of earnings which is taken into account in calculating the loss of earnings figure must not exceed one-and-a-half times the gross average industrial earnings at the time of the assessment.

16.1.3 Compensation for special expenses

If the applicant has been incapacitated for longer than 28 weeks as a direct result of the injury, the applicant can claim for certain special expenses incurred. Examples of such special expenses are adaptations to the applicant's accommodation, the cost of private medical treatment and the cos t of care.

16.1.4 Compensation for fatal accident cases

The scheme provides for the following classes of applicant.

(1) The spouse of the deceased who was formally married to the deceased, living with the deceased as husband and wife in the same household immediately before the date of death, or as a same-sex partner in the same household immediately before death, and who, if not formally married to the deceased, had been so living throughout two years before that date.
(2) The spouse of the deceased who, although not living with the deceased immediately before the date of death, was at that time financially supported by the deceased.
(3) A former spouse of the deceased who was financially supported by the deceased immediately before the date of death. (A former spouse does not qualify for the standard amount of compensation – see below.)
(4) A parent of the deceased whether or not the natural parent, provided that person was accepted by the deceased as a parent of the deceased's family.
(5) A child of the deceased whether or not the natural child, provided he was accepted by the deceased as a child of his family or was dependent on him. (The definition of child is not restricted to a person below the age of 18.)

Provided the deceased died as a result of the injury, one or more of the following types of payment can be made under the scheme:

(1) standard amount of compensation;
(2) dependency;
(3) loss of parental services for a child under 18 years of age.

Standard amount

Where there is only one qualifying payment, the standard amount of compensation will be at level 13 of the tariff. Where there is more than one qualifying payment, the standard amount of compensation for each claimant will be at level 10 of the tariff. The scheme does not provide for the standard amount of compensation to be paid to a former spouse of the deceased.

Dependency

The period of loss will begin at the date of the deceased's death and the normal multiplier/multiplicand approach will be adopted.

Loss of parental services

A claimant who is under the age of 18 may be eligible not only for the dependency claim but also for compensation for loss of parental services at an annual rate of level 5 of the tariff. Compensation may also be payable to meet other resultant losses, for example child care costs, or loss of earnings suffered by an adult looking after the child. An appropriate multiplier, applied to the period until the child reaches the age of 18, will be used.

16.1.5 Funeral expenses

The scheme provides that in fatal accidents no compensation will be paid other than reasonable funeral expenses for the benefit of the estate.

16.1.6 Maximum award

The scheme imposes an overall limit of £500,000 payable in respect of fatal injuries, irrespective of the number of claimants.

16.1.7 Deductions from calculations

All awards under the scheme (save for the tariff-based amounts of compensation) are subject to reduction to take into account social security benefits or insurance payments made in respect of the same event.

The scheme also provides that an award will be reduced by the full value of any payment made in the following circumstances:

(1) a civil court has made an order for payment of damages;
(2) a claim for damages and/or compensation has been settled on terms providing for the payment of money;
(3) payment of compensation has been ordered by a criminal court in respect of personal injury.

The scheme provides that the reduction will also include the full value of any payment to which the applicant has any present or future entitlement. If the applicant receives the compensation award by the CICA, and subsequently receives any of the payments referred to above, he is required to repay in full the equivalent of the subsequent payment to the CICA.

16.1.8 Review and appeals procedure

If the applicant disagrees with the decision of the CICA, the application for review must be made in writing within 90 days from the date of the letter giving notice to the applicant of the CICA's original decision, and the letter should state the reasons why a review is sought. At the review, the matter is considered again by a more senior claims officer. If this is still considered to be inadequate, it is possible to appeal the review within 90 days from the date of the letter giving notice of the review decision. The review is to the Criminal Injuries Compensation Appeals Panel.

16.1.9 Costs

The CICA will not pay solicitors' costs in respect of applications under the scheme.

Table B

Criminal Injuries Compensation Scheme

Levels of compensation	Amount
Level 1	£1,000
Level 2	£1,250
Level 3	£1,500
Level 4	£1,750
Level 5	£2,000
Level 6	£2,500
Level 7	£3,300
Level 8	£3,800
Level 9	£4,400
Level 10	£5,500
Level 11	£6,600
Level 12	£8,200
Level 13	£11,000
Level 14	£13,500
Level 15	£16,500
Level 16	£19,000
Level 17	£22,000
Level 18	£27,000
Level 19	£33,000
Level 20	£44,000
Level 21	£55,000
Level 22	£82,000
Level 23	£110,000
Level 24	£175,000
Level 25	£250,000

Table C

Examples from the tariff of injuries

Description of injury	Levels	Standard amount
Loss of ear	13	£11,000
Uncontrolled epilepsy	20	£44,000
Permanent clicking jaw	10	£5,500
Loss of smell	13	£11,000
Fractured pelvis – substantial recovery	9	£4,400
Fractured femur – one leg, substantial recovery	8	£3,800

16.1.10 Claims prior to 1 April 2001

Claims prior to 1 April 2001 were dealt with by the 1996 Scheme.

(The tables and other information contained within this section have been reproduced with the kind permission of the Board.)

16.2 CLAIMS ON BEHALF OF CHILD CLAIMANTS

16.2.1 Bringing the proceedings

In civil law, a child is a person who is not yet 18 years old. Under that age, a child is termed 'a person under a disability' (although this term is not used in the CPR 1998). Whilst under a disability the limitation period does not run against the child (see Chapter 6), but during that time the child cannot normally bring proceedings in his own name. The solutions therefore are either:

(1) to wait until the child reaches the age of 18; or
(2) during his minority to bring proceedings through a 'litigation friend' (usually a parent).

It is important to ensure that there is no conflict of interest between the child and the person who is bringing the action on the child's behalf. For example, if a child is injured in a road traffic accident whilst a passenger in a car being driven by his father, it would be sensible to appoint the child's mother as litigation friend (rather than the father) as the father may eventually be a defendant in the proceedings.

16.2.2 Court's approval of settlements

In all settlements involving a child (including the acceptance of money paid into court and a claim in a fatal accident case where there is a child dependant), the court's approval of the proposed settlement should be sought in order to validate the settlement, bind the claimant and give a discharge to the defendant.

16.2.3 Procedure for court settlement

If an agreement is made between the parties prior to proceedings being issued and the sole purpose of issuing proceedings is to obtain the court's approval, then the solicitor must follow the procedure set out in Part 8 of the CPR 1998 and a specific request must be included with the claim form for approval of the settlement. In addition, a draft consent order must be provided to the court using practice form N292. If the child reaches a settlement during the course of an action, or the defendant makes a Part 36 payment which is accepted, then the claimant will require an order from the court seeking:

(1) the court's approval of the settlement; and
(2) directions for investment of the damages.

16.2.4 The approval hearing

The aim of the hearing is to ensure that the settlement agreed is a reasonable one, and is in the child's best interests. At the hearing, the court will wish to have made available a number of documents including the following:

(1) the child's birth certificate (certainly details of the child's age);
(2) the statements of case and other documents already on the court file;
(3) evidence on liability (information as to whether liability is in dispute or the extent to which the defendant admits liability) and documents such as the police accident report, inquest report and details of any prosecutions brought;
(4) up-to-date calculation of past and future losses (with supporting documentation);

(5) up-to-date medical report or reports;
(6) litigation friend's approval of the settlement;
(7) interest calculation to date; and
(8) a copy of an opinion on the merits of the agreed settlement given to counsel or a solicitor (whilst the case is a simple one).

Full details of the court's requirements are set out in Part 21 of the CPR 1998 and the accompanying Practice Direction.

16.2.5 Further requirements at the hearing

The litigation friend should also provide a CFO form 320 (request for investment) which the district judge will complete.

16.2.6 The order

If the proposed settlement is approved, the court will give directions as to the investment of the damages. In the case of *Beatham v Carlisle Hospitals NHS Trust* (1999) *The Times*, May 20, it was held that the court's approval of a settlement on behalf of a child or indeed a patient (see **16.3**) should normally be given in public.

16.2.7 Investment of the damages

Money recovered on behalf of a child must be dealt with in accordance with directions of the court, which will be concerned that the damages are invested wisely for the child's benefit.

The court and the claimant's solicitor may need to know such things as whether:

(1) regular income is required;
(2) capital growth is required;
(3) the child has other income;
(4) the child is liable for tax;
(5) there are any specific liabilities;
(6) an address to which all future income is to be sent.

16.2.8 Possible orders with regard to investment

It is likely that the court will consider the following options when making an order for investment:

Payment out of part of or the whole sum immediately

In the case of small sums the court may consider that proper investment can be achieved by placing the sums in the hands of the litigation friend, for example to invest in a National Savings Bank investment account or building society account. In the case of a larger sum of damages, the court may authorise the immediate payment out of part of those damages to meet expenses already incurred on behalf of the child (eg the accrued cost of care) or expenses to be incurred in the immediate future.

Investment of the sum in court

The precise nature of the investment (eg government or local government stock, unit trusts, special account) is likely to be decided by the investment managers of the

Public Trust Office according to the policy of investment laid down by the court at the hearing, bearing in mind the requirements of the child (eg a requirement as to capital growth rather than income).

16.2.9 Refusal of approval by the court

If there is no dispute on liability, the court's refusal to approve the settlement will inevitably lead to renegotiation of the settlement figure or an appeal of the decision. If liability is in dispute, the defendant may wish to continue to defend the case.

16.3 CLAIMS ON BEHALF OF MENTAL PATIENTS

A 'patient' means a person who by reason of mental disorder within the meaning of the Mental Health Act 1983, is incapable of managing and administering his property and affairs and is regarded as being unable to bring proceedings on his own account. A 'patient' must have a litigation friend to conduct proceedings on his behalf.

With regard to the limitation period, if the person is injured whilst he is already a patient or the accident immediately renders him so (eg severe brain injury), the limitation period does not start to run until he ceases to be under a disability (Limitation Act 1980, s 28) and, therefore, in the case of a person rendered permanently mentally disordered in an accident, the limitation period is effectively infinite (see Chapter 6).

If the disability arises after the accrual of the cause of action, this may be taken into account by the court as a factor in considering whether to override the normal limitation period (Limitation Act 1980, s 33(3)(d)).

As with children, any settlement on behalf of a patient should be approved by the court.

16.4 PROVISIONAL DAMAGES

16.4.1 The problem which provisional damages are intended to solve

When the court makes a lump sum award of damages, it will be designed to cover both past and future pain and suffering (and other losses). The court will operate on the 'balance of probabilities', ie if it is probable that an event will occur, the court will work on the basis that it will occur, and if it is probable that the claimant will suffer, for example, from osteo-arthritis in the future, the court will work on the basis that the claimant will suffer from osteo-arthritis in the future.

The problem lies in cases where the deterioration, although possible, is less than probable.

> *Example*
> Fred is injured. At the time of the trial he has no loss of sight, but there is a 10% possibility that in the future he will lose the sight in one eye. Bearing in mind that quantum for pain and suffering and loss of amenity for the loss of sight in one eye is, say, £20,000, how does the judge award damages to Fred?

If the judge awards £2,000 (10% of £20,000) and Fred does lose the sight in his eye in the future, Fred will be under-compensated by £18,000, but cannot return to court for more damages. If Fred does not lose the sight in his eye in the future, Fred is unjustly enriched by £2,000 and the defendant cannot recover the excess damages.

Provisional damages are aimed at solving the above problem by providing an exception to the basic rule that, once a compensation payment has been made, it is in full and final settlement and further compensation cannot be claimed if the client's condition deteriorates unexpectedly. Therefore, in certain limited circumstances the claimant can be compensated for his injuries with the proviso that if a specific condition occurs in the future, he will be allowed to return to court so that further damages can be awarded.

16.4.2 The statutory provision

Section 32A of the Supreme Court Act 1981 provides:

> 'This section applies to an action for damages for personal injuries in which there is proved or admitted to be a chance that at some definite or indefinite time in the future the injured person will, as a result of the act or omission which gave rise to the cause of action, develop some serious disease or suffer some serious deterioration in his physical or mental condition.'

A similar provision applies in the county court (County Courts Act 1984, s 51).

The CPR 1998 state that the court may make an order for provisional damages providing the claimant comes within the definitions set out in s 32A of the Supreme Court Act 1981 or s 51 of the County Courts Act 1984.

'Chance'

The expression 'chance' is not defined in the Supreme Court Act 1981. It clearly indicates something less than a probability. However, it must be measurable rather than merely fanciful (*Willson v Ministry of Defence* [1991] 1 All ER 638, in which it was held that the possibility that the claimant would incur further injury from a fall as a result of an ankle injury was held not to be within s 32A of the Supreme Court Act 1981).

Whilst it is difficult to say with great certainty, where the likelihood can be expressed in the terms of single figure percentages, this is likely to be sufficient 'chance'. Provisional damages have been awarded in an unreported case where the chance was merely 2%.

'Serious deterioration'

'Serious deterioration' is not defined in the Supreme Court Act 1981. In *Willson* (above) it was held that 'serious deterioration' meant:

(1) a clear and severable risk of deterioration (not merely the natural progression of the injury); and
(2) something beyond ordinary deterioration.

(On the facts of *Willson*, the court held that the chance of arthritis was merely a natural progression of the injury and was not a suitable case for provisional damages.)

Clearly, the claimant will base his claim for provisional damages on medical evidence indicating that there is a 'chance' of a 'serious disease or deterioration' developing.

The most common examples of conditions in which provisional damages have been awarded in practice are where there is the chance of the claimant suffering from epilepsy or from a disease such as cancer or asbestosis as a result of exposure to a dangerous substance.

The mere fact that the claimant's medical prognosis will not be certain for a considerable time (eg 2 or 3 years) does not justify a claim for provisional damages. In such circumstances, consideration should be given to an application for an interim payment (see *Adefunke Fashade v North Middlesex Hospital* (2001) PMILL, January as an example of a recent case where provisional damages had been refused).

For a provisional damages award to be made, there must be sufficient certainty as to which circumstances must arise before the claimant is allowed to return to court. The court will wish to avoid a situation where there would be a dispute as to whether the proper circumstances had arisen.

16.4.3 The court's approach to provisional damages

If the court considers that there is a suitable case for provisional damages (see Part 41 and PD 41 to the CPR 1998), it will:

(1) assess damages on the assumption that the injured person will not develop the disease or suffer the deterioration in his condition;
(2) identify the disease or deterioration that has been disregarded;
(3) stipulate a period (which may be indefinite) during which the claimant may return to court for further damages if he develops the disease or suffers the deterioration;
(4) make an order that relevant documents are to be kept by the court.

Even where the claimant's claim falls within the realm of provisional damages, the claimant may not want to pursue an open-ended claim, preferring, instead, that the claim is satisfied once and for all by the award of a lump sum. The claimant's solicitor must take careful instructions on this aspect. It must be explained to the client that he will be able to return to court only if the deterioration is the 'specified disease or deterioration', and not for any other reason.

16.4.4 The claim for provisional damages must be included within the court documents

The claim for provisional damages must be included in the particulars of claim, and, if the possibility of provisional damages emerges after these documents have been served, the documents must be amended. Part 16 of the CPR 1998 and the accompanying Practice Direction set out the necessary information which must be included.

16.4.5 Consequences of a provisional damages claim

If the claimant claims provisional damages, the client must be informed of the consequences of the court's order and any time-limit imposed. Solicitors must also ensure that they preserve their own files for the appropriate length of time.

16.4.6 The court order

The only basis for an award of provisional damages is a court order. The order will be along the terms outlined in **16.4.3**. Any application by consent for an award of provisional damages should follow the procedure set out in Part 23 of the CPR 1998.

16.4.7 Further award

If the specified disease or deterioration occurs within the specified period, the claimant must give at least 28 days' written notice to the defendant of his intention to apply for further damages.

It is possible to apply to extend the period of time for claiming further damages, and a medical report should be filed in support of such an application. Such an application must be made within the original time-limit.

16.4.8 Provisional damages and the Fatal Accidents Act 1976

Section 3 of the Damages Act 1996 now allows an application to the court under the FAA 1976 where a person is awarded provisional damages and subsequently dies.

16.4.9 Provisional damages and Part 36 of the CPR 1998

The Part 36 payment notice must specify whether or not the defendant is offering to agree to the making of a provisional damages award (see CPR 1998, r 36.7).

16.5 STRUCTURED SETTLEMENTS

The basis of a structured settlement is that, instead of the entire award of damages being in the form of a lump sum, some (or all) of the damages may be in the form of an annuity bought or provided by the person by whom the compensation payment would otherwise have been made. The claimant therefore receives a large part of his damages as a number of slices of capital over a number of years, and, being capital, the payments are not subject to income tax. In contrast, if the claimant accepts his damages as a lump sum and then himself purchases an annuity, the payments are normally treated as income and are taxable as such.

16.5.1 Why a structured settlement?

The advantages of a structured settlement arise because of the (arguable) problems of a conventional award of damages in a lump sum.

The conventional award for future financial losses may under-compensate the victim

It may be argued (by the claimant's representatives) that the fund of money calculated on the conventional basis is inadequate as the fund will be exhausted before the period it is designed to cover has expired.

The investment of damages is a daunting prospect for the claimant

A claimant who is not used to handling large sums of money may find it daunting to be required to invest several thousands of pounds of damages.

The claimant needs protection from himself, his friends and family

The award of damages will need careful investment if it is to come close to compensating the actual period of loss. If the claimant is not used to dealing with large sums of money, he may 'squander' a large proportion of the damages on himself, his family and friends, and thus have very little to invest to meet the needs the damages were designed to cover.

The conventional award of damages does not allow the claimant to make provision for dependants

A prudent family person may wish to make provision for his family after his death. An injured claimant (who was formerly the family breadwinner) may wish to do the same, although his only asset is the damages received. If the invested damages are not likely to last for the claimant's own period of need, there will certainly be no scope to make provision for dependants.

The conventional award is unfair to defendants

The damages are awarded on the basis of the claimant's probable needs, but there is no control over the way in which he actually spends the award (the damages may be expended unjustifiably on purposes entirely different from those for which the award was designed). For example, damages awarded may be designed to cover future private medical care but, after the trial, the claimant undergoes National Health Service treatment. In this case, it could be argued that the claimant has 'defrauded' both the defendant (who cannot recover the 'excess' damages) and the State.

A structured settlement may tackle some of these problems and can be of particular use in cases involving minors, those without mental capacity and those who need long-term care.

16.5.2 The form of a structured settlement

A structured settlement cannot be imposed by the court on the claimant; it will come into existence only by agreement of the parties (*Burke v Tower Hamlets Area Health Authority* (1989) *The Times*, August 10). If the parties have agreed that a structured settlement is appropriate prior to the issue of proceedings, then a consent order should be made in accordance with the CPR 1998, Part 23.

PD 40C to the CPR 1998 sets out the procedure to be adopted by the court and details documents that need to be filed if there is to be a hearing.

16.5.3 Tax position

The structured settlement in a personal injury case is financed usually by the defendant's insurers using part of the damages to purchase an annuity from a life insurer.

Payments under the structure are treated as a payment of an antecedent debt. The receipt of the annuity by the claimant is treated as a payment to him of slices of capital rather than income and is not, therefore, subject to income tax.

Structured settlements are not only appropriate in personal injury cases but are also relevant to clinical negligence compensation payments. The NHS Executive in July 1996 issued guidance to all health authorities and trusts requiring that their procedures for handling clinical negligence and personal injury litigation ensure that structured settlements be considered where any settlement involves in excess of £250,000. In the case of a health authority trust, there are two types of structured settlements available: annuity-based (as described above) or self-financed structured settlements, where the health authority/trust gives an undertaking to provide the payments in the future. Self-financed structured settlements are more economical to the NHS but solicitors were originally concerned that if a trust could not meet its obligations under the agreement, the client would be without recompense to any alternative source. This fear had been thought to have been dealt with by s 6 of the Damages Act 1996 which gives Ministers a power to guarantee payments under a structure entered into by a health authority or trust (see also the National Health Service (Residual Liabilities) Act 1996); however, it appears that in practice health authorities are reluctant to use s 6. In a self-financed structured settlement, there is also the advantage to the NHS that the damages need not be paid out in one lump sum.

It is possible for the CICA and the MIB to make a structured settlement (see s 8 of the Criminal Injuries Compensation Act 1995).

16.5.4 Drafting the agreement

The involvement of an experienced, forensic accountant or specialist in setting up the structure is essential. The accountant may act exclusively for one party, or may act as 'honest broker' for both parties. The Law Society Working Party, however, recommends that each party should employ a separate accountant and the NHS litigation authority suggests that the practice of obtaining joint forensic accountant reports should not be undertaken.

The agreement must be drafted with care so as to comply with the appropriate Inland Revenue rules and also, once the structure is set up it cannot be easily undone. The claimant's future requirements (eg as to housing and nursing) will need to be ascertained.

There is usually a requirement for some capital to remain outside the structure to meet the claimant's setting-up costs, to reimburse the claimant for expenditure already incurred, and to provide an emergency fund should the structure fail or unforeseen circumstances arise.

It is important to note that, in order to obtain the benefits of a structured settlement, the parties' agreement should be obtained before any judgment for a money sum has been given or the claimant has received the compensation money or accepted money paid into the court.

16.5.5 At what level of award is a structure appropriate?

It is thought that the lowest structured settlement agreed in this jurisdiction was approximately £50,000. In claims where, on a conventional award basis, the claim would approach £100,000, the solicitor should discuss with the client the possibility of a structured settlement (and, indeed, it may be negligent not to do so).

16.5.6 Consequences on benefit claims

Following the case of *Beattie (A Patient) v Secretary of State for Social Security* [2001] 1 WLR 1404, care must be taken to advise clients as to the possible implications of receiving payments under a structured settlement on their benefit claims. In that case, it was held that the payments fell to be taken into account for the purposes of entitlement to Income Support.

16.5.7 Examples of structured settlements

The following are examples of structured settlements which have been agreed in practice:

Examples
(1) *Kelly v Dawes* (1990) *The Times*, September 27

The claim settled at £410,000, of which £110,000 (including an interim payment of £60,000) was paid immediately, with the balance purchasing an annuity of £2,146.99 per month until 2023 (index linked with 120 minimum payments regardless of the claimant's death in the interim).

(2) *Everett v Everett and Norfolk County Council* (1991) (unreported)

On a conventional basis, the claim was valued at £981,000. The award was discounted (in favour of the insurer) to £911,000, made up as follows:

Interim payment	£30,000
Pre-trial care	£50,000
Contingency fund	£118,622
Structured settlement	£706,378

The structured settlement was planned to produce the following stream of payments:

(1) an initial £17,000 per annum (plus 6% increase per annum) for life (minimum payment period 10 years);
(2) after 5 years, a further £18,735 per annum (plus 6% increase per annum) for life (minimum payment period 10 years);
(3) after 20 years, a further £29,186 per annum (plus 5% increase per annum) for life (no minimum payment period).

The projected cash value of the scheme if the claimant lives 50 years is £9 million.

(3) *Re B* (unreported)

The award on the conventional basis was valued at £400,000, discounted to £375,000. This was divided into a lump sum of £175,000 and £200,000 into the structure. This will produce an annuity of £12,474 per annum for life (plus 5% per annum indexing) for life (with a minimum payment period of 30 years). The projected cash value if the plaintiff lives to 70 is £2,345,000.

16.6 CHOICE OF JURISDICTION

A personal injury solicitor may have a client who has been injured abroad or who wishes to bring a claim in a different jurisdiction, normally on the basis that a higher level of damages may be awarded. (Eg clients may have heard of the case against McDonalds where the claimant was awarded $2.9 million (this amount was reduced on appeal) following hot coffee being spilt.) In such circumstances, the solicitor can refer the client to a specialist or seek the assistance of a barrister who is experienced in the area. However, the solicitor should be familiar with a basic outline of the law and procedure, and further details are supplied in the LPC Resource book *Civil Litigation* (Jordans).

16.6.1 Claims within the European Union

The main statute dealing with jurisdictional matters between Member States of the European Union (EU) is the Civil Jurisdiction and Judgments Act 1982 (CJJA 1982), which incorporates the Brussels Convention on Jurisdiction and the Enforcement of Judgments in Civil and Commercial Matters 1968 ('the Convention'). Reference should be made to CJJA 1982 when being instructed by a client who is considering bringing a claim within the European Union.

The Channel Islands and the Isle of Man are not part of the UK or EU, and, whilst the UK is a Member State of the EU, its internal jurisdiction includes England and Wales, Scotland and Northern Ireland.

If the defendant is domiciled in the EU then the basic rule is that he must be sued in his home court, ie where he is domiciled. However, where the action is based upon a tort, under Art 5(3) of the Convention there is jurisdiction in the courts of the country where the tort was committed or the State where the harm occurred (see *Handelskwekwerij GJ Bier BV v Mines de Potasse d'Alsace SA* [1978] QB 708). Therefore, if the client was injured in a road traffic accident in France by a French defendant, the claimant must sue the defendant in France. However, if a French manufacturer negligently makes a piece of machinery and sells it to an English customer who is harmed by a defect in England, the customer can sue in England where the harm occurred, or in France (where the defendant has its base).

If a claim is brought within another EU country then it must be remembered that there are many differences between the various legal systems of the Member States. For example, many European countries' judicial authorities have a far more inquisitorial role, with 'statutory settlement procedures' and obligations on the parties to participate in the judicial investigation if they wish to pursue a civil claim. The economics of pursuing the case also have to be considered. It also needs to be explained to the client that, in certain countries, costs are not recoverable from the defendant in addition to damages. For example, in France and Spain only limited costs are awarded in certain circumstances.

It must also be remembered that limitation periods differ between EU Member States, ranging from one to 30 years.

Consideration should be given as to which jurisdiction will give rise to the most satisfactory outcome for the client (often the highest level of damages is a significant factor). In *Edmunds v Simmonds* [2001] 1 WLR 1003, it was held that, despite the accident occurring in Spain, where both parties were English and the major heads of damages arose wholly in England, it was possible under Private International Law (Miscellaneous Provisions) Act 1995, s 12(1)(b) for English law to be the applicable law (see also *Hulse and Others v Chambers* (2001) *The Times*, July 13 relating to the quantification of damages being a matter of procedure and being governed by English law).

16.6.2 Claims outside the EU

The main non-European country where a personal injury solicitor may consider bringing proceedings is the USA. It is very likely that a US court will award a higher level of damages for a personal injury case than an English court, and this is the potential attraction of a US claim. As a consequence, any defendant is likely to object to the proceedings being taken in the USA and will seek to rely on the doctrine of *forum non conveniens* to show that an alternative forum is available and that private and public interests favour the case being dealt with outside the USA.

16.6.3 Package holidays

If an accident occurs whilst a client is on holiday, then consideration must be given to whether the holiday falls within the provisions of the Package Travel, Package Holidays and Package Tours Regulations 1992 as they might be able to provide the easiest form of remedy.

16.7 CONCLUSION

Some of the areas dealt with in this chapter arise infrequently in day-to-day practice, and reference must always be made to the appropriate Rules of Court and more specialist practitioner works. The aim of this chapter is simply to serve as an introduction to these topics and reference should be made to other sources including, for example, the Foreign Limitations Act 1984 and the Private International Law (Miscellaneous Provisions) Act 1995.

16.8 KEY POINTS

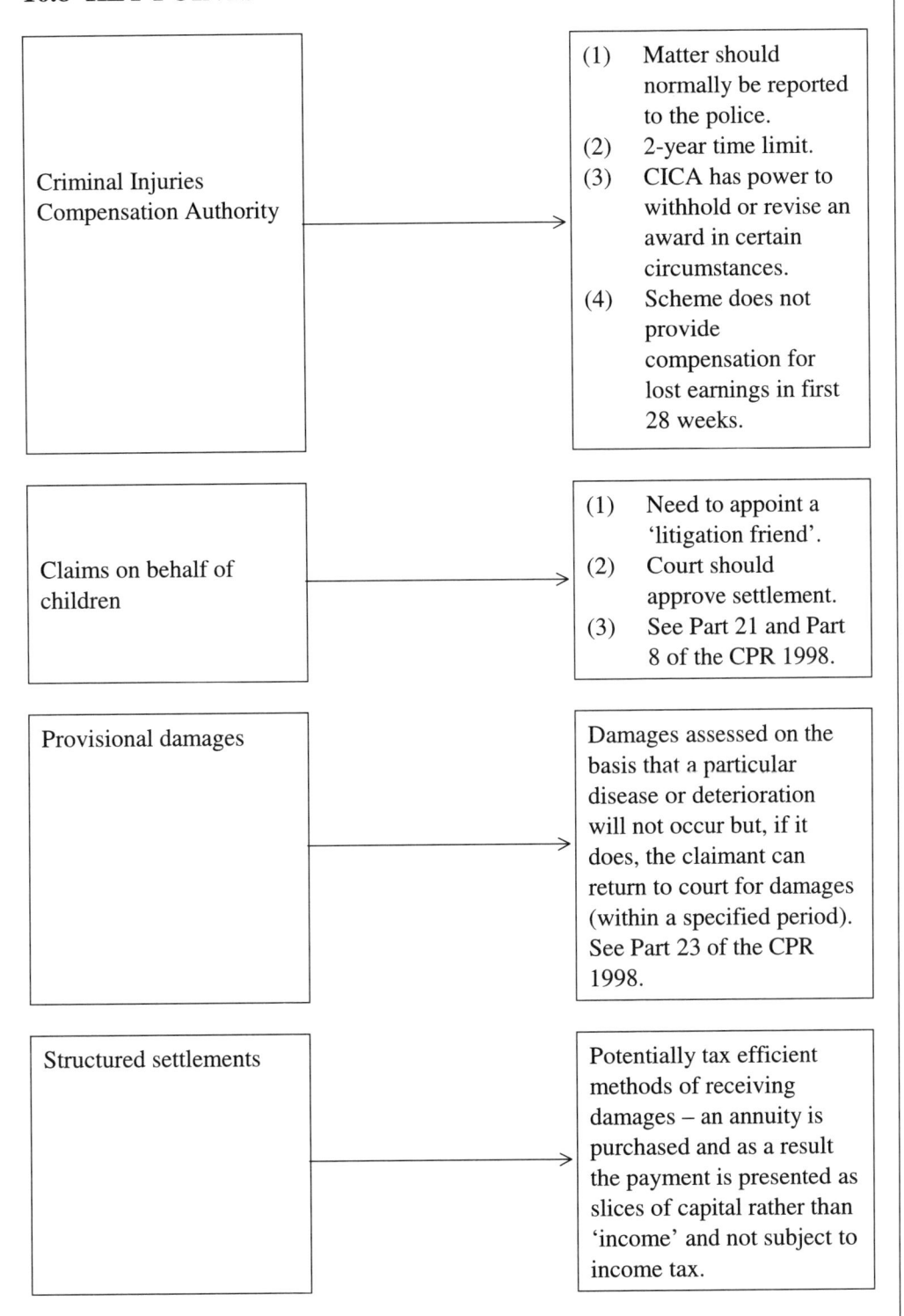

Criminal Injuries Compensation Authority	(1) Matter should normally be reported to the police. (2) 2-year time limit. (3) CICA has power to withhold or revise an award in certain circumstances. (4) Scheme does not provide compensation for lost earnings in first 28 weeks.
Claims on behalf of children	(1) Need to appoint a 'litigation friend'. (2) Court should approve settlement. (3) See Part 21 and Part 8 of the CPR 1998.
Provisional damages	Damages assessed on the basis that a particular disease or deterioration will not occur but, if it does, the claimant can return to court for damages (within a specified period). See Part 23 of the CPR 1998.
Structured settlements	Potentially tax efficient methods of receiving damages – an annuity is purchased and as a result the payment is presented as slices of capital rather than 'income' and not subject to income tax.

16.9 FURTHER READING

Kemp and Kemp *The Quantum of Damages* (Sweet & Maxwell).
Powers and Harris *Medical Negligence* (Butterworths).

APPENDICES

Appendix 1

CONDITIONAL FEE DOCUMENTS

Conditional Fee Protection Plan

> (explanatory leaflet and proposal form reproduced with the kind permission of Litigation Protection Limited)

Policy of Insurance

> (specimen policy reproduced with the kind permission of Litigation Protection Limited)

The Law Society's Conditional Fee Agreement

> (reproduced with the kind permission of The Law Society)

Conditional Fee Protection Plan

The first CFA insurance policy in the UK to cover all categories of cases

■ Provides cover for Opponent's legal costs and disbursements and the Assured's own disbursements from the start of the case

■ Covers cases where proceedings have already been issued

■ Free initial case consultation

■ No requirement to take out insurance on all cases

LITIGATION PROTECTION
LIMITED
Your experienced and innovative partner

The first Conditional Fee Agreement policy in the UK to cover all categories of cases

Litigation Protection Limited is recognised as the most experienced and innovative company in 'after the event' legal expenses insurance. LPL has provided insurance to meet the costs of a lost action, through its Litigation Insurance product, since 1993.

The introduction of Conditional Fees in 1995 saw the launch of the Conditional Fee Protection Plan to cover all classes of action allowed under the arrangements. LPL has developed these products and created a range of facilities for the challenges of the new civil justice regime.

LITIGATION PROTECTION
LIMITED

Conditional Fee Protection Plan

Solicitors and their clients can now use Conditional Fee or 'No win, no fee' Agreements for all money and damages claims. There are many opportunities, but also some difficulties, when working on this basis. Help is, however, now at hand for both Solicitors and their clients.

The Conditional Fee Protection Plan (CFPP), exclusively available from Litigation Protection Limited (LPL), takes care of the 'Buts', and offers your clients peace of mind knowing that they can initiate and pursue legal action to protect their rights, virtually free of the terrifying worry of enormous and unquantifiable expense.

The CFPP, essentially, is an insurance policy that complements a Conditional Fee Agreement already made between you and your client and that made with Counsel in appropriate cases, by providing an indemnity which can protect your client against some or all of the following risks:

■ **If the case is unsuccessful,** from having to pay:

- Any of the Opponent's Costs • Your client's Disbursements
- Own Counsel's fees • Expert Witnesses' fees.

■ **If your client wins the case in court** (optional cover):

- Being out of pocket on the legal costs through a shortfall in costs and damages awarded in your client's favour.

The Plan can also be used to provide a 'top-up' cover over any existing Legal Expenses Insurance which your client may have and provides a very useful option if the cover is insufficient.

WHY IS CFPP THE BEST?

CFPP offers your practice a unique combination of benefits:
- The most comprehensive Conditional Fee Insurance in the market
- Fast handling of enquiries and e-mail administration
- Access to instalment financing
- Invitation to a Partnership in RAIL - Risk Assessment in Litigation - a research project funded by the European Social Fund
- 100% Lloyd's security.

FURTHER BENEFITS

MODERN COMMUNICATIONS
Save time and save money on your case administration. LPL is at the cutting edge of after-the-event insurance products and actively encourage Solicitors utilising the CFPP to contact LPL using e-mail and the Internet. Utilising the latest technology will enable us all to reduce the paperwork associated with most insurances, saving you time and money.

SECURITY FOR COSTS
One of the many benefits of the CFPP for commercial clients is that the policy can be used to satisfy the court in respect of an order for security for costs, although this may require a bond to be issued. LPL can arrange this for an additional premium.

RISK ASSESSMENT
When working with CFAs, it is essential that your risk assessment capability is fully developed. It is one of the cornerstones of profitable and effective use of CFAs. If you are unhappy or uncertain about risk assessment, Workshops are organised by LPL at its Training Centre to develop these skills. We work with your staff in a professional partnership offering expert advice and tuition. A comprehensive Compendium of Conditional Fee Agreements will be available shortly from LPL - covering a wide selection of case categories, not just personal injury matters. Another opportunity that may well be of interest is the 'Risk Assessment in Litigation' project - details of this project are on page 8 of this brochure.

Conditional Fee Protection Plan

HOW DOES THE CFPP WORK?

When discussing the options with your client, you will, as required under practice rule 15, have spoken about the availability of insurance to cover any liability your client may have for the Opponent's Costs. Assuming that you enter into a CFA at or near the time of instruction, we expect you to apply for the CFPP within three months. Insurance is available outside these times (indeed all the way up to trial!) but a different premium may apply to those shown in our 'Premium Calculator' on page 5 - we will provide a precise quotation following assessment of the case.

To apply for cover, what we need from you is a completed proposal form (supplies available on request) together with enough information to enable us to assess the prospects of the case - depending on the stage of the case this will often be a statement from the client or a summary of the case prepared by you. If you are unsure about what to send us, please telephone LPL at the time of completing the proposal form. If you send the cheque with the proposal form we can issue the policy document following assessment - usually within 48 hours.

An assessment fee of £425 is payable on all Clinical Negligence and £295 on non-Personal Injury cases, although this amount is deducted from the Premium if the insurance is taken out. The assessment fee *does not* apply to Personal Injury cases unless the cover required is in excess of £50,000. Once the case has been approved for insurance by its Underwriters, LPL will provide a quotation.

As soon as we have received your instruction to proceed we will process the proposal and will send you the policy document confirming that your client is covered against the risks selected in the proposal form.

WHO CAN TAKE OUT A PLAN?

The CFPP can be taken out by almost anyone; private individuals, groups of individuals and firms, as well as professional practitioners such as Administrators, Liquidators and Receivers.

The major criterion is that a Conditional Fee Agreement must be completed and must be maintained throughout the duration of the legal action. There are no pre-requisites for you to fulfil before using the CFPP, e.g. no need to be a member of the Personal Injury, Clinical Negligence or any other Panels.

Conditional Fee Protection Plan

HOW MUCH COVER IS AVAILABLE AND WHAT DOES IT COST?

We believe the CFPP is both comprehensive and cost-effective and provides your client with the level of protection needed when pursuing a claim.

If you lose your case, the Conditional Fee Protection Plan under Standard Cover provides the following:

- Cover for having to pay Opponent's legal Costs and Disbursements
- Cover for Own Disbursements
- Cover for Own Counsel's Fees, unless under a CFA (unlike many other insurance policies)
- Cover for Expert Witnesses to attend the trial.

Optional cover is available for 'Deficiency of Damages' which covers any shortfall between costs charged to your client and the actual costs and damages paid by the Opponent when the case is won. The amount of cover provided under this section is 25% of the Limit of Indemnity selected and the premium payable is 25% of the premium payable for the Standard Cover.

In every case, the CFPP is retrospective - that means if you have already started acting for a client, the policy will protect the client's position regarding liability for Own Disbursements and Opponent's Costs and Disbursements incurred prior to the policy being issued. We do not believe you will find a more comprehensive insurance package anywhere in the market.

As a guide we have shown standard premium levels of cover, although we can provide quotations for cover to suit an individual case and can arrange cover up to £5,000,000 if required. Please indicate on the proposal form the level of cover required.

If, as the case progresses, the Limit of Indemnity selected proves to be inadequate, we may be able to help you purchase additional cover. The premium required for additional cover will depend on a number of factors including the stage that the case has reached. We will provide a quotation in each case.

Premium financing arrangements are available to pay the Premium over ten months at a service charge of 10%. LPL has made arrangements with Singer and Friedlander Insurance Finance, part of a major City based commercial bank, to provide funding facilities for both Solicitors and their clients. Please contact us for an application form.

Conditional Fee Protection Plan

PREMIUM CALCULATOR

These are a guide only and may vary according to each case

Limit of Indemnity Per Claim	Personal Injury (excl. Clinical Negligence & Special Category PI)	Special Category PI Post Traumatic Stress Disorder, RSI, Ind Disease etc	Clinical Negligence	Insolvency	All Other Cases
£10,000	£250	£450	£1,425	£1,500	From 10% of the amount of cover selected
£25,000	£500	£950	£2,500	£3,375	
£50,000	£1,000	£1,800	£5,000	£6,750	
£100,000	£2,000	£3,150	£10,000	£13,500	

NOTES
1. Insurance Premium Tax (IPT) at the prevailing rate is payable on all premiums
2. All cases are individually underwritten and Underwriters reserve the right to vary the premium or terms and conditions
3. Changes to the policy after the date of issue may be subject to a £25 administration fee.

WHAT ARE THE CLIENT'S OBLIGATIONS AND ARE THERE ANY LIMITATIONS?

The plan has been kept simple and there are very few 'exclusions', but so that there may be no misunderstandings:

- The client must have, and maintain, a Conditional Fee Agreement with you for the CFPP to remain in force
- The client must not change Solicitors after the CFPP is in force, without our agreement
- The client must co-operate fully with you during the case. If the client does not co-operate and this results in increased costs, we may withhold that amount from any claim, or in certain circumstances the policy would become void
- You must tell us of any payments or any material change in circumstances affecting the case
- The Plan does not cover you if you win and your Opponent does not pay the damages and costs awarded in your favour.

CONDUCT OF THE LEGAL PROCEEDINGS

The actual conduct of the legal proceedings will be entirely your responsibility. We expect only to be kept informed of the progress of the case.

As mentioned earlier, one of the many benefits of the CFPP for commercial clients is that the policy can be used to satisfy the court in respect of an order for security for costs, although this may require a bond to be issued which we can arrange for an additional premium.

WHAT HAPPENS WHEN THE CASE ENDS?

If your client wins, the Opponent will usually be ordered to pay your client's damages, Costs and Disbursements.

If your client loses, they pay nothing further. The Opponent's legal Costs and Disbursements and your Own Disbursements are paid by the CFPP policy.

THE POWER BEHIND THE CONDITIONAL FEE PROTECTION PLAN

The CFPP has been devised by Litigation Protection Limited which introduced the first Conditional Fees Insurance to the UK in 1995 and is recognised as the market leader in the rapidly developing 'after the event' insurance market.

LPL offers a wide range of legal expenses insurance policies, most are underwritten 100% in the most prestigious insurance market in the world - Lloyd's, London; others by certain specialist companies.

Conditional Fee Protection Plan

ANY QUESTIONS?

The CFPP is a simple, efficient and cost-effective means of enabling individuals, groups of individuals, companies, organisations and their professional advisors to achieve a just and fair result to their dispute, with minimal risk and at affordable cost.

If you require further information before completing the proposal form, please do not hesitate to contact our Customer Services Department on:

Telephone: 01903 883 911
Facsimile: 01903 885 911
E-mail: info@litigationprotection.co.uk

WHAT SHOULD I DO NOW?

Once you have agreed to enter into a Conditional Fee Agreement with your client, please complete and sign the proposal form. The client should also sign it.

Send the completed proposal form, together with:
For Personal Injury Cases requiring cover of up to £50,000:
■ Your cheque for the appropriate premium plus IPT
or
For all Clinical Negligence Cases, non-Personal Injury Cases and Personal Injury Cases requiring cover of over £50,000:
■ Completed proposal form
■ Assessment Fee £295 or £425 for Clinical Negligence

Cheques should be made payable to Litigation Protection Limited and sent to:

Litigation Protection Limited
Arundel Court
Park Bottom
Arundel
West Sussex
BN18 0AA
DX: 86906 Arundel

A copy of the proposal form should be retained by the client.

YOUR PRACTICE MAY ALSO BE INTERESTED IN

ACCESS TO JUSTICE ACCREDITATION

As the Lord Chancellor said recently

"The quality of legal services people receive is often depressingly poor. The large number of complaints which the Office for the Supervision of Solicitors received is testimony to the public's dissatisfaction."

In order to provide a quality standard which anyone can recognise, LPL has introduced the 'Access to Justice Accreditation'. This detailed but efficient Accreditation process means that your firm can join the elite in the litigation market and become a fully fledged partner with LPL. In the future, this vital kitemark will ensure an improved flow of quality business.

The scheme is available only to Solicitor firms who accept the quality control requirements imposed by the comprehensive Accreditation Procedure. This procedure is required as assurance to the Underwriters and SFIF or Investec as well as by ourselves, if we are to recommend clients to utilise your practice's services.

First you will need to apply to join the LPL 'List of Accredited Solicitors'. To become an LPL Accredited practice, an Application Form and Initial Questionnaire will need to be completed. Once these have been reviewed it will be followed by a visit to your premises by LPL's Accreditation team in order to be taken through your financial and case management procedures, and your current/proposed IT facilities. The final step will involve a financial status report on the practice by SFIF or Investec. For information, please contact LPL at their Head Office.

RISK ASSESSMENT IN LITIGATION (RAIL)

RAIL is a research programme funded by the European Social Fund to investigate methods of evaluating the risks in litigation. The project is now up and running and will run for one year. The first stage is to examine existing methods of risk assessment by extensive interviews and case studies with litigators across a broad range of experience and fields of activity.

Prompted by the extension of CFAs to all money and damages claims and the changes to legal aid, the project has a wide ranging remit to investigate risk assessment in any area of litigation.

Your participation in the research would be very welcome. If you would like more information contact the project director, David Chalk on 01903 883811, or via e-mail: d.j.chalk@anglia.ac.uk

Appendix 1

Conditional Fee Protection Plan   LITIGATION PROTECTION

NOTES: This Proposal will be considered by the Underwriters to assist in the assessment of the Proceedings or proposed Proceedings.
The completion of this Proposal does not bind either the Insurers or the Proposer to any contract of insurance. It is important that all questions are answered completely and accurately and that all relevant information which may affect the Underwriters' decision on the Proposal are disclosed. Any failure to do so may invalidate the Policy. In the event of the Policy being issued pursuant to this Proposal, the Proposal form, together with the Policy wording shall constitute the Policy contract. A copy of the Policy wording is available upon request.
This Proposal should be completed jointly by the Proposer and his/her Legal Adviser, and be signed by both of them.

THE ASSURED

1. Name
2. Address

   Postcode   Tel No

3. Legal Status: Company/Firm/Organisation/Individual (delete as appropriate)

4. If Individual, Date of Birth

5. If Company/Firm/Organisation (a) Date established   (b) Company Reg No

   (c) Annual income or turnover (approx) £

6. Party in this action: Claimant/Defendant (delete as appropriate)

THE APPOINTED REPRESENTATIVE

7. Firm

   Address

   Postcode   DX

   Tel No   Email address

8. Supervising Partner

9. Fee Earner

10. Are you a member of LawNet? YES ☐   NO ☐

THE OPPONENT

11. Name

12. Legal Status: Company/Firm/Organisation/Individual (delete as appropriate)

13. Please provide name of Solicitors acting (if known)

14. Is Opponent insured? YES ☐   NO ☐   DO NOT KNOW ☐

15. If Yes, name of Insurer

DETAILS OF CLAIM

16. Date of Incident

17. Date Instructed

18. Please enclose   Client Statement ☐   OR   Statement of Case ☐

19. Amount in dispute/damages expected to be recovered:

   General Damages £ _____ (approx)   Special Damages £ _____ (approx)

20. Details of injury/damage/loss

21. Current state of proceedings:

   (a) Have proceedings been issued?   YES ☐ NO ☐   If Yes, when _____
   (b) Has defence been received?   YES ☐ NO ☐
   (c) Is there a counterclaim?   YES ☐ NO ☐

   (d) Please give trial date/window allocated

   If not allocated, please estimate date

   (e) Have any Part 36 offers or payments been received?   YES ☐ NO ☐   If Yes, for how much? £ _____

   (f) Have you made a Part 36 offer?   YES ☐ NO ☐   If Yes, for how much? £ _____

22. If you have received any correspondence from the Opponent/Solicitor/Insurers which details the reason for your client's claim being disputed, please enclose copies   ENCLOSED ☐   NOT AVAILABLE ☐

CASE ASSESSMENT

23. **Own Costs**   **Total Estimated Costs up to and including Trial**

   Solicitor's Costs   £
   Counsel's Fees   £
   Disbursements incl. Expert Witness Fees   £
   Total   £

   Are any of these costs covered by Legal Aid or another insurer?   YES ☐ NO ☐

   If Yes, please give figure   £

24. **Opponent's Costs**

   If you expect these to be greater than your Own Costs, please estimate a total figure (including disbursements)   £

   If applicable, please explain why you expect a difference

25. Hourly rate being charged to your client (not including success fee) £ [   ]

26. Is this figure recoverable on assessment? YES ☐ NO ☐

27. Have any adverse costs awards been made? YES ☐ NO ☐
    If Yes, please provide details separately ENCLOSED ☐

28. Please give prospects of success (%) <50 ☐ 50-60 ☐ 60-70 ☐ 70-80 ☐ >80 ☐

29. How has this case been funded to date? Privately ☐   By another insurer ☐
                                             Legal Aid ☐   CFA from beginning ☐
    If not CFA from beginning, why is a CFA being offered now?

    [   ]

30. (a) Has an application for insurance in respect of this incident been made to another insurer? YES ☐ NO ☐

    (b) Has this application been declined by another insurer? YES ☐ NO ☐

    (c) Has the Legal Aid Board refused to support this claim? YES ☐ NO ☐
    (If yes to any of above, please give full details on a separate sheet)

THE CONDITIONAL FEE AGREEMENT

31. Please give date of CFA or confirm that a CFA will be entered into if the insurance is granted [   ]

32. Amount of success fee (%) [   ]

33. Have you consulted Counsel regarding this claim? YES ☐ NO ☐

    If Yes, please give name of Counsel [   ]

34. Is Counsel providing his/her services under a CFA? YES ☐ NO ☐

35. Is an Advice from Counsel available? YES ☐ NO ☐ If Yes, please forward *all* available Advices

FUNDING (Only applicable for premiums over £1,000)

Do you want to pay the premium by instalments? YES ☐ NO ☐
(10 payments over 10 months, Service charge 10%, APR 29.1%)

INSURANCE REQUIRED

Sections Required   **Category of Case**   **Limit of Indemnity**   **Premium**
                              eg personal injury, contractual dispute etc

Section A
Opponent's Costs and   Min. £10,000 [   ]   £ [   ]
Disbursements and Assured's   £25,000   [   ]   £ [   ]
own Disbursements   £50,000   [   ]   £ [   ]
                                                                        £100,000   [   ]   £ [   ]
*NB Disbursements includes Counsel's
Fees and Experts' Fees.*   Other   £ BY QUOTATION

NB Some case premiums are by quotation. We will provide full details following the case assessment.

Section B
Deficiency of Damages   YES ☐ NO ☐

                                            If required, add 25% of Section A £ [   ]

                                                          Premium Payable £ [   ]

                                            Add Insurance PremiumTax at 5% £ [   ]

                                                                    Total £ [   ]

IMPORTANT – ENCLOSURES

- Premium cheque ☐
- Client Statement OR Statement of Case ☐
- Substantive correspondence from Opponent/Solicitors/Insurers ☐
- Pleadings ☐
- Assessment Fee (not applicable to Personal Injury cases requiring up to £50,000 cover) ☐
- Counsel's opinion re: liability and/or quantum ☐
- Expert's reports ☐

DECLARATION BY PROPOSER

1. I declare that the contents of this Proposal Form are true to the best of my knowledge and belief and agree that the contents of the Proposal Form will form the basis of the Policy of Insurance issued.
2. I authorise the Appointed Representative to give to the Underwriters, financing institutions and their representatives all such information as they may require and I agree that the Appointed Representative may give information to Underwriters and financing institutions notwithstanding that this would otherwise be in breach of privilege and a duty of confidentiality owed to me.
3. I agree to the Appointed Representative giving the irrevocable undertaking set out in the Declaration below.

Signed _____

Name _____ Date _____

DECLARATION BY APPOINTED REPRESENTATIVE

1. I declare that the information set out above is true to the best of my knowledge and belief.
2. I certify that in my judgment, the Proposer has at least a 50% prospect of success and I am not aware of any other facts affecting the Proposer's prospects of success in the Proceedings or the prospects of a judgment in the Proceedings being successfully enforced.
3. If a Policy is issued by the Underwriters then in consideration of the issue of such Policy, I irrevocably undertake that I will immediately advise the Insurers in writing of:
   (a) the date on which the Proceedings are set down for Trial;
   (b) the date of the trial/trial window;
   (c) the cessation of the case;
   (d) the discovery of any fact or evidence or other matter materially affecting the Proposer's prospects of success in the Proceedings or the prospects of any judgment in the Proceedings being successfully enforced; or,
   (e) any failure by the Proposer to provide instructions or otherwise co-operate in the conduct of the Proceedings, or any requirement by the Proposer for the case to be conducted unreasonably or so as to incur an unjustifiable expense.
4. In addition to the above I undertake to keep Insurers informed of the progress of the Proposer's case and of any offer of settlement, payment into Court, Part 36 offer made or received, or changes affecting the prospects of success.
5. I will give the Underwriters, financing institutions and their representatives all such information as they require notwithstanding that this would otherwise be in breach of privilege and a duty of confidentiality owed to the Proposer.

Signed _____

Name _____ Date _____

LITIGATION PROTECTION
LIMITED

Litigation Protection Limited
Arundel Court, Park Bottom,
Arundel, West Sussex, BN18 0AA
Telephone: 01903 883911
Facsimile: 01903 885911
DX: 86906 Arundel
City Office: 69/70 Mark Lane,
London EC3R 7HS Tel: 0171 488 9080
Web site: www.litigationprotection.co.uk
e-mail: info@litigationprotection.co.uk

A member of the Access to Justice 2000 Group
Registered in England No. 2724102
The Conditional Fee Protection Plan is
underwritten by certain Underwriters at
Lloyd's, London

007/12/99/A

The brochure and a copy of the completed Proposal form should be retained by the Proposer for his/her records.
The Proposal form together with the Policy wording shall constitute the Policy contract.
A copy of the Policy wording is available upon request.

The Law Society Conditional Fee Agreement (for use in personal injury cases (non-clinical negligence))

Conditional Fee Agreement

For use in personal injury cases, but not clinical negligence

This agreement is a binding legal contract between you and your solicitor/s. Before you sign, please read everything carefully.

Words like 'our disbursements', 'basic charges', 'win' and 'lose' are explained in condition 3 of the Law Society Conditions which you should also read carefully.

Agreement date

[……………………………..]

I/We, the solicitor/s [……………………………………………………………………..]

You, the client [……………………………………………………………………………..]

What is covered by this agreement

- Your claim against […………………………..] for damages for personal injury suffered on […………………………..].
- Any appeal by your opponent.
- Any appeal you make against an interim order during the proceedings.
- Any proceedings you take to enforce a judgment, order or agreement.

What is not covered by this agreement

- Any counterclaim against you.
- Any appeal you make against the final judgment order.

Paying us

If you win your claim, you pay our basic charges, our disbursements and a success fee. The amount of these is not based on or limited by the damages. You are entitled to seek recovery from your opponent of part or all of our basic charges, our disbursements, a success fee and insurance premium. Please also see conditions 4 and 6.

It may be that your opponent makes a Part 36 offer or payment which you reject and, on our advice, your claim for damages goes ahead to trial where you recover damages that are less than that offer or payment. We will not add our success fee to the basic charges for the work done after we received notice of the offer or payment.

If you receive interim damages, we may require you to pay our disbursements at that point and a reasonable amount for our future disbursements.

If you receive provisional damages, we are entitled to payment of our basic charges our disbursements and success fee at that point.

If you win but on the way lose an interim hearing, you may be required to pay your opponent's charges of that hearing. Please see conditions 3(h) and 5.

If on the way to winning or losing you win an interim hearing, then we are entitled to payment of our basic charges and disbursements related to that hearing together with a success fee on those charges if you win overall.

If you lose, you pay your opponent's charges and disbursements. You may be able to take out an insurance policy against this risk. Please also see conditions 3(j) and 5. If you lose, you do not pay our charges but we may require you to pay our disbursements.

If you end this agreement before you win or lose, you pay our basic charges. If you go on to win, you pay a success fee. Please also see condition 7(a).

We may end this agreement before you win or lose. Please also see condition 7(b) for details.

Basic charges

These are for work done from now until this agreement ends.

How we calculate our basic charges

These are calculated for each hour engaged on your matter [from now until the review date on [...]...]. Routine letters and telephone calls will be charged as units of one tenth of an hour. Other letters and telephone calls will be charged on a time basis. The hourly rates are:

- Solicitors with over four years' experience after qualification
  £ [............]
- Other solicitors and legal executives and other staff of equivalent experience
  £ [............]
- Trainee solicitors and other staff of equivalent experience
  £ [............]

[We will review the hourly rate on the review date and on each anniversary of the review date. We will not increase the rate by more than the rise in the Retail Prices Index and will notify you of the increased rate in writing.]

Success fee

This is [......]% of our basic charges

The reasons for calculating the success fee at this level are set out in Schedule 1 to this agreement.

You cannot recover from your opponent the part of the success fee that relates to the cost to us of postponing receipt of our charges and disbursements (as set out at paragraphs (a) and (b) at Schedule 1). This part of the success fee remains payable by you.

Value added tax (VAT)

We add VAT, at the rate (now [.........]%) that applies when the work is done, to the total of the basic charges and success fee.

Law Society Conditions

The Law Society Conditions are attached because they are part of this agreement. Any amendments or additions to them will apply to you. You should read the conditions carefully and ask us about anything you find unclear.

Other points

Immediately before you signed this agreement, we verbally explained to you the effect of this agreement and in particular the following:

(a)   the circumstances in which you may be liable to pay our disbursements and charges;

(b) the circumstances in which you may seek assessment of our charges and disbursements and the procedure for doing so;
(c) whether we consider that your risk of becoming liable for any costs in these proceedings is insured under an existing contract of insurance;
(d) other methods of financing those costs, including private funding, Community Legal Service funding, legal expenses insurance, trade union funding;
(e)(i) In all the circumstances, on the information currently available to us, we believe that a contract of insurance with [……………………..] is appropriate. Detailed reasons for this are set out in Schedule 2.
(e)(ii) In any event, we believe it is desirable for you to insure your opponent's charges and disbursements in case you lose.
(e)(iii) We confirm that we do not have an interest in recommending this particular insurance agreement.

Signatures

Signed for the solicitor/s

Signed by the client

I confirm that my solicitor has verbally explained to me the matters in paragraphs (a) to (e) under 'Other points' above.

Signed……………………………………………………………………..(Client)

I specifically confirm that I verbally explained to the client the matters in paragraphs (a) to (e) under 'Other points' and confirm the matters at (e) in writing in Schedule 2.

Signed……………………………………………………………………(Solicitors)

This agreement complies with the Conditional Fee Agreements Regulations 2000 (S.I.2000 No.692).

Schedule 1

The Success Fee

The success fee is set at [………..]% of basic charges and cannot be more than 100% of the basic charges.

The percentage reflects the following:

(a) the fact that if you win we will not be paid our basic charges until the end of the claim;
(b) our arrangements with you about paying disbursements;
(c) the fact that if you lose, we will not earn anything;

(d) our assessment of the risks of your case. These include the following:

(e) any other appropriate matters.

The matters set out at paragraphs (a) and (b) above together make up [......]% of the increase on basic charges. The matters at paragraphs (c), (d) [and (e)] make up [.......]% of the increase on basic charges. So the total success fee is [.........]% as stated above.

Schedule 2

The Insurance Policy

In all the circumstances and on the information currently available to us, we believe, that a contract of insurance with [................] is appropriate to cover your opponent's charges and disbursements in case you lose.

This is because

We are not, however, insurance brokers and cannot give advice on all products which may be available.

Law Society Conditions

1. Our responsibilities

We must:

- always act in your best interests, subject to our duty to the court;
- explain to you the risks and benefits of taking legal action;
- give you our best advice about whether to accept any offer of settlement;
- give you the best information possible about the likely costs of your claim for damages.

2. Your responsibilities

You must:

- give us instructions that allow us to do our work properly;
- not ask us to work in an improper or unreasonable way;
- not deliberately mislead us;
- co-operate with us;
- go to any medical or expert examination or court hearing.

3. Explanation of words used

(a) *Advocacy*
Appearing for you at court hearings.

(b) *Basic charges*
Our charges for the legal work we do on your claim for damages.

(c) *Claim*
Your demand for damages for personal injury whether or not court proceedings are issued.

(d) Counterclaim
A claim that your opponent makes against you in response to your claim.

(e) Damages
Money that you win whether by a court decision or settlement.

(f) Our disbursements
Payment we make on your behalf such as:

- court fees;
- experts' fees;
- accident report fees;
- travelling expenses.

(g) *Interim damages*
Money that a court says your opponent must pay or your opponent agrees to pay while waiting for a settlement or the court's final decision.

(h) *Interim hearing*
A court hearing that is not final.

(i) *Lien*
Our right to keep all papers, documents, money or other property held on your behalf until all money due to us is paid. A lien may be applied after this agreement ends.

(j) *Lose*
The court has dismissed your claim or you have stopped it on our advice.

(k) *Part 36 offers or payments*
An offer to settle your claim made in accordance with Part 36 of the Civil Procedure Rules.

(l) *Provisional damages*
Money that a court says your opponent must pay or your opponent agrees to pay, on the basis that you will be able to go back to court at a future date for further damages if:

- you develop a serious disease; or
- your condition deteriorates;

in a way that has been proved or admitted to be linked to your personal injury claim.

(m) *Success fee*
The percentage of basic charges that we add to your bill if you win your claim for damages and that we will seek to recover from your opponent.

(n) *Win*
Your claim for damages is finally decided in your favour, whether by a court decision or an agreement to pay you damages. 'Finally' means that your opponent:

- is not allowed to appeal against the court decision; or
- has not appealed in time; or
- has lost any appeal.

4. What happens if you win?

If you win:

- You are then liable to pay all our basic charges, our disbursements and success fee – please see condition 3(n).
- Normally, you will be entitled to recover part or all of our basic charges, our disbursements and success fee from your opponent.
- If you and your opponent cannot agree the amount, the court will decide how much you can recover. If the amount agreed or allowed by the court does not cover all our basic charges and our disbursements, then you pay the difference.
- You will not be entitled to recover from your opponent the part of the success fee that relates to the cost to us of postponing receipt of our charges and our disbursements. This remains payable by you.

- You agree that after winning, the reasons for setting the success fee at the amount stated may be disclosed:
    (i) to the court and any other person required by the court;
    (ii) to your opponent in order to gain his or her agreement to pay the success fee.
- If the court carries out an assessment and disallows any of the success fee percentage because it is unreasonable in view of what we knew or should have known when it was agreed, then that amount ceases to be payable unless the court is satisfied that it should continue to be payable.
- If we agree with your opponent that the success fee is to be paid at a lower percentage than is set out in this agreement, then the success fee percentage will be reduced accordingly unless the court is satisfied that the full amount is payable.
- It may happen that your opponent makes an offer that includes payment of our basic charges and a success fee. If so, unless we consent, you agree not to tell us to accept the offer if it includes payment of the success fee at a lower rate than is set out in this agreement.
- If your opponent is receiving Community Legal Service funding, we are unlikely to get any money from him or her. So if this happens, you have to pay us our basic charges, disbursements and success fee.

You remain ultimately responsible for paying our success fee.

You agree to pay into a designated account any cheque received by you or by us from your opponent and made payable to you. Out of the money, you agree to let us take the balance of the basic charges; success fee; insurance premium; our remaining disbursements; and VAT. You take the rest.

We are allowed to keep any interest your opponent pays on the charges.

Payment for advocacy is explained in condition 6.

If your opponent fails to pay

If your opponent does not pay any damages or charges owed to you, we have the right to take recovery action in your name to enforce a judgment, order or agreement. The charges of this action become part of the basic charges.

5. What happens if you lose?

If you lose, you do not have to pay any of our basic charges or success fee. You do have to pay:

- us for our disbursements;
- your opponent's legal charges and disbursements.

If you are insured against payment of these amounts by your insurance policy, we will make a claim on your behalf and receive any resulting payment in your name. We will give you a statement of account for all money received and paid out.

If your opponent pays the charges of any hearing, they belong to us.

Payment for advocacy is dealt with in condition 6.

6. Payment for advocacy

The cost of advocacy and any other work by us, or by any solicitor agent on our behalf, forms part of our basic charges. We shall discuss with you the identity of any barrister instructed, and the arrangements made for payment.

Barristers who have a conditional fee agreement with us

If you win, you are normally entitled to recover their fee and success fee from your opponent. The barrister's success fee is shown in the separate conditional fee agreement we make with the barrister. We will discuss the barrister's success fee with you before we instruct him or her. If you lose, you pay the barrister nothing.

Barristers who do not have a conditional fee agreement with us

If you win, then you will normally be entitled to recover all or part of their fee from your opponent. If you lose, then you must pay their fee.

7. What happens when this agreement ends before your claim for damages ends?

(a) Paying us if you end this agreement

You can end the agreement at any time. We then have the right to decide whether you must:

- pay our basic charges and our disbursements including barristers' fees when we ask for them; or
- pay our basic charges, and our disbursements including barristers' fees and success fees if you go on to win your claim for damages.

(b) Paying us if we end this agreement

(i) We can end this agreement if you do not keep to your responsibilities in condition 2. We then have the right to decide whether you must:

- pay our basic charges and our disbursements including barristers' fees when we ask for them; or
- pay our basic charges and our disbursements including barristers' fees and success fees if you go on to win your claim for damages.

(ii) We can end this agreement if we believe you are unlikely to win. If this happens, you will only have to pay our disbursements. These will include barristers' fees if the barrister does not have a conditional fee agreement with us.

(iii) We can end this agreement if you reject our opinion about making a settlement with your opponent. You must then:

- pay the basic charges and our disbursements, including barristers' fees;
- pay the success fee if you go on to win your claim for damages.

If you ask us to get a second opinion from a specialist solicitor outside our firm, we will do so. You pay the cost of a second opinion.

(iv) We can end this agreement if you do not pay your insurance premium when asked to do so.

(c) Death

This agreement automatically ends if you die before your claim for damages is concluded. We will be entitled to recover our basic charges up to the date of your death from your estate.

If your personal representatives wish to continue your claim for damages, we may offer them a new conditional fee agreement, as long as they agree to pay the success fee on our basic charges from the beginning of the agreement with you.

8. What happens after this agreement ends

After this agreement ends, we will apply to have our name removed from the record of any court proceedings in which we are acting unless you have another form of funding and ask us to work for you.

We have the right to preserve our lien unless another solicitor working for you undertakes to pay us what we are owed including a success fee if you win.

Notes for Accident Line Protect cases

For Accident Line Protect cases, you need to annex the following clause to the agreement

'Accident Line Protect insurance (ALP)

Accident Line Protect is an insurance policy only made available to you by solicitors who have joined the Accident Line Protect scheme.

You agree to pay a premium of £[……………………] for Accident Line Protect Insurance when you sign this agreement. We undertake to send this to the broker on your behalf. If you lose after proceedings have been issued, Accident Line Protect will cover our disbursements and your opponent's charges and disbursements. It will not cover fees to your barristers or advocates. The maximum cover is £100,000.

If this agreement ends before your claim for damages ends, Accident Line Protect ends automatically at the same time.'

Appendix 2

MEDICAL INFORMATION

Common abbreviations used in medical records

COMMON ABBREVIATIONS USED IN MEDICAL RECORDS

AAL	Anterior axillary line
ACTH	Adrenocorticotrophic hormone
ADH	Antidiuretic hormone
AE	Air entry
AF	Atrial fibrillation
AFB	Acid fast bacillus (TB)
AFP	Alpha-fetoprotein
AJ	Ankle jerk (reflex)
Alk	Alkaline (phos = phosphatase)
An	Anaemia
ANF	Antinuclear factor
Anti-D	This gamma globulin must be given by injection to Rhesus negative mother who delivers/aborts Rhesus positive child/fetus to prevent mother developing antibodies which could damage a subsequent Rhesus positive baby
Apgar	Apgar score: means of recording baby's condition at and shortly after birth by observing and 'scoring' (0, 1 or 2) 5 parameters
AP	Anteroposterior
APH	Antepartum haemorrhage
ARM	Artificial rupture of membranes (labour)
ASO	Antistreptolysin O
ATN	Acute tubular necrosis
A/V	(i) Anteverted (ii) Arterio venous
AXR	Abdominal X-ray (plain)
Ba	Barium
BD	To be given/taken twice a day
BJ	Biceps jerk (reflex, see AJ)
BMJ	British Medical Journal
BMR	Basal metabolic rate
BO	Bowels open
BP	British Pharmacopoeia
BP	Blood pressure
BS	(i) Breath sounds (ii) Bowel sounds (iii) Blood sugar

C_2H_5OH	Alcohol
ca	Carcinoma/cancer
Ca	Calcium
Caps	Capsules
CAT scan	Computed axial tomograph scan
CBD	Common bile duct
cc	(i) Carcinoma (cancer) (ii) Cubic centimetre
CCF	Congestive cardiac failure
Ch VS	Chorionic villus sampling
CI	Contraindications
Cl	Clubbing (of finger or toe nails)
CLL	Chronic lymphocytic leukaemia
CML	Chronic myeloid leukaemia
CMV	Cytomegalovirus
CN I-XII	Cranial nerves 1 – 12
CNS	Central nervous system
C/O	Complaining of
CO_2	Carbon dioxide
COETT	Cuffed oral endotracheal tube
COT	Cuffed oral tube (an endotracheal tube used for ventilating a patient who cannot breath unaided)
CPD	Cephalo-pelvic disproportion (baby too large to fit through pelvis)
CSF	Cerebro-spinal fluid
CT	Computerised tomography
CTG	Cardiotocograph (trace during labour of baby's heart and mother's contractions)
CVA	Cardiovascular accident (stroke)
CVP	Central venous pressure
CVS	Cardiovascular system
Cx	Cervix
CXR	Chest X-ray
Cy	Cyanosis
DB	Decibel
D&C	Dilation (cervical) and curettage
DM	Diabetes mellitus

DNA	Deoxyribonucleic acid (also 'did not attend')
DOA	Dead on arrival
D&V	Diarrhoea and vomiting
DVT	Deep venous thrombosis
D/W	Discussed with
Dx	Diagnosis
ECG	Electrocardiography
ECT	Electroconvulsive therapy
EDC	Expected date of confinement
EDD	Expected date of delivery
EEG	Electroencephalogram/graph (brain scan)
ENT	Ear, nose and throat
ERCP	Endoscopic retrograde choledochopancreatico/graphy/scope
ERPC	Evacuation of retained products of conception
ESR	Erythrocyte sedimentation rate (blood)
ETR	Examined through clothes
EtoH	Alcohol
ET(T)	Endotracheal (tube)
EUA	Examined under anaesthesia
FB	(i) Finger's breadth (ii) Foreign body
FBC	Full blood count
FBS	Fetal blood sampling (a procedure which is carried out during labour to check on the baby's condition)
FH	Family history
FHH	Fetal heart heard
FHHR	Fetal heart heard regular
FHR	Fetal heart rate
FMF	Fetal movements felt
FSE	Fetal scalp electrode
FSH	Follicle-stimulating hormone
G	gram
GA	General anaesthesia
GB	Gall bladder
GFR	Glomerular filtration rate
GI	Gastro-intestinal

GIT	Gastro-intestinal tract
G6PD	Glucose 6 phosphate dehydrogenase
GP	General practitioner
GTT	Glucose tolerance test (for diabetes)
GU	Genito-urinary
GUT	Genito-urinary tract
h	Hour
Hb	Haemoglobin
Hct	Haemocrit
HOCM	Hypertrophic obstructive cardiomyopathy
HPC	History of presenting complaint
HRT	Hormone replacement therapy
HS	Heart sounds
HVS	High vaginal swab
Hx	History
ICP	Intracranial pressure
ICS	Intercostal space
IDA	Iron deficiency anaemia
IDDM	Insulin dependent diabetes mellitus
Ig	Immunoglobulin
IJ	Internal jugular vein
IM	Intramuscular
ISQ	In status quo
IT	Intrathecal
ITP	Idiopathic thrombocytopenic purpura
ITU	Intensive therapy unit
iu	International unit
IUCD	Intrauterine contraceptive device
IV	Intravenous
IVC	Inferior vena cava
IVI	Intravenous infusion (drip)
IVU	Intravenous urography
Ix	Investigations
J	Jaundice
°JACCO	No jaundice, anaemia, cyanosis, clubbing or oedema

JVP	Jugular venous pressure
K⁺	Potassium
kg	Kilogram
KJ	Knee jerk (reflex, see AJ)
kPa	Kilopascal, approximately 7.5 mmHg
L	(i) Litre (ii) Left
LA	Local anaesthesia
LBBB	Left bundle branch block
LFTs	Liver function tests
LH	Luteinising hormone
LIF	Left iliac fossa
LIH	Left inguinal hernia
LMN	Lower motor neurone
LMP	First day of the last menstrual period
LN	Lymph node
LOA	Left occiput anterior (position of baby's head at delivery, see also LOP, ROA, ROP, LOL, ROL, OA, OP)
LOC	Loss of consciousness
LOL	Left occipitolateral (see LOA)
LOP	Left occiput posterior (see LOA above)
LP	Lumbar puncture
LS	Letter sent
LSCS	Lower segment caesarean section (the 'normal' type of caesarean section)
LSKK	Liver, spleen and kidneys
LUQ	Left upper quadrant
LVF	Left ventricular failure
LVH	Left ventricular hypertrophy
mane	In the morning
mcg	Microgram
MCL	Mid clavicular line
MCV	Mean cell volume
µg	Microgram
mg	Milligram
mist	mixture

mitte 1/12	Supply/give/send/provide
ml	Millilitres
mmHg	Millimetres of mercury (pressure)
mMol	Millimol
MRI	Magnetic resonance imaging (=NMRI)
MS	Multiple sclerosis
MSU	Mid stream urine
N&V	Nausea and vomiting
Na	Sodium
NaHCO$_3$	Sodium bicarbonate
NAD	Nothing abnormal diagnosed/detected
NBM	Nil by mouth
ND	Notifiable disease
ng	Nanogram
NG	(i) Naso-gastric (ii) Carcinoma/cancer (neoplastic growth)
NLM	(Used by male paediatricians) Nice looking mother
NMCS	No malignant cells seen
NMR	Nuclear magnetic resonance (scan)
noct/nocte	At night
NOF	Neck of femur
N/S	Normal size
NSAID	Non-steroidal anti-inflammatory drugs
O$_2$	Oxygen
OA	(i) Occipito-anterior (see LOA) (ii) Osteoarthritis
OCP	Oral contraceptive pill
OE	On examination
OP	Occipito-posterior (see LOA)
Orthop.	Orthopnoea (breathlessness on lying flat)
P	Pulse
P or π	Period
PA	Posteroanterior
PAN	Polyarteritis nodosa
PC	Post cibum (after food)
pCO$_2$	Partial pressure of carbon dioxide (normally in blood)

PCV	Packed cell volume
PERLA	Pupils are equal and react to light and accommodation
PE	(i) Pulmonary embolism (ii) Pre eclampsia
PEFR	Peak expiratory flow rate
PET	Pre-eclamptic toxaemia
pg	Picogram
pH	Acidity and alkalinity scale. Low is acidic. High is alkaline. pH7 is about neutral
PH	Past/previous history
PID	(i) Pelvic inflammatory disease (ii) Prolapsed intervertebral disc
PIP	Proximal interphalangeal
PL	Prolactin
PMH	Past/previous medical history
PND	Paroxysmal nocturnal dyspnoea
PN (R)	Percussion note (resonant)
po	Per os (by mouth)
pO_2	Partial pressure of oxygen (normally in blood)
POH	Past/previous obstetric history
POP	Plaster of Paris
PoP	Progesterone only pill
PPH	Post-partum haemorrhage
pr	Per rectum (by the rectum)
prn	As required – of eg pain killers
PRV	Polycythaemia rubra vera
PTH	Parathyroid hormone
PTT	Prothrombin time
PU	Peptic ulcer
PV	Per vaginam (by the vagina)
QDS	To be given/taken 4 times a day
R	Right *or* respiration
RA	Rheumatoid arthritis
RBBB	Right bundle branch block
RBC	Red blood cell (erythrocyte)
RE	Rectal examination

Rh	Rhesus factor
RIC	Raised intracranial pressure
RIF	Right iliac fossa
RIH	Right inguinal hernia
ROA	Right occiput anterior (see LOA)
ROL	Right occipito-lateral (see LOA)
ROM	Range of movement
ROP	Right occiput posterior (see LOA)
RS	Respiratory system
RT	Radiotherapy
RTA	Road traffic accident
RTI	Respiratory tract infection
RUQ	Right upper quadrant
SB	Serum bilirubin
S/B	Seen by
SBE	Subacute bacterial endocarditis
SC	Subcutaneous
S/D	Systolic/diastolic (heart and circulation)
SE	Side effects
SH	Social history
SJ	Supinator jerk (reflex: see AJ)
SL	Sub linguinal (under the tongue)
SLE	Systemic lupus erythematosus
SOA	Swelling of ankles
SOB (OE)	Shortness of breath
SOS	(i) if necessary (ii) see other sheet
SROM	Spontaneous rupture of membranes
stat	Immediately
Supp	Suppositories
SVC	Superior vena cava
SVD	Spontaneous vaginal delivery
SVT	Supraventricular tachycardia
SXR	Skull X-ray
Ts and As	Tonsils and Adenoids

TCI 2/52	To come in (to be admitted to hospital), in 2 weeks' time
tds	To be given/taken 3 times a day
TGH	To go home
THR	Total hip replacement
TIA	Transient ischaemic attack
TJ	Triceps jerk (reflex: see AJ)
TPR	Temperature, pulse and respiration
TSH	Thyroid stimulating hormone
TTA	To take away
TVF	Tactile vocal fremitus
TX	Transfusion
UC	Ulcerative colitis
U&E	Urea and electrolytes (biochemical tests)
UG	Urogenital
UMN	Upper motor neurone
URTI	Upper respiratory tract infection
USS	Ultra sound scan
UTI	Urinary tract infection
VA	Visual acuity
VE	Vaginal examination
VF	Ventricular fibrillation
VT	Ventricular tachycardia
V/V	Vulva and vagina
VVs	Varicose veins
WBC	White blood corpuscle/white blood cell count
WCC	White blood cell count
WR	Wasserman reaction
wt	Weight
XR	X-ray

Appendix 3

PRE-ACTION PROTOCOL FOR THE RESOLUTION OF CLINICAL DISPUTES AND PRE-ACTION PROTOCOL FOR PERSONAL INJURY CLAIMS

PRE-ACTION PROTOCOL FOR THE RESOLUTION OF CLINICAL DISPUTES

Contents

Executive Summary

1 Why this Protocol?
2 The Aims and Objectives
3 The Protocol

    (a) Best Practice Commitments

    (b) Steps

4 Experts
5 Alternative approaches for resolving disputes

Annexes

A Illustrative Flowchart
B Medical Records Protocol
C Templates for letters of claim and response
D Lord Woolf's recommendations on Medical Negligence and Protocols in his Access to Justice Final Report 1996
E How to contact the Forum

Executive Summary

1 The Clinical Disputes Forum is a multi-disciplinary body which was formed in 1997, as a result of Lord Woolf's 'Access to Justice' inquiry. One of the aims of the Forum is to find less adversarial and more cost effective ways of resolving disputes about healthcare and medical treatment. The names and addresses of the Chairman and Secretary of the Forum can be found at Annex E.

2 This protocol is the Forum's first major initiative. It has been drawn up carefully, including extensive consultations with most of the key stakeholders in the medico-legal system.

3 The protocol—

- encourages a climate of openness when something has 'gone wrong' with a patient's treatment or the patient is dissatisfied with that treatment and/or the outcome. This reflects the new and developing requirements for clinical governance within healthcare;
- provides general guidance on how this more open culture might be achieved when disputes arise;
- recommends a timed sequence of steps for patients and healthcare providers, and their advisers, to follow when a dispute arises. This should facilitate and speed up exchanging relevant information and increase the prospects that disputes can be resolved without resort to legal action.

4 This protocol has been prepared by a working party of the Clinical Disputes Forum. It has the support of the Lord Chancellor's Department, the

Department of Health and NHS Executive, the Law Society, the Legal Aid Board and many other key organisations.

1 Why this Protocol?

MISTRUST IN HEALTHCARE DISPUTES

1.1 The number of complaints and claims against hospitals, GPs, dentists and private healthcare providers is growing as patients become more prepared to question the treatment they are given, to seek explanations of what happened, and to seek appropriate redress. Patients may require further treatment, an apology, assurances about future action or compensation. These trends are unlikely to change. The Patients' Charter encourages patients to have high expectations, and a revised NHS Complaints Procedure was implemented in 1996. The civil justice reforms and new Rules of Court should make litigation quicker, more user friendly and less expensive.

1.2 It is clearly in the interests of patients, healthcare professionals and providers that patients' concerns, complaints and claims arising from their treatment are resolved as quickly, efficiently and professionally as possible. A climate of mistrust and lack of openness can seriously damage the patient/clinician relationship, unnecessarily prolong disputes (especially litigation), and reduce the resources available for treating patients. It may also cause additional work for, and lower the morale of, healthcare professionals.

1.3 At present there is often mistrust by both sides. This can mean that patients fail to raise their concerns with the healthcare provider as early as possible. Sometimes patients may pursue a complaint or claim which has little merit, due to a lack of sufficient information and understanding. It can also mean that patients become reluctant, once advice has been taken on a potential claim, to disclose sufficient information to enable the provider to investigate that claim efficiently and, where appropriate, resolve it.

1.4 On the side of the healthcare provider this mistrust can be shown in a reluctance to be honest with patients, a failure to provide prompt clear explanations, especially of adverse outcomes (whether or not there may have been negligence) and a tendency to 'close ranks' once a claim is made.

WHAT NEEDS TO CHANGE

1.5 If that mistrust is to be removed, and a more co-operative culture is to develop—

- healthcare professionals and providers need to adopt a constructive approach to complaints and claims. They should accept that concerned patients are entitled to an explanation and an apology, if warranted, and to appropriate redress in the event of negligence. An overly defensive approach is not in the long-term interest of their main goal: patient care;
- patients should recognise that unintended and/or unfortunate consequences of medical treatment can only be rectified if they are brought to the attention of the healthcare provider as soon as possible.

1.6 A protocol which sets out 'ground rules' for the handling of disputes at their early stages should, if it is to be subscribed to, and followed—

- encourage greater openness between the parties;

- encourage parties to find the most appropriate way of resolving the particular dispute;
- reduce delay and costs;
- reduce the need for litigation.

WHY THIS PROTOCOL NOW?

1.7 Lord Woolf in his Access to Justice Report in July 1996, concluded that major causes of costs and delay in medical negligence litigation occur at the pre-action stage. He recommended that patients and their advisers, and healthcare providers, should work more closely together to try to resolve disputes co-operatively, rather than proceed to litigation. He specifically recommended a pre-action protocol for medical negligence cases.

1.8 A fuller summary of Lord Woolf's recommendations is at Annex D.

WHERE THE PROTOCOL FITS IN

1.9 Protocols serve the needs of litigation and pre-litigation practice, especially—

- predictability in the time needed for steps pre-proceedings;
- standardisation of relevant information, including records and documents to be disclosed.

1.10 Building upon Lord Woolf's recommendations, the Lord Chancellor's Department is now promoting the adoption of protocols in specific areas, including medical negligence.

1.11 It is recognised that contexts differ significantly. For example, patients tend to have an ongoing relationship with a GP, more so than with a hospital; clinical staff in the National Health Service are often employees, while those in the private sector may be contractors; providing records quickly may be relatively easy for GPs and dentists, but can be a complicated procedure in a large multi-department hospital. The protocol which follows is intended to be sufficiently broadly based, and flexible, to apply to all aspects of the health service: primary and secondary; public and private sectors.

ENFORCEMENT OF THE PROTOCOL AND SANCTIONS

1.12 The civil justice reforms will be implemented in April 1999. One new set of Court Rules and procedures is replacing the existing rules for both the High Court and county courts. This and the personal injury protocol are being published with the Rules, Practice Directions and key court forms. The courts will be able to treat the standards set in protocols as the normal reasonable approach to pre-action conduct.

1.13 If proceedings are issued it will be for the court to decide whether non-compliance with a protocol should merit sanctions. Guidance on the court's likely approach will be given from time to time in practice directions.

1.14 If the court has to consider the question of compliance after proceedings have begun it will not be concerned with minor infringements, eg failure by a short period to provide relevant information. One minor breach will not entitle the 'innocent' party to abandon following the protocol. The court will look at the effect of non-compliance on the other party when deciding whether to impose sanctions.

2 The Aims of the Protocol

2.1 The **general** aims of the protocol are—

- to maintain/restore the patient/healthcare provider relationship;
- to resolve as many disputes as possible without litigation.

2.2 The **specific** objectives are—

OPENNESS

- to encourage early communication of the perceived problem between patients and healthcare providers;
- to encourage patients to voice any concerns or dissatisfaction with their treatment as soon as practicable;
- to encourage healthcare providers to develop systems of early reporting and investigation for serious adverse treatment outcomes and to provide full and prompt explanations to dissatisfied patients;
- to ensure that sufficient information is disclosed by both parties to enable each to understand the other's perspective and case, and to encourage early resolution;

TIMELINESS

- to provide an early opportunity for healthcare providers to identify cases where an investigation is required and to carry out that investigation promptly;
- to encourage primary and private healthcare providers to involve their defence organisations or insurers at an early stage;
- to ensure that all relevant medical records are provided to patients or their appointed representatives on request, to a realistic timetable by any healthcare provider.
- to ensure that relevant records which are not in healthcare providers' possession are made available to them by patients and their advisers at an appropriate stage;
- where a resolution is not achievable to lay the ground to enable litigation to proceed on a reasonable timetable, at a reasonable and proportionate cost and to limit the matters in contention;
- to discourage the prolonged pursuit of unmeritorious claims and the prolonged defence of meritorious claims.

AWARENESS OF OPTIONS

- To ensure that patients and healthcare providers are made aware of the available options to pursue and resolve disputes and what each might involve.

2.3 This protocol does not attempt to be prescriptive about a number of related clinical governance issues which will have a bearing on healthcare providers' ability to meet the standards within the protocol. Good clinical governance requires the following to be considered—

(a) **Clinical risk management:** the protocol does not provide any detailed guidance to healthcare providers on clinical risk management or the adoption of risk management systems and procedures. This must be a matter for the NHS Executive, the National Health Service Litigation Authority, individual trusts and providers, including GPs, dentists and the private sector. However, effective co-ordinated, focused clinical risk management strategies and procedures can help in managing risk and in the early identification and investigation of adverse outcomes.

(b) **Adverse outcome reporting:** the protocol does not provide any detailed guidance on which adverse outcomes should trigger an investigation. However, healthcare providers should have in place procedures for such investigations, including recording of statements of key witnesses. These procedures should also cover when and how to inform patients that an adverse outcome has occurred.

(c) **The professional's duty to report:** the protocol does not recommend changes to the codes of conduct of professionals in healthcare, or attempt to impose a specific duty on those professionals to report known adverse outcomes or untoward incidents. Lord Woolf in his final report suggested that the professional bodies might consider this. The General Medical Council is preparing guidance to doctors about their duty to report adverse incidents and to co-operate with inquiries.

3 The Protocol

3.1 This protocol is not a comprehensive code governing all the steps in clinical disputes. Rather it attempts to set out **a code of good practice** which parties should follow when litigation might be a possibility.

3.2 The **commitments** section of the protocol summarises the guiding principles which healthcare providers and patients and their advisers are invited to endorse when dealing with patient dissatisfaction with treatment and its outcome, and with potential complaints and claims.

3.3 The **steps** section sets out in a more prescriptive form, a recommended sequence of actions to be followed if litigation is a prospect.

GOOD PRACTICE COMMITMENTS

3.4 **Healthcare providers** should—

(i) ensure that **key staff**, including claims and litigation managers, are appropriately trained and have some knowledge of healthcare law, and of complaints procedures and civil litigation practice and procedure;

(ii) develop an approach to **clinical governance** that ensures that clinical practice is delivered to commonly accepted standards and that this is routinely monitored through a system of clinical audit and clinical risk management (particularly adverse outcome investigation);

(iii) set up **adverse outcome reporting systems** in all specialties to record and investigate unexpected serious adverse outcomes as soon as possible. Such systems can enable evidence to be gathered quickly, which makes it easier to provide an accurate explanation of what happened and to defend or settle any subsequent claims;

(iv) use the results of **adverse incidents and complaints positively** as a guide to how to improve services to patients in the future;

(v) ensure **that patients receive clear and comprehensible information** in an accessible form about how to raise their concerns or complaints;

(vi) establish **efficient and effective systems of recording and storing patient records**, notes, diagnostic reports and X-rays, and to retain these in accordance with Department of Health guidance (currently for a minimum of eight years in the case of adults, and all obstetric and paediatric notes for children until they reach the age of 25);

(vii) **advise patients** of a serious adverse outcome and provide on request to the patient or the patient's representative an oral or written explanation of what happened, information on further steps open to the patient, including where appropriate an offer of future treatment to rectify the problem, an apology, changes in procedure which will benefit patients and/or compensation.

3.5 **Patients and their advisers** should—

(i) **report any concerns and dissatisfaction** to the healthcare provider as soon as is reasonable to enable that provider to offer clinical advice where possible, to advise the patient if anything has gone wrong and take appropriate action;

(ii) consider the **full range of options** available following an adverse outcome with which a patient is dissatisfied, including a request for an explanation, a meeting, a complaint, and other appropriate dispute resolution methods (including mediation) and negotiation, not only litigation;

(iii) **inform the healthcare provider when the patient is satisfied** that the matter has been concluded: legal advisers should notify the provider when they are no longer acting for the patient, particularly if proceedings have not started.

PROTOCOL STEPS

3.6 The steps of this protocol which follow have been kept deliberately simple. An illustration of the likely sequence of events in a number of healthcare situations is at Annex A.

OBTAINING THE HEALTH RECORDS

3.7 Any request for records by the **patient** or their adviser should—

- **provide sufficient information** to alert the healthcare provider where an adverse outcome has been serious or had serious consequences;
- be as **specific as possible** about the records which are required.

3.8 Requests for copies of the patient's clinical records should be made using the Law Society and Department of Health approved **standard forms** (enclosed at Annex B), adapted as necessary.

3.9 The copy records should be provided **within 40 days** of the request and for a cost not exceeding the charges permissible under the Access to Health Records Act 1990 (currently a maximum of £10 plus photocopying and postage).

3.10 In the rare circumstances that the healthcare provider is in difficulty in complying with the request within 40 days, the **problem should be explained** quickly and details given of what is being done to resolve it.

3.11 It will not be practicable for healthcare providers to investigate in detail each case when records are requested. But healthcare providers should **adopt a policy on which cases will be investigated** (see paragraph 3.5 on clinical governance and adverse outcome reporting).

3.12 If the healthcare provider fails to provide the health records within 40 days, the patient or their adviser can then apply to the court for an **order for pre-action disclosure**. The new Civil Procedure Rules should make pre-action applications to the court easier. The court will also have the power to impose costs sanctions for unreasonable delay in providing records.

3.13 If either the patient or the healthcare provider considers **additional health records are required from a third party**, in the first instance these should be requested by or through the patient. Third party healthcare providers are expected to co-operate. The Civil Procedure Rules will enable patients and healthcare providers to apply to the court for pre-action disclosure by third parties.

LETTER OF CLAIM

3.14 Annex C1 to this protocol provides **a template for the recommended contents of a letter of claim**: the level of detail will need to be varied to suit the particular circumstances.

3.15 If, following the receipt and analysis of the records, and the receipt of any further advice (including from experts if necessary – see Section 4), the patient/adviser decides that there are grounds for a claim, they should then send, as soon as practicable, to the healthcare provider/potential defendant, a **letter of claim**.

3.16 This letter should contain a **clear summary of the facts** on which the claim is based, including the alleged adverse outcome, and the **main allegations of negligence**. It should also describe the **patient's injuries**, and present condition and prognosis. The **financial loss** incurred by the plaintiff should be outlined with an indication of the heads of damage to be claimed and the scale of the loss, unless this is impracticable.

3.17 In more complex cases a **chronology** of the relevant events should be provided, particularly if the patient has been treated by a number of different healthcare providers.

3.18 The letter of claim **should refer to any relevant documents**, including health records, and if possible enclose copies of any of those which will not already be in the potential defendant's possession, eg any relevant general practitioner records if the plaintiff's claim is against a hospital.

3.19 **Sufficient information** must be given to enable the healthcare provider defendant to **commence investigations** and to put an initial valuation on the claim.

3.20 Letters of claim are **not** intended to have the same formal status as a pleading, nor should any sanctions necessarily apply if the letter of claim and any subsequent statement of claim in the proceedings differ.

3.21 **Proceedings should not be issued until after three months from the letter of claim**, unless there is a limitation problem and/or the patient's position needs to be protected by early issue.

3.22 The patient or their adviser may want to make an **offer to settle** the claim at this early stage by putting forward an amount of compensation which would be satisfactory (possibly including any costs incurred to date). If an offer to settle is made, generally this should be supported by a medical report which deals with the injuries, condition and prognosis, and by a schedule of loss and supporting documentation. The level of detail necessary will depend on the value of the claim. Medical reports may not be necessary where there is no significant continuing injury, and a detailed schedule may not be necessary in a low value case. The Civil Procedure Rules are expected to set out the legal and procedural requirements for making offers to settle.

THE RESPONSE

3.23 Attached at Annex C2 is a template for the suggested contents of the **letter of response**.

3.24 The healthcare provider should **acknowledge** the letter of claim **within 14 days of receipt** and should identify who will be dealing with the matter.

3.25 The healthcare provider should, **within three months** of the letter of claim, provide a **reasoned answer**—

- if the **claim is admitted** the healthcare provider should say so in clear terms;
- if only **part of the claim is admitted** the healthcare provider should make clear which issues of breach of duty and/or causation are admitted and which are denied and why;
- it is intended that any **admissions will be binding**;
- if the claim is denied, this should include specific comments on the allegations of negligence, and if a synopsis or chronology of relevant events has been provided and is disputed, the healthcare provider's version of those events;
- where additional documents are relied upon, eg an internal protocol, copies should be provided.

3.26 If the patient has made an offer to settle, the healthcare provider should **respond to that offer** in the response letter, preferably with reasons. The provider may make its own offer to settle at this stage, either as a counter-offer to the patient's, or of its own accord, but should accompany any offer by any supporting medical evidence, and/or by any other evidence in relation to the value of the claim which is in the healthcare provider's possession.

3.27 If the parties reach agreement on liability, but time is needed to resolve the value of the claim, they should aim to agree a reasonable period.

4 Experts

4.1 In clinical negligence disputes expert opinions may be needed—

- on breach of duty and causation;
- on the patient's condition and prognosis;
- to assist in valuing aspects of the claim.

4.2 The civil justice reforms and the new Civil Procedure Rules will encourage economy in the use of experts and a less adversarial expert culture. It is recognised that in clinical negligence disputes, the parties and their advisers will require flexibility in their approach to expert evidence. Decisions on whether experts might be instructed jointly, and on whether reports might be disclosed sequentially or by exchange, should rest with the parties and their advisers. Sharing expert evidence may be appropriate on issues relating to the value of the claim. However, this protocol does not attempt to be prescriptive on issues in relation to expert evidence.

4.3 Obtaining expert evidence will often be an expensive step and may take time, especially in specialised areas of medicine where there are limited numbers of suitable experts. Patients and healthcare providers, and their advisers, will therefore need to consider carefully how best to obtain any necessary expert help quickly and cost-effectively. Assistance with locating a suitable expert is available from a number of sources.

5 Alternative Approaches to Settling Disputes

5.1 It would not be practicable for this protocol to address in any detail how a patient or their adviser, or healthcare provider, might decide which method to adopt to resolve the particular problem. But, the courts increasingly expect parties to try to settle their differences by agreement before issuing proceedings.

5.2 Most disputes are resolved by discussion and negotiation. Parties should bear in mind that carefully planned face-to-face meetings may be particularly helpful in exploring further treatment for the patient, in reaching understandings about what happened, and on both parties' positions, in narrowing the issues in dispute and, if the timing is right, in helping to settle the whole matter.

5.3 Summarised below are some other alternatives for resolving disputes—

- The revised NHS Complaints Procedure, which was implemented in April 1996, is designed to provide patients with an explanation of what happened and an apology if appropriate. It is not designed to provide compensation for cases of negligence. However, patients might choose to use the procedure if their only, or main, goal is to obtain an explanation, or to obtain more information to help them decide what other action might be appropriate.
- Mediation may be appropriate in some cases: this is a form of facilitated negotiation assisted by an independent neutral party. It is expected that the new Civil Procedure Rules will give the court the power to stay proceedings for one month for settlement discussions or mediation.
- Other methods of resolving disputes include arbitration, determination by an expert, and early neutral evaluation by a medical or legal expert. The Lord Chancellor's Department has produced a booklet on 'Resolving Disputes Without Going to Court', LCD 1995, which lists a number of organisations that provide alternative dispute resolution services.

Annex A

Illustrative Flowchart

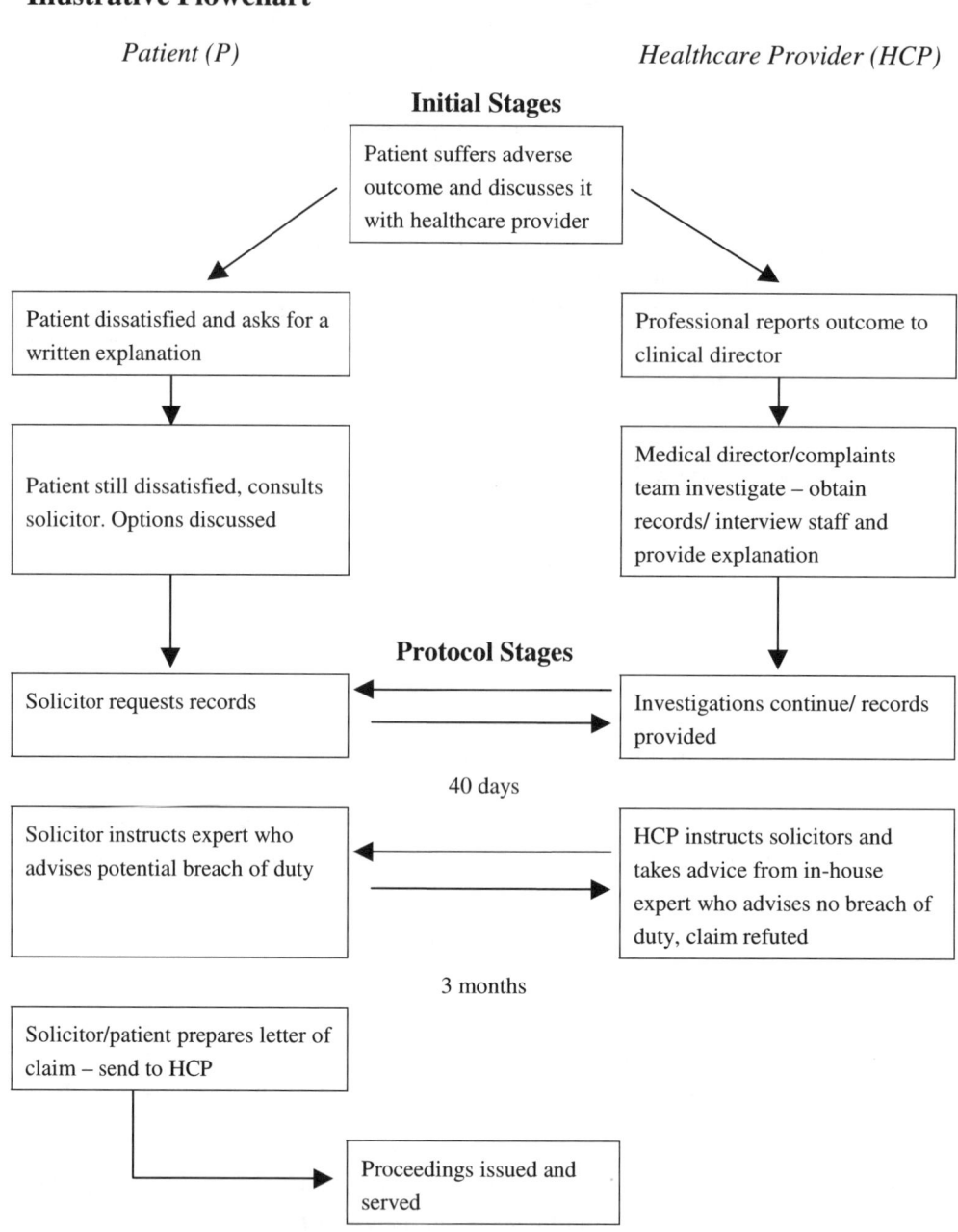

Patient (P) — *Healthcare Provider (HCP)*

Initial Stages

- Patient suffers adverse outcome and discusses it with healthcare provider

Patient side:
- Patient dissatisfied and asks for a written explanation
- Patient still dissatisfied, consults solicitor. Options discussed

HCP side:
- Professional reports outcome to clinical director
- Medical director/complaints team investigate – obtain records/ interview staff and provide explanation

Protocol Stages

- Solicitor requests records ↔ Investigations continue/ records provided

40 days

- Solicitor instructs expert who advises potential breach of duty ↔ HCP instructs solicitors and takes advice from in-house expert who advises no breach of duty, claim refuted

3 months

- Solicitor/patient prepares letter of claim – send to HCP
- Proceedings issued and served

Annex B

**Protocol for Obtaining Hospital Medical Records
(Revised Edition (June 1998); Civil Litigation Committee, The Law Society)**

Application on Behalf of a Patient for Hospital Medical Records for Use When Court Proceedings are Contemplated

PURPOSE OF THE FORMS

This application form and response forms have been prepared by a working party of the Law Society's Civil Litigation Committee and approved by the Department of Health for use in NHS and Trust hospitals.

The purpose of the forms is to standardise and streamline the disclosure of medical records to a patient's solicitors, who are investigating pursuing a personal injury claim against a third party, or a medical negligence claim against the hospital to which the application is addressed and/or other hospitals or general practitioners.

USE OF THE FORMS

Use of the forms is entirely voluntary and does not prejudice any party's right under the Access to Health Records Act 1990, the Data Protection Act 1984, or ss 33 and 34 of the Supreme Court Act 1981. However, it is the Department of Health policy that patients be permitted to see what has been written about them, and that healthcare providers should make arrangements to allow patients to see all their records, not only those covered by the Access to Health Records Act 1990. The aim of the forms is to save time and costs for all concerned for the benefit of the patient and the hospital and in the interests of justice. Use of the forms should make it unnecessary in most cases for there to be exchanges of letters or other enquiries. If there is any unusual matter not covered by the form, the patient's solicitor may write a separate letter at the outset.

CHARGES FOR RECORDS

The Access to Health Records Act 1990 prescribes a maximum fee of £10. Photocopying and postage costs can be charged in addition. No other charges may be made.

The NHS Executive guidance makes it clear to healthcare providers that 'it is a perfectly proper use' of the 1990 Act to request records in that framework for the purpose of potential or actual litigation, whether against a third party or against the hospital or trust.

The 1990 Act does not permit differential rates of charges to be levied if the application is made by the patient, or by a solicitor on his or her behalf, or whether the response to the application is made by the healthcare provider directly (the medical records manager or a claims manager) or by a solicitor.

The NHS Executive guidance recommends that the same practice should be followed with regard to charges when the records are provided under a voluntary agreement as under the 1990 Act, except that in those circumstances the £10 access fee will not be appropriate.

The NHS Executive also advises—

- that the cost of photocopying may include 'the cost of staff time in making copies' and the costs of running the copier (but not costs of locating and sifting records);
- that the common practice of setting a standard rate for an application or charging an administration fee is not acceptable because there will be cases when this fails to comply with the 1990 Act.

RECORDS: WHAT MIGHT BE INCLUDED

X-rays and test results form part of the patient's records. Additional charges for copying X-rays are permissible. If there are large numbers of X-rays, the records officer should check with the patient/solicitor before arranging copying.

Reports on an 'adverse incident' and reports on the patient made for risk management and audit purposes may form part of the records and be discloseable: the exception will be any specific record or report made solely or mainly in connection with an actual or potential claim.

RECORDS: QUALITY STANDARDS

When copying records healthcare providers should ensure—

1 All documents are legible, and complete, if necessary by photocopying at less than 100% size.
2 Documents larger than A4 in the original, eg ITU charts, should be reproduced in A3, or reduced to A4 where this retains readability.
3 Documents are only copied on one side of paper, unless the original is two sided.
4 Documents should not be unnecessarily shuffled or bound and holes should not be made in the copied papers.

ENQUIRIES/FURTHER INFORMATION

Any enquiries about the forms should be made initially to the solicitors making the request. Comments on the use and content of the forms should be made to the Secretary, Civil Litigation Committee, The Law Society, 113 Chancery Lane, London WC2A 1PL, telephone 0171 320 5739, or to the NHS Management Executive, Quarry House, Quarry Hill, Leeds LS2 7UE.

The Law Society

May 1998

Application on Behalf of a Patient for Hospital Medical Records for Use when Court Proceedings are Contemplated

This should be completed as fully as possible

Insert Hospital Name and Address   **TO: Medical Records Officer**   Hospital

1 (a)		Full name of patient (including previous surnames)	
	(b)	Address now	
	(c)	Address at start of treatment	
	(d)	Date of birth (and death, if applicable)	
	(e)	Hospital ref no if available	
	(f)	N.I. number, if available	
2		This application is made because the patient is considering	
	(a)	a claim against your hospital as detailed in para 7 overleaf	YES/NO
	(b)	pursuing an action against some one else	YES/NO
3		Department(s) where treatment was received	
4		Name(s) of consultant(s) at your hospital in charge of the treatment	
5		Whether treatment at your hospital was private or NHS, wholly or in part	
6		A description of the treatment received, with approximate dates	
7		If the answer to Q2(a) is 'Yes' details of	
		(a) the likely nature of the claim,	
		(b) grounds for the claim,	
		(c) approximate dates of the events involved	
8		If the answer to Q2(b) is 'Yes' insert	
		(a) the names of the proposed defendants	
		(b) whether legal proceedings yet begun	YES/NO
		(c) if appropriate, details of the claim and action number	
9		We confirm we will pay reasonable copying charges	
10		We request prior details of	

	(a) photocopying and administration charges for medical records	YES/NO
	(b) number of and cost of copying x-ray and scan films	YES/NO
11	Any other relevant information, particular requirements, or any particular documents not required (eg copies of computerised records)	
	Signature of Solicitor	
	Name	
	Address	
	Ref.	
	Telephone number	
	Fax number	
	Please print name beneath each signature. Signature by child over 12 but under 18 years also requires signature by parent	
	Signature of patient	
	Signature of parent or next friend if appropriate	
	Signature of personal representative where patient has died	

First Response to Application for Hospital Records

NAME OF PATIENT Our ref Your ref		
1	Date of receipt of patient's application	
2	We intend that copy medical records will be dispatched within 6 weeks of that date	YES/NO
3	We require pre-payment of photocopying charges	YES/NO
4	If estimate of photocopying charges requested or pre-payment required the amount will be	£ / notified to you
5	The cost of x-ray and scan films will be	£ / notified to you
6	If there is any problem, we shall write to you within those 6 weeks	YES/NO
7	Any other information	
	Please address further correspondence to	
	Signed	
	Direct telephone number	
	Direct fax number	
	Dated	

Second Response Enclosing Patient's Hospital Medical Records

Address   Our Ref
                                                                    Your Ref

1	NAME OF PATIENT: We confirm that the enclosed copy medical records are all those within the control of the hospital, relevant to the application which you have made to the best of our knowledge and belief, subject to paras 2–5 below	YES/NO
2	Details of any other documents which have not yet been located	
3	Date by when it is expected that these will be supplied	
4	Details of any records which we are not producing	
5	The reasons for not doing so	
6	An invoice for copying and administration charges is attached	YES/NO
	Signed	
	Date	

ANNEX C

Templates for Letters of Claim and Response

C1 LETTER OF CLAIM

Essential Contents

1. Client's name, address, date of birth, etc

2. Dates of allegedly negligent treatment

3. Events giving rise to the claim:
- an outline of what happened, including details of other relevant treatments to the client by other healthcare providers.

4. Allegation of negligence and causal link with injuries:
- an outline of the allegations or a more detailed list in a complex case;
- an outline of the causal link between allegations and the injuries complained of.

5. The client's injuries, condition and future prognosis

6. Request for clinical records (if not previously provided)
- use the Law Society form if appropriate or adapt;
- specify the records required;
- if other records are held by other providers, and may be relevant, say so;
- State what investigations have been carried out to date, eg information from client and witnesses, any complaint and the outcome, if any clinical records have been seen or expert's advice obtained.

7. The likely value of the claim
- an outline of the main heads of damage, or, in straightforward cases, the details of loss.

What investigations have been carried out

An offer to settle without supporting evidence
Suggestions for obtaining expert evidence
Suggestions for meetings, negotiations, discussion or mediation

Possible enclosures

Chronology
Clinical records request form and client's authorisation
Expert report(s)
Schedules of loss and supporting evidence

C2 LETTER OF RESPONSE

Essential Contents

1. Provide **requested records** and invoice for copying:
- explain if records are incomplete or extensive records are held and ask for further instructions;
- request additional records from third parties.

2. **Comments on events and/or chronology**:
- if events are disputed or the healthcare provider has further information or documents on which they wish to rely, these should be provided, eg internal protocol;

- details of any further information needed from the patient or a third party should be provided.

3 **If breach of duty and causation are accepted**:
- suggestions might be made for resolving the claim and/or requests for further information;
- a response should be made to any offer to settle.

4 **If breach of duty and/or causation are denied**:
- a bare denial will not be sufficient. If the healthcare provider has other explanations for what happened, these should be given at least in outline;
- suggestions might be made for the next steps, eg further investigations, obtaining expert evidence, meetings/negotiations or mediation, or an invitation to issue proceedings.

Optional Matters

An offer to settle if the patient has not made one, or a counter offer to the patient's with supporting evidence

Possible Enclosures

Clinical records
Annotated chronology
Expert reports

ANNEX D

Lord Woolf's Recommendations

1 Lord Woolf in his Access to Justice Report in July 1996, following a detailed review of the problems of medical negligence claims, identified that one of the major sources of **costs and delay** is **at the pre-litigation stage** because—

(a) Inadequate incident reporting and record keeping in hospitals, and mobility of staff, make it difficult to establish facts, often several years after the event.
(b) Claimants must incur the cost of an expert in order to establish whether they have a viable claim.
(c) There is often a long delay before a claim is made.
(d) Defendants do not have sufficient resources to carry out a full investigation of every incident, and do not consider it worthwhile to start an investigation as soon as they receive a request for records, because many cases do not proceed beyond that stage.
(e) Patients often give the defendant little or no notice of a firm intention to pursue a claim. Consequently, many incidents are not investigated by the defendants until after proceedings have started.
(f) Doctors and other clinical staff are traditionally reluctant to admit negligence or apologise to, or negotiate with, claimants for fear of damage to their professional reputations or career prospects.

2 Lord Woolf acknowledged that under the present arrangements **healthcare providers**, faced with possible medical negligence claims, have a number of **practical problems** to contend with—

(a) Difficulties of finding patients' records and tracing former staff, which can be exacerbated by late notification and by the health-care provider's own failure to identify adverse incidents.

(b) The healthcare provider may have only treated the patient for a limited time or for a specific complaint: the patient's previous history may be relevant but the records may be in the possession of one of several other healthcare providers.

(c) The large number of potential claims do not proceed beyond the stage of a request for medical records, or an explanation; and that it is difficult for healthcare providers to investigate fully every case whenever a patient asks to see the records.

ANNEX E

How to Contact the Forum

The Clinical Disputes Forum

Chairman

Dr Alastair Scotland
Medical Director and Chief Officer
National Clinical Assessment Authority
9th Floor, Market Towers
London
SW8 5NQ
Telephone : 020 7273 0850

Secretary

Sarah Leigh
c/o Margaret Dangoor
3 Clydesdale Gardens
Richmond
Surrey
TW10 5EG
Telephone: 0181 408 1012

PRE-ACTION PROTOCOL FOR PERSONAL INJURY CLAIMS

Contents

1 Introduction
2 Notes of guidance
3 The protocol

Annexes
A Letter of claim
B Standard disclosure lists
C Letter of instruction to medical expert

1 Introduction

1.1 Lord Woolf in his final Access to Justice Report of July 1996 recommended the development of pre-action protocols:

'To build on and increase the benefits of early but well informed settlement which genuinely satisfy both parties to dispute'.

1.2 The aims of pre-action protocols are:
- more pre-action contact between the parties
- better and earlier exchange of information
- better pre-action investigation by both sides
- to put the parties in a position where they may be able to settle cases fairly and early without litigation
- to enable proceedings to run to the court's timetable and efficiently, if litigation does become necessary.

1.3 The concept of protocols is relevant to a range of initiatives for good litigation and pre-litigation practice, especially:
- predictability in the time needed for steps pre-proceedings
- standardisation of relevant information, including documents to be disclosed.

1.4 The courts will be able to treat the standards set in protocols as the normal reasonable approach to pre-action conduct. If proceedings are issued, it will be for the court to decide whether non-compliance with a protocol should merit adverse consequences. Guidance on the court's likely approach will be given from time to time in practice directions.

1.5 If the court has to consider the question of compliance after proceedings have begun, it will not be concerned with minor infringements, eg failure by a short period to provide relevant information. One minor breach will not exempt the 'innocent' party from following the protocol. The court will look at the effect of non-compliance on the other party when deciding whether to impose sanctions.

2 Notes of Guidance

2.1 The protocol has been kept deliberately simple to promote ease of use and general acceptability. The notes of guidance which follow relate particularly to issues which arose during the piloting of the protocol.

SCOPE OF THE PROTOCOL

2.2 This protocol is intended to apply to all claims which include a claim for personal injury and to the entirety of those claims: not only to the personal injury element of a claim which also includes, for instance, property damage.

2.3 This protocol is primarily designed for those road traffic, tripping and slipping and accident at work cases which include an element of personal injury with a value of less than £15,000 which are likely to be allocated to the fast track. This is because time will be of the essence, after proceedings are issued, especially for the defendant, if a case is to be ready for trial within 30 weeks of allocation. Also, proportionality of work and costs to the value of what is in dispute is particularly important in lower value claims. For some claims within the value 'scope' of the fast track some flexibility in the timescale of the protocol may be necessary – see also paragraph 3.8.

2.4 However, the 'cards on the table' approach advocated by the protocol is equally appropriate to some higher value claims. The spirit, if not the letter of the protocol, should still be followed for multi-track type claims. In accordance with the sense of the civil justice reforms, the court will expect to see the spirit of reasonable pre-action behaviour applied in all cases, regardless of the existence of a specific protocol.

2.5 The timetable and the arrangements for disclosing documents and obtaining expert evidence may need to be varied to suit the circumstances of the case. Where one or both parties consider the detail of the protocol is not appropriate to the case, and proceedings are subsequently issued, the court will expect an explanation as to why the protocol has not been followed, or has been varied.

EARLY NOTIFICATION

2.6 The claimant's legal representative may wish to notify the defendant and/or his insurer as soon as they know a claim is likely to be made, but before they are able to send a detailed letter of claim, particularly for instance, when the defendant has no or limited knowledge of the incident giving rise to the claim or where the claimant is incurring significant expenditure as a result of the accident which he hopes the defendant might pay for, in whole or in part. If the claimant's representative chooses to do this, it will not start the timetable for responding.

THE LETTER OF CLAIM

2.7 The specimen letter of claim at Annex A will usually be sent to the individual defendant. In practice, he/she may have no personal financial interest in the financial outcome of the claim/dispute because he/she is insured. Court imposed sanctions for non-compliance with the protocol may be ineffective against an insured. This is why the protocol emphasises the importance of passing the letter of claim to the insurer and the possibility that the insurance cover might be affected. If an insurer receives the letter of claim only after some delay by the insured, it would not be unreasonable for the insurer to ask the claimant for additional time to respond.

REASONS FOR EARLY ISSUE

2.8 The protocol recommends that a defendant be given three months to investigate and respond to a claim before proceedings are issued. This may not always be possible, particularly where a claimant only consults a solicitor close to the end of any relevant limitation period. In these circumstances, the claimant's solicitor should give as much notice of the intention to issue proceedings as is practicable and the parties should consider whether the court might be invited to extend time for service of the claimant's supporting documents and for service of any defence, or alternatively, to stay the proceedings while the recommended steps in the protocol are followed.

STATUS OF LETTERS OF CLAIM AND RESPONSE

2.9 Letters of claim and response are not intended to have the same status as a statement of case in proceedings. Matters may come to light as a result of investigation after the letter of claim has been sent, or after the defendant has responded, particularly if disclosure of documents takes place outside the recommended three-month period. These circumstances could mean that the 'pleaded' case of one or both parties is presented slightly differently than in the letter of claim and response. It would not be consistent with the spirit of the protocol for a party to 'take a point' on this in the proceedings, provided that there was no obvious intention by the party who changed their position to mislead the other party.

DISCLOSURE OF DOCUMENTS

2.10 The aim of the early disclosure of documents by the defendant is not to encourage 'fishing expeditions' by the claimant, but to promote an early exchange of relevant information to help in clarifying or resolving issues in dispute. The claimant's solicitor can assist by identifying in the letter of claim or in a subsequent letter the particular categories of documents which they consider are relevant.

EXPERTS

2.11 The protocol encourages joint selection of, and access to, experts. Most frequently this will apply to the medical expert, but on occasions also to liability experts, eg engineers. The protocol promotes the practice of the claimant obtaining a medical report, disclosing it to the defendant who then asks questions and/or agrees it and does not obtain his own report. But it maintains the flexibility for each party to obtain their own expert's report, if necessary after proceedings have commenced, with the leave of the court. It would also be for the court to decide whether the costs of more than one expert's report should be recoverable.

2.12 Some solicitors choose to obtain medical reports through medical agencies, rather than directly from a specific doctor or hospital. The defendant's prior consent to the action should be sought and, if the defendant so requests, the agency should be asked to provide in advance the names of the doctor(s) whom they are considering instructing.

NEGOTIATIONS/SETTLEMENT

2.13 Parties and their legal representatives are encouraged to enter into discussions and/or negotiations prior to starting proceedings. The protocol does not specify when or how this might be done but parties should bear in mind that the courts increasingly take the view that litigation should be a last resort, and that claims should not be issued prematurely when a settlement is in reasonable prospect.

STOCKTAKE

2.14 Where a claim is not resolved when the protocol has been followed, the parties might wish to carry out a 'stocktake' of the issues in dispute, and the evidence that the court is likely to need to decide those issues, before proceedings are started. Where the defendant is insured and the pre-action steps have been conducted by the insurer, the insurer would normally be expected to nominate solicitors to act in the proceedings and the claimant's solicitor is recommended to invite the insurer to nominate solicitors to act in the proceedings and do so 7–14 days before the intended issue date.

3 The Protocol

LETTER OF CLAIM

3.1 The claimant shall send to the proposed defendant two copies of a letter of claim, immediately sufficient information is available to substantiate a realistic claim and before issues of quantum are addressed in detail. One copy of the letter is for the defendant, the second for passing on to his insurers.

3.2 The letter shall contain **a clear summary of the facts** on which the claim is based together with an indication of the **nature of any injuries** suffered and of **any financial loss incurred**. In cases of road traffic accidents, the letter should provide the name and address of the hospital where treatment has been obtained and the claimant's hospital reference number.

3.3 Solicitors are recommended to use a **standard format** for such a letter – an example is at Annex A: this can be amended to suit the particular case.

3.4 The letter should ask for **details of the insurer** and that a copy should be sent by the proposed defendant to the insurer where appropriate. If the insurer is known, a copy shall be sent directly to the insurer. Details of the claimant's National Insurance number and date of birth should be supplied to the defendant's insurer once the Defendant has responded to the letter of claim and confirmed the identity of the insurer. This information should not be supplied in the letter of claim.

3.5 **Sufficient information** should be given in order to enable the defendant's insurer/solicitor to commence investigations and at least put a broad valuation on the 'risk'.

3.6 The **defendant should reply within 21 calendar days** of the date of posting of the letter identifying the insurer (if any). If there has been no reply by the defendant or insurer within 21 days, the claimant will be entitled to issue proceedings.

3.7 The **defendant's** (insurers) will have a **maximum of three months** from the date of acknowledgment of the claim to **investigate**. No later than the end of that period the defendant (insurer) shall reply, stating whether liability is denied and, if so, giving reasons for their denial of liability.

3.8 Where the accident occurred outside England and Wales and/or where the defendant is outside the jurisdiction, the time periods of 21 days and three months may reasonably be extended up to 42 days and six months.

3.9 Where **liability is admitted**, the presumption is that the defendant will be bound by this admission for all claims with a total value of up to £15,000.

DOCUMENTS

3.10 If the **defendant denies liability**, he should enclose with the letter of reply, **documents** in his possession which are **material to the issues** between the parties, and which would be likely to be ordered to be disclosed by the court, either on an application for pre-action disclosure, or on disclosure during proceedings.

3.11 Attached at Annex B are **specimen**, but non-exhaustive, **lists** of documents likely to be material in different types of claim. Where the claimant's investigation of the case is well advanced, the letter of claim could indicate which classes of documents are considered relevant for early disclosure. Alternatively these could be identified at a later stage.

3.12 Where the defendant admits primary liability, but alleges contributory negligence by the claimant, the defendant should give reasons supporting those allegations and disclose those documents from Annex B which are relevant to the issues in dispute. The claimant should respond to the allegations of contributory negligence before proceedings are issued.

SPECIAL DAMAGES

3.13 The claimant will send to the defendant as soon as practicable a Schedule of Special Damages with supporting documents, particularly where the defendant has admitted liability.

EXPERTS

3.14 Before any party instructs an expert he should give the other party a list of the **name**(s) of **one or more experts** in the relevant speciality whom he considers are suitable to instruct.

3.15 Where a medical expert is to be instructed the claimant's solicitor will organise access to relevant medical records – see specimen letter of instruction at Annex C.

3.16 **Within 14 days** the other party may indicate **an objection** to one or more of the named experts. The first party should then instruct a mutually acceptable expert.

3.17 If the second party objects to all the listed experts, the parties may then instruct **experts of their own choice**. It would be for the court to decide subsequently, if proceedings are issued, whether either party had acted unreasonably.

3.18 If the **second party does not object to an expert nominated**, he shall not be entitled to rely on his own expert evidence within that particular speciality unless:

(a) the first party agrees,
(b) the court so directs, or
(c) the first party's expert report has been amended and the first party is not prepared to disclose the original report.

3.19 **Either party may send to an agreed expert written questions** on the report, relevant to the issues, via the first party's solicitors. The expert should send answers to the questions separately and directly to each party.

3.20 The cost of a report from an agreed expert will usually be paid by the instructing first party: the costs of the expert replying to questions will usually be borne by the party which asks the questions.

3.21 Where the defendant admits liability in whole or in part, before proceedings are issued, any medical report obtained by agreement under this protocol should be disclosed to the other party. The claimant should delay issuing proceedings for 21 days from disclosure of the report, to enable the parties to consider whether the claim is capable of settlement. The Civil Procedure Rules Part 36 permit claimants and defendants to make offers to settle pre-proceedings.

ANNEX A

Letter of Claim

To

    Defendant

    Dear Sirs

        <u>Re: Claimant's full name</u>
            <u>Claimant's full address</u>
            <u>Claimant's Clock or Works Number</u>
            <u>Claimant's Employer (name and address)</u>

We are instructed by the above named to claim damages in connection with an *accident at work/ road traffic accident / tripping accident* on   day of   (*year*) at (*place of accident which must be sufficiently detailed to establish location*)

Please confirm the identity of your insurers. Please note that the insurers will need to see this letter as soon as possible and it may affect your insurance cover and/or the conduct of any subsequent legal proceedings if you do not send this letter to them.

The circumstances of the accident are:
(***brief outline***)

The reason why we are alleging fault is:
(***simple explanation eg defective machine, broken ground***)

A description of our client's injuries is as follows:
(***brief outline***)

(***In the cases of road traffic accidents***)

Our client (state hospital reference number) received treatment for the injuries at (name and address of hospital).

He is employed as (*occupation*) and has had the following time off work (***dates of absence***). His approximate weekly income is (*insert if known*).

If you are our client's employers, please provide us with the usual earnings details which will enable us to calculate his financial loss.

We are obtaining a police report and will let you have a copy of the same upon your undertaking to meet half the fee.

We have also sent a letter of claim to (***name and address***) and a copy of that letter is attached. We understand their insurers are (***name, address and claims number if known***).

At this stage of our enquiries we would expect the documents contained in parts (***insert appropriate parts of standard disclosure list***) to be relevant to this action.

A copy of this letter is attached for you to send to your insurers. Finally we expect an acknowledgment of this letter within 21 days by yourselves or your insurers.

Yours faithfully

ANNEX B

Standard Disclosure Lists

(Fast Track Disclosure)

RTA CASES

SECTION A

In all cases where liability is at issue –

(i) Documents identifying nature, extent and location of damage to defendant's vehicle where there is any dispute about point of impact.
(ii) MOT certificate where relevant.
(iii) Maintenance records where vehicle defect is alleged or it is alleged by defendant that there was an unforeseen defect which caused or contributed to the accident.

SECTION B

Accident involving commercial vehicle as potential defendant –

(i) Tachograph charts or entry from individual control book.
(ii) Maintenance and repair records required for operators' licence where vehicle defect is alleged or it is alleged by defendants that there was an unforeseen defect which caused or contributed to the accident.

SECTION C

Cases against local authorities where highway design defect is alleged –

(i) Documents produced to comply with Section 39 of the Road Traffic Act 1988 in respect of the duty designed to promote road safety to include studies into road accidents in the relevant area and documents relating to measures recommended to prevent accidents in the relevant area.

HIGHWAY TRIPPING CLAIMS

Documents from Highway Authority for a period of 12 months prior to the accident –

(i) Records of inspection for the relevant stretch of highway.
(ii) Maintenance records including records of independent contractors working in relevant area.
(iii) Records of the minutes of Highway Authority meetings where maintenance or repair policy has been discussed or decided.
(iv) Records of complaints about the state of highways.
(v) Records of other accidents which have occurred on the relevant stretch of highway.

WORKPLACE CLAIMS

(i) Accident book entry.
(ii) First aider report.
(iii) Surgery record.
(iv) Foreman/supervisor accident report.
(v) Safety representatives accident report.

(vi) RIDDOR report to HSE.
(vii) Other communications between defendants and HSE.
(viii) Minutes of Health and Safety Committee meeting(s) where accident/matter considered.
(ix) Report to DSS.
(x) Documents listed above relative to any previous accident/matter identified by the claimant and relied upon as proof of negligence.
(xi) Earnings information where defendant is employer.

Documents produced to comply with requirements of the Management of Health and Safety at Work Regulations 1992 –

(i) Pre-accident Risk Assessment required by Regulation 3.
(ii) Post-accident Re-Assessment required by Regulation 3.
(iii) Accident Investigation Report prepared in implementing the requirements of Regulations 4, 6 and 9.
(iv) Health Surveillance Records in appropriate cases required by Regulation 5.
(v) Information provided to employees under Regulation 8.
(vi) Documents relating to the employees health and safety training required by Regulation 11.

WORKPLACE CLAIMS – DISCLOSURE WHERE SPECIFIC REGULATIONS APPLY

SECTION A – WORKPLACE (HEALTH SAFETY AND WELFARE) REGULATIONS 1992

(i) Repair and maintenance records required by Regulation 5.
(ii) Housekeeping records to comply with the requirements of Regulation 9.
(iii) Hazard warning signs or notices to comply with Regulation 17 (Traffic Routes).

SECTION B – PROVISION AND USE OF WORK EQUIPMENT REGULATIONS 1992

(i) Manufacturers' specifications and instructions in respect of relevant work equipment establishing its suitability to comply with Regulation 5.
(ii) Maintenance log/maintenance records required to comply with Regulation 6.
(iii) Documents providing information and instructions to employees to comply with Regulation 8.
(iv) Documents provided to the employee in respect of training for use to comply with Regulation 9.
(v) Any notice, sign or document relied upon as a defence to alleged breaches of Regulations 14 to 18 dealing with controls and control systems.
(vi) Instruction/training documents issued to comply with the requirements of Regulation 22 insofar as it deals with maintenance operations where the machinery is not shut down.
(vii) Copies of markings required to comply with Regulation 23.
(viii) Copies of warnings required to comply with Regulation 24.

SECTION C – PERSONAL PROTECTIVE EQUIPMENT AT WORK REGULATIONS 1992

(i) Documents relating to the assessment of the Personal Protective Equipment to comply with Regulation 6.
(ii) Documents relating to the maintenance and replacement of Personal Protective Equipment to comply with Regulation 7.

(iii) Record of maintenance procedures for Personal Protective Equipment to comply with Regulation 7.

(iv) Records of tests and examinations of Personal Protective Equipment to comply with Regulation 7.

(v) Documents providing information, instruction and training in relation to the Personal Protective Equipment to comply with Regulation 9.

(vi) Instructions for use of Personal Protective Equipment to include the manufacturers' instructions to comply with Regulation 10.

SECTION D – MANUAL HANDLING OPERATIONS REGULATIONS 1992

(i) Manual Handling Risk Assessment carried out to comply with the requirements of Regulation 4(1)(b)(i).

(ii) Re-assessment carried out post-accident to comply with requirements of Regulation 4(1)(b)(i).

(iii) Documents showing the information provided to the employee to give general indications related to the load and precise indications on the weight of the load and the heaviest side of the load if the centre of gravity was not positioned centrally to comply with Regulation 4(1)(b)(iii).

(iv) Documents relating to training in respect of manual handling operations and training records.

SECTION E – HEALTH AND SAFETY (DISPLAY SCREEN EQUIPMENT) REGULATIONS 1992

(i) Analysis of work stations to assess and reduce risks carried out to comply with the requirements of Regulation 2.

(ii) Re-assessment of analysis of work stations to assess and reduce risks following development of symptoms by the claimant.

(iii) Documents detailing the provision of training including training records to comply with the requirements of Regulation 6.

(iv) Documents providing information to employees to comply with the requirements of Regulation 7.

SECTION F – CONTROL OF SUBSTANCES HAZARDOUS TO HEALTH REGULATIONS 1988

(i) Risk assessment carried out to comply with the requirements of Regulation 6.

(ii) Reviewed risk assessment carried out to comply with the requirements of Regulation 6.

(iii) Copy labels from containers used for storage handling and disposal of carcinogenics to comply with the requirements of Regulation 7(2A)(h).

(iv) Warning signs identifying designation of areas and installations which may be contaminated by carcinogenics to comply with the requirements of Regulation 7(2A)(h).

(v) Documents relating to the assessment of the Personal Protective Equipment to comply with Regulation 7(3A).

(vi) Documents relating to the maintenance and replacement of Personal Protective Equipment to comply with Regulation 7(3A).

(vii) Record of maintenance procedures for Personal Protective Equipment to comply with Regulation 7(3A).

(viii) Records of tests and examinations of Personal Protective Equipment to comply with Regulation 7(3A).

(ix) Documents providing information, instruction and training in relation to the Personal Protective Equipment to comply with Regulation 7(3A).

(x) Instructions for use of Personal Protective Equipment to include the manufacturers' instructions to comply with Regulation 7(3A).
(xi) Air monitoring records for substances assigned a maximum exposure limit or occupational exposure standard to comply with the requirements of Regulation 7.
(xii) Maintenance examination and test of control measures records to comply with Regulation 9.
(xiii) Monitoring records to comply with the requirements of Regulation 10.
(xiv) Health surveillance records to comply with the requirements of Regulation 11.
(xv) Documents detailing information, instruction and training including training records for employees to comply with the requirements of Regulation 12.
(xvi) Labels and Health and Safety data sheets supplied to the employers to comply with the CHIP Regulations.

SECTION G – CONSTRUCTION (DESIGN AND MANAGEMENT) REGULATIONS 1994

(i) Notification of a project form (HSE F10) to comply with the requirements of Regulation 7.
(ii) Health and Safety Plan to comply with requirements of Regulation 15.
(iii) Health and Safety file to comply with the requirements of Regulations 12 and 14.
(iv) Information and training records provided to comply with the requirements of Regulation 17.
(v) Records of advice from and views of persons at work to comply with the requirements of Regulation 18.

SECTION H – PRESSURE SYSTEMS AND TRANSPORTABLE GAS CONTAINERS REGULATIONS 1989

(i) Information and specimen markings provided to comply with the requirements of Regulation 5.
(ii) Written statements specifying the safe operating limits of a system to comply with the requirements of Regulation 7.
(iii) Copy of the written scheme of examination required to comply with the requirements of Regulation 8.
(iv) Examination records required to comply with the requirements of Regulation 9.
(v) Instructions provided for the use of operator to comply with Regulation 11.
(vi) Records kept to comply with the requirements of Regulation 13.
(vii) Records kept to comply with the requirements of Regulation 22.

SECTION I – LIFTING PLANT AND EQUIPMENT (RECORDS OF TEST AND EXAMINATION ETC) REGULATIONS 1992

(i) Record kept to comply with the requirements of Regulation 6.

SECTION J – THE NOISE AT WORK REGULATIONS 1989

(i) Any risk assessment records required to comply with the requirements of Regulations 4 and 5.
(ii) Manufacturers' literature in respect of all ear protection made available to claimant to comply with the requirements of Regulation 8.
(iii) All documents provided to the employee for the provision of information to comply with Regulation 11.

SECTION K – CONSTRUCTION (HEAD PROTECTION) REGULATIONS 1989

(i) Pre-accident assessment of head protection required to comply with Regulation 3(4).

(ii) Post-accident re-assessment required to comply with Regulation 3(5).

SECTION L – THE CONSTRUCTION (GENERAL PROVISIONS) REGULATIONS 1961

(i) Report prepared following inspections and examinations of excavations etc to comply with the requirements of Regulation 9.

(ii) Report prepared following inspections and examinations of work in cofferdams and caissons to comply with the requirements of Regulations 17 and 18.

NB Further Standard Discovery lists will be required prior to full implementation.

ANNEX C

Letter of Instruction to Medical Expert

Dear Sir,

Re: (*Name and Address*)

D.O.B. –

Telephone No. –

Date of Accident –

We are acting for the above named in connection with injuries received in an accident which occurred on the above date. The main injuries appear to have been (**main injuries**).

We should be obliged if you would examine our Client and let us have a full and detailed report dealing with any relevant pre-accident medical history, the injuries sustained, treatment received and present condition, dealing in particular with the capacity for work and giving a prognosis.

It is central to our assessment of the extent of our Client's injuries to establish the extent and duration of any continuing disability. Accordingly, in the prognosis section we would ask you to specifically comment on any areas of continuing complaint or disability or impact on daily living. If there is such continuing disability you should comment upon the level of suffering or inconvenience caused and, if you are able, give your view as to when or if the complaint or disability is likely to resolve.

Please send our Client an appointment direct for this purpose. Should you be able to offer a cancellation appointment please contact our Client direct. We confirm we will be responsible for your reasonable fees.

We are obtaining the notes and records from our Client's GP and Hospitals attended and will forward them to you when they are to hand/or please request the GP and Hospital records direct and advise that any invoice for the provision of these records should be forwarded to us.

In order to comply with Court Rules we would be grateful if you would insert above your signature a statement that the contents are true to the best of your knowledge and belief.

In order to avoid further correspondence we can confirm that on the evidence we have there is no reason to suspect we may be pursuing a claim against the hospital or its staff.

We look forward to receiving your report within ___ weeks. If you will not be able to prepare your report within this period please telephone us upon receipt of these instructions.

When acknowledging these instructions it would assist if you could give an estimate as to the likely time scale for the provision of your report and also an indication as to your fee.

Yours faithfully

Appendix 4

QUESTIONNAIRE – ACCIDENT AT PLACE OF WORK

QUESTIONNAIRE – ACCIDENT AT PLACE OF WORK

Section A – Personal Details

Your name:

Your address:

Your telephone number   daytime:

                           evening:

Your age:

Your date of birth:

If you are under 18, the full names and address of your parents:

Your marital status:

Your spouse's name:

Your spouse's age:

Your spouse's date of birth:

Do you have children? If so, please state their names and ages:

Your National Insurance number:

What do you earn net (take home pay) each week?
(please bring with you your wages slip for the last month)

What does your spouse earn net (take home pay each week)?

Are you a member of a trade union?

If so, which trade union?

Have you asked your trade union to help you make a claim regarding the accident?

If so, what was the result?

Are you covered by insurance for legal costs?

Section B – Details of your Present Employer

Your present employer's name:

Your present employer's address:

Your employee number:

What is your present job?

What is your job title?

What is your present employer's business?

How long have you worked for your present employer?

Section C – Details of your Employer at the Time of the Accident

Name and address of your employer at the time of your accident:

Your employee number at the time of the accident:

What was your job at the time of the accident?

What was your job title at the time of the accident?

How long had you worked for your employer at the time of the accident?

How many other employees did your employer have at the time of your accident?

Please give the details of your employer's insurers:

Section D – Details of the Accident

On what date did the accident occur?

At what time of day did the accident occur?

Did the accident occur in your normal working hours?

Were you doing your job when the accident occurred?

Where did the accident take place?

If the accident occurred in a building:

> what is the address of the building where the accident took place?
> who owns that building?
> what type of building is it?
> was this building your usual place of work at the time of the accident?
> if not, where was your usual place of work?

What were you doing at the time of the accident?

What caused the accident?

What equipment were you using at the time of the accident?

Who gave you this equipment?

Who do you think was to blame for the accident?

Why do you think that this person was to blame for the accident?

What job is this person employed to do?

What is this person's job title?

Has this person admitted he was to blame for the accident?

Do you think you were to blame for the accident?

Do you know if anyone has made a complaint about similar accidents?

Have you reported the accident to your employer?

To whom did you report it?

When did you report it?

Were details of the accident recorded in your employer's accident report book?

Did anyone else witness the accident?

If so, give the names and addresses of the witnesses.

Have you made a written statement about the accident to anyone?

Have you been asked to make a statement?

Have you made a claim for compensation against your employer or anyone else regarding the accident?

If so, to whom did you make your claim?

What was his response?

Do you know whether your employer was prosecuted as a result of your accident?

If so, what was the result?

Section E – Details of your Injuries and Medical Treatment

What injuries did you receive as a result of the accident?

Who is your doctor (general practitioner)?

What is his address?

What is your patient number?

Have you consulted him about your injuries?

When did you consult him?

Please bring with you to the interview your appointment card (if you have one).

Have you received hospital treatment for your injuries?

If so, what was the name and address of the hospital?

Name of the doctor who treated you:

Your hospital record number:

Please bring with you to the interview your appointment card (if you have one).

What was your state of health before the accident?

What has your state of health been since the accident?

Did you have time off work as result of the accident?

If so, how long?

How long did you spend in hospital?

Did you receive any money while you were off work?

If so, how much did you receive?

Who paid you the money?

Did anyone look after you after you left hospital?

    professional help (eg district nurse):
    non-professional help (eg your spouse, another relative, a friend):

How long did you receive this care?

What sort of care was it?

Did you have to pay for this care?

If so, how much?

Section F – Expenses you have Incurred as a Result of the Accident

What expenses have you incurred as a result of the accident?

Please make sure to keep a careful note of all expenses you incur from now on as a result of the accident (and, if possible, please obtain a receipt for these expenses).

INDEX

References are to paragraph and Appendix numbers.

Access (to documents), *see* Medical records
Accident, *see also* Incident
    abroad   16.6
        package holiday, on   16.6.2
    coroner's verdict   14.2.6
    fatal, *see* Fatal accident
    road, *see* Road traffic incident
    tripping/slipping, *see* Incident, tripping/slipping
    work, *see* Employee; Health and safety at work
Accident book   3.6.2, 5.6.7
Accident Line   1.5, 4.3.1
Accident Line Protect   4.3.7
Accident report
    employer, by   3.6.2
Accident site
    photographs   4.4.3
    visit   4.4.3, 4.6.2
Accountant
    structured settlement, for   16.5.4
Acknowledgment of service   9.5.4
Action for Victims of Medical Accidents (AVMA)
    1.5
Adaptations
    cost of   13.2.5
Admissions   11.9.4
Adopted child   15.6.1
Alcohol   3.2.5
    blood, in, post-mortem reveals   14.2.2
Alternative Dispute Resolution   11.6
    civil procedure reforms   11.6.2
    clinical negligence cases, and   11.6.6
    personal injury claims, and   11.6.3
    timing of   11.6.4
    types   11.6.1
Amenity, loss of   13.3.1
Amputation
    damages example   13.3.3
    impact of   2.2.1
Annuity   16.5.3
Asbestosis   2.2.8
Association for Victims of Medical Accidents
    8.3.2
Association of Personal Injury Lawyers   1.5,
    8.3.1, 13.1
Asthma, occupational   2.2.9
Attendance allowance   4.7.1, 4.7.2, 12.5, 12.7
Automatism   3.2.5

Barrister
    child, for settlement for   16.2.5

conditional fee agreement 'uplift'   4.3.4,
    4.3.7
conduct of trial   11.10.3
conference with   8.9
court bundle, copy to in advance   11.9.6
fee   4.3.7
instructing   11.9.3
statements of case in clinical negligence case,
    drafting of   8.9.1
Benefits Agency   4.7, *see also* Welfare benefits
Bereavement claim   15.6, 15.6.4
    amount of   15.6.4
    claimants   15.6.4
    interest on   15.7
Bundle, court   11.9.6
Byssinosis
    benefit for   4.7.1

Car, *see* Road traffic accident; Vehicle
Carer
    cost of   13.2.4, 13.3.5
        recoupment of benefit   12.4–12.6
Case management   10.1 *et seq*
    allocation to track   10.3
    conference   10.4, 11.6.2
    directions in fast track   10.3.2
    fast track   10.3.2
    fixing trial date   10.3.2
    listing questionnaire   10.3.2, 10.4.1
    multi-track   10.3.3
    notice of allocation   10.3.2
    pre-trial review   10.4.2
    small claims track   10.3.1
    stay to allow settlement of case   10.2.1
    variation of timetable   10.4.1
Case tracking   10.1 *et seq*
Charitable payment   13.2.2
Child
    claim for   16.2
        who brings   16.2.1
    dependant, as   15.6.1, 15.6.2, 16.2.2, 16.2.3
        criminal injury compensation claim
            16.1.4
        loss of dependency claim   15.6.2
    health and safety at work   3.3.2
    illegitimate   15.6.1
        mother of, bereavement claim   15.6.4
    limitation period for action by   6.5, 16.2.1
    medical treatment   3.10.3
    medical report on   16.2.4
    nanny for, cost of   15.6.2, 16.1.4

Child *cont*
   next friend   16.2.1
   payment into court for   16.2.3
   settlement for, approval of court   16.2.2–16.2.6
      counsel and solicitor, requirements for   16.2.5
      investment, directions for   16.2.7–16.2.8
      need for   16.2.2
      order   16.2.6
      procedure   16.2.3–16.2.5
      refusal to approve   16.2.9
Child-minding fees
   benefit help with   4.7.1
   nanny, cost of   15.6.2, 16.1.4
Civil action
   breach of statutory duty, for   3.3.2
Claim
   statement/particulars of   8.8, 15.6.1
Claim form   9.5
Clinical negligence claim   1.1, 1.3
   action diagram   1.6.1
   benefit recoupment, and   12.11
   causation in   3.8.3
      expert to be told   8.7.1
   claimant's solicitor
      advice at first interview   4.5.1
      aims of   1.3.1
   consent to treatment and knowledge of risks   3.10.1, 3.10.2
      child, and   3.10.3
      consent form   3.10.4
      refusal of consent   3.10.4
   coroner's inquest prior to   14.2, 14.2.2, 14.2.4, 14.2.5, 14.2.6
      statements for   14.2.8
   see also Coroner's inquest
   cost   1.3.1, 4.5.1
   counsel, conference with   8.9
   defendant   5.2.3
   defendant's solicitors' aims   1.3.2
   duty of care
      breach of, test for   3.8.2
      who owes   3.8.1
   emergency treatment   3.10.2
   equipment, injury from   3.10.6
   expert
      choice for   8.3.2, 8.7.1
      instructing and access to notes   8.7.1
      preliminary letter to   8.7.1
      separate liability and quantum reports   8.7
      see also Expert(s)
   explanation request   5.8.1
   hospital/GP records, *see* Medical records
   initial investigations   1.3.1
   letter before action in   5.3.2
   liability   1.3.1, 3.1, 3.8, 3.10
      contractual (private treatment)   3.10.5
      diagram of initial investigations   5.11
      invitation to admit   5.8.1
      negligence as basis   3.10.5
      shared   3.10.7
   loss of recovery, balance of probabilities   3.8.3
   LSC funding   4.3.3
      claims not exceeding £10,000   4.3.3
      full representartion   4.3.3
      Investigative Help   4.3.3
   negotiations in   11.5
   practice accepted at the time   3.8.1, 3.8.2, 8.7.1
   pre-action protocol   3.2.1, 5.3.2, 9.3, 11.5, App 3
   proof   3.8, 4.5.2
   proof of evidence for   4.6.2
   reputation and publicity as factors in   1.3.2
   res ipsa loquitur   3.9
   special damages   11.9.5
   statements of case
      drafting of   8.9.1
Clinical Negligence Scheme for Trusts   11.7
Clothing
   damages for   13.2.1, 15.5.5
   protective, for employee   3.3.2
Codes of Practice
   health and safety at work   3.1, 3.2.2
   medico-legal reports, for   8.6.1
Cohabitee
   dependant, as, circumstances   15.6.1
   exclusion from bereavement claim   15.6.4
Commission for Health Improvement   7.1
Community Legal Service   4.3.2
   see also First interview, Legal help, Legal representation, Legal Services Commission
Compensation, *see* Criminal Injuries Compensation Authority; Damages; Motor Insurers' Bureau
Compensation recoupment, *see* Welfare benefits
Compensation Recovery Unit   12.6, 12.10, 12.11, 12.12, 12.16, *see also* Welfare benefits
Compensators   12.10
Complaints (NHS procedure)   7.1 *et seq*
   access to health records, for refusal of   7.13
   coroner, reference to, and   7.14
   end of procedure   7.10
   flow charts   7.19
   health authority's response   7.11
   Health Service Commissioner, to, *see* Ombudsman
   independent review   7.2, 7.4–7.9, 7.17
      access to records   7.6
      advisors to panel   7.6, 7.7
      convenor, role of   7.4.1, 7.5.1
      decision to convene   7.4, 7.4.1
      panel composition and role   7.5
      procedure   7.5.3
      written reports, *see* 'reports' *below*

Complaints (NHS procedure) *cont*
   local resolution   7.2, 7.3, 7.17
      GPs and dentists   7.3.2
      hospitals   7.3.1
   personnel covered   7.2
   referral to complaints manager   7.3.1, 7.3.2
   reports
      assessors, by   7.7
      confidentiality   7.8.1
      independent review panel, by   7.6, 7.8, 7.9
   scope of complaints   7.2
   time-limits   7.3.3, 7.4.2, 7.9
      investigation refused when outside   7.12.1
Complementary health practitioner   5.2.3
Conditional fee agreement   4.3.2–4.3.7, App 1
   advising on   4.3.4, 4.3.6
   after the event insurance   4.3.5
   contents of   4.3.4
   counsel's fees   4.3.4, 4.3.7
   early end to   4.3.4
   examples   4.3.4
   exclusions   4.3.4
   insurance cover   4.3.4, App 1
   leaflet on   4.3.6
   legal help, and   4.3.4
   model agreement   4.3.4
   success fee   4.3.4
Consent order   11.8.2
Consulting engineer
   expert, as   8.6.2, 14.2.6
Consumer protection   3.10.6
Contractor
   employee working for, employer's liability   3.2.3, 5.2.2
   independent, injury to visitor caused by   3.4.4
Contractual claim
   private medical treatment, for   3.10.5
Contributory negligence   3.2.4, 4.5.1, 4.6.2
   examples of   3.2.5
   increase in allegations likely   3.3.1
   recoupment of benefit, and   12.9
   reduction of damages   3.2.5
Coroner's inquest   5.6.9, 14.2
   assessor, role of   14.2.1
   burden of proof   14.2.6
   circumstances for   14.2.2, 14.2.3
   clinical negligence case, *see* Clinical negligence claim
   coroner
      duty to inform on post-mortem   14.2.2
      opinion, expressing   14.2.6
      reference of complaint to   7.14
      role and qualifications   14.2.1
      summing up   14.2.6
   coroner's officer   14.2.1
   deputy coroner   14.2.1
   effect of referral on complaint   7.14
   evidence   14.2.2, 14.2.6–14.2.8
   family, and   14.2, 14.2.7, 14.2.9
      examination of witness by   14.2.6
   formal opening and adjournment   14.2, 14.2.6
   funding representation   14.2.4
   legal advice and assistance scheme covers   14.2.4
   hearing, preparation for   14.2.5
   identification of body   14.2.7
   jury   14.2.6
   'lack of care' verdict   14.2.6
   'neglect', and   14.2.6
   notification of date of   14.2.1
   personal injury case   14.2.8
   post-mortem   14.2.2
   public inquiry, after   14.2.6
   procedure   14.2.6, 14.2.7
   publicity   14.2.9
      statement to press   14.2.9
   purpose of   14.2, 14.2.6, 14.2.7, 14.2.8
   refusal to call, solicitor's options   14.2.3
   solicitor's aims   14.2
   transcript   14.2.6
   venue   14.2
   verdict   14.2.6, 14.2.7
   'violent' or 'unnatural' death   14.2.3
   witnesses   14.2.5, 14.2.6
      examination of   14.2.6
      self-incrimination   14.2.6
      solicitor's request for   14.2.6
Corporate group
   identifying defendant in   6.3.3
Corporate homicide
   Parliamentary bill   14.3.1
Corporate manslaughter   14.3
Costs   4.3
   expert, of   8.11
   order   11.10.5
Council tax benefit   4.7.1
Counsel, *see* Barrister
Counterclaim   9.5.8
County court
   order   11.10.6
   pre-action disclosure   5.7
   provisional damages in   16.4.2
Court bundle   11.9.6
Crash helmet   3.2.5
Criminal Injuries Compensation Authority   16.1
   claim   16.1, 16.1.10
   compensation
      deductions from   16.1.7
      earnings loss, for   16.1.2
      funeral expenses, for   16.1.5
      level of   16.1.1, 16.1.9
      maximum   16.1.6
      special expenses   16.1.3
   conditions   16.1

Criminal Injuries Compensation Authority *cont*
   costs, solicitor's   16.1.9
   fatal accident provision   16.1.4
   penalty point system   16.1
   review and appeal   16.1.8
   structured settlement   16.5.3
Criminal proceedings
   conviction in, use of   5.6.8, 14.4
   death by dangerous driving, for   14.4
      definition   14.4
   manslaughter prosecution   14.3
   note of evidence from   5.6.8
   work-place fatal accident, for   14.3

Damage
   remoteness of   3.2.3
Damages
   appeal   13.5
   award of lump sum   16.4.1, 16.4.4
      problems with   16.5, 16.5.1
   bereavement, for   15.6, 15.6.4, 15.7
   child, for   16.2
      investment of   16.2.7–16.2.8
   criminal injury compensation, *see* Criminal Injuries Compensation Authority
   date for assessment   13.1
   dependency, claim for loss of   15.6, 15.6.1, 15.6.2
      example   15.6.2
      financial loss, need for   15.6.1
      multiplicand and multiplier   15.6.2
      wife and mother, services of   15.6.2
   estate of deceased, to   15.5, 15.6.7
      distribution of   15.5.6
   explanation to client   4.5.1
   fatal accident, schedule for   15.11
   funeral expenses   15.5.3, 15.6, 15.6.5
      criminal injury compensation   16.1.5
      reasonableness of   15.6.5
   general   4.5.1, 13.1, 13.3
      case reports, use of amounts in   13.3.1
      employment prospects, loss of   13.3.2
      future loss of earnings   13.3.3, 15.5.2, 15.5.7
      heads of   13.3
      job satisfaction, loss of   13.3.4
      life expectancy, reduced   13.3.1
      loss of amenity   13.3.1, 15.5.1
      pain and suffering   13.3.1, 15.5.1
      pension, loss of   13.3.6
      recoupment   12.4
      vehicle use, loss of   13.3.7
   inflation   13.3.1, 13.3.3
   insurance money, and   13.2.2, 15.5.6, 15.6.6
   interest on   13.4, 15.7
   likely, solicitor to assess   11.3
   maximising   1.2.1, 13.1 *et seq*
   medical expenses   13.2.3
   nursing, etc, services, valuing   13.2.4
   pension loss   13.3.6, 15.8
   provisional   16.4
      approach of court   16.4.3
      CPR 1998, and   16.4.9
      defendant's position on   16.4.4, 16.4.5
      deteriorating condition, for   16.4.1, 16.4.2
      documents for court file   16.4.6
      fatal accident, and   16.4.8
      further damages claim after   16.4.7
      order for   16.4.6
      purpose of   16.4.1
      'serious deterioration'   16.4.2
      tender offer   16.4.5
   quantification   13.1 *et seq*
      no minimum or maximum   13.3.1
   quantum   1.2.1
      report on   8.7, 8.12
   recoupment
      estate of deceased, from   15.5.6, 15.6.7
      see also Welfare benefits
   reduction of   3.2.5
   special   4.5.1, 13.1, 13.2, 15.7
      amounts left out of account   13.2.2
      clinical negligence claim   11.9.5
      deduction of sums from   13.2.2
      employment of another while incapacitated   4.6.1, 13.2.4, 15.5.4
      evidence of   13.2.6
      heads of   13.2
      hire car charges   13.2.1
      loss of dependency   15.6.1, 15.6.2
      loss of earnings   5.6.4, 12.4, 13.2.2, 15.5.2
      record of   4.5.1, 5.1, 13.2.1
      recoupment   12.4, 12.5
      rehabilitation and adaptation expenses   13.2.5
      schedule of   11.9.5
      specific loss items   13.2.1
      statement of, filing of   8.7
   tax, and   13.5
Dangerous occurrence   5.6.6
Dangerous substance   3.3.2
Data protection   5.8.4
Deafness, industrial   2.2.5
Death
   see also Coroner's inquest; Fatal accident
   cause of, doctor's duty as to   14.2.2
   dangerous driving, caused by   14.4
   employee, report to HSE   5.6.6
   exclusion of liability   3.4.5
   instantaneous   15.5.7
   investigation for victim's family, or for person causing   14.1 *et seq*
   neglect, caused by   14.2.6

Death *cont*
   post-mortem examination   14.2.2
   unnatural   14.2.3
Defective equipment   3.2.1
Defence   9.5.5
   contents   9.5.7
   extension of time for filing   9.5.6
Defendant
   identifying   5.2
      limitation period, and   6.3.3
   letter before action to   5.3
   multiple, and benefit recoupment   12.10
   offer to settle   11.4
Dentist   5.2.3, 7.3.2
Dependant
   see also Child
   criminal injury compensation for   16.1.4
   fatal accident action   6.4.2, 15.1 *et seq*
      cause of action   15.3
      cohabitee   15.6.1
      damages   15.5, 15.6
      dependency, claim for loss of   15.6.1, 15.6.2
      limitation period   15.2
      statutory definition of 'dependants'   15.6.1, 15.12
   see also Fatal accident
   inquest, at, *see* Coroner's inquest: family
Dermatitis, occupational   2.2.10
Directions   8.8
   see also Disclosure
   expert's report, *see* Expert(s)
   High Court   8.8
   investment of damages for child   16.2.7–16.2.9
   summons for   10.2, 10.6
Directive, *see* European Union
Disability, *see* Injury
Disability, person under
   see also Child; Patient
   limitation period   6.5
   meaning   6.5
Disability living allowance   4.7.1, 4.7.2, 12.5, 12.7
Disabled person's tax credit   4.7.1
Disablement pension   12.7
Disclosure
   clinical negligence claim, in   5.8
   expert evidence, of   8.6.1, 8.8
   pre-action   5.7.1
Disclosure and inspection of documents   10.7
   procedure   10.7.1
   specific disclosure   10.7.2
Diseases   2.1 *et seq*, *see also* Medical terms
   reporting of   5.6.6
Doctor
   see also clinical negligence claim
   consultant, expert report from   8.6.1, 14.2.8
   defendant, identification as   5.2.3
   duty of care and negligence   3.8.1, 3.8.2
      clinical judgment and errors distinguished   3.8.2
      state of knowledge, date for   3.8.2
   employee of practice, complaint on   7.3.2
   expert, instructing as   8.6.1, *see also* Expert(s)
   general practitioner   5.2.3
      complaints resolution   7.3.2
   instructing   1.2.1, 1.3.1, 8.6.1
   private treatment   3.10.5
Doctors, disciplinary proceedings against   7.15.1
   appeals   7.15.9
   'convictions', meaning   7.15.2
   Preliminary Proceedings Committee   7.15.4, 7.15.6
   procedure   7.15.5
   Professional Conduct Committee   7.15.4, 7.15.7, 7.15.8
   serious professional misconduct, meaning   7.15.3
   statutory provisions   7.15.1
Documents
   court, for   11.9.6
Document access   5.7
   see also Disclosure
Driver   5.2.1
   see also Road traffic accident
   intoxication of   3.2.5
Drugs   3.2.5

Earnings
   criminal injury compensation, and   16.1.2
   dependency claim for loss of   15.6.2
   general damages, and future loss   13.3.3
      multiplicand and multiplier   13.3.3
   Ogden tables   13.3.3, 13.3.5
   reduced earnings allowance   12.5, 12.7
   reduced life expectancy, and   13.3.3
   special damages, and loss of   5.6.4, 13.2.2
      amounts left out of account   13.2.2
      deduction of sums   13.2.2
      estate of deceased, claim for   15.5.2
      tax rebate, deduction of   13.2.2
Emergency
   medical treatment   3.10.2
Employee
   carelessness of
      employer to protect him   3.2.4
      vicarious liability for   3.5.2, 3.5.3
   co-employee as witness   5.6.2
   competent staff, employer's duty to provide   3.2.1
   contributory negligence, *see* Contributory negligence

Employee *cont*
    death, report of   5.6.6
    details   5.6.4
    disability of, extra precautions for   3.2.2
    disobedience   3.5.3
    duties
        equipment, etc, use of   3.3.2
        informing employer of danger   3.3.2
        take care of self   3.3.1
    earnings, loss of   5.6.4, 13.2.2
        amounts included in   13.2.2
    health and safety, *see* Health and safety at work
    mistake by   3.5.2
    protective equipment   3.3.2
    reckless disregard for own safety   3.2.5
    State benefits, *see* Welfare benefits
    work-place injuries/diseases   2.2.7–2.2.10, 2.2.13
        accident book   3.6.2, 5.6.7
        benefits for   4.7.1
        liability of employer for   3.1 *et seq, see also* Employer
        proof of evidence details   4.6.2
        questionnaire   4.2.1, App 4
Employer
    breach of statutory duty, *see* Statutory duty, breach of
    cost of precautions   3.2.2
    defendant, identification as   5.2.2
    delegation   3.2.3, 3.4.4
    details from   5.6.4
    duty of care   3.2, *see also* Negligence
    health and safety duties, *see* Health and safety at work
    injury or disease, etc, reporting duty   5.6.6
    insurance   5.3, 3.6.2
    knowledge of risk to employee   3.2.2
    liability   1.1, 3.1, 3.3, 3.6.3, 5.3
        consideration of heads of claim   3.9
        enforcement through criminal proceedings   3.6.3
        see also Statutory duty, breach of
    negligence, *see* Negligence
    payment to employee, deduction from damages   13.2.2
    risk assessment   3.3.2
        duty to carry out   3.3.2
        noise level   2.2.5
    slipping and tripping accident avoidance   3.2.1, 4.6.2
    trade practices   3.2.2
    vibration injury, avoidance methods   2.2.7
    vicarious liability, *see* Vicarious liability
    wages of employee, details from   13.2.2
Employers' liability claim   1.1, 3.1, 3.3, 3.9, 5.2.2, 5.3, *see also* Negligence; Statutory duty, breach of
Employment
    job satisfaction, loss of   13.3.4
    prospects, loss of
        damages for   13.3.2, 13.4
        medical evidence of   13.3.3
        pleading of   13.3.2
        proof of evidence, in   4.6.1
        '*Smith v Manchester*' claim   13.3.2
    wages, loss of, *see* Earnings
Equipment (aids)
    future cost, general damages   13.3.5
Equipment (work)
    latent defect   3.2.1
    protective   3.3.2
    safety and maintenance of   3.2.1, 3.3.2
    use of and training   3.3.2
European Union
    claim in   16.6.1
    Directives on health and safety   3.3, 3.3.1, 3.3.2
        common law principles unaffected   3.3.2
        introduction of   3.3.2
        Regulations implementing   3.3.2
Evidence
    see also Witness; Witness statement
    co-employee, from   5.6.2
    criminal conviction, admissibility   5.6.8, 14.4
    defendant, as to   5.2
    expert, *see* Expert(s)
    general damages, of   13.3.1
    labour market handicap, of   13.3.2
    obtaining   5.1 *et seq*
    oral, advice on   11.10.2
    order   11.10.4
    photographic   4.4.3, 11.9.7
        admissibility   11.9.7
    proof of (client's), *see* Proof of evidence
    quick action desirable   5.9, 14.5
    special damages, of   13.2.6
    statements from non-witnesses   5.6.3
Expenses
    see also Damages: special
    funeral, of   15.5.3, 15.6.5, 16.1.5
    medical, *see* Medical treatment
    record of   4.5.1, 5.1, 13.2.1
    rehabilitation   13.2.5
Expert(s)   1.2.1, 1.3.1
    access to medical notes   8.6.1, 8.7.1
    accident reconstruction   14.4
    agreed issues   8.10
    choice of   8.3, 8.4
    clinical negligence case   8.3.2, 8.7, 8.9.1, 8.9.2
        choice   8.7.1
    counsel, conference with   8.7.1, 8.9
        after proceedings issued   8.9.2
        before proceedings issued   8.9.1
    doctor as   8.5.1, 8.7.1, 8.12
    engineer, as   8.6.2, 8.12

Expert(s) cont
   employment prospects of claimant, on   13.3.2
   fee/payment for   8.6.1, 8.7.1, 8.11
   instructing   8.1 *et seq*
   joint instruction   8.5, 8.6.4, 8.7.2
   joint selection   8.6.4
   joint statement   8.10
   letter of instruction, drafting   8.6.1, 8.7.1
   meaning   8.2
   meeting between   8.10
   number of   8.8
   personal injury case, in   8.3.1, 8.6, 8.9.2
   qualities required in   8.4
   report
      approval by client   8.6.1, 8.8
      child, on   16.2.4
      clinical negligence, types   8.7
      disclosure   8.6.1, 8.8
      exchange of   8.8, 11.9.2
      'medical report'   8.8
      scope of   8.1
      solicitor must analyse   8.8
      time taken for   8.6.1
      use of   8.8
   road traffic accident, for   8.6.3
   types of   8.12
Expert evidence   10.10
Eyesight
   problems from use of VDU   3.3.2

Fares
   special damages, as   13.2.1
Fatal accident
   see also Coroner's inquest
   cause of action   15.3
   compensation payment prior to death   15.3
   criminal injury causing, compensation   16.1.4
   contributory negligence of deceased   15.2
   criminal prosecution   14.3
   damages   15.5, 15.6, 15.9, *see also* Damages
      loss of dependency head   15.6.1, 15.6.2
      non-wage earner deceased   15.6.2
      schedule of loss for   15.11
   liability, establishing   15.9
   limitation period   6.4, 15.2
      dependant, for   6.4.2
      personal representative, for   6.4.1
   loss of dependancy   15.6.3
   personal representatives, *see* Personal representative
   procedure in claim   15.1 *et seq*
   proof of evidence, obtaining before death   15.9
   provisional damages prior to death   16.4.8
First interview
   arrangements for   4.2
   cost and funding of   4.3
   client paying fees   4.3.10
   conditional fee agreement, *see* Conditional fee agreement
   duty to advise private client on   4.3.10
   free   4.3.1
   insurance   4.3.4, 4.3.9
   trade union funding   4.3.8
   clinical negligence claim advice   4.5.2
   diagram   4.12
   importance of   4.10
   legal help matters
      conditional fee agreement, and   4.3.2, 4.3.4
      duty to advise on   4.3.2, 4.3.10
      emergency application   4.4
      legal help scheme   4.3.1
   length of   4.2
   personal injury claim advice   4.5.1
   photographic evidence of injuries, site, etc   4.4.3
   proof of evidence, *see* Proof of evidence
   questionnaire   4.2, 4.2.1, App 4
   urgent issues   4.4.1
   welfare benefits information   4.7
Floor (workplace)   3.3.2
France, claim in   16.6.1
Funeral expenses   15.5.3, 15.6, 15.6.5
   amount   15.6.5
   criminal injury compensation   16.1.5
   one claim only   15.6.5

General practitioner   5.2.3, 7.3.2
   notes, access to, *see* Medical records
Goods
   patient injured by   3.10.6
Group litigation   10.5
   order   10.5

Hazardous substances   3.3.2
Health and safety at work   3.1, 3.2.1
   audit   3.3.2
   breach of statutory duty, *see* Statutory duty, breach of
   child   3.3.2
   Codes, *see* Code of Practice
   competent assistant for compliance   3.3.2
   emergency procedures   3.3.2
   enforcement   3.6
   EU Directives   3.3, 3.3.2
      Regulations implementing   3.3.2
      'six pack'   3.3.2
   fatal accident
      criminal prosecution for   14.3

Health and safety at work *cont*
    inquest after   14.2.2, 14.2.6, 14.2.8, *see also* Coroner's inquest
    good practice, and Codes   3.2.2, 3.3
    health surveillance, duty   3.3.2
    inspectors   3.6.1
    place of work, and   3.3
    policy   3.3.2, 3.6.2
    risk assessment and information   3.3.2
    safe system of work, duty and extent   3.2.1, 3.2.2, 3.3.2
    training   3.3.2
    young person   3.3.2
Health & Safety Executive
    documents from   3.2.2, 5.6.6
    enforcement role   3.6
    Guidance Notes   3.2.2
    report   5.6.6
    report to   3.6.2
        reportable occurrences   5.6.6
Health authority   5.2.3
    defendant, as   5.2, 5.2.3
    duty of care   3.8.1
    solicitor for, at inquest   14.2.8
    structured settlement by   16.5.3
Health Information Service   7.2
Health records, *see* Medical records
Health trust   5.2.3, 14.2.8
Healthcare providers   7.1 *et seq, see also* Complaints (NHS procedure)
    complaints procedure   7.1 *et seq*
    disciplinary procedures   7.1 *et seq*
High Court
    pre-action disclosure   5.7
    provisional damages in   16.4.2
Highway
    fall on   4.6.2
Hire car charges   13.2.1
Hit and run case   5.5.5
Hospital (NHS/Trust/Private)
    complaints resolution   7.3.1
    deduction from damages for stay in   13.2.2
    defendant to action against   5.2.3
Housing benefit   4.7.1

Illness, *see* Injury
Improvement notice   3.6.1
Incapacity benefit   4.7.1, 4.7.3, 12.7
Incident, see also Accident
    road, see Road traffic incident
    tripping/slipping   3.2.1, 3.3.2, 4.6.2
Income support   4.7.1, 12.7
Incontinence
    costs associated with   13.2.5
Industrial injuries disablement benefit   4.7.1
Information
    employee's duty to provide   3.3.2
    employer's duty to provide   3.3.2
Injunction
    preventing hospital treatment   3.8.2
Injury
    see also Medical terms
    Criminal Injuries Compensation Authority   16.1
    damages for, quantification of   13.3.1, *see also* Damages
    deteriorating   16.4
    expenses of
        equipment and care   13.3.5
        rehabilitation and adaptation   13.2.5
    pre-existing condition   4.6.1, 4.6.2
        post-mortem may reveal   14.2.2
Inquest, coroner's, *see* Coroner's inquest
Inquest (organisation)   14.6
Inspection
    equipment and plant, of   3.2.1
    health records   5.8.4
Inspector (health and safety)   3.6.1
Insurance
    'after the event'   4.3.4, App 1
    cost of defending prosecution, covering   14.4
    damages, effect on   13.2.2, 15.5.6, 15.6.6
        criminal injury compensation   16.1.7
    employers' liability   3.6.2, 5.2.2
    legal expenses   4.3.9
    Motor Insurers' Bureau   5.5
    private   4.3.9
Insurance company/Insurer
    acting for insured   1.2.2
    aims of   1.2.2
    ascertaining, for road traffic case   5.2.1, 5.3
    child's claim, settlement of   16.2.2
    instructing solicitor   14.2, 14.2.8
    letter before action, response to   5.3
    letter of authority   1.2.2
    negotiations with   11.3
    notice of proceedings not given   5.4.2
    traffic accident, enforcement of judgment against   5.4
Interest
    damages, on   13.4, 15.7
        calculation   13.4.1
        claim for   13.4
    Nelson-Jones table   13.4.1
    payment into court, on   11.10.5
Interim payments   10.6
Interlocutory stage, *see* Directions: Interim payment; Interrogatories; Payment into court
Interim payment
    settlement after   11.8.2
Intoxication
    driver, of   3.2.5

Invalid care allowance 4.7.1
Invalidity pension and allowance 12.7
Investment
    damages, of, difficulties 16.5.1
    damages for child, of 16.2.7–16.2.8
Issues, narrowing 11.9.4
Issuing proceedings 9.5

Jobseeker's allowance 12.7
Judgment
    note of 11.10.5
Jurisdiction 16.6
Jury
    gross negligence, question for 14.3
    inquest, at 14.2.6

Knowledge, date of, see Limitation period

Law Society, The 1.5, 4.3.2
    guidelines for press statements 14.2.9
Legal help 4.3.1, 4.3.2
    see also Community Legal Service, First
        interview, Legal representation, Legal
        Services Commission
    complaint on NHS 7.1
    emergency 4.4, 6.8
    European Union, in 16.6.1
    expert, authority for use 8.6.1, 8.11
    leading counsel, authority for 11.9.3
    legal help scheme 4.3.1,
        5.6.5, 14.2.4
    negotiations, effect on 11.3
    taxation, order for 11.10.5
Legal representation 4.3.2
    see also Community Legal Service, First
        interview, Legal help, Legal Services
        Commission
Legal Services Commission 4.3.2
    see also Community Legal Service, First
        interview, Legal help, Legal representation
    funding 4.3.2, 4.3.3
Less adversarial culture 1.4
Letter of claim 5.3, 9.2.3
Liability
    clinical negligence claim, in, see Clinical
        negligence claim
    personal injury claim, in, see Personal injury
        claim
    settlement, and 11.4
Life expectancy
    reduced, damages for 13.3.1
Lifting
    regulation of 3.3.2

Lighting 3.3.2
Limitation period 4.4.1, 6.1 et seq
    action outside, claim against solicitor 6.6,
        6.9
    contribution, for recovery of 6.7
    date of knowledge 6.3
        constructive knowledge 6.3.2
        definition 6.3.1
        identity of defendant 6.3.3
        test for 6.3.1
    disability, person under 6.5
    European Union, in 16.6.1
    extension of, court discretion 6.6
        cases 6.3.1, 6.6
        test for reason for delay 6.6
    fatal accident claim, for 6.4, 15.2
    minor, and 6.5, 16.2.1
    'personal injury', meaning for 6.1
    primary period 6.2, 6.4
    solicitor, matters for 6.8
        ex parte application 6.8
        negligence claim against 6.6, 6.9
        records, importance of 4.4.2, 6.1
    specal periods 6.7
Litigation, group 10.5
Local authority
    cost of care services, recovery of 13.2.4
    highway responsibility 4.6.2

Machinery 3.2.1
    expert on, instruction of 8.6.2
    provision and use of 3.3.2
Maintenance
    plant, of 3.2.1, 3.3.2
Manslaughter 14.3
Manual handling regulation 3.3.2
Medical condition
    pre-existing 4.6.1, 4.6.2
Medical defence union 5.2.3, 14.2, 14.2.4
Medical information App 2
Medical negligence claim, see Clinical negligence
    claim
Medical records 8.6.1, 8.7.1
    access right 5.8.4, 7.13
        deceased individuals, for 5.8.4
        exclusion of 5.8.4
        fee 5.8.4
        human rights 5.8.4
    client's authority for 5.8.2
    correction of 5.8.4
    data protection 5.8.4
    examining and checking 5.8.7
    expert, and 5.8.5, 5.8.7, 8.6.1, 8.7.1
    inquest, for 14.2.5
    obtaining from GP and hospital 5.8.1–5.8.6
        information in response, examples 5.8.6

Medical records *cont*
   obtaining from GP and hospital *cont*
      order for   5.8.4
   terms used in, *see* Medical terms
   undertaking for copy costs   5.8.2
Medical report
   see also Expert(s)
   definition   8.8
Medical terms   2.1 *et seq*, App 2
   asbestosis   2.2.8
   asthma, occupational   2.2.9
   cerebral palsy   2.2.12
   dermatitis, occupational   2.2.10
   fracture types and treatments   2.2.1
   hand/arm vibration syndrome   2.2.7
   hand, wrist and fingers   2.2.7, 2.2.11
   head injuries   2.2.4
   hearing loss from employment   2.2.5
   obstetrics/birth   2.2.12
   orthopaedic injuries   2.2.1
   pneumoconiosis   2.2.8
   post-traumatic stress disorder (PTSD)   2.2.6
   skeleton, diagram   2.3
   skin injuries   2.2.3
   stress, employment-induced   2.2.13
   understanding of, need for   2.4, 8.6.1
   VWF   2.2.7
Medical treatment
   consent   3.10.1–3.10.4
   private
      damages, as   13.2.3
Mental Health Act
   person of unsound mind under, *see* Patient
Mental patient, *see* Patient
Minor
   see also Child
   meaning   16.2.1
Misadventure
   coroner's verdict   14.2.6
Mobility benefit   12.7
Mobility, loss of
   recoupment from damages   12.4–12.7
Mother
   bereavement claim, illegitimate child   15.6.4
   loss of services of   15.6.2
Motor bike
   crash helmet law   3.2.5
Motor car
   see also Road traffic accident; Vehicle
   seat belt law   3.2.5
Motor Insurers' Bureau   5.5
   First Agreement (uninsured driver)   5.5.1
   New Agreement (Compensation of Victims of Uninsured Driver)   5.5.2–5.5.4
   Second Agreement (untraced driver)   5.5.5

National Health Service (NHS)
   see also Health authority; Healthcare providers
   complaints, *see* Complaints (NHS procedure)
   Commission for Health Improvement   7.1
   costs recovery scheme   4.8
   doctor, *see* Doctor
   hospital   5.2.3, *see also* Health authority
   Litigation Authority (NHSLA)   11.7
   shared liability between professionals in   3.10.7
   Trusts   5.2.3, 14.2.8
      Clinical Negligence Scheme   11.7
      duty of quality   7.1
      structured settlements   16.5.3
National insurance
   contributions, and benefit claim   4.7.1, 4.7.3
   number, note of   4.6.1
Neglect
   verdict at inquest   14.2.6
Negligence
   clinical, *see* Clinical negligence claim
   common law liability   1.2.1, 3.2, 3.3.3
   contributory   3.2.4, 3.2.5
   defences   3.2.4
   duty of care of employer   3.2
      personal nature of, and delegation   3.2.3
      'reasonable care'   3.2.1, 3.2.2
      remoteness of damage   3.2.3
   exclusion or restriction of liability   3.4.5
   neglect found in inquest, distinction from   14.2.6
   proof   3.3.3
   res ipsa loquitur   3.2.3
   solicitor, of   6.6, 6.9
   vicarious liability of employer   3.5
Negotiations   11.1–11.4
   clinical negligence claim   11.5
   issues for solicitor   11.3, 11.4
   'splitting the difference'   11.4
   techniques for   11.3
   'without prejudice'   11.2
Nervous shock   3.7, *see also* Psychiatric illness
   meaning   3.7.1
Notice of proceedings
   insurers, to (road accident)   5.4.2
Nurse
   complaint on   7.2, 7.3.2
   statement for inquest   14.2.8
Nursing profession, disciplinary proceedings against   7.16
   Preliminary Proceedings Committee   7.16.4, 7.16.5
   Professional Conduct Committee   7.16.3, 7.16.6, 7.16.7
   serious professional misconduct   7.16.2
   statutory provisions   7.16.1
Nursing services
   cost of   13.2.4

Occupiers' liability 3.4, 5.2.2
    contractor, injury caused by 3.4.4
    duty of care 3.4.2
        delegation of 3.4.4
        discharge of 3.4.3
        exclusion or restriction of 3.4.5
    'occupier' 3.4.1
    'visitor' 3.4.1
Offer to settle 10.11
Ogden Tables 15.6.3
Ombudsman 7.4, 7.10, 7.12
    role and scope 7.12.1
Osteopath 5.2.3

Pain and suffering
    damages for 13.3.1, 15.5.1
Parent
    bereavement claim 15.6.4
    criminal injury compensation claim 16.1.4
    dependent on unmarried child, claim by 15.6.2
Part 17 claims 9.5.8
Part 36 offer 10.11
    acceptance by defendant 10.11.4
    compensation recovery 10.11.7
    contents 10.2
    consequences where claimant fails to match 10.11.5
    defendant's failure to obtain more than offered 10.11.6
    effective acceptance 10.11.3
    payments 10.11.2
Particulars of claim 9.5.2
    statement of 11.9.5
Pathologist 14.2.2, 14.2.6
Patient
    claim for 16.3
    limitation period for 6.5, 16.3
    meaning 16.3
    settlement approval 16.3
Pavement
    injury caused by tripping etc
        details and records 4.4.3, 4.6.2
        statements from neighbours 5.6.3
Pay, *see* Earnings
Payment into court 10.11
    benefit recoupment, and 12.13
    child, for 16.2.3
    interest on 11.10.5
    notice of 12.13
    order for payment out 11.10.5
    provisional damages claim, countering 16.4.5
Pension rights
    loss of 13.2.2, 13.3, 13.3.6

    dependants, claim for 15.8
Personal injury
    meaning for limitation purposes 6.1
Personal injury claim 1.2
    action diagram 1.6.2
    claimant's solicitor
        advice at first interview 4.5.1
        aims of 1.2.1
    compensation
        explanation of 4.5.1
        quantum 1.2.1
    counsel, conference with 8.9
    defendant's solicitors' aims 1.2.2
    deteriorating condition 16.4
    directions in, *see* Directions
    evidence
        collecting 1.2.1
    expert 1.2.1, 8.3.1, *see also* Expert(s)
    expenses, record of 4.5.1
    expert report, *see* Expert(s)
    interim payment, *see* Interim payment
    letter of claim 5.3.1
    liability 1.2.1, 3.1 *et seq*
        breach of statutory duty, *see* Statutory duty, breach of
        diagram of initial investigations 5.11
        negligence, in, *see* Negligence
        occupiers' liability, *see* Occupier's liability
        work accidents, *see* Employer
    losses of function/incapacity
        details of 4.6.1
        record of 4.5.1
    meaning 1.1
    narrowing issues 11.9.4
    pre-action protocol 9.2 *et seq*, App 3
    proof of evidence, *see* Proof of evidence
    settlement 11.1, 11.4
        order giving terms 11.8
    time-scale 1.2.1
Personal representative
    see also Fatal accident
    action by 15.4
    appointment 15.4, 15.10
    limitation period for claim by 6.4.1
    taking over claim started by deceased 15.4
Pharmacist
    liability shared with doctor 3.8.7
Photograph
    evidence, as 11.9.7
    road traffic case 4.4.3
    specialist medical 4.4.3
    time for, and importance of 4.4.3, 4.6.2
    use of, at trial 11.9.7
Plans, photographs and models as evidence at trial 10.9
Plant
    defective 3.2.1

Plant *cont*
    employer's duty to provide adequate 3.2.1
    maintenance 3.2.1
Pleadings
    bundle, in 11.9.6
    deteriorating condition, and
        provisional damages claim 16.4.4
    handicap in labour market, fact of 13.3.2
Pneumoconiosis 2.2.8
    benefit for 4.7.1
Police accident report 4.4.3, 4.6.2, 5.6.5
    obtaining 5.6.5
    release of 5.3, 5.6.5, 14.2.8
Police custody
    death in 14.2.6
Post-mortem examination 14.2.2
Post-traumatic stress disorder 2.2.6, 3.7.1
Pre-action disclosure 9.4
    offers to settle 9.4.4
    orders against person who is non-party 9.4.1
    procedure 9.4.2
    rules in relation to inspection of property before commencement or against non-party 9.4.3
Pre-action disclosure, *see* Disclosure
Pre-action protocol 9.2
    clinical disputes 9.3, App 3
        claimant's offer to settle 9.3.6
        form of request for records 9.3.4
            good practice commitments 9.3.3
            letter of claim 9.3.5
            obtaining health records 9.3.4
            proposed defendant's offer to settle 9.3.8
            proposed defendant's response 9.3.7
            quantification of claim 9.3.9
            steps 9.3.4
    personal injury claims 9.2 *et seq*, App 3
    selection of experts 9.2.7
Pre-commencement steps 9.1 *et seq*
    documents to be produced by claimant 9.2.6
    early disclosure of documents 9.2.5
    letter of claim 9.2.3
    reasons for and against commencing proceedings early 9.1.1
    response by defendant 9.2.4
Premises
    safe 3.2.1
Preservation
    medical records, request for 5.8.6
Prison
    death in 14.2.2, 14.2.6
Product 1.1, 3.10.6
Prohibition notice 3.6.1
Proof of evidence 4.6
    clinical negligence claim 4.6.2
    contents 4.6.1, 4.6.2
    specific accident types, for 4.6.2
    use of 4.6, 4.6.1

Prosthesis 2.2.1
Protective equipment 3.3.2
Provisional damages, *see* Damages
Psychiatric illness 3.7, *see also* Nervous shock
    bystanders as victims 3.7.6
    employee victims 3.7.4
    foreseeability of primary and secondary victims 3.7.3
    primary victims 3.7.2
    rescuers as victims 3.7.5
    secondary victims 3.7.2
Public funding
    see also Community Legal Service, First interview, Legal help, Legal representation, Legal Services Commission
    transitional provisions 4.3.2
Public liability claim 1.1

Quantum 1.2.1, 8.7
Questionnaire
    use in interview with client 4.2, 4.2.1, App 4

Recoupment, *see* Welfare benefits
Redundancy payment
    deduction from damages 13.2.2
Rehabilitative treatment 4.9
Relative
    see also Dependant
    deceased, of, acting for 14.1 *et seq*, *see also* Fatal accident
Reply 9.5.9
    contents 9.5.10
Report
    expert, by, *see* Expert(s)
    police accident, *see* Police accident report
    post-mortem, of 14.2.2
Res ipsa loquitur 3.9
Retirement pension (State)
    damages, and 13.2.2
Risk
    assessment 3.3.2
    information on, employer to provide 3.3.2
Road traffic accident 1.1, 4.4.3
    blood alcohol level 14.2.2
    death from 14.4, *see also* Coroner's inquest; Criminal proceedings; Fatal accident; Post-mortem examination
    defendant, identification of 5.2.1, 5.3
    details from client 4.6.2
    evidence 5.6.3, *see also* Evidence; Witness
    inquest after 14.2.8
    judgment enforcement against insurers 5.4
    NHS costs recovery scheme 4.8
    photographs 4.4.3
    reconstruction expert 8.6.3

Road traffic accident *cont*
   special damages   13.2.1
   uninsured or untraced driver   5.5

Safety, *see* Health and safety at work
Safety audit   3.3.2
Safety committee   3.6.2
Safety representative   3.6.2
Seat belt
   law on   3.2.5
Self-employed person   5.6.4, 13.2.2
Service of proceedings   9.5.3
Services
   third party rendering, damages for   4.6.1, 13.2.4, 15.5.4
      valuing   13.2.4
   wife and mother, of, valuing   15.6.2
Settlement   11.1
   child, for, *see* Child
   court order stating terms   11.8
   funding   11.7
   negotiating   11.3, 11.4–11.6
   patient, for   16.3
   structured   16.5
      agreement for   16.5.2, 16.5.4
      approval and 'standard agreements'   16.5.2
      benefit recoupment   12.12, 16.5.5
      circumstances for   16.5.1, 16.5.3, 16.5.5, 16.5.7
      drafting of   16.5.4
      examples   16.5.7
      tax   16.5, 16.5.2, 16.5.3
   time for   11.4
Severe disablement allowance   4.7.1, 12.5, 12.7
Sex life
   effect on   4.6.1
      damages   13.3.1
Site visit   4.4.3
Skeleton, diagram of   2.3
Solicitor
   see also First interview
   Accident Line scheme referral   1.5, 4.3.1
   approach of   4.1
   day of trial, checklist   11.10.1
   expert, choosing   8.3, *see also* Expert(s)
   familiarising self with file   11.3
   fatal accident claim, conduct of   15.10, 15.11
   Law Society specialist panels   1.5, 4.3.1
   letter before action   5.3
   medical terms, need to understand   2.4, 8.5.1, *see also* Medical terms
   negligence   6.6, 6.9, 16.5.5
   negotiations   11.1 *et seq*
   nominated   4.3.8, 4.3.9
   preparation for trial if no settlement   11.9
Spouse
   see also Dependant; Fatal accident
   bereavement claim   15.6.4
   criminal injury compensation claim   16.1.4
   defendant and carer, as   13.2.4
   dependant, as   15.6.1
      former   15.6.1
   dependency, claim for loss of   15.6.2
   remarriage prospects   15.6.2
State benefits, *see* Welfare benefits
Statement of claim
   see also Pleadings
   dependants, details in   15.6.1
   documents to be served with   8.8
Statements of value   9.5.1
Statutory duty, breach of
   civil liability   3.3.1
      causation   3.3.1
      duty owed and breached   3.3.1
      health and welfare provision   3.3.1
      'mischief of statute', and   3.3.1
      Parliament's intentions, construction of   3.3.1
      proof   3.3.1, 3.3.3
      safety provision   3.3.1
      statutory duty, and   3.3.3
Statutory sick pay   4.7.1, 12.7
Structured settlement, *see* Settlement
Suicide
   inquest verdict   14.2.6

Tax
   damages, and   13.5
   refund   13.2.2
   structured settlement, and   16.5.3
      Inland Revenue approval   16.5.2
Third party
   defective equipment, liability   3.2.1
   no claim for loss following injury to claimant   13.2.4
Time-limit, *see* Limitation period
Tobacco-related diseases   2.2.14
Tort, *see* Negligence, Vicarious liability
Traction   2.2.1
Trade union
   examination of witness at inquest   14.2.6
   funding of legal advice by   4.3.8
Training
   employer's duty (health and safety)   3.3.2
Transcript
   coroner's inquest, of   14.2.6
Treatment, rehabilitative   4.9
Trial   11.10
   conduct of   11.10.3

Unemployed person
   earning capacity etc   5.6.4

Unemployed person *cont*
    incapacity benefit   4.7.1
    recoupment of benefit   12.7
Unfair contract term   3.4.5
Unlawful killing
    coroner's verdict   14.2.6
Upper limb disorders
    work-related   2.2.2

Vehicle
    see also Road traffic accident
    adaptation to, cost of   13.2.5
    damage, etc, to, as special damages   13.2.1, 15.5.5
    hire car charges   13.2.1
    loss of use of   13.2.1, 13.3.7
    reconstruction of accident, and   8.5.3
    seat belt law   3.2.5
Ventilation   3.3.2
Vibration white finger   2.2.7
Vicarious liability   3.5
    behaviour of employee, and   3.5.2, 3.5.3
    'course of employment'   3.5.2, 3.5.3
    definition   3.5.1
    limitation period, and   6.3.3
Video
    use in court   11.9.7
Violence, victim of
    compensation for, *see* Criminal Injuries Compensation Authority
Visual aids   11.9.7
Visual display unit   3.3.2

Wages, *see* Earnings
Warnings   3.2.1, 3.4.3
Water
    drinking and washing, work-place provision of 3.3.2
Welfare benefits   4.7
    see also specific benefits
    appeals system   12.15
    benefit types   4.7.1
    certificate of recoverable benefit   12.6.2
    Compensation Recovery Unit ('CRU') 12.6, 12.10, 12.11, 12.12, 12.16,
    eligibility   4.7.3
    employer's duty to complete form   3.6.2
    exempt payments   12.8
    medical examination for   4.7.3
    notifying CRU   12.6.1
    payment   4.7.2
    recoupment, old Scheme   12.2, 12.12
    recoupment and offsetting, revised Scheme 12.1 *et seq*
    clinical negligence claim   12.11
    'compensation payment'   12.3.1
    compensators or multiple defendants 12.10
    contributory negligence, and   12.9
    criminal injury compensation, and   16.1.7
    fatal accident damages   15.5.6, 15.6.7
    general damages   12.4
    Guide (Benefits Agency)   12.2
    exempt payments   15.6.7
    'like-for-like'   12.5, 12.7
    payment into court, and   12.13
    'recoverable benefit'   12.3.3, 12.7
    'relevant period'   12.4
    special damages   12.4, 12.5
    structured settlements, and   12.12
    role of compensator   12.6
Wheelchair
    cost of   13.3.5
    injury caused by   3.10.6
Widow, *see* Spouse
Widower
    remarriage prospects   15.6.2
Wife and mother
    death of, value of services   15.6.2
Witness
    advising on procedure   11.10.2
    coroner's inquest, at, *see* Coroner's inquest
    evidence-in-chief   11.10.2
    expert, *see* Expert(s)
    order of   11.10.4
    police officer   5.6.5
    proof of evidence   5.6.2
    tracing and interviewing   4.6.2, 5.6.2
Witness evidence   10.8
    procedure   10.8.2
    statements to stand as evidence-in-chief 10.8.4
    use at trial   10.8.3
    witness summary   10.8.5
Witness statement   5.6.2
    counsel to   11.9.3
    evidence of damages in   13.2.6, 13.3.1, 13.3.2, 13.3.4
    importance of   4.6.1
    police accident report, in   4.6.2
    proof of evidence as basis of   4.6.1
Work-place
    see also Health and safety at work; Machinery
    accident in, *see* Criminal proceedings; Employee
    health etc regulations   3.3.2
Working families' tax credit   4.7.1
Workman's compensation scheme   4.7.1

Young persons   3.3.2